BALANCING READING & LANGUAGE LEARNING

How do I lern English

I lern English reading books in English. in the library I read two books English I rent one book and I read. when I go to the library I put the book on his place. I rent one book I read all the books of the library when I read one book I know English. and I talk more English and the school'and the teacher say Janzeel you lean me Englesh.

BALANCING READING & LANGUAGE LEARNING

A Resource for Teaching English Language Learners, K–5

MARY CAPPELLINI

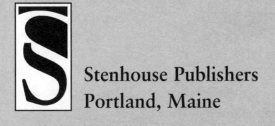

Stenhouse Publishers
Portland, Maine

INTERNATIONAL
Reading
Association
Newark, Delaware

Stenhouse Publishers
480 Congress Street
Portland, Maine 04101-3400
www.stenhouse.com

International Reading Association
800 Barksdale Road, PO Box 8139
Newark, Delaware 19714-8139
www.reading.org

Credits
Reprinted with permission of Harcourt Achieve:
Dressing with Pride by Maria Herminio Acuña and Maly Ny. Copyright © 1997 by Rigby.
The Story of Doña Chila by Mary Cappellini. Copyright © 1997 by Rigby.
Bringing Water to People by Katacha Díaz. Copyright © 1997 by Rigby.
The Big Catch by Mary Cappellini. Copyright © 1997 by Mary Cappellini and Shortland Publications.
Green Footprints by Connie Kehoe. Copyright © 1989 by Mimosa Publications Pty Ltd.
Shells by Coral White. Copyright © 2000 by Rigby.
Dad Didn't Mind at All by Ngarangi Naden. Copyright © 2000 by Shortland Publications Ltd.
Pets by Jennifer Beck. Copyright © 1998 by Shortland Publications Ltd.
Storm Trackers by Katacha Díaz. Copyright © 1997 by Rigby.
Car Trouble by Kathryn Sutherland. Copyright © 1999 by Rigby Education and Stephen Harrison.

Reprinted with permission of The McGraw-Hill Companies:
Huggles' Breakfast by Joy Cowley. Copyright © 1989 by Wright Group.
Poor Old Polly by June Melser and Joy Cowley. Copyright © 1998 by Wright Group.
Cranes by Sally Cole. Copyright © 2000 by Wright Group.
Dance My Dance by Ned Osakawa. Copyright © 2000 by MacMillan Education Australia Ltd.

Reprinted with permission of Learning Media:
Canoe Diary by Nic Bishop. Copyright © 1999 by Learning Media.
Whale Watching by Mary Cappellini. Copyright © 2000 by Learning Media.
The Living Rain Forest by Nic Bishop. Copyright © 2000 by Learning Media.

Learning Media titles are distributed in the United States of America by Pacific Learning, P.O. Box 2723, Huntington Beach, CA 92647-0723. Web site: www.pacificlearning.com

Library of Congress Cataloging-in-Publication Data
Cappellini, Mary, 1961–
    Balancing reading and language learning : a resource for teaching English language learners, K–5 / Mary Cappellini.
        p. cm.
        Includes bibliographical references and index.
        ISBN 1-57110-367-8
        1. English language—Study and teaching (Primary)—Foreign speakers. 2. Reading (Primary) I. Title.
PE1128.A2C344 2005
372.652'1044—dc22   2005047124

Cover and interior design by Martha Drury
Photographs by Maria Acuña on p. 51
Photographs by Sarah Maher on pp. 197, 241
Photograph by Julie Duddridge on p. 113
All other photographs including cover by Mary Cappellini

Manufactured in the United States of America on acid-free paper
12 11 10 09 08 07 06 05   10 9 8 7 6 5 4 3 2

*To my love, my husband, César,
who has enriched my life so much by
sharing his world with me.*

CONTENTS

ACKNOWLEDGMENTS

Writing this book has been an arduous but rewarding process. I have been working on it continuously the last three years, but the journey started over ten years ago. Along the way I have had the pleasure to meet and work with wonderful children, teachers, administrators, consultants, and colleagues. Many have become great friends whom I will always cherish. I have learned a lot from all of them, and many of their stories are part of this book.

I thank first the Mayras, the Jonathons, the Nayelis and the Edis of this world—the beautiful children that come to school speaking a language other than English, full of rich experiences and with eyes full of hope and amazement. Their joy of learning and thirst for knowledge always keeps me smiling and makes me extremely happy that I chose education as a career.

Next I have to thank the hundreds of hard-working teachers in whose schools and classrooms I've consulted over the years who encouraged me to write a book about "their kids." They welcomed me into their classrooms and shared with me their thoughts on how best to teach reading and lan-guage to their English language learners. They encouraged me to do demonstration lessons in their rooms, they questioned and self-reflected on their practices, and they were always thirsting to learn.

One of those teachers is Darlene Johnson of Sunview Elementary School, Ocean View School District in Huntington Beach, California, now retired, which is a sad loss for the children. I have to thank Darlene for allowing me to come into her first/second-grade combination class over a three-year period. My trips to her classroom started as an opportunity to visit a dear friend and to share com-mon beliefs about literacy—little did I know that I would become a welcome fixture in her room! I can't thank her enough for sharing of herself, her classroom, and her children over those years. Many of the detailed descriptions of primary children you will find in this book come from her rich, diverse community of learners.

Two other talented upper-grade teachers who I would like to thank are Sarah Knaus Maher of Sunset Elementary in San Ysidro, California, and Lizeth Villalobos of Kimbrough Elementary in San Diego City Schools in San Diego, California. They shared their print-rich rooms with me, discussed how they balanced all of their numerous guided reading groups, shared their reading assessments, allowed me to take pictures of them in action during reading workshop, and helped gather permissions. Many of the upper-grade children discussed in this book are from these two classrooms. It was nice to go back and visit them and work with their children after spending more than a year consulting at each of their schools.

Numerous other dedicated teachers helped me obtain permissions for this book, provided notes and assessments on their students, shared student samples, and allowed me to take pictures of them working in their guided reading groups and reading conferences. Many have since moved, but I want to thank Kim Swoboda and Ila Dawson of Carson Elementary and Elsy Romero of Kimbrough Elementary from the San Diego City Schools; Saida Valdez of Paramount Elementary, Azusa Unified School District in Los Angeles County; Chris Thom, Katie Unland, and Kendy Bjorndahl of Moffet Elementary, Huntington Beach School District; Lynn Takacs of Kinoshita Elementary, Capistrano Unified School District in San Juan Capistrano; Daryl Fowler of Jefferson Elementary School, Santa Ana Unified School District, now retired; and Julie Duddridge, Kristen Oswald, Dawn Calvert, Laura Parker, Tiffany Harris, Lori Wilburn, and many dedicated teachers in the Newport-Mesa Unified School District who spent a good part of their summers in Literacy Institutes to learn how to provide a balanced literacy program for their English language learners; and I especially need to thank Dr. Julie Chan, Director of Literacy at the district, who set up those institutes with the children and the teachers in mind. Julie is a wealth of information and knowledge, and I thank her for the support she has given me as a consultant and as a friend.

For their help and support, I thank the many principals who saw the importance of focusing on the needs of their English language learners and facilitated programs for them including Margie Lincoln and Carol Barry of San Diego City Schools, as well as Antonio Villar, who was a true spokesman for English language learners within the Literacy Department, now a principal within the district; Manuel Paúl of San Ysidro School District;

Billie Baker of Huntington School District; and Marti Baker of Santa Ana Unified School District, my friend, mentor, and collaborator at Madison Elementary, who along with our resource team including Maria Acuña, Darlene Staab, and Renelle McQuiston continue to help set up a strong learning environment for parents as well as children. I thank them all for their support and friendship.

Many people supported me professionally over the years and took the time to read my early drafts. I respect them as educators, appreciate their love of literacy and their interest in helping improve the education of all children, and I feel honored to call them friends. In addition to Julie Chan and Antonio Villar, these include Barbara Flores, Professor at Cal State University, San Bernardino; Debra Crouch, Literacy Consultant; Karen Valdes, Regional Director of Murietta Office of Education, Riverside County; and Victoria Velasquez, Literacy Coach for the Azusa Unified School District.

Many friends and book reps helped me with permissions and helped gather materials for this book, and I thank them. Among these are Mary Milton, Sherry McCrossen, Susan Cossaboom, Phil Ellis, Adrian Roberts, Lynelle Morgenthaler, and Bill Gaynor. Numerous other friends and all of my siblings and their spouses helped me constantly at home, listening to my stories, helping me with my children, and just being a support. They are too many to name, but they know who they are!

Bill and Pat Eastman, for their long friendship and belief in me, and their interest in connecting me to wonderful people who care about children's literacy, deserve a special thanks, especially since they helped me start my writing career, and they also introduced me to Philippa Stratton so many years ago.

I can't thank Philippa enough, my wonderful editor and the guiding force at Stenhouse, for all her support and encouragement through numerous drafts of this very long book. With a sense of humor, and a sense of compassion, she acknowledged that we all work while life still "happens" around us. "Keep writing" she would nudge through the seasons. My husband only wished she pushed harder! She is a lovely person, and I thank her so much for her kindness and for sharing her stories of Maine and England with me. We have developed a friendship that I will always treasure, and I thank her for helping me make this book the best it could be.

There are numerous other people at Stenhouse that have seen this book from beginning stages to the final production and marketing, and I thank them for their time and talents, including Bill Varner, Tom Seavey, Martha Drury, Doug Kolmar, Nathan Butler, Chuck Lerch, and Jay Kilburn.

I would especially like to thank my Mom and Dad, my constant teachers and cheering section, who have always supported me in everything I do. My Mom, the English teacher, was always willing to help read any chapter I would give her, and she would make wonderful suggestions to help clarify my writing. She was always there to also help with my three kids. I couldn't survive without her support and love. My Dad, my cheerleader, was always asking, "How's it going?" His love and encouragement and his interest in what I am doing has always enriched my life. I feel so blessed to live so close to them and to have them as role models for me. It is through their example of keeping a rich balance in life that has helped me always juggle family, career, volunteering, and writing. By being raised as one of their seven children, they taught me the important qualities of being a teacher—to see the best in every child, to treat each of them with love and respect, and to motivate them with their individual strengths to be all that they can be. Thanks Mom! Thanks Dad!

I have to also thank Coco and Nelida for treating me like a daughter and for sharing their love and their son with me—*muchas gracias*! They constantly take an interest in what I write and always ask if I am going to write it in Spanish! I have been so lucky to have another family in another land and to be able to go there with my husband and our children and celebrate their world, which is actually so similar to ours.

To my three lovely and talented daughters—Francesca, Jackie, and Natalie—how can I thank them enough? They deserve the patience award! They often waited for me and beautifully entertained themselves as I was trying to finish a deadline. My girls would tell their friends—"My mom always writes"—not necessarily in a good way. But I also appreciate their pride when I heard them say to others: "My mom's a writer." They and their dad have been my strength and motivation through it all. I have learned so much from them, and I am so proud of them. I love them dearly, and I thank them so much for the joy they bring to my life.

My biggest support, and my life, however, is my husband. His love and encouragement allowed me to finish this book. He was constantly encouraging me to write, and he was always saying how proud he was of me when I was down, and when I worried if the book would ever come to be. He would tease me by asking: "When will you finish this book?" And my daughters all started to answer him: "She'll never finish it, Dad!" Then they all laughed. It was a constant joke, and he always kept the humor going in the house. I actually had doubts myself. César, though, always had it in perspective. He kept taking the delays in stride and always helped me with the kids and the house as I worked. He has taught me so much, not only about learning a second language, but also about sacrifice and about courage and about never giving up. He's a wonderful dad and a wonderful husband, and I am so lucky to share my life with him.

César said to me: "Now I know why people say that in their lifetime they want to have a baby, write a book, and plant a tree—they are all such an accomplishment—and all such a long process!" Seeing the final fruits of your labor is definitely rewarding. Next I guess I'll have to plant a tree. And of course I will also dedicate that to my husband.

LIST OF
ACRONYMS

CABE—California Association for Bilingual Education

CATESOL—California Association of Teachers of English to Speakers of Other Languages

CDE—California Department of Education

CELDT—California English Language Development Test

CREDE—Center for Research on Education, Diversity & Excellence

DRA—Developmental Reading Assessment

DRS—Developmental Reading Stage

ELA—English Language Arts

ELD—English Language Development

ELL—English Language Learner

ELP—English Language Proficiency

ESL—English as a Second Language

FEP—Fully English Proficient

GR—Guided Reading (level)

IL—Intervention Level

IPT—Idea Proficiency Test

IRA—International Reading Association

IRAs—Informal Reading Assessments

IRI—Informal Reading Inventory

LAS—Language Assessment Scales

NABE—National Association for Bilingual Education

NCBE—National Clearinghouse for Bilingual Education

NCLB—No Child Left Behind

NCTE—National Council of Teachers of English

OELA—Office of English Language Acquisition (U.S. Department of Education)

QRI—Quantitative Reading Inventory

RR—Running Record (level)

RR—Reading Recovery (level)

SOLOM—Student Oral Language Observation Matrix

TEA—Texas Education Agency

TABE—Texas Association for Bilingual Education

TESOL—Teachers of English to Speakers of Other Languages

USDE—U.S. Department of Education

WIDA—Wisconsin, Delaware, Arkansas, District of Columbia, Maine, New Hampshire, Rhode Island, Vermont, and Illinois Consortium

INTRODUCTION

Working with children whose first language is not English has been a joy and challenge for me for twenty-two years.

For many teachers, our classrooms look very different today than they might have even five years ago. They are filled with children from a variety of backgrounds, not with homogeneous groups of children from the same ethnic origins. An increasing number of students are immigrants, children who live between two languages and two cultures. They come with rich cultural and language heritages with many fascinating things to teach us. Their families may be from Mexico, or Afghanistan, South Korea, Ukraine, Vietnam, El Salvador, Iraq, or China. But it doesn't matter where they are from: they are all English language learners (ELLs) who need to learn to speak, read, and write English.

We have the challenge of figuring out how to teach them effectively and of setting up an environment where all of them can succeed. As we educate them to their highest potential, we need to treat them with affection and kindness, as one of my favorite book titles, *Literacy con cariño* ("literacy with affection") emphasizes. We need to show them that we value both their primary languages and cultures and their learning of English reading and language skills. In this book I have chosen to use the more commonly accepted term English language learner (ELL) rather than limited-English-proficient (LEP) because it stresses a positive view of students' ability to succeed in English learning rather than focusing on their present deficits.

During the decade over which this book took shape, I moved back and forth like the tides deciding how to focus it based on educational and political changes that occurred. When I started, the focus was going to be on helping bilingual teachers provide a balanced reading program in both Spanish and English. Yet now the focus must be to help all teachers educate ELLs in mainstream English-only classes because that is where the majority of our ELLs are being taught. Starting in California with Proposition 227 (1998), a strong political shift in society's views of how best to teach ELLs has made bilingual education almost extinct in parts of the United States. Only 10 percent of the one million ELLs in California schools are receiving instruction in their primary language. In California, which has over 25 percent of the nation's ELL population, most teachers now have ELLs in their classrooms, and nationally 40 percent do. The U.S. Department of Education states a 32 percent rise in ELLs in classrooms across the nation, including a dramatic increase of over 300 percent in states like Indiana, North and South Carolina, Georgia, Nevada, and Alabama. Thus many teachers are facing a new, great challenge with very little preparation or experience in the specialty of teaching children whose primary language is not English. Less than 20 percent of such teachers feel they are qualified to meet this challenge (National Center for Education Statistics). And the federal No Child Left Behind Act, instituted in January 2002, adds to the burden of teachers and school districts: it requires all teachers of ELLs to be certified and qualified to teach them as of 2005 (U.S. Department of Education), and all English language learners must be assessed annually on their language proficiency and in reading and writing on standardized tests. Thus all teachers must now look upon the education of ELLs not only as their responsibility but also as their priority because most ELLs must master additional skills in order to reach specified standards at the same time as their English-speaking peers.

This book is designed to help all teachers—both mainstream and bilingual—instruct ELLs in English reading and English language development. For instance, I highlight for mainstream teachers the benefit of tapping into students' literacy in their primary languages when possible, including the use of Spanish cognates (words that are almost identical in English) because 79 percent of all ELLs come from Spanish-speaking homes (National Center for Education Statistics). And I stress for bilingual teachers the effectiveness of using the same good teaching strategies, such as guided reading, in both primary-language and second-language work.

Each teacher needs to provide a balanced reading program within a strong literacy block that includes a reading workshop and a writing workshop, with specific language instruction in both sections. Since I believe the connection between reading and writing is paramount, I include shared writing and response writing within the reading workshop to enhance the higher-level reading strategies and specific language functions and structures being learned. But I also think that learning to write well is a very complicated and important process that deserves its own time, and I encourage teachers to allot a full hour per day for writing workshop. This allows students to learn writing strategies and to practice by producing and publishing their own written pieces. There are many books on the teaching of writing, and this is not intended to be another one. But I encourage an emphasis on writing to enable children to become better readers and language users.

I also hope to enrich the dialogue of effective English as a second language (ESL) and English language development (ELD) instruction. We have progressed to a deeper understanding of what constitutes effective ELD; it is no longer just oral language development. Starting in kindergarten, children are expected to read some English even if they are beginning speakers (California Department of Education, Texas Education Agency, and WIDA Consortium). An effective English Language Arts program for ELLs would include reading, writing, listening, and speaking throughout the day based on the ELD and Content Area Standards. We cannot expect ELLs to become proficient English readers and speakers with only 45 minutes or an hour of English language development. If English language learners need more help in language instruction, this must be provided, just as certain children who lag in mathematics receive extra help in that subject in the course of the school day. And we need to make sure that language study based on individual students' needs is done within the context of a balanced literacy program that encourages the integration of content and themes.

I outline in this book how to use the framework of a balanced reading program to teach language and reading together. I detail the importance of Reading To, With, and By children, always noting what this means for different levels of ELLs and emphasizing the importance of discussion and talk. Some experienced mainstream teachers who are familiar with a balanced reading program may not know how to help ELLs in guided or shared reading. And some experienced bilingual teachers may not know how to use guided or shared reading to help ELLs develop language as well as reading proficiency in English. Of course, new teachers might need help in all these areas. I hope this book will be a resource for all teachers working with ELLs. The book examines English language proficiency levels (with California standards as a guide) and how they correlate with children's developmental reading levels. Many ELLs come into the classroom already reading and writing in their primary languages, or perhaps even in English, and we cannot necessarily align their instruction perfectly with the recommendations set out in the ELD standards.

Once a child is "reclassified"—the child has passed various language, reading, and writing tests and has been designated a fluent English speaker—that child is no longer considered to be an ELL. It sometimes happens that the reclassification is premature because the child may still have English language and literacy needs. I try to help teachers evaluate both the language and the reading strengths and weaknesses of each child, and then suggest how instruction can be individualized.

Many of us as adults could only wish for ourselves what we are asking of our students—to become proficient in a second language. In order to put ourselves in their shoes, I have included vignettes of adults' humorous yet often difficult experiences with learning a second language. For many of our students, English may actually be a third or fourth language. It is amazing to see how quickly children learn to fit into their new environment. But it is also easy to forget the daily difficulties they must go through to learn to speak and read in another language.

At the start of each chapter I have also included "Guiding Questions" to help guide the readers' thinking while reading, focusing on questions that teachers have asked me over the years that are addressed in the chapter.

I have dedicated several chapters in this book to guided reading, one of the strongest teaching techniques in a balanced reading program and an extremely important strategy to use with ELLs. Many educators consider it the key or heart of any balanced reading program (*Reading for Life* 1996; Fountas and Pinnell 1996). Some teachers are still not sure how to use guided reading effectively with English language learners. I give detailed instructions on how to lead a guided reading session, and I highlight guided reading lessons with children at varying levels of language proficiency and literacy development.

Guided reading and language development should be part of a carefully planned out, balanced program that supports children in a nonthreatening, welcoming environment; that empowers children to talk, emphasizes academic language proficiency, builds on children's background knowledge and primary language, uses models to demonstrate effective strategies in reading and language, meets students at their individual language and literacy levels, and encourages families to become involved in the learning community at school. All this can and does occur at wonderful schools across the country. I hope this book will help readers make this a reality at their own schools also.

1

SETTING UP THE LEARNING ENVIRONMENT

"I Felt Like My Tongue Was Cut Off"

When my husband first arrived in the United States from Argentina, he felt as if his tongue had been cut off. He was unable to communicate as he had in his homeland. His sense of humor, which normally attracted a crowd, was lost. His quick wit in the context of a testy conversation disappeared. His knowledge of the world and of his profession could not be tapped. His opinions on politics could not be shared. His sense of fun and teasing were not understood. When he did start to speak English, his jokes, which he insisted on telling, never translated right. His newly acquired swear words were always spoken at the wrong times. His incorrect sentence structures often hid the meaning of his words. And he found that most people would not accept his imperfect speech.

He also found that he had to start over not only with a new language but with new experiences in "America." It was as if his previous existence in South America didn't count. He became a clean slate. He had to prove himself and start from scratch. His years of experience as an engineering consultant didn't count when he looked for a job because he didn't have any work experience here in the United States, even though he had consulted for large U.S. multinational corporations overseas and had a master's degree. They still wanted to know what he had done here. "I just arrived!" he would say, but they didn't care. When he tried to get car insurance, they would not accept his impeccable driving record from Argentina. Instead, they treated him like a teenager with five accidents and gave him the highest rate. Socially, even my friends didn't think he was able to do the sports we liked to do, like play tennis, ski, and windsurf. When they saw him do all those things very well, they wondered where he had learned them. In Argentina, we'd say. Yes, just as in the States, they have sports there, and mountains with snow, and oceans with breezes. He was constantly amazed and disappointed at how little people assumed he was capable of. It was quite a culture shock.

How many of the children in our classrooms feel the way César felt? How many of our students feel frustrated at people's expectations of them? How many of them are silent in our classrooms? Do we know what each and every one of our English language learners is capable of? How much do we really know about their true selves or their true potential?

Many of our students are immigrants themselves, children who have just arrived speaking different languages and coming from diverse backgrounds and experiences. Many are refugees coming with the clothes on their backs with families fleeing from dangerous situations. My husband was a lucky immigrant. He didn't come to this country to escape war or poverty or persecution. Most immigrants are poor, and the children among them therefore live below the poverty line.

Some of these children were educated in their homelands in their primary languages and have a rich knowledge base that needs to be tapped. These children like César have it easier than those who arrive uneducated. If they already know how to read, they don't need to learn to read all over again; they just need to learn new vocabulary in English to help them be successful in their new language. César didn't need to learn to be an engineer again. He already had that knowledge which transfers to any language.

Cummins (2001) calls this ability to transfer knowledge from one language to another Common Underlying Proficiency (CUP). It doesn't matter what language we use to learn the concepts or demonstrate our knowledge of the concepts. The concepts are separate from the language, forming what Cummins now calls an underlying academic proficiency. Speakers who are truly bilingual can move between two languages easily, explaining a concept or idea in either language. Cummins does not agree that what we learn in one language cannot be accessed in another. He calls this the Separate Underlying Proficiency (SUP) view of learning and language development. For example, instead of just learning a new vocabulary for food, a child would have to relearn each concept of food as if he had never seen or eaten it before. I would agree with Cummins that this view of learning and language development doesn't make sense. Traveling in foreign countries, I knew enough about food to figure out what to order. Although I may not have known the exact word for what I was ordering, once I received the food I knew exactly what was on my plate, even though it may not have been what I had wanted. And I sure remembered the vocabulary the next time. Prior knowledge, regardless of the language it is stored in, is a powerful tool to help children gain meaning. If English language learners know about something in Spanish or Vietnamese, for example, we can tap into that knowledge to help them speak and read about it in English.

Other immigrant children have little background knowledge in content areas because they have not been educated in their own languages. That doesn't mean that they have not acquired life experience in their five to ten years of life, just that they don't have the academic concepts that could help them succeed in school and that could be transferred to English. With these children we need to teach new concepts in a new language, which is a much more difficult task. If they don't know how to read or write in their primary languages, they do not have the advantage of transferring literacy skills to their second language.

There are still many other children, also English language learners, who were born in the United States into families whose parents are immigrants, and who speak their primary language at home. These children have seen their parents suffer and work two or three jobs to make ends meet for their families. These parents are trying to provide a better life for their children than the one that they left behind in their homeland, and they often have little time to help their children adjust to their school setting, help them with homework, or read to them even in their native language. These children also usually have no language support in English at home to support the development of their new language. They do not receive the modeling of English that our native speakers do, which is so vital for their development. Yet these children, as well as the other immigrant children I described above with

different background and educational experiences, may be in our classrooms. We need to provide a nurturing and structured environment where they can all flourish and become readers and literacy learners and speakers of English.

The ELLs who come into our classrooms never having heard English spoken before need time to catch up to their English-speaking peers, but unfortunately they are not given much time. In many states they are required to take the same standardized tests as native English speakers even if they have been in the United States for less than one year. With the passage of the federal No Child Left Behind Act (NCLB) in 2001, school districts and states are required to show substantial gains on standardized tests by all students, including ELLs. We as educators must find the best and fastest way to educate these English language learners. It takes time to learn a language proficiently, but unfortunately the U.S. educational system is not that patient. Cummins (1981; 2001) estimates that it takes five to seven years to learn a language proficiently. Children might sound fluent in one to two years as they converse socially, yet it takes much longer to reach a level of academic fluency on par with their English-speaking peers. Research by Collier (1992) and others supports Cummin's claim. Cummins (1981; 2003) differentiates between social and academic language skills—basic interpersonal communication skills (BICS) and cognitive academic language skills (CALP), or conversational language and academic language. We need to develop the academic language of all English language learners in order for them to become successful readers, writers, and speakers of English.

Even though there may be a language barrier, we need to look carefully through the screen and diagnose what each ELL knows about literacy and then teach her accordingly. Together with the students and with colleagues, we can plan a balanced curriculum in reading and language that will meet the needs of all English language learners in our classrooms, value their cultures, and motivate them to work to their full potential. The elements necessary to provide a balanced literacy program for English language learners are shown in Figure 1.1 and are discussed throughout the book.

In this chapter I discuss the diversity we have in our classrooms and our responsibility to make

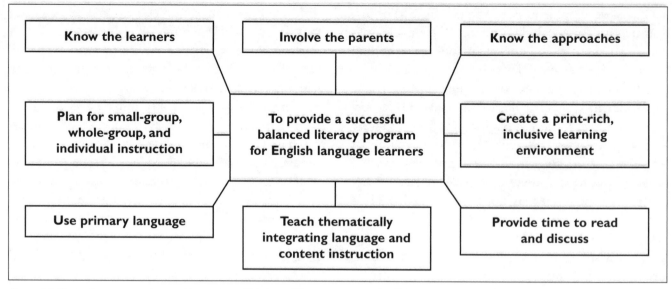

Figure 1.1 Elements necessary to provide a successful balanced literacy program for ELLs.

everyone feel welcome and the need to set up an environment of acceptance where talk is not only encouraged, but also a critical part of a balanced program for English language learners.

GUIDING QUESTIONS

What type of environment do I need to create to support all my diverse English language learners?

How do we make English language learners feel comfortable to participate in discussions?

What is the best way to use an Instructional Assistant to help my students?

What is the difference between language functions and higher-level reading strategies?

How can we develop students' thinking skills while we are developing their language?

What are the conditions that need to be in place for learning to take place in my classroom?

How can I use my English language learners' own speech to help teach them to use more effective language patterns?

How can I get better prepared for all my diverse children before they arrive?

TEACHING ALL OUR STUDENTS

Driving into a middle-class neighborhood in Huntington Beach, California, on my first visit to a friend teaching in a public school, I never imagined the diversity I would find in her first/second-grade combination class. The beautiful mix of children and the warm accepting environment were intoxicating, and I returned to her classroom for regular visits over a three-year period. I always looked forward to my visits and to watching this master teacher work. I also enjoyed talking with and getting to know individual children, leading small guided reading groups, and conferring with and assessing the English language learners in her classroom. The children were from a mix of languages and cultures. Most were first-generation Americans with parents from Mexico, South Korea, Afghanistan, El Salvador, Dominican Republic, Vietnam, Russia, or the Ukraine. Others were second-generation Mexican Americans, and there were also two Anglo Americans. Each child was aware of his or her special worth, strengths, needs, and developmental level in reading. They all worked independently. They had their own book boxes, journals, reading and writing folders, and math journals. They also worked well together; buddy reading, discussing in the science center, creating a skit or a project. The walls were covered with their work, and overflowing bookshelves stood around the room organized in different ways, by themes, by authors, by genres, by levels, or just displaying beautiful book art or the latest book purchase.

Mayra was one of the children with whom I developed a special bond, mainly because she

Mayra.

always greeted me, "Mary," and gave me a big hug as I walked in. She was thrilled that I spoke Spanish and would share with me in Spanish something new about her family each time I came in. She mainly talked to me in English, however, being proud of the progress she was making in her new language. She also wrote me notes and shared her writing. Mayra came into the classroom in first grade as a beginning speaker and an emergent reader. She left in second grade as a strong intermediate speaker and a fluent reader. She was lucky to be in an environment where her individual needs were met on a daily basis. From the first day she entered class, she was placed in a guided reading group that matched her language and reading levels, and she started writing in a journal (she filled up four journals that year). She was also lucky to be able to stay with the same teacher for one more year, just as the other first-graders in her class did. She was lucky to be in an environment where all children not only were encouraged to participate in group discussions, in shared reading, in the Daily News, but also were expected to do so. The expectations for Mayra

(The Powerpuff girls are waiting for Santa Claus.)

A sample of Mayra's first-grade writing.

> I got a new
> frend name Alexa Sandi
> she is cool and she
> is nice to me. She
> was My reading Bude,
> in frist Grade and
> now she is not
> because I am in
> second Grade and
> I like her mom and
> her name is relieve
> and : she is beotufl
> and she is My best
> frend ans she nosme
> and we are best
> Erend.

A sample of Mayra's second-grade writing.

were just as high as those for the native speakers in the classroom, and Mayra, as well as all the children, excelled in that environment.

Many people view the diversity in our classrooms as an asset, as Mayra's teacher does. Others see it as an unexpected hindrance in the national pursuit to raise test scores. We need to view all our students as assets and have high expectations for all of them. We also need to view English language learners as individuals and realize that they come from a range of experiences and backgrounds. It is not appropriate to lump them all together and assume their needs are all the same.

AN ENVIRONMENT OF INCLUSION

In order to educate children from so many different backgrounds we need to create an environment of inclusion. We need to accept and include in our classrooms different languages, cultures, and learning styles. We need to welcome parents who may not speak English. We need to welcome the larger community, including cultural leaders and local shop owners, who will help bridge the gap between the classroom and the neighborhoods in which our children live. And most important, we need to make every child feel welcome in and an important part of the classroom. We need to carefully plan for each child's individual instruction and to motivate and engage the child in meaningful learning opportunities based on his interests and curiosity. We can also include that child's language in our instruction, for instance, by stopping to ask how to say a word in Spanish or Korean or Chinese or Armenian, thus validating that child's capability in his primary language.

I have been in classrooms where *hello, please,* and *thank you* in every language of the children are posted on the walls. I have been in rooms where charts, graphic organizers, and wall murals show the variety of topics and themes that the children are investigating. There are other charts that focus on effective reading strategies or on academic vocabulary or language patterns. This language that covers the walls provides all children with the opportunity to read and revisit the ideas discussed over and over again. These types of classrooms, which also include extensive libraries and research materials, provide children with a print-rich environment. They help those who might come from homes with very few books or any type of reading material. Research has shown a strong correlation between print-rich environments and literacy development (Krashen 1996; Snow et al. 1991).

Learning environments are only as effective as the instruction that goes on inside them. We need to have a strong literacy block where English language instruction is a crucial part of every ELL's reading development and not seen as a separate subject. We should not expect that an ESL teacher's pulling ELLs out of the classroom for an hour should be the entire extent of the children's language and reading program. Are we expecting that teacher to teach them all the academic vocabulary they need or to teach them to read? We are responsible for all the English language learners in our classrooms, and we need to make sure—possibly in coordination with an ESL teacher—that they receive a balanced reading program with specific instruction in

A print-rich environment.

language development as well as reading development within our classrooms.

Our English language learners must be provided with the opportunity to work with their English-speaking peers in the classroom so that they can hear students modeling correct speech and can practice speaking themselves. Even if there are few native speakers in the classroom, the different English language proficiency levels will ensure the children's learning from one another. They need to be able to interact with other children in the classroom and not be pulled out during important instructional time, such as small-group work, literature circles, or discussion groups. What are they missing when they are pulled out? And do they feel comfortable coming back when the rest of the children have moved on to other things? A preferable alternative is offered in schools that have after-school programs to provide extra support for ELLs.

If we are lucky enough to have a specialized and credentialed ESL teacher at the school, we should look at that person as a resource to supplement, not supplant, what we are already doing in the classroom. That person could serve as a language or lit-

eracy coach to help the classroom teacher look more closely at the needs of ELLs. She could help with ongoing assessments of the children's developmental proficiency levels in language and reading, and with planning for these developmental needs. She could offer support by coming into the classroom to work side by side with the teacher in small groups or to model whole-group lessons. That would show our students that we are all working together to achieve the same goals. The English language learners would be enriched by the individualized help they receive within their normal classroom routine, and the rest of the class would benefit from receiving help from an additional teacher. If the teachers worked collaboratively, all students would feel a sense of belonging in the class, and all would receive support from team teachers for part of the day.

I encourage classroom teachers to feel responsible for the students assigned to them regardless of the children's language proficiency levels. It is not the sole job of the ESL teacher to care for the children's English language development, and it is not the sole job of a fellow teacher if one switches for

ESL or ELD. I do not encourage teachers to switch children for part of the literacy or language block, or to expect someone else to teach their English language learners. Language and reading instruction are so closely connected that it doesn't make sense to have them taught separately. Children need to see the importance of using language for real functions, such as reading and talking about what they have read.

If teachers do switch students for part of the language block, hopefully both will have time daily to share what has been taught—what the children were capable of doing in reading and speaking that day—and to plan what will be taught next based on the children's needs. Otherwise, valuable instructional time is lost. I find that it is most effective for many reasons to keep the same students in class throughout the day. Planning is one. It is much easier to plan for children whom one knows very well. Because one can observe them closely all day, one can plan lessons that are tied together thematically and built on the same academic language. More important, children learn from each other, and they need the language modeling of their more fluent peers to help them. If all the beginning speakers from various classrooms are grouped together, they have no fluent role models except for the teacher, and it is more difficult for them to learn from each other.

Although it is not my preference, I do acknowledge that there have been successful models where teachers teamed together for effective ELD instruction for their English language learners. But the basis for these models is that teachers work and plan together on a daily basis. That takes a very large commitment, and it takes a group of teachers with the same philosophical outlook on educating ELLs. In these good cases, the teachers view all the students from all the classrooms as their own and take on the responsibility for all the children's success.

THE ROLE OF INSTRUCTIONAL ASSISTANTS

Not all schools have ESL or ELD teachers, but many have instructional assistants or bilingual paraprofessionals. These bilingual speakers can play an important part in helping English language learners feel comfortable at school. They can work in small groups, explaining ideas or experiences that are culturally different from the ones the children know from their homes or homelands. Bilingual paraprofessionals are usually hired because of their primary languages, yet they are often asked to replace an ESL teacher or to support ELLs in English.

Instructional assistants are best utilized to support ELLs in the primary language so that the students can develop a deeper understanding of what they are reading and transfer that knowledge to their second language. Working in small groups in the primary language, the assistants can help the children gain a better comprehension of the content they are studying. Then, when they rejoin the whole class, they will be better prepared to participate in English discussion. That helps them build confidence and feel a part of the classroom community while at the same time helping them develop cognitively.

Instructional assistants can also help with the preview/view/review strategy for content area instruction (Freeman and Freeman 2001). The concepts being taught can be previewed with the ELLs in the primary language. Then, after they have viewed the material and participated in an English discussion at their developmental level, the instructional assistant can review what the children learned by having them ask questions or summarize the important concepts in the primary language. This technique allows the students to develop concepts in the first language and transfer them to English as they acquire new vocabulary (Cummins 2001; Krashen 1996). Instead of someone's just translating everything, which often has the effect of making ELLs tune out English as they wait for the translation, the preview/view/review helps them to be engaged in the learning and to try to participate in the English discussion with the whole class. If the teacher is fluent in the children's native language, she does not need an instructional assistant for this technique but could do it herself in the context of a lesson or discussion with the whole class.

SETTING UP A CLIMATE OF ACCEPTANCE

In order for children to feel a part of the classroom community and to feel free to join in discussions, there needs to be a climate of acceptance regardless of background, language level, or reading level. Children feel empowered to participate in classroom discussions when they can relate to the subject or have experience with it either first-hand or through their family's experiences. By participating in discussions in which they can contribute something, they can demonstrate their full knowledge and feel part of the mainstream group. This helps with developing the academic language necessary to be successful in reading and content areas (Krashen 1996). It is important to include all our students in classroom discussions because children from diverse backgrounds have unique points of view that can enliven and enrich any discussion regardless of their language or reading levels. As Freire (1978) states, it is important to bring the child's world into the language of the classroom.

Often English language learners don't feel like they are a part of the classroom, especially as they move into the upper grades. They often feel that their home experiences aren't similar to what is being discussed or that their oral English proficiency level isn't high enough to permit them to share in a group. The attention we place on individual comfort zones as well as on cultural perspectives and attitudes is critical in fostering healthy discussions. We need to accept one word or short phrases as well as incomplete or incorrect sentences when ELLs try to share their ideas. The main point of what they are saying is more important than the grammar or syntax while they are learning English. We have to be careful not to correct their speech in front of their peers but rather to model correct sentences in our responses. We also have to encourage others to listen to what ELLs are saying and interact with them. We can do this by asking children to respond to the speaker's comments ("What do you think of José's ideas?") or to rephrase what he just said. By doing this we are validating the speaker's contribution even if it was not in correct English.

We need to read our children's faces and body language to see how we can facilitate their participation in the discussion. If we notice a child looks uncomfortable participating, we have to find a way to make him feel less awkward. That might require offering an easier task, having the child share with a friend rather than the whole group, or just providing more positive feedback and encouragement.

We have to keep anxiety low, and motivation and self-esteem high; these are the three "affective variables" that influence language acquisition (Krashen 1981; Freeman and Freeman 2001).

If you have tried to include beginning speakers in class discussions but it just hasn't worked, I encourage the use of the primary language. If you speak the child's primary language, you could validate his comments and translate his words for the rest of the class. That shows that the child and his primary language are valued and that he has something worthwhile to say even though it is not in English. Many students understand much more than they can share verbally. If you don't speak the primary language, you could have another child or an instructional assistant translate and share the comments with the class.

Another important factor in helping children feel comfortable contributing in classroom discussions is to make sure the topic is one to which we know all the children would have something to add. They might comment because they are interested in the subject, can make a personal connection with it, or know something about it. Using background knowledge, personal connections, or connections to the world or to another text are critical strategies to help children improve their reading comprehension and language development (Harvey and Goudvis 2000; Keene and Zimmerman 1997; Cummins 2001).

In selecting books for read-aloud, it is important to choose books that the children can relate to in some way. But if certain children cannot relate to a character in the book because their background is so different, we might try to connect the character with a concrete example of something that happened in our own lives or with a character in another book. By modeling making connections, we might trigger a remembrance of something children have experienced in their own lives, which then helps them make their own connections. This can be a launching point for them to take part in a discussion by sharing their own experiences.

Amelia's Road is a wonderful book for ELLs to connect to. It is about a Hispanic child in a family of migrant farmworkers who hates to move. She hates the road that takes her to new camps, new destinations, new schools. Her parents remember her birth date only by the crops they were harvesting at the time ("I remember we were picking peaches at the time . . . which means you were born in June"). Although most ELLs in our classroom may not be from migrant worker families, many have experienced moving to a new place and having to start over in a new school. They know how it feels to have to make new friends and find a new place to call home. They can relate to Amelia's experience of having to start over. If we can help children make these types of connections, we can help them not only empathize with the character in the book but also with other children in the same position as the character. They can learn how that character dealt with a situation similar to theirs, and then reflect on and react to it. Connecting, reflecting, reacting, and commenting are important language functions and reading strategies.

Another book that has sparked children's interest is *Dear Abuelita*. The young child in the story has just arrived with his family at his new home in a large city in California, leaving his grandmother behind on their farm in Mexico. We learn about his experiences and his feelings about adjusting to a new place from his letters to his grandmother, his *abuelita*. In one fourth-grade class where I was working, we read the book in a guided reading group. One of the Hispanic girls, Esmeralda, was so taken by the story that she couldn't stop talking about it. She said it was "just like my life." The group's discussion about the child's point of view—

comparing the noise of the city to the peacefulness of his Mexican farm or his large new school to the tiny school back home, and articulating his feelings of loneliness—was enriched by Esmeralda's sharing of her own similar experiences. After the discussion, she was still so excited about the book that she went back to her seat and wrote down, both in English and in Spanish, her own feelings about the story and the connections she saw to her own life. There are many other multicultural books that stimulate English language learners to engage in class discussions (see Appendix D2).

LINKING LANGUAGE FUNCTIONS AND READING STRATEGIES

Allowing children to share and speak about what they know helps them develop cognitively and helps us assess their cognitive academic language proficiency. It helps us analyze the types of reading strategies and language functions that they are using effectively. How many of us could speak intelligently about the difference between the British House of Commons and the House of Lords? If not, does that mean we don't know how to compare and contrast? Or could we do a lot better if asked to explain the difference between the U.S. Senate and the House of Representatives? Too often

The book I read named "Dear Abuelita" remainded me alot about when I got hear 4 years ago. I went into school and I had no friends. I also mised my best Priend her name was mariela. We Practice were like Sisters, We spend all the time together. I felt really bad some of the nights I even cryed becouse I mized all of my family. All my family was in Mexico and me and my father, Mother and 2 sister's were only the ones that were in th U.S. Thats why I liked this story.

El libro que lei "Dear Abuelita me recordo mucho de cuando llege a los estado Unidos ase cuatro años. Tambien cuando entre ala escuela, no tenia ningun amigo o amiga y tambien estrañaba mucho a mi mejor amiga se llama mariela. Eramos como ermanas siempre estabamos juntas. Unas noches asta llore, Porque estraño Da a mi familia en Mexico. Todos estaban alla, Nadamas mi Papá y mama y mis dos ermanas estaba aqui. y llo me sentia muy Sola.

Esmeralda's writing about *Dear Abuelita.*

we don't encourage our students to discuss what they know, and thus we misjudge their thinking abilities as well as their language skills.

For children who are learning English, gaining meaning is always paramount. They are constantly trying to make sense of what is being said, trying to understand the teacher's message while she is speaking or the author's message while they are reading a book. They learn language in context by asking questions to clarify meaning, discussing their observations with peers, and listening to native speakers.

Many people separate the use of language from the ability to read; even state English Language Arts standards have separate sections for language (speaking) and reading. But can we really separate them? Don't we need a strong language base in order to read effectively? And don't we need an understanding of higher-level thinking strategies in order to discuss what we are reading? The link between language and reading is too strong to pull apart. Children develop language in the context of real purposes, including understanding what they are reading. As they discuss what they are reading, they develop their language skills. The more they read, the better readers they become (Smith 1994; Goodman 1982). And the more they talk, the better speakers they become (Krashen 1996).

In the study of language acquisition, researchers look at how children use language for set purposes (Collier 1992; Krashen 1994), which Gibbons (1991) and Halliday (1989) call *language functions*. They also look at the grammatical structures that children use as they are developing language, which Gibbons (1991) calls *language patterns*. According to ELD standards, children are expected to use language for a variety of purposes as well as to use correct speech at different stages of their development. They are also expected to use their knowledge of language to read at varying levels depending on their developmental language levels (California Department of Education).

It is our job as educators to understand how we can encourage language to be used for a variety of purposes in our classrooms and also to help children develop language effectively to become fluent readers of English. I feel that it is important, therefore, to teach and assess language in the context of the purposes for which children use it in the class-

room. I have divided the language functions into two categories—social and academic—and have given some examples here.

Social Language Functions

Greet someone
Answer simple questions
Ask simple questions
Respond to commands
Describe how one is feeling
Share an exciting event
Communicate with adults
Get along with peers
Work on a project with others
Play a game with friends
Chat on the playground
Share a snack or lunch
Chat with the lunch lady

Academic Language Functions

Retell a story
Describe how a character in a book is feeling
Compare and contrast two plots
Analyze an author's intent
Infer what else a character might do
Question one's own reading of a text
Predict what might occur in a story
Use background knowledge to make connections
    to own life
Create a play or reader's theater
Support one's own opinion
Participate in a role play
Interact in the science center
Negotiate with a partner how to do a science
    project
Write a hypothesis for a science experiment
Read a math word problem
Work on a history or social studies investigation
Summarize the plot of a story
Share a news article
Describe a genre
Synthesize information from two texts
Ask questions in an author interview

Notice that the list of academic language functions looks very similar to what one would see on a checklist of strategies to be used for higher-level reading development (see Appendixes A6 and A7).

These academic language functions or reading strategies should be developed as children develop their English language proficiency, but many children may have already developed them if they are fluent readers in their primary languages. They might just need the vocabulary to help them transfer the ideas into English. I feel, therefore, that we should look at the use of these language functions in context and teach children to synthesize texts, for example, or to analyze author's intent, in the context of reading texts during reading workshop. Also by teaching in thematic units (see Chapter 5), we can enable children to use the newly acquired academic language in the content areas.

In order to learn appropriate language for different purposes, children need to hear correct language patterns or structures modeled in context (Gibbons 2002). We need to set up times during the day to model correct patterns based on the children's developmental proficiency levels. Children can then practice using these language patterns or structures while they are using set language functions to help them learn to read. Chapter 2 talks about the different stages of language development and the language patterns that children use at each stage and how we can assess them while they naturally use their language.

In class discussions children should be encouraged to use the language they are acquiring. They need to think about what they have read—the motivation of the main character or the author's purpose for writing the book—and share what they think. These discussions need to go on during read-aloud, shared reading, guided reading, literature circles, or buddy reading. We need to spend less time on literal questions and more time on having children share in their own words what they think about a story. By helping them acquire thinking and language skills we can help them become independent learners (Gibbons 1991). We can verbally check the children's understanding and encourage them always to try to use the language they are learning at a deeper level while they participate in discussions. For us to assess them and for them to learn, they have to provide output (speak) as well as just take in comprehensible input (listen) (Swain 1985; Van Lier 1988).

As children advance up the grades, more cognitive demands are made on them. With longer, more challenging texts, they need to think critically about what they are reading, to interact with the text, and to share their opinions with their peers. It doesn't matter if their speech is in broken English. They might understand a concept and just need support in discussing it with correct language patterns. ELLs must practice speaking about what they are reading in order to improve both their language and their literacy skills. We cannot have reading time be passive; rather, we must encourage children to respond energetically, in discussions and writing, in small groups, whole group, and with reading partners. Does the class get noisy? Perhaps. But the noise is constructive noise that is important for learning to occur and for language to develop.

CONDITIONS OF LEARNING

The task of expanding the cognitive development of English language learners may seem difficult when we see very low language levels. But we must not stop modeling and talking to them just because they cannot respond in full sentences. Imagine a toddler acquiring language. We expect him to respond through gestures or with a word, and we interact to make sure he understands. When my sister-in-law asked her son how old he was, he held up one finger on each hand with a giant smile. "One!" he shouted. He didn't say, "I am one year old." He responded appropriately for his age and developmental level. The smiles and applause he got from her and his watching cousins were feedback enough for him to practice the concept and the language over and over again.

We need to interact with our ELLs, too, with smiles, encouragement, and positive feedback. When children are beginning speakers, they will respond with one or two words. When they are early intermediate speakers, they will respond with short phrases or incomplete sentences. But that doesn't mean they don't understand. It is our role to foster their language and cognitive development. We need to ask open-ended questions and give them the chance to use and show us the language they have. We have to be able to assess their comprehension from their language output and continue developing it by modeling correct language and encouraging them to participate in discussions.

How we respond to children and interact with them is critical in their reading and language development. Social interaction helps children acquire language (Van Lier 1988). Modeling, providing feedback, accepting, and encouraging language use in a natural way have been proven to be effective instructional techniques. They have also been shown to be part of the seven conditions of learning that Cambourne wrote about. He did research on the natural acquisition of language, wondering why a child by the age of five can speak so well in her native language without any formal instruction. The conditions Cambourne found necessary for the acquisition of language also apply to learning anything, from riding a bike, to reading, writing, or sewing, to name a few examples. He explains in his book *The Whole Story* (1988) that the following conditions need to be in place for children to learn to speak and read:

★ *Immersion.* They need to be immersed in the language and immersed in books and print.

★ *Expectation.* They need to be expected to speak and read.

★ *Responsibility.* They need to take on responsibility to talk, as toddlers do when they want something, and they need to be responsible in choosing to read.

★ *Approximation.* Their approximations need to be accepted and valued as they are learning to speak and read.

★ *Demonstration.* They need demonstrations (modeling) from experts on how to talk and how to read.

★ *Feedback.* They need constant feedback on their efforts at speaking and reading.

★ *Employment.* They need to be employed as a speaker and a reader; since it is their "job," they need time to speak and to read.

Add to these *engagement,* which is necessary for any learning to take place.

All these conditions of learning make sense to me, especially when I think of how I've learned anything in my life, including windsurfing, skiing, physics, or how to speak Spanish.

Even after years of studying Spanish in school, certain conditions were missing for me to be able to learn the language fluently. It wasn't until I was fully immersed in Spanish, when I was living with a Spanish-speaking family in Spain during college, that I felt I was truly learning the language. I received constant demonstration and feedback on my approximations at correct Spanish, including the laughter of the three-year-old in the family when I tried to ask for certain things in the kitchen. Her mother was much more kind, but I always knew right away when I used the wrong word or the wrong part of speech. My Spanish friends enjoyed correcting my speech as well. Luckily none of them knew English, so Spanish was my sole focus. It became my job to use Spanish to survive, communicate, make friends, and discuss coursework with my Spanish professors. I had to find my way around the city, catch the right bus to the university, and ask for the correct items at the pharmacy or local market. It was my full-time responsibility to speak and read Spanish to succeed at the university level. My friends, my adopted family, and my professors expected me to speak Spanish. Even I had high expectations of myself. And of course I was engaged in my learning of Spanish. I chose to be in Spain. I loved exploring the cities, the fiestas, the museums, the bullfights, the late-night bars, the narrow streets, the paella, the tapas, the castles, and the people. All of this culture just added to my rich language experience. It took many more years to consider myself an expert Spanish speaker, but I came back home pretty fluent in Spanish. I believe that all these conditions had to be in place for me to learn.

If we can implement Cambourne's conditions of learning in our daily classroom routines, we will be well on our way to providing ELLs with an environment where they can learn and be successful.

WELCOMING TALK IN THE CLASSROOM

English language learners need to practice speaking and listening to others, both in and outside the classroom, and we need to provide as many opportunities as we can for them to do so. The minute they walk into the classroom, we should encourage discussion, not ask them to be quiet and sit down as the day begins. Rather, we need to welcome chat about their day, their weekend, their new shoes or sweater, their new baby brother, their visit to the zoo, relatives that are staying with them, a new entry in their journal, a new poem they wrote, a new book they are reading, the new project they are working on. I reveled in the news the children would tell me as they came in the door, and the notes they would bring, which they had written the night before in English or their primary languages. They of course wanted to read their notes to me. And I enjoyed listening to them much more than I would have checking their homework as they came in. I usually saved the notes and placed them in the children's writing folders as samples of their writing ability. Their parents or other family members were also often there in the morning, and they too wanted to share something exciting that their child had done or just tell me about some part of their lives. Parents also liked seeing their child get out a reading book or looking around the room for samples of new work in progress.

This morning "buzz" was exciting and welcoming, especially for new ELLs, who listened to the English chat and joined in when they could. I found that it was critical to promote these discussions in the classroom, not only to develop the children's language but also to develop a sense of community. This was their room, and they were all a part of it, the families, too. Of course time is of the essence in our daily schedules, and we need to be aware of starting class on time. But don't we often begin serious conversations with small talk to get comfortable and to set the tone for the task at hand? We need to encourage such talk because children naturally want to make connections to the classroom from their own lives. And making parents and grandparents welcome encourages them to come back and volunteer.

To encourage talk as the day started, I always had on the board a morning message, which many would try to read and discuss as they entered the room. This allowed me to continue talking with other children and their parents or family members. At this time, too, children showed their parents books they were reading or a new story they had written. Perhaps five minutes was all it took to settle into the room, share the morning message, and start group meeting, but it was a critical five minutes. Children were talking about real-life situations that would become a basis for their writing

Morning message highlighting the letter *f*.

and reading connections. They were often sharing their love of literacy and coming to understand that their own and others' ideas were important.

Some teachers would then move right into independent reading time, when the teacher would confer with individual children while the rest were reading books of their choice. This was seen as a warm-up to the day (Taberski 2000). Other teachers might ask the families to stay and read with the children. But I prefer to continue the dialogues that occur as children walk into the room, so I move into group meeting. By starting with group meeting, I hope to promote the children's use of natural language. We might start with a welcome song or an alphabet song, or we might read a favorite poem or chant together in a shared reading. We reread and discuss the morning message, and then focus briefly (not more than five minutes) on the set skill that I had incorporated into the message. We talk briefly about the calendar, the day's events, and any news that affects our classroom or school. But my favorite part of group meeting is shared writing, when we compose the Daily News.

LEARNING FROM THE DAILY NEWS

Not only does the Daily News promote a sense of community as children share the news of their lives but it also lets us teach about the structure of English—sentence patterns, adjectives, word study, phonics, punctuation, capitalization, sound-symbol relationships—by using the children's natural language. Many schools have some form of daily oral language (DOL), one or two sentences that teachers can use in a daily drill of language skills. These

The Daily News.

canned sentences from DOL programs are often not engaging to the children, or focus on skills they may not need. In contrast, asking children to supply their own sentences orally, and working as a group to write these down, proofread, and correct them, keeps them interested and actively learning. The language that the children share in the Daily News is theirs, from their own lives, not someone else's. And this allows us to learn about each other—to bring their world into the classroom. Some examples from my classes are the following:

"My daddy got a new car."

"We went to Mexico over the weekend."

"I got new shoes yesterday."

"We're going to the beach tomorrow."

"My baby sister kept me up all night last night."

"My mommy went to Las Vegas. She won a lot of money!"

"My cousin's birthday party got broken up by gang members."

"My uncle is really sick."

"I lost my tooth, and my brother said I look funny,"

"Maria and I always love it when my Great Aunt Berta comes over with *empanadas* to share."

Such sentences are a stimulus for celebration and discussion. The Daily News is a working document to look at and study, an absorbing one that the children want to reread and talk about. It is a wonderful tool for teaching the mechanics of writing and often goes into the reading corner to be used during independent reading time. Most important, it is by composing the text, and shaping the ideas into correct sentences that an audience will understand, that ELLs learn and practice language skills. Many ELLs cannot yet speak in complete sentences or even share complete ideas in English, yet the shared writing of the Daily News allows all to have a part in composing a grammatically correct text. The discussion necessary to getting the ideas correctly down on paper helps all children, no matter what their proficiency level, feel comfortable about contributing. This is true for primary and upper grades.

Sample Lesson with the Daily News

After the children tell me the date and help me write it correctly, filling in all the commas, I ask them, "Who has something to share today for the Daily News?" Most hands in the room shoot up, and I usually accept three or four responses before I decide on one that I'll use for that day's News. I try to keep the children guessing, never consistently choosing the first or last response. I try to choose a response from a child who didn't share the day before, but I never have preselected children to call on because I don't know what is going to happen in a child's life. Did her mother just have a new baby? Did new relatives just arrive from his homeland? Outstanding events in the children's lives always take precedence. Being flexible is important in accepting responses. If all hands are raised at the same time, which often happens, I ask everyone to turn to a partner and share. That way, every child has a chance to talk and listen to someone even if not with the whole group.

After selecting Juan's response to write down in the Daily News, I ask the group to repeat it:

"Where did Juan go over the weekend?"
"To the beach."
"Who can tell me that in a complete sentence?"
"Juan went to the beach."
"Good. Let's write that."

I write this down, asking for help in choosing the correct letters to spell each word—the letter that corresponds to a certain sound, for example, because I know that encoding helps with decoding and rereading the text later. We talk about capital letters, and before I write a period at the end of the sentence, I ask,

"When did Juan go to the beach?"
"The weekend."
"Yes, he went <u>over</u> the weekend. Can we add that to the sentence to make it longer? Let's read the sentence together now."
"Juan went to the beach over the weekend."

We then discuss what Juan did at the beach. Juan responds with one word: "swimming." I ask him whom he swam with, was it cold, and did he use a boogie board? Once again, Juan's responses were single words: "brother," "sister," "no," "yes." The other children were not bothered by these short responses. Instead, they joined in modeling more advanced language patterns, which then helped us compose the sentences that would go into the Daily News:

"I go swimming with my brother."
"My sister and I go swimming in the waves."
"I use a boogie board with my dad."
"It's fun."
"The water isn't cold when you get used to it."

The final version of the News for that day:

Today is Monday, August 5th.
Juan went to the beach over the weekend.
He went swimming in the waves with his brother and his sister.
The water wasn't cold.
They used a boogie board to ride the waves.
They had fun.

All this discussion happens very naturally and quickly. I try to encourage a free flow of discussion, drawing the children out but still keeping them on topic. Together we write a short description of Juan's trip to the beach, continually checking with him to see if it is right and using complete sentences, which helps ELLs of all proficiency levels. All the children are engaged, from beginning speakers like Juan to intermediate and advanced speakers. The Daily News session makes all feel they are involved in the task. But of course each hopes that tomorrow she will be called, and her story will be written down.

After we had composed and written down the Daily News from Juan's contribution, we used it as a focus for highlighting set phonics skills and word recognition. I noticed there were a lot of words that began with the letter *w*. This is a difficult letter and sound to teach certain ELLs because in Spanish, for example, it is not part of the alphabet. A Spanish dictionary does contain the letter *w* but only in words that come directly from English, like *windsurf* or *Westerns* (movies). So I knew that many children were not familiar with using the letter *w* in their writing or reading. I then asked if anyone could find a word that started with *w*. I gave them the phoneme, or sound, in case they were unfamiliar with it. One by one, I gave the children a pen and had them tell me a word with *w*, circle the word, and underline the letter. If a child could see a word with a *w* but had trouble reading it aloud, we often reread the sentence together, or I asked other children to help him figure it out. I wanted to make sure they could not only distinguish the letter but could recognize the word and read it either alone or in context. (Individual modeling of skills is discussed in Chapters 7 and 8, on shared reading, and in Chapter 14, on planning for students' individual needs.)

Teachers have used the Daily News in their classrooms for years to teach specific skills and writing strategies in the context of using natural language. They have extended the Daily News by highlighting punctuation, phonics, adjectives, compound words, verbs, or whatever the language focus might be after they have composed the News. Many have also used interactive writing with the Daily News: The teacher passes the pen to a child while the class is constructing the message together, and the child writes part of the sentence on the chart paper; the focus is on encoding—writing letters to match the sounds one hears. I think it is also important though to highlight the composing of sentences as the Daily News is being written in order to help English language learners develop their oral language. The syntax that is naturally modeled by rephrasing sentences correctly is invaluable for ELLs, who often do not have English models at home to hear correct speech. Through this natural approach of speaking and writing for a real purpose, the children benefit from more than just an exercise in writing. With ELLs in our classrooms, every moment of the day should be spent on developing and using language constructively and for real purposes. The Daily News allows us to do this as well as it helps create a strong sense of community while we learn about each other's lives.

DOING OUR HOMEWORK

In order to set up a nurturing, inviting, and vigorous environment for our students, a lot of preparation needs to take place before the school year even begins. Although it is difficult to start planning any type of instruction without first getting to know the incoming children in person, there is a lot we can do to prepare before they arrive. Besides setting up the classroom and organizing the schedule, we need to know as much as we can about each student. That means we need to review records that are already available to us.

Looking at each child's cumulative record is a good place to start. Also, the child's portfolio, which should have been passed on from the previous teacher, is usually filled with a wealth of information about the student. I am amazed at how few of us take the time to read the information that is provided in these two sources before the school year begins. I think it is because we get so overwhelmed with the task of setting up the classroom, getting it to look beautiful for the children, that we forget that getting to know each child is the most important thing to do. Research takes time, but we need to do research on each child.

If we don't do research, we have to start from scratch, evaluating the details of each child's language level and developmental reading level. This steals time from instruction. We need to do our homework by seeking information from records and from the previous teacher so that we can build on it to form our own assessments as we meet the children. We need to trust each other as professionals, and validate the time, effort, and energy that our colleagues have invested into compiling a child's portfolio, assessing a child's strategy use and developmental reading level, and assessing a child's language proficiency. We should use that information as a starting base to begin instruction for our students and then fine-tune our teaching as we get to know each child day by day through ongoing assessment and careful observation. I find children take a few weeks to get comfortable anyway to really show me what they can do. The best way I can assess them at the beginning is informally through real reading and speaking situations in the classroom.

We can acknowledge the information our colleagues have gathered, and we can also acknowledge that a child may have grown since the previous year or perhaps needs some updating of skills. But at least we know where the child left off. Hopefully we can create an environment in our schools where we have ongoing dialogues with other teachers in order to advance the best interests of the child. Ideally, we all speak a common language as we assess and evaluate the children, so that when we start to assess our new students, we will see some continuity with what our colleagues did.

These are some of the documents we should review for every child prior to his coming into the classroom. We might find this information in the child's cumulative record or in his portfolio.

★ Home language survey, which lists the languages spoken in the home
★ Results of a state-mandated language test (CELDT) with the child's language proficiency level
★ Scores on the standardized test, both in English and in the primary language, if available
★ Child's last report card, to see if he was working at, above, or below grade level and to see what type of study skills and habits he has
★ Child's developmental reading progress card, which marks progress on a continuum from

emergent to fluent reading with regard to reading strategies and reading level

★ Child's developmental language progress card, which marks progress on a language continuum from beginning to advanced with regard to functions and structures

★ Developmental checklists on reading—emergent; sustaining and expanding meaning

★ Developmental checklists on language—beginning to intermediate; early advanced to advanced

★ Reading assessments (DRA, IRI, QRI)

★ Language assessments (IPT, LAS, SOLOM)

★ Samples of retellings of text from inventories or benchmark books

★ Samples of the child's response to the text from reading response journals or literature circle logs

★ Samples of the child's reading log, or list of books and genres the child has read, which will show his reading habits

★ Assessment notebook, which will include anecdotal records on the child's reading development as well as his language development

★ Running records

★ Informal language assessments which might be included in the assessment notebook

★ Recorded interviews and booktalks on tape

★ Letter/sound recognition, phonemic awareness assessments (K–2)

★ High-frequency word recognition (San Diego Quick)

Many of these formal and informal assessments are discussed in Chapter 2.

Based on the information we learn from this research, we can form preliminary groups and start instruction the first day. Children come in eager to start. Many wait all summer to begin, or begin again; others in year-round schools have far fewer days to get prepared. But prepared and eager they do arrive. Setting the scene is critical. We need to prepare to let children jump in, not wait four weeks to get their feet wet. Disappointment, frustration, and boredom set in if we don't get moving with our teaching. Parents too are expecting a lot from us the first week of school. They want to feel that we know who their child is and what her needs are. Often the wait for back-to-school night to hear about the program and what we are teaching their children is too long for them to wait. And of course if we are not prepared to start instruction right away, we lose valuable time in setting our ELLs on the path to becoming successful fluent readers and speakers.

Many teachers make home visits before school begins. They introduce themselves to the children and get to know the family in order to start forming the bond of trust so that learning can take place from the outset in a rich and welcoming environment.

2 KNOWING EACH ENGLISH LANGUAGE LEARNER

"I'm So Embarrassed!"

The night I arrived in Valencia, Spain, as a young college student, it seemed like chaos. There was a crowd of Spanish host families waiting in the university parking lot for us to get off the bus. We had all arrived from different parts of the United States. Those from the West Coast had left families almost 24 hours ago to embark on a semester abroad and had boarded a bus in Madrid for the five-hour bus ride to Valencia. When we got off the bus to greet our host families, most of us had not slept or eaten, and we were extremely jet lagged.

When my new friend, whom I had met on the bus, stepped off, retrieved her suitcase, and found her host family, she fainted right there in the middle of the crowd. She woke up to a circle of strangers huddled around her anxiously, with her host family looking a little startled. She so wanted to make them feel at ease that she didn't stop babbling, lo siento, lo siento *("I'm sorry, I'm sorry"). She must have said it ten times, and then she tried to say, "I'm so embarrassed!" Unfortunately, she said,* ¡Estoy tan embarazada! *("I'm very pregnant"). Well, you can imagine the response. After the jaw dropping, the shouting began, and the mother of the host family very understandably asked the program director why they had sent her a nineteen-year-old pregnant American girl. "What am I going to do with her?" wailed the mother. That's how my friend first learned about false cognates, words that sound alike in both languages but have very different meanings. After much discussion and assurances from my friend that she was just embarrassed, not pregnant, the family finally agreed to take her home. They decided she just needed a little rest and feeding—simple cures.*

How many of us have been in an embarrassing situation where we thought we were saying the right thing, yet it came out all wrong? How many of the children in our classrooms feel embarrassed lest they say the "wrong" thing? Some ELLs have just enough language to get by socially but not enough to get by academically. We need to look very closely at both the developmental language and developmental reading levels of each child in order to identify what we must teach her so that she can move ahead from her actual level of learning.

In order to do so, we must value the importance of looking at each child individually and decide how to teach to that child's strengths. We need to know which strategies and skills children should have at each developmental language and reading stage and assess each child's abilities against these, keeping in mind that she may have mastered more advanced strategies in the primary language than are apparent in her English speaking and reading. We then need to encourage her to use these strategies, regardless of the language, to help her acquire academic English and reading fluency.

All children are unique and all children seem to cry out to us to see their uniqueness, if we could only hear them and discover their special qualities. Often if we don't speak their language, it is even harder to discover their uniqueness, and even easier to lump them together in a group.

In the hundreds of classrooms and demonstration lessons with which I have been involved over the years as a consultant or a teacher, I have never seen two alike. That is because no two children are alike. Oh, they may look alike; there might be a classroom full of children with black hair and brown eyes or all speaking the same primary language. But they do not all have the same personalities, interests, families, life experiences, or language and literacy levels. Does a child like to read and have opportunities to read at home? Does her family speak any English? What are her happiest or most anxious concerns? We need to acquire such details about individual students so that we can choose appropriate books for them, plan pertinent lessons and thematic units, and try to build a community of learners and risk takers who love to read and write.

In this chapter I discuss formal and informal assessments of both English language proficiency and developmental reading levels. These should be done on an ongoing basis and the results recorded in a reading and language folder that is accessible to teacher and students during the reading block. I mention the importance of taking informal language assessments as well as running records and anecdotal notes on what we observe during the reading block about language interactions or reading strategies used. The development stages of language acquisition and reading are outlined with an emphasis on sustaining and expanding meaning. The chapter concludes with a case study of how to assess individual children's strengths and weaknesses and how to analyze them as both readers and language users. Then I mention what we need to do to meet their individual needs, which will lead into the chapters that focus on instruction.

TYPES OF ASSESSMENTS AND HOW TO TRACK THEM

What types of assessments do we use to shape our instruction? When I ask teachers that, I usually get a recital of the standardized tests they are required to give. These formal assessments are given once a year, and teachers get back the results many months later or often the following school year. They are high-stakes tests, and we all feel the pressure of

them, but they do not really drive our day-to-day planning for the needs of individual children.

Formal Language and Reading Assessments

State-adopted language tests like the California English Language Development Test (CELDT) are given under scrutiny and scored by the state, the results being sent back to schools approximately three months later. That is clearly not an assessment tool that can be used to group children or to inform language instruction on a daily basis (although many teachers hand-score the test themselves to get an idea of the proficiency level of each child). Teachers need to assess the language level of their students themselves on an ongoing basis, and they need to use some form of informal or formal assessment of their children's language level to do so (O'Malley and Valdez Pierce 1996).

There are some formal assessments that teachers can give once every quarter or three times a year to monitor children's language levels so that their development over stages becomes apparent. The Idea Proficiency Test (IPT), for instance, assesses set structures and use of language functions at each developmental level. It was first used at school sites to assess all ELLs upon their arrival in school. When teachers analyzed IPT results and looked closely at the speech errors the children made, the IPT gave instant feedback on the children's language levels as well as their use of sentence patterns and vocabulary. Now that state standardized language tests for ELLs have come into our schools, many teachers unfortunately no longer use the IPT or similar forms of assessment. Because it can provide a formal, accurate way to keep track of children's language development, I encourage teachers to continue to use this instrument. It is helpful in showing any gaps that ELLs may have in language development and enables teaching to their needs as they move along the continuum of English language proficiency (see use of IPT in case studies at the end of the chapter).

Schools and districts also use formal reading assessments like the Developmental Reading Assessment (DRA) or the Quantitative Reading Inventory (QRI). I consider these formal rather than informal assessments, although they may not have been designed that way, because they are usually used two times a year to compare the child to a benchmark, to see how the child is progressing through that year. They provide a formal way to compare reading progress to grade-level standards.

I encourage teachers to use a formal reading assessment like the DRA and a formal language assessment like the IPT at least twice a year and to keep the results of these two types of assessments together. That way, we can see the children's progress in reading and language and the correlation between them, and we can analyze if the child needs to work more on language development, on reading development, or both. By analyzing the results, we can effectively plan our groupings for instruction.

Informal Language and Reading Assessments

Besides formal assessments we should also use ongoing informal assessments, which I feel give even more information about our students and help us more effectively plan for individual instruction. We should keep track of our observations of children's developmental levels of reading and language in the form of anecdotal records, checklists, running records, miscue analysis, informal language assessments and reviews of retellings, and responses to literature, as well as reading interviews. We should keep all this information about each child in one assessment folder—the reading *and* language folder—because it is important to analyze children's language in the context of their reading. (I have a separate writing folder on each child, which we use during the writing workshop. In this book I talk only about reading and language development, however, even though writing development is just as important.)

The reading and language folder should be a working folder that you and the children have access to. I would include a reading and language assessment notebook, in which are recorded running records with miscue analysis, notes from conferences (Taberski 2000), and notes on language structures and functions or strategies that the child is using well. Informal language assessment notes can be recorded in the notebook or on separate record sheets (see Appendix A1 and sample on p. 26)

One-on-one reading conference.

kept in the folder. Comments about the child's language development and progress in reading should be included, as well as developmental checklists.

Why do I not recommend a separate language assessment notebook? Because it is in the context of listening to children read and discussing their reading where we can assess and analyze their language most effectively. By having the information in the same place, I am working on the connection between language development and reading development, which can then help me plan mini-lessons for my ELLs. I might notice that a child is having difficulty decoding multisyllabic words and speaking in longer sentences, and thus that he might have problems reading longer sentences with two clauses, for example. All might be connected to the child's sustaining meaning as he is reading. With this information on both language and reading, I would be able to analyze the connection between the two and plan mini-lessons based on what I observe in order to target the child's language patterns or his strategy use or both.

As we are conferencing with a child, we can learn a lot about his language proficiency and can write down sentence structure that we hear the child using in order to better assess his language

Reading Conference Sheet

To Monitor Reading and Language Development and to Plan for Instruction

Week of _March 8_

Date/ Name of Child	Type of Conference Title of Book	Observed Reading Strategies and Language Used	Future Mini-Lessons Reading	Future Mini-Lessons Language
3/8 Maria	Making connections <u>Tomas and the Library Lady</u>	Made good predictions. Was making connections to Tomas with own experiences. Speaking in complete sentences but not in future tense.	(Had trouble) self-correcting, sustaining meaning.	Future tense, conditional
Jose 3/8	Retelling <u>Amelia's Road</u>	Retold with lots of insight into character - how she was feeling. Skipped over lots of detail. Language: had trouble in past tense and asking questions.	Reread text for details to support main idea.	Asking questions Past tense
Adrian 3/9	Retelling <u>Esperanza Rising</u> (sharing story)	Great connections! Shared feelings about character- related to Miquel. Had some questions but had difficulty asking them.	Reread - dig deeper - to help clarify.	Asking questions
Marta 3/9	Inferring <u>Camila and Clay Old Woman</u>	Had trouble inferring what Camila would do - what she would do if placed in her shoes. Spoke in present tense mainly.	More lessons on inferring.	Future tense to talk about what she would do

Anecdotal notes on a variety of children during reading conferences.

development. What better way than in a one-on-one conference to hear how children are speaking as well as how they are reading? After I write notes in the individual reading and language assessment notebook of the child I am conferring with, I quickly write down what occurred on a reading conference sheet (Appendix A2).

The reading conference sheet allows me to record brief anecdotal notes on conferences with many children and serves as a quick way to see if there are any similarities in what I need to focus on for a variety of children either in reading or language. I can use it as a tool to help plan future mini-lessons in reading strategies or language patterns or both. The example shown tells me Jose and Adrian need help in asking questions and Maria and Marta need help with the future tense in language development. And all would benefit from a mini-lesson on rereading for meaning.

As educators we need to be kidwatchers, as Yetta Goodman (1985) said years ago. We need to observe children in order to learn as much as we can about them and to plan for their instruction. We also have to set up opportunities to interact with them individually and in small groups in order to assess them better. We have to engage them in reading texts and in conversation, and assess not only their reading strategies but also their language ability. When we get a new student, we watch how he participates in the class and interacts with other children. We ask what we can learn about this new child or other children by their attitudes in class, their body language, their verbal output, and their participation.

These first observations help us make some quick assessments, but they are very general and may not be accurate. A child who I think has a very low level of English proficiency may just be very shy. Or perhaps the types of questions I ask her may only require a yes or no response, but if I followed up with more thoughtful questions, perhaps she would be able to speak much more. The boy who seems bored today and doesn't want to participate in shared reading may be at a much higher level than I had anticipated, or perhaps he is just distracted by something that happened at home this morning. The child who speaks beautifully and seems to have a much higher level of English than his peers does not necessarily read better than his

fellow students who are struggling with English speech. He might be a fluent speaker, but that doesn't mean he has well-developed strategies to help him while he is reading.

What can we do to get to know our students in more detail? We need to assess them individually or in small-group work. Part of that assessment needs to be anecdotal, through ongoing observation. Here are some questions we can keep in mind:

What did I observe about this child today that I didn't observe yesterday?

What did I notice about this child's language as she participated in a small group or in an individual conference with me?

What strategies did I notice this child using as I observed her in a small group or during a running record?

What did I learn about this child's attitudes about reading by observing her in independent reading?

What did I learn about this child's language use while observing her participate in a variety of activities in class?

Here is an example of how to engage a child in conversation for the purpose of assessing his language proficiency.

In my friend's same first- and second-grade combination class, I often notice Kevin, who seems quiet and rarely speaks in class. One day, curious about his language level, I notice that he is in the science center with his friend Janty, and I think it would be a good time to eavesdrop on his use of natural language. Kevin's parents are from Vietnam, but he was born in the United States. His family speaks Vietnamese at home, and I presume the only English he is learning is in school. This year the classroom has a few new immigrant children from Mexico, Russia, Panama, and Korea. There are also three new Anglo-American children, one with autism. Janty's parents immigrated from Ukraine, but he was born here.

Hoping to take notes on Kevin's language as he and Janty talk while drawing dinosaurs, I approach the pair. But Kevin stops speaking when I come up. I therefore try to engage him in a discussion about his drawing, which seems to be a rendering of the cover of a book in the science center. I recorded my questions and his responses on a blank sheet of paper.

He is drawing a T-Rex. I want to ask him, "What type of dinosaur are you drawing?" but first I want to know if he even has the word *dinosaur* in his vocabulary.

What are you drawing?
A dinosaur.
I can see that. Wow, you are quite the artist. Do you know a lot about dinosaurs?
I know like about T-Rex.
What do you know about the T-Rex?
T-Rex . . . he eat.
Do you know anything else about him?
He like to fight with Triceratops.
Why do you think he fights with the Triceratops?
'Cause he has three horns.
Does the Triceratops beat the Tyrannosaurus Rex?
Sometimes Tyrannosaurus Rex win . . . just sometime.
How do you know?
'Cause I have the book.
What do they eat?
They eat small dinosaurs.

I decide to focus back on his drawing, because he has stopped drawing, and his drawing is incomplete. I use short questions to see if he can add vocabulary or ask me a question to clarify.

Can you tell me what you're drawing?
Like what did I draw? What part did I start?
Yes, can you tell me what part of the dinosaur you have drawn and what you are working on?
A neck.
Can you tell me in a complete sentence, starting with I?
I am drawing a long neck.
If you were going to describe the dinosaur, how would you describe it?
His teeth is like tight, and sometimes if he eat small dinosaur his teeth is bloody and like broke.

He points to the picture in the book and continues telling me what he knows about dinosaurs.

Some small dinosaurs are mean. If they stand up, they're bigger than Tyrannosaurus Rex.
Really? How does T-Rex then eat the small dinosaurs?

First they have to fight. Then the small dinosaur die and they eat it.

What did I learn in my short conversation with Kevin? Well, I learned that Kevin used language for real purposes. He could describe what he knew and what he was doing. He answered simple questions and could maintain a dialogue. He had no trouble understanding what I was asking, and his language functions were pretty high. He could also speak in complete sentences, and he used adjectives and comparisons with an advanced sentence structure using cause and effect ("If they stand up, they're bigger than Tyrannosaurus Rex."). He also asked some questions in the past tense, and he showed knowledge of abstract time ("Sometimes T-Rex win . . . just sometime."). He often used correct subject-verb agreement ("they eat," "he has") and correct contractions ("they're"). From our conversation I also found, however, that Kevin needed to work on some language patterns or structures to improve his English fluency. He needed to work on subject-verb agreement, especially the third person ("he eat," "he like," "his teeth is") and to improve his sentence structure without using *like* so much. This type of speech might be appropriate in some informal conversations but not in academic English. Kevin also needed to improve his questioning skills, although the questions he asked were pretty close to being correct.

Kevin's informal language assessment record sheet on the next page shows how I analyzed what I recorded from our conversation. I used this after I had dictated his direct speech onto a piece of paper, just as with running records. Sometimes I record these informal conversations on an audiotape. That is much easier, if the child is comfortable. The audiotape can stay in the child's reading and language folder; it is a wonderful way to go back and review the child's progress in oral language. So where is he on the developmental language continuum? What is Kevin's developmental level of English language proficiency? And how can we help him? Well, let's look at the developmental levels and then we will go back to Kevin to see if we can match his language output to his appropriate level.

Informal Language Assessment Record Sheet

Name ___Kevin_____ Grade __1__ Current ELD Level _Advanced_

Date ___Nov. 8_____ Type of Interaction _Conversation in Science Center_

Language Structures Used Correctly	Language Structures Used Incorrectly	Types of Language Functions Used
Used complete sentences		Maintained dialogue
Used adjectives "They eat small dinosaurs."		Answered questions fine
Used conjunctions "fight with Triceratops"		
Subject-verb agreement "I have" "He has"	Subject-verb agreement "He eat" "He like"	
Present progressive effectively "I am drawing a long neck."		Used descriptions
		Compared and contrasted
Past-tense questions "Like what did I draw?"	Questions "What part did I start?"	
Conditional form "If they stand up"		Used cause and effect to describe dinosaur fight
Sequential words "first, then"		Used sequence, abstract time ("sometimes")

Comments, Analysis

Kevin is functioning quite well in English. He is using his language for many purposes, including holding a conversation with me, answering my questions, describing his drawing, comparing and contrasting, and using cause and effect in his explanation. He is speaking in complete sentences and uses some complex sentence patterns, including past-tense questions and the use of cause and effect. He uses adjectives effectively to describe his drawing and the dinosaurs in his discussion. I question his advanced fluency level, however, since I see numerous errors which are at the intermediate fluency level. He needs to work more on subject-verb agreement, especially the third person. He also needs to work on asking questions.

Kevin's informal language assessment record sheet.

TABLE 2.1 Developmental Levels of English Language Proficiency

Developmental Proficiency Levels Based on ELD State Standards	Stages of Language Acquisition	Language Output
I Beginning	A or B Preproduction Speech	Often silent; uses gestures to communicate; then one-word responses, yes/no answers, a few two-word phrases
II Early Intermediate	C Speech Emergence	Uses short phrases and sentences; answers a variety of questions but makes simple speech errors
III Intermediate	D Intermediate Fluency	Has basic command of conversational English; uses full sentences and narratives; basic proficiency with academic language; makes common grammatical errors
IV Early Advanced	E Advanced Fluency	Has command of conversational English; uses complete and longer sentences and narratives; nearly native proficiency with academic language; makes some grammatical errors
V Advanced	F Fluency	Has full command of conversational English; native proficiency with academic language

DEVELOPMENTAL LEVELS OF LANGUAGE

By state and national standards, children are assessed according to five developmental levels of English language proficiency. They move through these levels based on stages of language acquisition, which Krashen and Terrell (1983) described as a natural process that children go through while learning language. Table 2.1 shows the correspondence between the stages of language acquisition and the developmental levels of English language proficiency. Throughout this book, I use the terminology of the state standards—beginning, early intermediate, intermediate, early advanced, and advanced—in discussing language proficiency. Once we know our student's language levels, we need to teach them based on their individual proficiencies.

If we look at the language skills listed in Table 2.1, we can see that Kevin is not an advanced speaker. Yet he was placed at level F (fluency) by his classroom teacher, and so I had classified him as an advanced speaker on his informal language assessment record sheet. He had carried on a pretty good conversation with me but had made numerous errors, and he sounded closer to what an interme-

diate-level speaker would sound like. Then why was he listed as a fluent speaker?

Many children in the primary grades are listed as fluent, or advanced English speakers even though they don't sound like native speakers. Often they come from homes that do not have English as a primary language. The reason for the discrepancy is that children may have enough conversational English at four or five years old—from preschool experiences, watching television, or speaking to older siblings—to pass the language assessment test when they enter school, and they are "FEPed out." That means they are listed as fluent English proficient (FEP) and not put into any special language program. Yet as they approach six or seven years of age, we can see gaps in their English language ability as they are asked to use academic language in classroom discussions and in reading and writing. A key to helping a child improve his English language proficiency regardless of his listed level is to assess the language patterns he has trouble with and teach them to him in natural ways, through mini-lessons in shared reading or language development. It is also important to give him many opportunities to practice in small-group discussions and while reading texts at his instructional levels in language and reading.

WHAT ARE
LANGUAGE PATTERNS?

Language patterns are sentence structures, syntax, and grammar. Children naturally develop this syntactic knowledge in their native languages without any formal instruction and thus become skilled native speakers by about age five. It may be difficult for a kindergarten or first-grade teacher to think about teaching such young ELLs syntax or grammar, yet the ELD standards require it, and it can be done in a natural process. These children have gone through a developmental process to learn their primary languages and will do the same in their second language. First they speak with one or two words, then they put phrases together into short sentences and then longer sentences (see Table 2.1). As children get older and read more advanced texts, we naturally teach higher levels of grammar, which will help them in their language development.

To better understand which language proficiency level a child is performing at, we need to know the language patterns characteristic of each level (see Table 2.2). For instance, children speak in the present tense and the present progressive tense before they start speaking in the past or future tense. Noticing these patterns, we would know that if we hear a child speaking only in the present tense, she is probably an early intermediate speaker, and if we hear a child speaking correctly in the past tense using even irregular verbs, she is probably an early advanced speaker. If a child consistently uses the habitual present tense incorrectly ("We goes," "He go"), she is probably not an intermediate speaker because intermediate-level speakers consistently use that tense correctly. That tense is more difficult than the present progressive tense ("We are going," "He is going"), which is used at the early intermediate level. We need to be aware of these nuances in order to help our students in both reading and language. We need to know that it is more natural for a child who is just learning English to read "He is sitting" than "He sits," even though *sits* looks like an easier word to read. If a child is not using intermediate-level patterns in his speaking, he won't be able to read them either.

Looking back at Kevin's informal language assessment record sheet, we can see that he was using past-tense questions at the early advanced stage yet was having difficulty with subject-verb agreement at the intermediate stage. He had also started to use the conditional tense at the advanced level yet needed more work to improve his use of it. He also used comparatives effectively at the intermediate level. Overall, I would say that based on his speech patterns he is speaking at a range between an intermediate and an early advanced level of language proficiency. As I mentioned, he was classified in kindergarten as a fluent speaker, but these discrepancies start to show up in first or second grade. A child like Kevin is often hard to diagnose because he uses language patterns across a variety of levels. This shows that he has some gaps that need to be filled, and by continuing these types of ongoing informal assessments to listen to his speaking and reading, we can effectively plan mini-lessons to best meet his needs.

I find that having sentences to use as examples for the developmental levels (see Table 2.2) helps me understand which level the children are speaking at. As children develop in language and as they read better, they start to internalize higher-level sentence structures. But we need to make sure that their language progress keeps up with the more advanced sentence structures they encounter in their texts. If they get confused by a relative pronoun, for instance, in the sentence, "She was the lady who lived down the street," they might ask, "*Who* lived down the street?" and miss the meaning of the sentence or even the passage they are reading. Or, if they don't understand the use of various conjunctions, they might miss how ideas are linked together by cause and effect.

Some children pick up correct language patterns and vocabulary naturally and easily; others need more exposure and explicit teaching on how to use them for set purposes. For example, to compare and contrast two characters in a book, a child would need to use adjectives, comparatives, and conjunctions. We could have a chart labeled "Language Used to Compare and Contrast" that lists words like *bigger, prettier, larger, smaller, more, less, as, like, unlike*. The chart would be displayed in the classroom after comparing and contrasting had been taught and modeled in a shared reading lesson with an actual text. Then we would be modeling not only how to compare and contrast but also the language patterns and vocabulary nec-

TABLE 2.2 Language Patterns Used at Each Developmental Level of English Language Proficiency

Developmental Level	English Language Patterns with *Sample Sentences*
Beginning	Yes/no responses Regular plurals Prepositions Verb *to be* Common nouns Simple sentences: *I am a girl.*
Early Intermediate	Pronouns Subject statements: *there is/are, here is/are* Negative statements Verbs, present progressive tense: **She is going to school.** Prepositional phrases: *on the table* Basic adjectives Coordinating conjunctions: *and, or, but*
Intermediate	Possessive pronouns Verbs, habitual present tense: **She goes to her friend's house every day.** Past tense: **He played soccer yesterday.** Subject-verb agreement Adjectives Coordinating conjunctions: *for, so, yet* Clauses linked by conjunction: **We go to the market so we can buy some food.** Subordinating conjunctions: *because, when, before, after* Contractions: *it's, isn't* Comparatives Questions, future tense
Early Advanced	Reflexive pronouns Abstract nouns Verbs, irregular past tense Coordinating conjunctions: *however, therefore, neither/nor* Clauses linked by more advanced conjunction: **I liked the play; however, I didn't like the main character.** Gerunds Superlatives Questions, past tense: **Did you go to the museum yesterday?** Difficult idioms
Advanced	Verbs, conditional tense, past perfect tense Auxiliary verbs: *could, would, should, might* Auxiliary verb contractions: *couldn't, wouldn't, shouldn't* Relative Pronouns: *who, whom, whose, which, that* Clauses linked by relative pronoun: **She was the lady who lived down the street.** Subordinating conjunctions: *although, whenever, until* Adverbial clauses: **Whenever you finish your homework, you can watch TV.** Abstract language Passive voice Metaphors and similes

Based on California ELD Standards and on the Idea Placement Test (IPT), used for assessment upon entrance to school and for exit from English language development programs.

essary to carry out this purpose. The ELLs in the classroom could refer to the chart at other times during literacy block.

I find the best form of assessing is daily and ongoing, so I record anecdotal notes on the Informal Language Assessment Sheet and use checklists to monitor children's developing language patterns. One is designed for beginning to intermediate speakers (Appendix A3), and the other for early advanced to advanced speakers (Appendix A4—see examples of their use in case studies at the end of the chapter). Even if children sound almost as if they were native speakers, they still need help with the nuances of English, which has many varied sentence structures that cause English language learners difficulty. The checklists may be kept in the child's language and reading folder and may be updated once a month, just as you would use a developmental reading checklist to show progress. They are meant to allow notations over a variety of levels because children who are intermediate speakers, for example, may make some errors at the beginning or early intermediate levels. This may be noted on the checklist by marking Developing, Secure, or No Evidence for each skill.

The various functions of language are assessed in the context of children actually reading and using language for real academic purposes, such as discussing their literature book or content area material, or summarizing, comparing, and contrasting during a guided reading lesson or in a literature circle. Or in the case with Kevin, we learned he could use higher-level language functions, like cause and effect, through an interview. These language functions or strategies used can be recorded on the Expanding Meaning and Sustaining Meaning Checklists highlighted in the discussion of the developmental levels of reading in this chapter (see Appendixes A6, A7). Also, Appendixes E4 and F3 provide you with observation sheets to write anecdotal notes on academic language functions children use in shared and guided reading.

In the first chapter I talked about the functions of language, and in Chapter 5 on Thematic Planning, I also discuss the importance of looking at the functions or purposes for using language within the context of learning content rather than learning it in isolation. Language actually allows children to function in numerous situations, and I

therefore prefer to analyze its use (or function) in the context of actually reading and discussing text. I provide you, therefore, with checklists to analyze children's ability to use expanding meaning strategies while reading, which cover a broad level of language functions, and which also overlap with the content area thinking process discussed in Chapter 5. The national ESL standards developed by TESOL (1997) have children using English to achieve academically in all content areas as one of its three main goals. We can teach the functions of language as strategies to use while the child is reading content, with meaning making at the forefront.

DEVELOPMENTAL LEVELS OF READING

Once we are familiar with the children's developmental language levels, we also need to know their developmental reading levels. We need to look at the reading strategies that a child uses, regardless of his language level, in order to help us decide what a child's developmental reading level is. That means we assess a child's ability to track or use pictures or reread to find meaning or use prior knowledge and personal connections to predict and understand text. It doesn't matter in what language a child does these. As was discussed in Chapter 1, if a child knows how to use any of these strategies, she doesn't have to learn them again in a new language.

Many English language learners already know how to read in the primary language and use effective reading strategies to expand and sustain meaning. We have to be careful to acknowledge what the child is able to do in reading, even if the child is barely speaking in English. We shouldn't label a beginning speaker an emergent reader just because of his language level. Perhaps that child *is* an emergent reader. But if he is a recent immigrant in fourth or fifth grade and knows how to read in his primary language, it is doubtful that he is starting out as an emergent reader. The strategies for emergent readers listed in Table 2.3 correlate with a child who is having his first experiences with text, not to a child who has had many years of reading experiences in his own language. It is important to verify accurately the strategies that a child is already using, whether in his primary language or in

TABLE 2.3 Developmental Stages of Reading

Characteristics of the Developmental Stages of Reading

The Emergent Reader

Holds book appropriately; tries to understand what book is about

Highlights title and author/illustrator on cover and title page

Knows that writing on page can be read orally; knows pictures help to tell story

Turns pages; knows the difference between beginning and end of book

Relies on pictures as best clue to gain meaning

Tracks from left to right and top to bottom with a return sweep

Begins to understand punctuation

Identifies some high-frequency words

Uses predictable patterns to help read

Uses sound-symbol relations at beginning of words to figure out words and check predictions

Predicts and retells stories

Begins to understand cause and effect, and main idea, in simple stories

Relates stories to own experiences; shares opinion of stories

Shares favorite parts of stories and why he likes them

The Early Reader

Uses pictures to help gain meaning but not for full understanding of text

Increasingly uses phonics and graphophonics to figure out unknown words

Uses decoding strategies: chunks words, blends sounds

Uses knowledge of syntax and language patterns to gain meaning

Uses background and semantics knowledge to gain meaning

Begins to cross-check using semantic, syntactic, and graphophonic cues

Self-questions while reading to see if it makes sense

Rereads, reads on, and goes back to gain meaning

Uses punctuation (quotations, question marks, commas) to gain meaning

Predicts and retells longer stories

Understands cause and effect, and main idea, in stories

Relates stories to own experiences; shares opinion of stories

Shares favorite parts of stories and elaborates on why he likes them

Compares two stories and describes both

Begins to use nonfiction text features to gain information

The Early Fluent Reader (Transitional)

Applies earlier strategies to longer texts

Predicts before and during reading to understand author's message

Makes connections to text, other texts, and prior experiences

Uses strategies for sustaining meaning to gain meaning when stuck

Knows when meaning is lost; stops and uses strategies to regain meaning

Reads a greater variety of texts and genres

Maintains meaning over longer passages and more complex story lines

Understands more complicated language structures

Self-questions while reading to understand text

Infers while reading to understand text

Summarizes chapters to predict later chapters

Uses nonfiction text features to gain information

Begins to understand complex plots and character development

The Fluent Reader

Uses strategies for sustaining meaning while reading more complex fiction and nonfiction

Focuses on overall text rather than small details to figure out difficult text

Copes with difficult text by continuing to read for information and a deeper understanding

Reads a wider range of genres, including novels, historical fiction, nonfiction

Summarizes book's main idea and gives supporting details

Analyzes plot and important parts of story to understand author's purpose

Evaluates more complex characters to decide whether their actions in story were appropriate

Infers author's message; predicts what characters might do in other situations

Synthesizes new nonfiction information to gain insight into a topic

Can deal with longer time periods in which the plot fluctuates from the past to the present and perhaps back again

Is able to self-question as he is reading in order to gain a deeper understanding of the text

Sets a purpose for his reading and uses his own questions and knowledge to gain more information about a topic

Is able to integrate a variety of sources of information effectively while he is reading

Can compare and contrast different characters from within the same book or from a variety of books

Can reflect on what he is reading and respond critically and emotionally to the text, whether fiction or nonfiction

English. Then we are able to build on his strengths to move him forward on the literacy continuum, by matching him with the right level of text to challenge him in guided reading and to support him while he reads independently. And with the support of language assessment, we can develop his English language proficiency as we continue to develop his reading strategies and skills.

We have to use appropriate reading assessments, both in the child's primary language and in English, in order to shape instruction to his needs. I mentioned the DRA as a formal reading assessment. This can also be given in Spanish. You can also give informal reading assessments, such as analyzing retellings, in the child's primary language, whether it is Vietnamese, Hmong, or Russian. An instructional assistant or fluent native speaker of the child's primary language can assist you in analyzing the retelling if you are not proficient in the language. By assessing the child in his primary language, we can build on his strengths as he transfers his strategies and skills to the new language. We also need to use ongoing informal assessments in reading, as we do in language, to help us look at what the child is able to do on a daily basis and to plan instruction to meet his needs.

INFORMAL READING ASSESSMENTS

Once we have an understanding of the characteristics of the various levels of reading development, we can determine at what levels children are performing based on the strategies we see them using while reading. If a child is still an emergent reader, I use a developmental checklist for emergent readers (Appendix A5) for ongoing assessment. This checklist includes some higher-level strategies, such as "begins to understand cause and effect" and "retells a story maintaining the main idea," but it principally highlights the print awareness and word analysis characteristics of an emergent reader.

Since children keep using many of the same strategies as they become better readers, I find that individual checklists for each level are not that helpful. Rather, once a child goes beyond being an emergent reader, I prefer to use two checklists for each child: a sustaining meaning checklist

(Appendix A6) and an expanding meaning checklist (Appendix A7). We can divide the strategies a child uses into these two camps—strategies to help her sustain meaning and to continue when she is having difficulty, and strategies to expand meaning and help her go beyond the literal interpretation of the text (Fountas and Pinnell 2001). I put both these checklists, which also help me keep track of their language functions, in each child's reading and language folder along with the developmental checklists of language patterns.

These checklists serve as a reminder of what I should be watching for as I confer with children, take running records on their reading, or assess them during guided reading lessons. I keep notes on the children's reading and language development, including retellings, running records, and miscue analysis, in their assessment notebooks on a daily basis. (I suggest doing this daily and focusing on each child once or twice a week.) Then, as I review each child's assessment notebook, I use the checklists about once a month to record her developmental progress. This also serves to remind me what strategies children still need to work on and which children I might group together for mini-lessons or guided reading. I also use Appendix F3 during guided reading to help me. The reading and language folder, holding the checklists and assessments, truly drives my instruction.

A CASE STUDY

Let's now look at a case study to see how we can assess a new English language learner who arrives in the classroom. I use informal language and reading assessments, a formal language assessment, and developmental language and reading checklists to help analyze how to teach her effectively and plan for her instruction. I also describe another child for comparison to gain perspective on how to plan for both children in the classroom.

Miriam

I met Miriam in a summer literacy institute I was leading for teachers. They were working with ELLs who were below grade level in reading or having dif-

> Afrien dis... Miriam
> someone you like to
> spend time with h.
> A FRIEND IS...
> Toy
> Story
> Someone who is lo yal.

Miriam's writing sample.

ficulty in reading and writing. Miriam had just finished kindergarten and was entering first grade in the fall. I entered Miriam's room during writing workshop and sat down next to her to get to know her better. I looked at her writing, and my first reaction was, that's pretty good. She had written not only complete sentences but complicated ones with ellipses and words like *loyal*. Her spelling was perfect, which might seem like a difficult feat in itself for a five-year-old, let alone an ELL. I was a little suspicious, however, when I saw *A Friend Is . . .*, on her desk. (The title) was exactly what she had written in her journal. I asked her first to read her writing to me, and she couldn't do it. So I asked her to read the book to me, and when she turned each page, I saw she had copied each line from the book. But instead of reading about how to be a friend, using the characters of *Toy Story,* she "read" the pictures. This is what she said:

Woody
The soldier
Piggy
Woody and Toy Story
The dinosaur
I don't remember what it's called.
The soldiers

The radio
The Woody and the woman
Woody and Toy Story
Now these two are friendlys.

Q *What do I know about Miriam so far as a reader, a writer, and a language user?*

She knows that reading is about making meaning. She can hold a book, turn the pages, and use the pictures to help her make meaning. She named all the characters in the book as she turned each page and looked at the pictures. She knows how to form letters, she can write in a straight line from left to right and top to bottom, and she is a good copier. She can also speak in complete sentences, although they may not be grammatically correct, and she has a vocabulary that includes the characters of *Toy Story*.

Although I had learned some things about her, I had many more questions about this intriguing child:

Can she read a book more at her instructional level?
Can she track and match words one-to-one on the page?
What other strategies does she use as a reader?
Does she know letters, and can she match them to sounds to help her decode simple words?
Can she write on her own?
Does she use developmental spelling to help her write words in her stories?
How developed is her English language proficiency?

I decided to engage Miriam in more conversation to see if I could learn more about her language level. Then I would take a running record on an emergent-level text to see her developmental reading level and, if necessary, give her an Idea Placement Test to assess her language use. I would also ask her to write about her favorite part of the story, or about any other book she wanted to comment on, to see the level of her own writing.

Our talk and the running record took about ten minutes. If I had been the classroom teacher, I could perhaps have divided that into two five-minute intervals. In just a quick conference with a child, one can learn a lot about her strengths and instructional needs.

"Wow! You sure know a lot about *Toy Story*," I said. Miriam told me she had seen the movie and had "two toys of Woody and the glasses." She used *glasses* for *binoculars*. She said she had gotten the toys at McDonalds. I asked if she could tell me more about the story. I wrote every word down as quickly as I could. The punctuation is mine, based on how she told the story.

> The girl kissed Woody. The Toy Story was on the bed of Woody. "Get off my bed," said Woody. "This is my bed!" Then the Toy Story wouldn't get off the bed. Woody got off the bed. Then the girl, he used the glasses to see what was happening to Woody and Toy Story. That's all I remember.

Miriam was excited to tell me what she knew about the movie. It took me a few minutes to figure out that "Toy Story" meant the character Buzz Lightyear. That would have been much more difficult for her to say. I loved her retelling of the dialogue, which she thought was very amusing. Since she didn't want to say any more about the story, I shifted the subject to the book and her writing. She went back to her writing, drawing on the side of it as if I weren't there.

"What does the title say?" I asked, pointing to the cover of the book and to the first line of her writing. "The title says Woody and Friends," Miriam said. Well, the book *is* about Woody and his friends, and once again, she is trying to make meaning.

"I remember something else," Miriam said. "The dinosaur and Woody ... the dinosaur ... Woody was getting the television. 'Aaah!' says the dinosaur, and he said, 'If I scared you?' Woody says, 'No!' " She laughed, and I laughed, too, appreciating how much she enjoyed the dialogue and the wit of the movie, and how she was able to retell that so effectively, even though her question formation shows she is not a native speaker.

I then asked her to read her writing. And once again, instead of reading "A Friend Is ...," which she had copied, she said, "Woody and Friends." Then she started naming the letters, not reading the words. She named every letter correctly. When she got to the word *time*, she said /ē/ for both the letter *i* and the letter *e*. So I asked, "If this [letter *e*] is /ē/, what is this [letter *i*]? She said /ī/.

What else have I learned about Miriam?

Her strengths are her delight in a good story and her ability to retell it. Her English speech is very developed for a five-and-a-half-year-old whose first language is Spanish. She knows the names of all the letters, and although she did make an error, she can distinguish between the Spanish and English pronunciations of the letters *e* (/ā/ in Spanish) and *i* (/ē/ in Spanish). This shows she has knowledge of letters and sounds in both the primary and second languages.

I wanted to know more about her reading ability, so I asked her to read the emergent-level book *Huggles' Breakfast* and took a running record on a blank piece of paper. I told her the title but did not walk through the book, so this was a cold read of an unfamiliar text. She tracked across the page and looked at the pictures. In this eight-page book, each page has a picture and only two words: "A carrot, / a cake, / a fish, / a bone, / a banana, / a sausage, / a telephone." The two pictures showing telephones also show the words "Ring, Ring" in the picture.

From the first page on, Miriam embellished the text on each page with "I'm eating the." At the word *sausage*, she said, "I don't remember this word." *Sausage* might be difficult even for a native speaker if she didn't eat sausages at home. She automatically read "Ring, Ring" for the two pages where the telephone is shown. (See her running record on the next page.)

Now what do I know about Miriam's strengths and needs as a reader and an English speaker?

Miriam has a strong sense of story and tries to use that along with her strong language ability to create a meaningful sentence from each page. She added words to make meaning, and she knows what a telephone does. She also knows there are patterns in text, and she successfully used the same pattern throughout her "reading" of the book. She tracks and uses the pictures to help her.

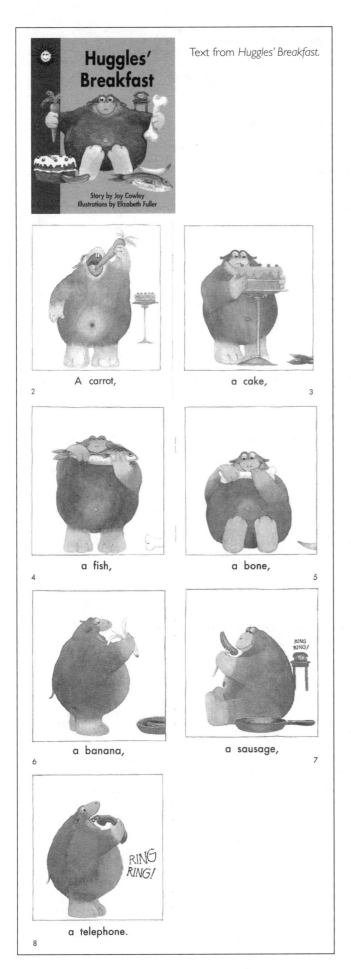

Text from *Huggles' Breakfast.*

A carrot,

a cake,

a fish,

a bone,

a banana,

a sausage,

RING RING!

a telephone.

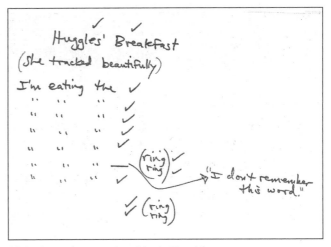

Miriam's running record on *Huggles' Breakfast.*

Q *What strategies does Miriam need to work on to become a better reader?*

She needs to focus on one-to-one word correspondence and to use her knowledge of sound-symbol relationship to check her predictions. If she used these two strategies, she would see that her four-word sentence ("I'm eating the ——") doesn't match the two-word pattern on each page. She would also notice that *I'm* doesn't start with *A* or *a* and therefore could not be the first word on each page. Based on the strategies listed on the developmental checklist for emergent readers, I would say that Miriam is an emergent reader (see page 36).

Q *What is Miriam's language proficiency level?*

Based on her conversation with me, I would probably classify her as an intermediate or early advanced speaker. However, because of her age and the complete sentences she is able to use, even though sometimes incorrectly, she might test out as a fluent English speaker because such tests are given developmentally by grade level. A kindergarten child, for example, is not expected to speak as articulately as a third-grader.

Miriam scored at a D stage of language acquisition (intermediate fluency), or a developmental proficiency level of intermediate (see Table 2.1), on the Idea Proficiency Test (IPT). As a kindergartner, she would be considered a fluent English speaker, yet she is starting first grade. She answered the question, "Are bananas blue?" with "No, they're yellow," which showed she could say a negative statement and use

Developmental Checklist for Emergent Readers

Name _Miriam_   **D = Developing, S = Secure, NE = No Evidence**

Reading Strategies and Language Functions	Date								
Pleasure Reading									
Participates in shared reading activities by memorizing rhymes, songs, repetitive phrases of Big Books									
Holds book and envisions self as reader	S								
Starts to read books independently	S								
Chooses own books out of classroom library	S								
Comprehension									
Develops a sense of story	S								
Uses pictures to gain meaning from stories	S								
Retells a repeated pattern in a book	D								
Tells an appropriate story to match a picture	S								
Retells a story maintaining the main idea	S								
Begins to understand cause and effect	S								
Begins to predict outcomes in new stories	S								
Print Awareness									
Recognizes print in books and the environment	NE								
Holds book and turns pages properly	S								
Follows and tracks lines of print left to right	S								
Has one-to-one correspondence when pointing to words	NE								
Word Analysis									
Begins to point to individual words in a familiar story	NE								
Recognizes common words	NE								
Develops an individualized sight word vocabulary	NE								
Names some beginning or ending letters in words	S								
Begins to use sound-symbol relations to read words	NE								
Matches words with predictions to self-correct	NE								
Vocabulary Development									
Develops speaking vocabulary from wide variety of thematic units	D								
Starts to use words in short sentences	S								
Starts to use words heard in books and songs in own sentences	D								

Miriam's assessment on developmental checklist for emergent readers.

Developmental Checklist of Language Patterns for Beginning to Intermediate English Language Learners

Name: Miriam   **D = Developing, S = Secure, NE = No Evidence**

English Language Proficiency Level	Skill	Date 7/14
Beginning	Uses regular plurals	S
	Uses prepositions	S
	Knows how to use the verb *to be*	S
	Can say a command	S
Early Intermediate	Knows subject pronouns	S
	Uses statements: *there is/are, here is/are*	S
	Knows present tense	S
	Uses present progressive	S
	Can state a negative statement	D
Intermediate	Uses habitual present: *she goes*	S
	Knows subject/verb agreement	S
	Uses adjectives correctly	D
	Uses past tense	S
	Uses simple contractions: *it's, isn't*	S
	Uses comparatives	D
	Asks questions in future tense	D
	Uses possessive pronouns	D

Developmental Checklist of Language Patterns for Early Advanced to Advanced English Language Learners

Name: Miriam   **D = Developing, S = Secure, NE = No Evidence**

English Language Proficiency Level	Skill	Date 7/14
Early Advanced	Uses superlatives: *most, least*	D
	Uses irregular past tense	S
	Uses adverbs: *well* (vs. *good*)	NE
	Uses abstract nouns: *freedom, citizenship*	NE
	Uses gerunds: *going to school*	D
	Uses conjunctions: *however, therefore*	NE
	Uses synonyms and antonyms	D
	Asks questions in past tense	D
Advanced	Uses perfect tenses: *has been, will have been*	NE
	Uses conditional perfect tense: *if he had worked harder, he would have finished*	NE
	Uses specialized adverbs: *already, still*	D
	Uses auxiliary verbs: *could, would, should*	NE
	Uses auxiliary contractions: *couldn't, wouldn't, shouldn't*	NE
	Uses relative pronouns: *who, whom, whose*	NE
	Uses metaphors	NE
	Uses similes	NE

Miriam's checklists.

contractions—two skills difficult for ELLs. She could also use the present progressive tense and regular plurals. However, she did have some gaps in her language development that a teacher could help her work on. She had difficulty with collective nouns like *corn* (she said "corns"); with asking questions correctly; with comparisons like "Ice water is colder than coffee"; and with using the habitual present tense as in "He rides his bike every day" (she said, "He's on his bike; he is going to his house."). She also couldn't name the days of the week, which is surprising because they spend so much time on that in kindergarten.

The above two checklists of developmental language patterns (Appendixes A3 and A4), which I filled out after listening to Miriam speak with me, and after analyzing her IPT, show her right in line with being an intermediate speaker. These assessments guided me and helped me suggest to the classroom teacher what to work on with Miriam in her language and reading development.

Eddie

I would like to briefly survey another child, Eddie, and compare the two children and then give suggestions on how to help them both. Eddie, also an ELL, had just entered first grade, and I assessed him in both language and reading, using the same book *Huggles' Breakfast,* and the Idea Proficiency Test (IPT).

Eddie had just read a book with a repetitive pattern of "I see," and he used patterns very effectively, so it is understandable that he would expect to use a pattern he had just read while reading an unfamiliar book, *Huggles' Breakfast* (see full text on p. 35). As his running record shows, he added "I see" to the first page of text ("A carrot") but then stopped and self-corrected *I* to *a.* He self-corrected a second time *I/a.* He touched every word. He knew all the vocabulary, possibly because I had previewed a couple of the words I thought he might have difficulty

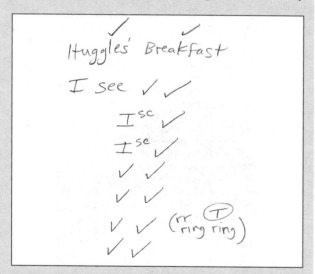

Eddie's running record on *Huggles' Breakfast.*

with, like *sausage.* When I pointed to "Ring, Ring," he didn't know what sound the telephone makes. He tried to sound it out by saying /r/ almost like a tiger sound and yet couldn't get it, so I then told him the word. Then he pointed to each word *ring* and was able to read it.

Q What strategies did Eddie use?

Eddie tracked from left to right. He had one-to-one correspondence. He looked at

the pictures to help himself. He self-corrected because he knew that what he had read wasn't on the page. He used his knowledge of graphophonics to help him check his predictions. He made sense of what he was reading. He repeated the word I gave him (*ring*) and used it to read other instances of it. Each time he wasn't sure of a word, he stopped and said, "Hmm," and put his finger to his head to show he was thinking. Eddie was at a strong emergent reading level on his way to being an early reader (see Table 2.3). Besides assessing him on a developmental checklist for emergent readers, I did so also on a checklist of strategies used by early to fluent readers to sustain meaning (Appendix A6) because he seemed to be using such strong strategies (see next page).

Q What is Eddie's language proficiency level?

Eddie scored at a B stage of language acquisition (preproduction speech), or a developmental proficiency level of beginning (see Table 2.1), on the IPT. He could produce basic vocabulary like *teacher, window, fish,* and *apple* but said *hand* for *arm,* for example. He knew how to say how old he was, his grade level, and his first and last names. He could respond to a silly sentence. Besides just checking the test answers, I recorded his responses to show the classroom teacher exactly what he had said. That way we had a better way to analyze the score. The developmental checklist of language patterns for beginning to intermediate ELLs (Appendix A3) confirmed that he was a beginning speaker (see page 40).

Eddie was developing a knowledge of the verb *to be,* subject pronouns, the statement *this is,* and the present tense ("I drive, I see"). He showed no evidence of knowing plurals, saying a command, using the present progressive tense, or saying a negative statement.

Planning for Eddie

Eddie needs the modeling of a good reader, a teacher who reads an exciting text with expressive pictures and a great story line to engage him. The text I would choose for a shared reading lesson would be a Big Book that supports his developmental language needs, a book with strong

Developmental Checklist for Emergent Readers

Name Eddie   **D = Developing, S = Secure, NE = No Evidence**

Reading Strategies and Language Functions	Date					
Pleasure Reading						
Participates in shared reading activities by memorizing rhymes, songs, repetitive phrases of Big Books						
Holds book and envisions self as reader	S					
Starts to read books independently	S					
Chooses own books out of classroom library	S					
Comprehension						
Develops a sense of story	S					
Uses pictures to gain meaning from stories	S					
Retells a repeated pattern in a book	S					
Tells an appropriate story to match a picture	D					
Retells a story maintaining the main idea	D					
Begins to understand cause and effect	S					
Begins to predict outcomes in new stories	S					
Print Awareness						
Recognizes print in books and the environment	S					
Holds book and turns pages properly	S					
Follows and tracks lines of print left to right	S					
Has one-to-one correspondence when pointing to words	S					
Word Analysis						
Begins to point to individual words in a familiar story	S					
Recognizes common words	S					
Develops an individualized sight word vocabulary	D					
Names some beginning or ending letters in words	S					
Begins to use sound-symbol relations to read words	S					
Matches words with predictions to self-correct	S					
Vocabulary Development						
Develops speaking vocabulary from wide variety of thematic units	D					
Starts to use words in short sentences	D					
Starts to use words heard in books and songs in own sentences	D					

Checklist of Strategies Used by Early to Fluent Readers to Sustain Meaning

Name Eddie   **D = Developing, S = Secure, NE = No Evidence**

Context of Observation (lesson, conference) _conference – running record_ **ELP Level** (B, EI, I, EA, A) _____

Reading Strategies	Date							
	10/23							
Predicts	S							
Uses context	D							
Uses background knowledge	D							
Uses pictures/visual cues	S							
Uses graphophonic cues	S							
Uses syntactic cues	D							
Recognizes miscues that disrupt meaning	NE							
Self-corrects miscues that disrupt meaning	NE							
Rereads/looks back	D							
Reads ahead	NE							
Cross-checks using multiple strategies	NE							
Asks for help	D							
Expects to get meaning from the text	S							
Uses punctuation to help gain meaning	D							
Makes connections to gain meaning	D							
Thinks what would make sense	S							

Eddie's developmental checklists on strategies used by emergent to fluent readers.

repetitive patterns in the present progressive tense. I would highlight the pattern in the text to help build on the sentence structure he is developing. Also, I might choose a text with plurals, perhaps with animals, which he seems to know and like. *A Farm's Not a Farm* might be a good book to use because it has both of these language components in it and also animals (see description in Chapter 7). By focusing on Eddie's interests and strengths, I can start where he is and move him forward. The key is to do this while trying to meet the needs of nineteen other children. Chapter 7 explains how to plan a shared reading lesson that focuses on the developmental levels of all the children in a class, including children like Eddie who are at beginning English language proficiency while demonstrating strong use of reading strategies.

Developmental Checklist of Language Patterns for Beginning to Intermediate English Language Learners

Name **Eddie**   **D = Developing, S = Secure, NE = No Evidence**

English Language Proficiency Level	Skill	Date							
		10/23							
Beginning	Uses regular plurals	NE							
	Uses prepositions	D							
	Knows how to use the verb *to be*	D							
	Can say a command	NE							
Early Intermediate	Knows subject pronouns	D							
	Uses statements: *there is/are, here is/are*	NE							
	Knows present tense	D							
	Uses present progressive	NE							
	Can state a negative statement	NE							
Intermediate	Uses habitual present: *she goes*	NE							
	Knows subject/verb agreement	NE							
	Uses adjectives correctly	NE							
	Uses past tense	NE							
	Uses simple contractions: *it's, isn't*	NE							
	Uses comparatives	NE							
	Asks questions in future tense	NE							
	Uses possessive pronouns	NE							

Eddie's assessment on developmental checklist for beginning to intermediate readers.

Planning for Miriam

Miriam could also benefit from a shared reading lesson in which the teacher models not only language patterns but also good emergent reading strategies. Since her command of sentence structure is much stronger than Eddie's, and her academic language proficiency much more developed, I would focus on highlighting reading strategies that would help her attend more to the text. I would model one-to-one correspondence by pointing to the words with a pointer or a bright-colored pen while reading. I would also model matching the text with the picture and trying to figure out which word would fit. I would use Post-it notes to cover up words or parts of words and have Miriam use her three cueing systems to figure out the correct word in context and to help her self-correct. I would model looking more closely at the words, and help her realize that although something might make sense, we still need to use our graphophonic cueing system by checking the spelling of words and using a knowledge of phonics to see if what we predicted is actually the word on the page. This can be done naturally in the context of a shared reading lesson.

Both Children

I placed all the notes, running records, and language assessments, including the IPT, I had taken on Miriam and Eddie as well as their developmental checklists on both language and reading into their reading and language folders. These could then be used by the classroom teacher in continuing to plan instruction for the children. Based on formal and informal assessments of both children, I felt pretty confident that I had identified their language and reading levels correctly, especially because I provided an "upper bound," an additional check, by assessing Miriam (a strong speaker) on a higher developmental language checklist and Eddie (a strong reader) on a higher checklist of reading strategies. Children don't just master one level and then move on to the next. They are constantly developing their language and reading abilities, making mistakes, learning new structures and strategies, and using them in context. Sometimes it makes sense to use checklists at two levels to assess a child in order to get a full picture of what the child can do and to confirm one's assessment of his reading or language level, allowing him to perform to his full potential.

Q *How would we compare Miriam with Eddie? Who is the better reader?*

Miriam is an emergent reader with a strong intermediate level of language proficiency, and Eddie is a strong emergent or even early reader with a beginning level of language proficiency. How can we teach them both in the same classroom? Hopefully we would plan shared reading lessons to model for their individual needs using their strengths in language or reading to help them. And there are many other ways to help them develop language and reading strategies, including guided reading, which I discuss in subsequent chapters.

The important thing is that we who have English language learners in our classrooms need to look closely at each child in order to know her skills completely and instruct her most effectively. We should not assume that a child who has a strong level of English language proficiency compared to her peers is necessarily a better reader, or that a child who is at a lower language level than his peers is necessarily at a lower reading level. As I have said, I regard language development and reading development as inseparable elements of a balanced literacy program, yet each needs to be looked at closely.

3

WELCOMING PARENTS AS PARTNERS

The Meeting of the Parents

I will never forget the first time my parents and my husband's parents met. César's parents arrived in the United States a week before the wedding, and we planned a dinner at my parents' house the night of their arrival. Neither set of parents spoke the others' language. I told Coco (César's dad) and Nelida (César's mom) that my parents were very informal and that they shouldn't worry about dressing up. That didn't convince them. They were going to their son's future in-laws' house for the first time, and they wanted to make a good impression. So Coco wore a suit and tie with a silk handkerchief sticking out of his pocket, and Nelida wore a semiformal dress with matching jacket. My dad opened the door to greet them—in his bare feet! Now, you have to know that shoes are not my dad's favorite. Although he was dressed nicely, he didn't have shoes on. My mother had kept warning him, "They'll be here any minute, get your shoes on," but he hadn't listened. Coco held out his hand to shake my dad's, but my dad enveloped him in a bear hug. My mom went to hug Nelida, but Nelida kissed my mom on the cheek. Greeting customs were a little mismatched but they all smiled, especially at my dad's feet. He held up his shoes, pointing to them, and thus started the conversation of hand gestures between the fathers. Within minutes, Coco had taken off his coat and Nelida her jacket, and they all began to settle in. They could see the sparkle in each other's eyes and the warmth that radiated from their mutual smiles, and although they couldn't converse in words, they all felt right at home. Although Coco and Nelida might have looked too formal on the outside (by my parents' standards), my parents learned right away that they had chosen to dress up to show respect for the other family, not because they were "stuffed shirts." And Coco and Nelida could see that even given my parents' informality, the two families had religion, education, and values in common. The respect and fondness conveyed by each couple toward the other were obvious regardless of the language barrier.

A face-to-face meeting was critical for our parents, and is critical for the joining of any two families. When cultural differences and language barriers exist, there isn't anything better than to meet personally. Then, through hand gestures, smiles, body language, and of course through their children as translators, diverse families can perceive that they are all good people who care about their children and deserve mutual respect.

All parents, regardless of language, culture, education, or relationship roles—which could mean stepparents or guardians—want the best for their children. So, when their child enters school, they want to know their child's teacher, what the teacher has planned for their child, and what they can do to help their child be successful regardless of whether or not we see them at school. Most immigrant parents come to the United States to make a better life for their children. They have suffered many hardships and still may be suffering from poverty. They often work two or three jobs and hope that their children will get the education that is the key to a better life. We need to help make the school experience a successful one for both parents and children. Often parents do not know how to act or how to become engaged in our school system, which may seem foreign to them. Their children often have to translate for them. We need to make them feel welcome, make them feel a part of our learning community, and give them many opportunities to become involved regardless of language. We need to build bridges between home and school so that the children can continue learning in the home environment and the home language. Parents are the first teachers of their children, and the values and concepts that they transmit at home in the primary language can be transferred to any language.

In this chapter I describe ways of involving parents in the classroom and in the larger school community. I also emphasize the importance of promoting literacy activities in the context of family, whether reading or speaking, at home or at school, in the primary language or in English.

GUIDING QUESTIONS

How can I get parents to come into my class-room?

I have so many different languages in my room, how can I highlight their languages and still emphasize English?

I don't speak the parents' languages, so how can I communicate with them?

How can my children's parents help them to read in English when they don't speak English themselves?

What types of programs could I use to promote family literacy?

INVOLVING PARENTS IN THE CLASSROOM

As a classroom teacher I always started the school year by sending a welcome letter to parents, which invited them to participate in their children's schooling:

Dear Parents:

Welcome to our classroom!

I would love you to come in and participate in the education of your child this year. You are an important part of making sure that your child is successful in school. Not only would I appreciate your help, but I know that your child would as well.

There are many ways that you can partici-pate and become involved in the classroom. You could help during reading time, writing time, or with math, science, history, or social studies. If you are talented in music, art, or physical education—or you have a special tal-ent like how to make homemade paper or how to sew or make model airplanes—your help in any of those areas would be much appreciated. If you could come in and help make copies, pre-pare materials for class, or help correct papers, that would be great.

On the next page is a short survey for you to fill out that will help me understand your

skills, strengths, and special talents, and how you might like to participate in the education of your child this year. Please add anything else in the blank lines that you might like to do. Also, you may not be able to come in during the day but could help me prepare for the class activities at home.

If you are not fluent in English, that is not a problem. I would still love you to come in and help, and if I can't communicate with you effec-tively, I will find a translator to help me; per-haps even your child could help. Language should not be a barrier to your coming in and participating in your child's education.

Thank you for your time and effort! I look forward to having you help and participate with us this year!

Mrs. Cappellini

Appendix B1 shows this letter in Spanish and the survey in both English and Spansih. Since I was a bilingual teacher of Spanish and English, the survey went out in those languages, but in sharing this practice with teachers at numerous school sites, I always encouraged them to adapt it to their own needs and the languages of their students, using translators to help.

Many families are really hoping to come in and help in their children's classrooms, but they may have logistical problems that get in the way. Sometimes there are younger children at home and the family cannot afford day care or a babysitter. To get over this obstacle, certain schools, with the prin-cipal's support, have offered space for a child care cooperative where parents take turns taking care of the younger children while other parents help in the classroom. Some parents work at night and sleep mornings but could help in school during the after-noon. To accommodate this, some teachers schedule literacy block in the afternoon instead of in the tra-ditional morning time. Other parents would be only too glad to help at home, preparing journals for the children to use in class, for instance, or putting new books into the home-school book bags, or stapling the pages of children's newly published books. They just have to be asked. Some prospective volunteers may never have attended school themselves and may be unfamiliar with the classroom or the school set-ting. Or they don't know where to go, and hesitate

Mother and daughter reading in Spanish before school starts.

to ask at the office. Many schools set up a "parent room," a welcoming place for parents to read notices, find supplies, work together on schoolwide or parent-teacher association projects, or meet other "room parents."

These are simple solutions to draw more parents into the classroom. More complicated is making parents feel comfortable to come into the school; this requires whole-school planning and a supportive climate created by everyone from the principal on down. It should be noted that parents who do not participate in the school community often have complex reasons for not doing so. I recommend focusing on school-based solutions rather than reaching too far into each family's complex background issues.

The tone that we set for parents is critical from day one. Every time we see them and have an opportunity to interact with them, we need to show them kindness and respect with the same patience we show their children. We need to be inviting and inclusive rather than just tolerating the many cultural, language, and educational differences. I have found that the schools with the highest percentage of parents involved at school are the ones that make them feel welcome and comfortable to be there. A map of the languages and countries of origin of the students is posted on a common wall of the school. Letters are sent home in several languages, and vol-

unteer speakers of various languages from the community act as liaisons to parents. The principal and staff greet parents with open arms. They open the school doors in the morning and welcome parents to walk their children to the classrooms, come in, and stay for a while. Parents mingling with each other, even for a few minutes, create a positive environment and allow teachers to see them on an ongoing basis so that relationships can develop. The children feel honored that their parents are regarded as valued members of the school community rather than only being called in when there is a problem or a scheduled conference.

The following are some ways in which schools can set up a welcoming environment and encourage ongoing home-school communication. It is assumed that all this communication will be presented bilingually and that efforts will be made to use the primary languages of all the children and families at the school.

★ *Open Campus in the Morning.* Allowing parents to walk onto campus with their children in the morning and up to the classroom door provides teachers and parents informal ways to interact and to build relationships.
★ *Greeters.* Bilingual parents and teachers can serve as greeters in the morning to welcome parents and children and set a positive tone.
★ *Morning Library Time.* If the school library is open before school starts, children and families can go in and read together.
★ *Family Reading in the Classroom.* Encourage family members to come in and read with their children the first twenty minutes of the school day (or at other times). Classroom libraries would be available for their book selections.
★ *School Bulletin Boards.* All types of events and curriculum information is posted for families.
★ *School Newsletters.* Include school curriculum issues, events, and letters from the principal, PTA, school site council, and bilingual advisory board each month.
★ *Class Newsletters.* These include themes, curriculum news, books read, and focus of study of the class and weekly notes from the teacher.
★ *Morning Teas.* Monthly social teas allow parents to get to know each other. Certain

Parents helping in the library.

faculty members speak about events, books, or special programs, and guest speakers are invited.

★ *Breakfast with the Principal.* Monthly breakfasts provide positive ongoing communication with the principal and allow parents to ask questions regarding the school as a whole.

★ *School Tours.* Three times a year tours lead parents through the classrooms and focus on the programs of instruction in reading, math, and content areas.

★ *Community Liaisons.* A community liaison can foster understanding with families who don't speak English or who are unfamiliar with prevailing customs.

★ *Family Storytellers.* Encouraging parents to come in and tell stories in the primary language with the support of a community translator celebrates diversity and validates all parents, including those who are not literate.

★ *Family Journals.* These make connections in writing that the whole family can participate in daily.

★ *Parent-Teacher Journals.* Letter writing back and forth on any topic furthers communication.

★ *Literary Journal.* A quarterly journal highlights student, teacher, and family work.

★ *School Web Page.* A school Web page is a convenient and inviting way for families to stay involved with the school. Curricular and extracurricular activities are highlighted.

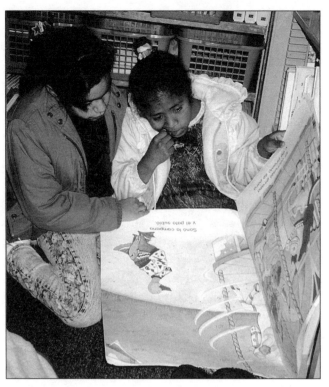
Reading together during the first twenty minutes of the day.

I'd like to expand on a couple of these ideas.

Family Storytellers

Many family members do not read in the primary language, but they do have great stories to tell. Providing them with an opportunity to tell their stories with the help of a community translator supports children's appreciation of diversity and pride in the primary culture and language. In one of the large urban schools I worked at in Santa Ana, California, many parents who were not literate in their native languages came in and told stories. Some of the parents spoke Hmong and Khmer, and since the school was mainly Hispanic, we had a translator from the Cambodian Community Center come in with these parents and translate the story for the children. Most children in the classroom had never heard Hmong or Khmer being spoken, and this gave them an opportunity to hear a new language and celebrate a classmate's culture. Each child sat next to his parent while the parent told the story in his native language. The translator then translated the story into English, and the teacher scribed what was being said. The child was then able to illustrate his parent's story and place it in the class library for all to read. These family stories became favorites of the class. They were also taken home through the class checkout book system.

Knowing the home languages of your students would be ideal, but often this is clearly impossible. That is why having community liaisons or translators or instructional assistants who speak the language of your students and their families goes a long way toward making families feel comfortable at school. Liaisons can also be asked to assist at morning teas or breakfast with the principal, or indeed at any events where families and school staff get together. It is extremely valuable to highlight the native languages of children at your school, especially if some minority languages are represented. These families, too, need to feel that their languages and culture are valued and that they are welcome in the community of learners at the school site.

School Tours

Public schools are open to the parents of children, and parents have the right to come in and visit anytime providing that the teacher or the principal knows they will be visiting. Often, however, parents just want to have a better understanding of the type of instruction that is occuring at the school and what they can do to support it. They don't want to disturb the teacher, and the teacher has very little opportunity to describe what is going on in the classroom except at back-to-school night or at parent conferences. But parents may still not be able to visualize the type of program the teacher is espousing. Providing opportunities for parents to see the school literacy program in action is an important part of creating ongoing dialogue and educating parents on schoolwide literacy goals as well as encouraging them to participate as classroom volunteers.

That is why we created school tours on our campus three times a year. Private schools provide tours to entice parents to enroll their children, and we felt we should do the same to arouse interest. Because our campus was large—over 1,200 children in K–5—we provided tours at two different times on the same day to accommodate different work schedules. We offered the tour two other times during the year and focused on math and content areas at that time. The first tour in the fall focused on the schoolwide literacy program of

Reading To, With, and By children, so we hoped that when we walked through various classrooms, parents would see a read-aloud, a shared reading lesson, a guided reading lesson, or children reading independently or in literature circles.

We first assembled in the school library and described the literacy program in both Spanish and English. We also had community liaisons and instructional assistants who translated in Khmer, Hmong, and Vietnamese. We then divided into smaller groups of twenty or less, and the resource teachers, principal, assistant principal, and liaisons and translators acted as tour guides. The parents divided into language groups, and they visited the track their children were in, since it was a year-round school with four tracks. As they walked through classrooms from kindergarten through grade 5, they did not interrupt the instruction; the tour guides described what was going on in the classroom and perhaps pointed out certain wall charts as well, which showed the current focus of instruction or unit of study.

The parents then met back in the multipurpose room for refreshments and to further discuss the schoolwide literacy program. The feedback was very positive: parents felt like they had gotten a bird's-eye view of real instruction. All questions were answered regarding the overall program, and parents then felt easier about asking the teacher questions regarding their individual children. Many new volunteers came in, and the communication between teachers, staff, and parents became stronger. Relationships between staff, administration, and parents are often difficult to forge because parents don't see them as often as they do classroom teachers. The tour and meeting allowed parents to feel as if they knew more people at school whom they could turn to if they had concerns.

ENCOURAGING PARENTS TO SUPPORT LITERACY

Reading in the Primary Language

Today we see messages all around us for parents to be involved in their children's reading development. Ads in newspapers and on television show famous movie stars, sports figures, or other celebrities advocating the importance of reading to children.

Yet what is the conclusion immigrant parents might draw from these? Read to them in English! Does that mean parents should not read to their children in the primary language? Perhaps they will conclude, I can't read in English, so I can't read to my children.

Some parents don't read at all or don't discuss with their children what they read. Yes, it is important for parents to read to their children in English, but only if they have the language level not only to read to them but to discuss the reading afterwards. If they can't discuss the text because of their English level, they won't be able to encourage the higher-level thinking processes of analyzing what is read, summarizing it, or connecting it to their own lives.

Children need practice reading in the language they are learning, but they also need practice in developing the depth of understanding of a story, the detailed plot development, the character analysis, and the author's intent in writing the story. If their English proficiency is too low to benefit from such discussions in English, we should not just wait till the language level improves. They could be developing these higher-level thinking skills if their parents read to them and discussed literature in the primary language.

This cognitive development of children transfers from the primary language to English, but often our schools do not acknowledge that fact. Once a child learns how to retell a story, how to make inferences while reading, and how to compare and contrast, she can transfer that knowledge to her new language. She already knows the concept of how to do it; now she applies new vocabulary to the concept.

There's nothing I enjoy more while reading a book to my daughters than to see their eyes light up with excitement as they share their favorite parts of the story or ask questions or make comments as we are getting through the book. They each make their own connections to other books or to their own lives and develop their own understanding of the book. When they say, "Read it again!" after hearing *Click, Clack, Moo, Cows That Type* or "This is my favorite book!" to *Falling for Rapunzel*, I know they are truly enjoying reading. I would hope that all parents, regardless of whether they speak Spanish, Korean, Vietnamese, or any other language, can experience the same joy as I do at home reading and sharing books with my children in our primary language.

Because I am able to read to my daughters in Spanish, their second language, as well, I've seen firsthand that the experience is not the same as when we read in English because their second language level is too low. They do enjoy listening to the stories and looking at the pictures when we read in Spanish, but we can't talk, for instance, about what they think a character will do next or how this book compares to another or what the author is trying to say. Our conversations are limited to simple questions like which is your favorite character or part of the story (but not why). Frustrated by such constraints, we often just switch to our primary language to share our views and personal connections.

We need to encourage family members who are literate to read and talk about books with their children in any language with which they are comfortable. Imagine parents who are not fluent in English being asked to read in English to their children. What types of discussions can they have together in English? I would hope that they value the importance of having these discussions with their children regardless of the language. They can read the book in English if they are able to, for example, and then discuss it in Spanish. Or more important, they could read a book to their children in the language they are comfortable and fluent in. If they can read or discuss in English, so much the better, but the joys and benefits of reading should not be out of reach to families because of second language limitations. I would hope that more teachers encourage their students' parents or any adult that can read to just read to them!

Hopefully, your school has a large collection of literature in your students' primary languages whether or not you are teaching in a bilingual setting. Having access to primary language sections in libraries, and allowing children to check out books in Spanish, Korean, Vietnamese, Cantonese, or any of the many languages our students speak, not only conveys respect for their home languages in their new country but also lets children continue developing conceptual skills while they are developing English language proficiency. It also allows families to take part in fostering their literacy development.

Free reading in the large Spanish library collection.

In my city, the library made the headlines of the local paper for starting a literature section in Spanish both for adults and children. They emphasized what a help it will be for students taking Spanish to read literature in Spanish and how it will also be a service for those wanting to continue reading in their primary language. I wonder why the local school board doesn't make that same acknowledgement and allow Spanish speaking sections in the school libraries. What a gift for children to be able to read in two languages, and what a wonderful opportunity to read with their parents in one language and read with their classmates in another. Many children translate stories for their parents and many share their parents' stories with their classmates in English. Instead of worrying that our children should only read in English, I would hope that most schools and school boards would hope that children just continue to read!

Promoting Family Literacy

It is important to encourage the literacy development not only of our students but also of their families. Among the family literacy programs I have developed

or seen used at the many schools I've worked at are the following. It is assumed that all these programs are presented bilingually, with translation offered in the primary languages of the participating families.

★ *Before-School Reading Club.* Children and their parents read together English and primary language books in a "reading room" before school starts.

★ *Authors' Tea.* Grade-level or classroom teas planned with parents and teachers to highlight their children as authors.

★ *Family Literacy Night.* Four times a year families and their children's teachers participate in shared reading, read-alouds, guided reading, and independent reading with a focus on fostering the literacy development of the students and their families.

★ *Home-School Reading Program.* Take-home books are provided by teachers for all students in their classrooms.

★ *Library Night.* One evening per month families are invited into the school library to see featured books, use computer programs, and access the Internet.

Family literacy class.

Parents writing family histories.

★ *ESL Classes.* Classes are offered in the evenings or the mornings for families at all levels of English language proficiency.

★ *Parenting Classes.* Classes are offered on various topics of parenting responsibilities at different times of the day or evening, adjusted to parents' schedules.

I'd like to expand on a couple of these ideas.

Home-School Reading Program

Hopefully every school has some sort of home-school reading program that encourages all chil-

dren to take a book home and read it every night. Most schools have incentive programs to spur children to read, but I have found the best incentive is to allow children to share with the class the books they read at home the night before. Then the act of reading itself becomes a wonderful incentive. But in order for children to be excited about reading and sharing their books, a lot of time needs to be spent in the classroom to develop such excitement. Teachers should spend a lot of time modeling, sharing, and encouraging their children to read good books, not just send them to the library once a week for the library assistant to help them check out a book. Home–school reading programs should encourage children to take home books daily that they are interested in and that they would like to practice Reading To, With, and By their families.

Most schools with students who qualify for Title I or that are schoolwide Title I programs have a family component written into their site plans. This component usually includes a home-school reading program, or it should. This is the best way to fund the purchase of numerous books so that children can take home different ones every night.

I have found that if we give children responsibility for taking care of the books, even the smallest children have no problem doing so. The children who come from homes that most need the books, the homes where there are no other books, tend to be so thrilled that they have a book that they can't wait to bring it back and bring home another one. There are always families that move again, possibly for the fourth time that year and, yes, we might lose a few books, but in the overall picture that does not amount to many books. I taught in a school with a 40 percent transiency rate, yet we lost very few books.

There are several options for setting up a home-school reading program. In an English-only setting with ELLs, one of the best ways for parents to be involved in reading to their children is to send home bilingual texts or the same text in both English and the primary language, if available. Or send home a book at the child's independent reading level in English together with a higher-level text in the primary language for the parent to read to the child. That way a family member can listen to the child read his book in English and then read the higher-level text and have an in-depth discussion about it in the primary language.

How can we assemble primary language books for the classroom library? First, if a school has an immersion or English-only strand where a bilingual program is also offered, visit colleagues teaching bilingually and ask to share some of their primary language books. Second, search the school or district. After the dismantling of many bilingual programs in the past ten years, some schools had tons of books in Spanish, for example, that got placed in a closet somewhere or were sent to the district office. You would be surprised what can be found hidden away in school or district storage spaces. If this "site detection" comes up dry, well, then, start ordering some primary language books out of Title I funds or school improvement funds or other state funds. And appeal to the principal. I have found that principals are very good at finding resources for materials if they see the potential benefit for ordering them.

Many teachers have a home-school book program in which they send home English books (and sometimes the corresponding primary language books) at different reading levels in order to give the child and the parent the flexibility of reading different types of books together. But they include a To, With, or By bookmark in English or Spanish (Appendix B2) to tell family members the appropriate use for each book they send home. A **To** bookmark means that the book needs to be read **To** the child because it is above the child's independent reading level. A **With** bookmark means that the book needs to be read **With** the child because although the book is at the child's instructional level, and the child might be able to read most of it, he will need some assistance. A **By** bookmark means that the child can read the book **By** himself because the book is at the child's independent level. This guidance is a wonderful help for parents, because often a child takes home a book to share that is much too difficult, and the parents wonder why he can't read it. If the parents don't read English, they might not be able to help with the **To** or **With** books, but at least they will be aware of the level, and they might be able to find an older sibling, an aunt, or a neighbor who can read in English with their child. Ideally, if the teacher had a very large selection of books, the child would take home three books at the same time: one at the **To** level, one at the **With** level, and one at the **By** level. (The Spanish bookmarks say *lea a*, *lea con*, and *lealo solo*—see Appendix B2.)

Another option for a home-school reading program is for the children to take home the books they have read in guided reading that day. Or they could take home an independent reading book that they had read that day in case they had not met in guided reading. Some teachers send home two or three books from their independent reading book boxes in a special envelope or pouch. This allows the parents to see the books their children are working on in class. The parents can then see what the child's independent reading level is. A focus sheet or response journal might also go home with the books for the children and parents to write in together. Once again, although teachers may be concerned that the children will lose the books, most children have no problem returning the books every day if they are instilled with the idea that reading is important. Books then become like gold. They are so honored to have them that they care for the ones they take home and are eager to choose new ones to take home the next night.

Family Literacy Night

One way to kick off a home-school reading program is to plan a family literacy night at school, which should be repeated three more times during the year. This provides an opportunity for school personnel, parents, and children, as well as community volunteers who want to participate, to come together in the hope of developing a love of reading within their school community. The teachers or resource teachers who help run these family literacy nights will ideally be bilingual in order to communicate effectively with the families. If not, bilingual instructional assistants or volunteers from the community could help teachers with the different languages. Ideally, the teachers and the families, the young children and the older kids, will participate in read-alouds, shared reading, guided reading, and independent reading in both English and the primary language.

The Reading To, With, and By model would be presented, and the teachers would share the importance of discussing books, not just reading them.

Discussions could be modeled, and families could take turns rotating through the different types of reading activities, which would be set up around the large multipurpose room or school library. One group of families would participate in a shared reading of a Big Book, for example, and then they would use other Big Books to practice with their own children what the teacher had modeled. Another group of families would participate in a read-aloud and discussion, and then each family would choose its own book to read with the children.

Of course, one needs hundreds of books on hand for such a night because hopefully hundreds of people would attend. In the same school where we led the school tours, family literacy nights often drew three hundred people. We discovered through surveys that many parents worked night shift or swing shift and could not come to evening meetings. So, we planned successive family literacy meetings in the morning, afternoon, and evening. Of course, children and teachers are in school in the morning, so the morning meetings were primarily instruction for parents on how to read with their children at home, but these parents did get to prac-

tice with the toddlers they brought to the meetings. The afternoon meetings were held right after school, and the children could participate, so the meetings were nicely attended. The evening meetings were the best attended of the three meeting times, but we were surprised to have good attendance at the other two meeting times as well. This shows that we often have to think outside the box in planning meetings around the needs of families. If we can make it easy for them to come (even if it means more work for us), they will come because they want to help with their children's education.

Before-School Reading Club

One other opportunity to help instill the love of reading in children, and to have them practice reading as much as possible, is to have a before-school reading club. When I was a Title I Bilingual Resource Teacher at a school in Santa Ana, we realized that the children at our school did not spend enough time reading, so in addition to the home-school reading program and the schoolwide independent and silent reading time, we decided to set up a before-school reading club.

Before-school reading club.

Since 95 percent of our children were receiving free or reduced meals, most of them came to the campus thirty or forty minutes early to eat breakfast. The children would often finish their breakfast in a couple of minutes, and then they stood around with their parents, waiting for the classrooms to be open. They were anxious to get into their classrooms, yet teachers were making last-minute preparations and couldn't open the classrooms before the bell rang. We realized that we couldn't expect the teachers to open their rooms early every morning, yet we wanted a place for the children to read.

We decided to open two of our resource rooms as reading club rooms in the morning. That meant both rooms had to be manned by resource teachers or instructional assistants. One room was the Spanish reading club room, and the other was the English reading club room. All the children needed to do to enter either room was to have a parent sign a permission slip that they could enter the club and read before school, and then they received laminated reading club cards with their names on them. They were so proud of their cards. Many had never received a library card before. We wanted parents involved in this important process. We wanted them to be part of this exciting morning activity of coming to a special place to read. So, parents were encouraged to come in and read with the children. Although the city had a large public library, children rarely went there because it was too far away for them to walk and most of the parents didn't drive.

The reading club rooms were also used as bookrooms, and teachers would come in and check out literature books, Big Books, and guided reading books. So, in the morning we often saw teachers coming in to check out materials while children were sitting on parents' laps reading with them. Often siblings would read books to each other. There were bean bag chairs, and kids were sprawled out all over the floor reading books together. There were often sixty people in the Spanish room and thirty or forty in the English room. It was a wonderful sight, and much better, we thought, then seeing them just stand around outside waiting for school to begin.

We did have a school library, where the children went once a week to check out books, but it wasn't available in the morning. It was inside our multi-purpose room, which often had morning meetings or activities going on, and the library assistant was not available to have children come visit in the morning. Staffing is definitely an issue when planning a before-school or after-school reading program, but often it just takes flexibility and the desire for it to happen to put it in place. As resource teachers, we often were called to morning meetings, so we trained two instructional assistants and extended their day for half an hour in order to allow us the flexibility to move in and out of the rooms if we needed to. The important thing was that we had provided a wonderful space for English language learners to read with their families in a welcoming environment. Often immigrant families live in crowded living spaces, and many children do not have a place to read quietly. Both the children and the families seemed to really enjoy it.

BUILDING COMMUNITY

We need to provide opportunities during the school year for families to get to know each other, to build not only tolerance but respect and understanding of each other's cultures. That is what builds community—times to get to know each other through enjoyable planned events that highlight children's accomplishments and also build friendships. By working together on projects for the good of the school, parents who normally would not meet or socialize have the opportunity to interact and share their skills. And by helping with schoolwide projects, like a fall festival or an annual picnic, parents also get to know the school staff better. The connections they make with each other and with the school personnel help parents feel more connected to the school and perhaps more willing to be part of their children's educational experience. The school stops feeling so foreign, and they start feeling accepted by the people who work there—the office staff, the principal, the teachers. The faces that they see are not strangers anymore, but people with whom they have worked side by side at a school carnival or helped to make costumes for a school play.

The following community-building activities are examples of what many schools are doing to promote a sense of community:

* *School Carnival.* Halloween, fall, winter, or spring carnivals are great ways to bring the school and local communities together.
* *School International Festival.* With a focus on food, art, and music from various cultures, the day serves as a celebration of diversity.
* *School Fashion Show.* Great way to highlight the traditional costumes of home countries and learn about different cultures.
* *School Play.* An annual school play can highlight the talents not only of the children but of the parents as set designers, costume makers, directors, musicians, and so on.
* *Community Fundraisers.* These include family nights at local restaurants, pizza parlors, skating rinks, and so on (percentage of money spent goes toward the school).
* *Family Dances.* Bring the whole family to the school gym for a dance with teachers and school staff.
* *Family Astronomy Night.* Enjoy star gazing with the school community; experts from local universities or astronomy clubs participate.
* *School Holiday Programs.* These include songs from all languages and cultures in the school.
* *Ice Cream Socials and Art Festivals.* Traditional ice cream socials can be planned throughout the year, and children's art can be featured.
* *Family-School Annual Picnic.* A picnic at a local park, beach, or lake is a wonderful opportunity for socializing and for an end-of-year event.

Each of these events takes a lot of planning and coordination of families and school staff. I want to highlight one of the events—the school fashion show—to show the reasoning and planning behind it. I find that if there is a purpose in mind, in this case, to deepen our understanding of the different cultures at the school, the event can be entertaining and also educational.

At the same large school I mentioned previously, less than 10 percent of the children were from Asian countries. Over 90 percent were Hispanic, and they knew very little about their fellow classmates. Unfortunately, they called any child who didn't look like them "Chinitos," a derogatory term meaning little Chinese people. We were very concerned about the lack of respect they showed their peers and their ignorance of their classmates' cultures. Most of the Asian children were from Cambodia, with some from Vietnam and Laos. With the help of the neighborhood Cambodian Center, parents, and instructional assistants, we put on an Asian fashion show to educate the students about the diverse and rich cultures of these minority children.

Once we started planning the fashion show and interviewing the families who were going to participate, more and more people wanted to be in it, including parents and teachers who were immigrants from other countries. Soon the Asian fashion show became the school fashion show, with children, teachers, and families modeling traditional costumes from Japan, Mexico, Bolivia, Peru, and Argentina as well as Cambodia, Laos, China, Vietnam, and Thailand. Besides the interesting and beautiful costumes, including silk wedding gowns that parents had brought with them when they immigrated, the interviews we conducted of each individual were the highlight of the show. These interviews, which helped us introduce each model and gave us information to talk about as each person walked down the runway, gave us a deeper respect for the cultural heritage and background not only of the children and parents but of the teachers at our school. We learned things we had never known. We found out about the journeys many parents had made to come to the United States, including living in refugee camps, and we learned that one of the teachers had been born in a Japanese internment camp. We decided to have special bulletin boards placed in classrooms, the library, and the teachers' lounge to highlight children, parents, instructional assistants, and teachers each week or month. The fashion show was also the impetus for a children's book called *Dressing with Pride,* written by Maria Acuña and Mali Ny, both instructional assistants from the school (the book is also available in Spanish). The book had photographs of children who were models in the original fashion show and showed them both in ordinary American clothing and, posing with family members, in special traditional clothing of their cultures. (See pages from the book on page 56.)

Meet Gina, Mina, and Nancy Chang. Their parents came from Laos to the United States in 1979. The girls were born here. For New Year, the Chang family prepares special foods and wears traditional clothes. Gina, Mina, and Nancy feel very proud when they wear this clothing.

The girls pose with their mother. Laotian women have many types of traditional clothing. All are made with a special Asian silk. Gina is wearing a Laotian dress that covers only one shoulder. Mina and Nancy are wearing clothing and hats from the Hmong culture. The skirts are called *Tab*. In front of the Tab is a longer piece called the *Sev* with sequins and silver coins sewn onto it.

6

7

Two pages from *Dressing with Pride.*

There are many wonderful opportunities to build cultural understanding and foster deeper friendships between families, staff, and children at school from many diverse backgrounds. It just takes time, effort, and a desire to put the lives of the people first. We can learn many things from the families our students come from. We need to regard them as valuable resources in the education of their children regardless of the languages they speak.

4

READING TO, WITH, AND BY CHILDREN

The Demanding Tourist

On one of my trips back to Spain, I was traveling with a friend through the beach towns of southern Spain. I had been looking forward to using my Spanish, but everywhere we went, there were crowds of German tourists, who spoke either German, which I didn't understand, or English, which I didn't want to use. One morning I went into a camera repair shop, hoping to have the proprietor quickly fix my shutter, which wasn't closing properly, but it turned into a very long wait. A German tourist had walked into the shop just ahead of me. He too seemed to want his camera fixed, and he was trying to explain what he wanted in German. Unlike many of the other Spanish shopkeepers, the owner of the camera shop didn't seem to understand much German, but he was trying to communicate using gestures. In an attempt to find out what the tourist wanted, he pointed to the tourist's camera, then to the camera cases, lenses, and film packages on display in the store. In response, however, the tourist just kept on speaking louder in German. The shopkeeper kept trying to understand him, but instead of using gestures or choosing different words to convey his request, the tourist just kept repeating the same phrases over and over, louder and louder until he was almost shouting. I began to feel afraid as the voice of this man got more demanding and threatening. I was glad when the shopkeeper finally gave up and, shrugging his shoulders, showed the tourist the universal "get out" sign by pointing at the door.

How many times have we tried to explain something to a new student who doesn't speak our language, and we don't speak his, and it almost seems like a futile effort? Hopefully we don't just keep on talking louder, as this tourist did, thinking perhaps that the other person just can't hear us. Rather, we need to think of different ways to make ourselves understood to the ELLs in our classrooms. Perhaps we could phrase our sentences differently, use different key words they can latch onto, use visuals as a reference, or use total body language by pointing and perhaps even acting out what we are trying to say (Krashen and Terrell 1983). It was very obvious in the preceding scenario who was trying to make his language more comprehensible and who was not. One would've thought that, in the context of a camera shop, the tourist might at least have used the prop he had and all the props available to him in the shop to make himself understood. I think he just assumed that the shopkeeper should conform to his speech without making any adjustments. As teachers of English language learners, we have to constantly make adjustments so that our students can continue to grow and learn.

Research has taught us that we need to scaffold our instruction to support ELLs in both language and reading (Krashen 1996; Gibbons 2002; Graves and Fitzgerald 2003), to teach them within their zone of proximal development (Vygotsky 1978), to engage them in instructional conversations (Saunders and Goldenberg 1999), to build on their strengths and teach them from where they are at, and to help them acquire English by setting up opportunities to use it for real purposes and in the context of reading real texts (Krashen 1996; Ellis 1990; Freeman and Freeman 2002). We need to model for them, encourage them to try, support them, challenge them, interact with them, and then set them free to read and speak independently.

Children learn through direct teaching, guided practice, and trying out independently what they have learned. Cambourne's conditions of learning (see Chapter 1) must be in place, and the best practices of teaching reading and language must be synthesized to provide a balanced literacy program. We can do that by following a model that Mooney (1990) espouses of reading *To* the children, reading *With* the children, and having the children read *By* themselves.

In this chapter I describe what it means to read To, With, and By all children of all language and literacy levels through the important components of a balanced reading program, including read-alouds, shared reading, guided reading, and independent reading (including literature circles). I hope that readers who are familiar with these techniques will see them in a new light as they instruct English language learners. We must constantly be aware of the children's developing language and think of the importance of also talking To, With, and By the children as they are learning to read. The discussion or "talk" that needs to take place in our classrooms in order for our English language learners to be able to gain a deeper understanding of what they are reading and a stronger command of the language cannot be trivialized. Meaning making is paramount and discussion must be an important part of our program as children are not only learning to read, but are also learning to speak the language.

Subsequent chapters discuss read-alouds, shared reading, guided reading, and independent reading in detail, with examples of primary and upper-grade lessons. This chapter provides an overview of a balanced program where both reading and language skills and strategies are taught within these components of the To, With, and By model on a daily basis. Also included are sample schedules for putting this into effect.

GUIDING QUESTIONS

What should a balanced reading program for English language learners look like?

What is the benefit of reading to children if their English level is so low?

How do we teach strategies and skills in read-aloud and shared reading?

What is the purpose of guided reading?

How is guided reading different from other reading techniques?

How important is independent reading time for my English language learners?

Why do we have children share their reactions to what they are reading or what they have learned about themselves as readers?

How can I manage the needs of all of my English language learners and still fit everything in the day?

ORGANIZING A BALANCED PROGRAM OF READING TO, WITH, AND BY CHILDREN

I first read about organizing a balanced reading program in Hornsby and Sukarna's *Read On: A Conference Approach to Reading* (1986), in which the authors describe small- and whole-group literature instruction and individual conferences with children on what they have read. The authors wrote about modeling reading for children, Holdaway's (1979) shared reading model, and reading aloud to children daily. They also emphasized tailoring the teaching of skills and strategies to children's individual needs and keeping good track of their progress through ongoing assessment. That book provided me with a wonderful model on how to set up a balanced program, but it did not take up the important topic of guided reading.

Mooney's book *Reading To, With, and By Children* (1990) did include guided reading, and it made the organization of the program so easy for me. It seemed so simple, and it still does. I consistently share this model with teachers as I work in their classrooms because it is a great way to think about teaching reading—Reading To, With, and By children every day. I had tried organizing such a program with a first-grade class, and it worked great. I had thirty-six students, and of course all my colleagues had sent me their "favorite" children. Our district had a waiver from the state to increase class size without penalty. (This was before California went twenty to one in K–3.) All the children were ELLs, and one-third were new to the school. You could say I was a little overwhelmed. But as I've shared with teachers over the years, I clung to those three words—To, With, and By—as to a life preserver. I put them at the top of my lesson plans and the organization of my reading block seemed to fall into place. These words were a constant reminder of what I needed to do every day.

Every day I read *to* the children and modeled for them as an expert English reader and speaker. I showed them what a proficient reader does, how she thinks while reading a book, and how she describes her thinking. I also read *with* them and allowed them to join in as they started to enjoy reading and speaking. I engaged them in instructional conversations and helped them construct

Reading To Children

Read-Alouds. The teacher reads aloud *to* children at least two or three grade levels above the children's reading level, with the children participating interactively or the teacher modeling reading strategies in think-alouds and the use of rich language.

Reading With Children

Shared Reading. The teacher reads a Big Book *with* children in a whole heterogeneous group, modeling reading strategies, language functions, and language structures and teaching skills in context. Children join in the reading when they are ready and participate in discussions.

Reading By Children

Guided Reading. Children read *by* themselves an unfamiliar text at their instructional levels, with guidance from the teacher in small homogeneous groups, using the reading strategies and the language patterns that they learned in shared reading and read-alouds.

Independent Reading. Children read self-selected texts *by* themselves or in literacy centers, while other children are in guided reading groups or literature circles and the teacher reads one-on-one or confers with individual children. This could also be seen as DEAR time (drop everything and read) or SSR (sustained silent reading) time.

Literature Circles. Children read and discuss literature in small groups led *by* themselves or teacher assists if necessary.

meaning. I set aside time to meet with them in small guided reading groups, where they would read *by* themselves. I gave them guidance, encouraged them to read on their own, helped them use the strategies and skills they had learned through watching, listening, and participating in read-alouds and shared reading. I gave them opportunities to make choices and to have time to read: to read books they were interested in and books they could successfully read by themselves, to read along with a tape or with a buddy or volunteer, and to discuss their books in literature circles. I included these approaches to teaching reading in my classroom every day. I still share with teachers the importance of using all these approaches daily. The description above is an adaptation of Mooney's model.

Readers who are familiar with Mooney's model of how to organize a balanced reading program will see that I differ slightly with her description of where the components fit. I include guided reading in Reading *By* children along with independent reading rather than in Reading *With* children, as Mooney does. I believe it is important to make a clear distinction between shared reading and

guided reading, because I have seen the line blurred too often in classrooms. This is really where the bridge from dependence to independence occurs, with shared reading on one side of the bridge and guided reading on the other. Both are used in the classroom to support ELLs, but it is in guided reading that children start to read by themselves, albeit with guidance and support from the teacher. In guided reading the teacher is not reading the text aloud together with the children, as in shared reading, but rather every child in the group reads the text by herself.

MODELING LANGUAGE AND STRATEGIES IN READ-ALOUDS

Jim Trelease is known by many as the guru of reading aloud to children. He has published many books, including the *New Read-Aloud Handbook* (2001) and suggests that we continue reading aloud to children all the way through to college. He read to his daughter her whole life, and when she came back from Oxford University, she still asked him to

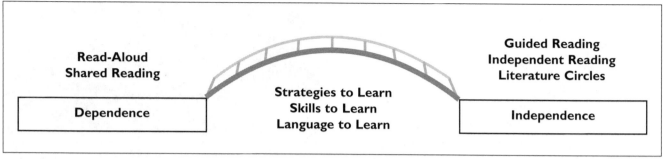

read to her. The pleasure the parent gets from this experience is as great as the child's. I treasure my time every night when I read to my three daughters.

In the classrooms where I work, if they just had me read a story aloud to the children, I'd be happy. Picture books are wonderful for English language learners, and they have become so sophisticated and the illustrations so beautiful that they are as suitable for reading to upper-grade children as to younger ones. The illustrations help children visualize the story as it is being read, which is extremely helpful for ELLs. Folk tales, fairy tales, family dramas, historical fiction, the alphabet, humorous stories, adventure stories, realistic narratives—all can be found in picture books. *Q Is for Quark: A Science Alphabet Book* is so detailed that each letter—for instance, Y is for Y chromosome—could be used to teach a whole science unit in the upper grades.

Often it is only in the classroom that ELLs hear English spoken or read, or get to interact with an expert reader of English. In their homes they might be fortunate to have such interactions in the primary language, but they also need to practice them in English. In read-alouds they are exposed to language that is more formal, with a wider range of vocabulary and language structures, than the language they hear on the playground or in normal conversations. They benefit from hearing rich language in a well-written story and from well-known literature that they otherwise wouldn't be exposed to. They need to hear

A told B and B told C "I'll meet you at the top of the coconut tree."

from the well known and much loved *Chicka Chicka Boom Boom* by Bill Martin Jr. and John Archambault. And they need to hear

"Pull back hard," old Abuela said. "Make it jolt, so the threads stay close, like family."
"Yes, Abuela."

from the Parents' Choice Award Honoree *Abuela's Weave* by Omar Castañeda. They need to hear

It was late one winter night, long past my bedtime, when Pa and I went owling.

from the famous book and Caldecott Medal winner *Owl Moon* by Jane Yolen. And they need to hear

Annemarie looked up, panting, just as she reached the corner. Her laughter stopped. Her heart seemed to skip a beat.
"Halte!" the soldier ordered in a stern voice.
The German word was as familiar as it was frightening. Annemarie had heard it often enough before, but it had never been directed at her until now.

from Lois Lowry's remarkable Newberry Medal winner *Number the Stars*.

English language learners also benefit from the teacher's modeling of reading strategies, or how she maneuvers her way through a text, even the tricky parts. They benefit from the chance to talk with the teacher and with each other about books even if they can make only a one- or two-word response. And they benefit from reading the text over again in independent reading time.

Read-aloud time is when I choose to model higher-level strategies while thinking aloud and encouraging the children to help me while I try to make meaning for myself and allowing them the opportunity to interact with me as well:

I wonder what they're going to find up the coconut tree?
Coconuts!
[*Chicka Chicka Boom Boom*—self-questioning, encouraging predictions]

I like the way the author compares the tight weave to family ties. I wonder if all families feel that close.
My *abuela* is a close part of my family.
[*Abuela's Weave*—commenting on author's craft, making connections]

I can see the moon and the giant trees, and I can almost hear that whistle. She makes it so real for me.
I've seen an owl.
[*Owl Moon*—visualizing]

I bet that Annemarie is so scared that she freezes. I bet if they ask her anything, she won't know what to say. I'd freeze, too.
I would be so scared. I would want to run, but my legs would be stuck.
[*Number the Stars*—inferring, making connections]

I model strategies like inferring, making connections, analyzing, synthesizing, building on what I know, questioning, rereading, and studying the plot. After modeling a strategy in read-aloud, I am careful to model it again and develop it further in shared reading that day. ELLs, like most children, need repeated emphasis (and practice) to learn. They need constant dosages of language.

It is not just the young ones who love to be read to, but the older students in upper grades as well. In *Reconsidering Read-Aloud* (2002), Hahn declares the importance of reading to older children and gives wonderful examples of read-alouds in fourth- and fifth-grade classrooms. ELLs who are just learning English need as many read-alouds as possible to help them. I try to do at least two per day. Regardless of grade level, one read-aloud is always a chapter or two from a novel we are reading, and the other is always a fiction or nonfiction picture book. Sometimes I read newspaper or magazine articles to help students learn how to read these as well.

Chart of Spanish-English cognates.

While I am reading, I am aware of metaphors or difficult phrases or sentences or even common words that don't seem to fit into the sentence and that can trip up ELLs. It is my job to stop and think aloud, vocalizing my thoughts and concerns about the meaning of a word, phrase, or sentence I've just read. I try not to say, "You probably don't know this word" or "You should know this word, and it means . . . ." Rather, I might say, "I wonder why the author [of *Saltwater Habitats*] chose the word *leathery* to describe the case that the shark eggs sit in. Is it because it is hard like the *leather* in my shoes, which protects my feet? I wonder if this *leathery* case actually protects all the eggs." This shows the children how to figure out words in context and how to make connections to things one already knows.

I also try to highlight or emphasize through intonation Spanish-English cognates if there are Spanish-speaking ELLs in the class (see chart above). Thousands of words sound almost the same in English and Spanish and have the same root and meaning. If one can tap into these words for the (many) ELLs whose first language is Spanish, one can use language they already know to advance their knowledge of English and improve their academic vocabulary (see Chapters 5, 6, and 8 and Appendix C4 for more on cognates).

Many picture books have themes dealing with complicated social issues in the United States yet are wonderfully told through the eyes of children. Most children enjoy *Baseball Saved Us* and *The Bracelet*, both set in the 1940s during World War II, when U.S. citizens of Japanese ancestry were rounded up and sent off to internment camps. Another book, *A Migrant Family*, tells the real story of a twelve-year-old boy and his family who lived in the underbrush in southern California, basically homeless with no running water, while the father worked as an itinerant day laborer picking crops. *Smoky Nights* deals with the Los Angeles riots of 1992 and with the tension between residents of different ethnic groups in that city. Some might argue that these themes may be difficult to explain in terms that children can understand, and more difficult perhaps because of the limited language levels of many ELLs. But they often touch on realities that immigrant children and their families have experienced in the United States and thus can help the children make connections to their own lives. They provide us with a wonderful opportunity to tap into the higher levels of reading strategies that our English language learners need to develop in order to master academic English proficiency (Cummins 1994).

TEACHING SKILLS AND STRATEGIES IN SHARED READING

In the daily sessions of shared reading, children are taught to use effective reading strategies for sustaining and expanding meaning as well as natural language patterns to improve their reading and language proficiency. In shared reading, where the text is a Big Book or enlarged on an overhead, children can follow along with the teacher's reading and join in when they feel comfortable. Shared reading is one of the most effective ways of helping children in all grades learn reading strategies and language skills, no matter what their language or reading levels, because they can engage with the text in such a natural and enjoyable way. Shared reading is also a good time to introduce a wide variety of genres, which gives children practice in reading different genres for themselves.

In a kindergarten classroom, the teacher, wearing an apron like the main character, might be reading *Mrs. Wishy-Washy*, pointing to the words in the Big Book. Children are wielding stuffed animals like those in the book—pigs, cows, ducks—while they read along with the teacher and chime in on the chorus of "wishy washy, wishy washy" with much laughter. At the end, of course, they ask to read it again, and this time children are called up to "handle" the Big Book by turning the pages and using the pointer stick to track the words, or called up to match Post-it notes inscribed with animals' names to the animal pictures or words in the Big Book.

In a third-grade classroom, one might see a shared reading lesson using a Big Book like *What Makes a Bird a Bird?* Together the teacher and children are using the illustrations and the author's pointed questions to figure out answers. They read the book's detailed information and follow the scientific method to answer the questions posed as hypotheses: "Is it a bird because it flies? Or are they birds because they have wings? A penguin can't fly. Penguins walk. An ostrich doesn't fly. It runs." and so on. While they are trying to make sense of the text, they reread aloud lines that the teacher points to. They go back to the text to check their predictions, eliminate incorrect assumptions, and read again. The emphasis is on making meaning and making sense. The lesson is happening in a welcoming, supportive environment where all levels of English output are accepted as the children participate in the discussion.

Shared reading benefits upper-grade ELLs just as much as younger learners. In an upper-grade classroom, the teacher might be using an overhead from *Time for Kids* on Ancient Civilizations of Mexico. Together, teacher and children are discovering "another type of skyscraper: stone pyramids that rise above tropical trees." They are reading for a purpose—to answer questions that they have posed together regarding these pyramids: Where do you find them? Who built them? What do we know

Teaching Strategies and Skills During Shared Reading

Students Complete a Sentence. Is there a repetitive phrase? If so, they can easily complete the sentence. If not, ask them to fill in the next word of the text, as in a close activity.

Talk About Print Awareness. Lead a discussion about directionality (left to right, top to bottom), spacing, turning pages, and checking the back and front book covers for clues.

Students Identify Words. Ask students to find words from the text that the teacher has written on chart paper and circle them: rhyming words, words that start with the same letter, or a specific word (perhaps a high-frequency word) that the teacher wants them to recognize.

Students Cross-Check. Ask students to decipher text by looking at pictures, sampling for information, checking their predictions, and confirming them. Remind them to ask, Does it look right? Does it sound right? Does it make sense?

Highlight Chunks of Language or Patterns in a Story. On chart paper write part of the story—a repetitive phrase or pattern or some lines of text. Ask students to reread it and interact with it using pens or Post-it notes to focus on the language structure.

Students Look for Graphophonic Clues. The focus is on the spelling of words and phonics instruction. Write on chart paper two words from the story. Ask students to find the difference between them, or to find words from the text that have a common letter or sound.

Analyze the Content of the Story Together. Have a class discussion on the story and record everything on chart paper. Ask students, What did we learn from this story? Together, write out descriptions of the characters or a story map. Locate information in the story for retelling, and check facts. Share experience of rereading, going back in the story.

Highlight Features in Nonfiction Text. Focus on the special features in nonfiction text that support the reader: table of contents, index, captions, section headings, photographs. How do these features help the reader understand the text?

Emphasize Punctuation. Ask students to find quotation marks, speech dashes, question marks, periods, exclamation marks in the text. How are capital letters used based on different punctuation?

---

about these ancient people? What language did they speak? Are any of our ancestors from Mexico? In the process of finding answers, they learn how to read nonfiction features like charts and paragraphs full of facts. Because the text is enlarged, the dimension of visual support is added to the teacher's modeling. The teacher's input becomes more comprehensible as children read the text along with her while she points at it and focuses on strategies, skills, or language patterns that she knows from assessments the children need to learn.

By reading with children, teachers encourage a love of good literature in a variety of genres and model what good readers do. They expose their students to rich academic language, to new patterns of speech, to the elements of story, to the conventions of print, and to "sustaining meaning" strategies like predicting, decoding, self-correcting, rereading, and cross-checking as well as "expanding meaning" strategies like analyzing, inferring, summarizing,

making connections, and evaluating the author's intent, which are important language functions. This is all done thoughtfully and carefully with ELLs in mind. One text may be used many times (or different texts may be chosen) to teach a variety of strategies and skills that meet the individual needs of the students.

Shared reading, with its multiple readings of the same text, has within it the components of Reading To, With, and By children. During the first reading, I do most of the reading *to* them, although some children may join in and read with me right away. This first reading is primarily for enjoyment. By the second or third reading, most children are reading *with* me, and it is at these readings (sometimes just of sections of the text) that I focus on teaching specific strategies, skills, or language patterns that I know the children need to work on. Finally, during independent reading, the children take the shared reading book, either in Big Book form or in small copies, and read it again *by* themselves. Often they read it with partners or groups of friends, or along with a tape in the listening center.

In shared reading lessons, we might have ELLs at all five developmental levels of language proficiency (see Table 2.1) and all four developmental levels of reading (see Table 2.3). The assessments we have made (see Appendix A) will guide us in planning what to focus on. Even though a shared reading lesson is conducted with the whole group, it is still necessary to think about the types of responses that we expect from each child, even beginning speakers. (See more detailed discussion on planning shared reading lessons for all levels of language users in Chapters 7 and 8.)

The list on page 64 suggests some ways to teach strategies and skills in the context of shared reading.

Keep in mind the difference between strategies and skills, defined by the *Merriam-Webster Collegiate Dictionary* as "plans toward a goal" and "developed aptitudes or abilities," respectively. Teachers sometimes overemphasize skills and underemphasize strategies in their lessons for English language learners. Children need both.

Strategies

The strategies children learn in shared reading will be the strategies they use as independent readers. It is therefore critical that we not only focus on strategies in our teaching but also make children aware of what good reading strategies are. Taberski (2000) writes about having children share what they learned about themselves as readers. One primary class of ELLs that I worked with answered the question: *What reading strategies did I use successfully today?* as follows:

I used the pictures to help me.
I thought about what the book might be about.
I reread a line.
I used the beginning letter and ending letter to help me figure out the word.
I started the sentence over when I got lost.
I used my best English.
I made a prediction and then checked it.
I tracked from left to right.
I thought about what made sense.
I asked myself if it sounded right.
I checked the word to see if it looked right.

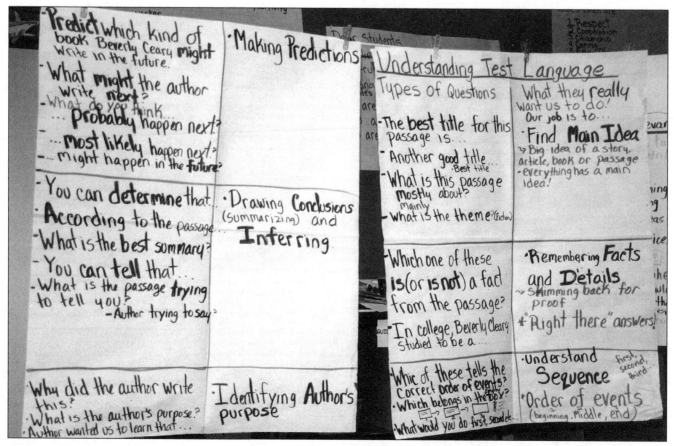

Strategy charts.

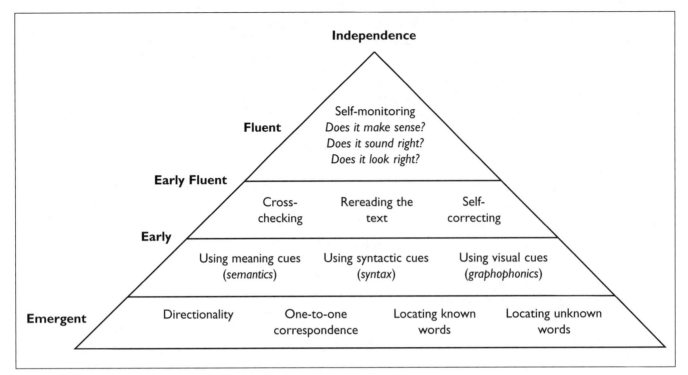

Pyramid of strategies to sustain meaning.

I think of strategies as problem solving, ways to gain access to the meaning of text. There are lower-level strategies that children use to figure out words they do not know and to help them sustain meaning as they read, as the list above shows. And there are higher-level strategies that help children gain a deeper understanding of text by expanding meaning. They have to learn both the "sustaining meaning" strategies and the "expanding meaning" strategies in order to become proficient readers and gain the academic language necessary to explain what they have learned. We need to keep track of these strategies for assessment and planning purposes (see Appendixes A6 and A7). Ideally we want children to self-monitor their reading and to become independent readers. Through the teaching of these strategies, we can help children become proficient.

This awareness of reading strategies starts in shared reading, when the teacher focuses on specific strategies she uses as a proficient reader and encourages the children to try them out and talk about them with the group. Although in read-alouds the teacher thinks aloud and models higher-level strategies, I feel that shared reading is a more natural place to teach lower-level or sustaining meaning strategies because of the enlarged texts that all children can see, which provide concrete

examples of what might otherwise be very abstract concepts. For instance, when a teacher says, "Track from left to right," the students can actually see the teacher move her arm or pointer across the page, along the line, and onto the next page, and thus understand what *tracking* means in this context. Without that visual input, ELLs might become "derailed" with confusing associations of railroad tracks or tire tracks because they are constantly trying to make sense of new speech that is thrown at them. Also, ELLs gain confidence from working with peers and observing other children trying out strategies they may not have thought of.

Readers use their knowledge of three cueing systems to gain meaning while they read: graphophonic, syntactic, and semantic cueing systems (see Chapter 9). And they use the following strategies to help them.

Decoding puts to use their knowledge of graphophonics—how to match the sounds they know with the letters they see. Their knowledge of *syntax* and the structure of English helps them understand sentences and the writing of the author. With *meaning clues* and their knowledge of *semantics* they can figure out if what they are reading makes sense. *Cross-checking* uses visual cues of the letters of words, syntactic cues of the placement of words in the sentence, and semantic cues including pictures and background knowledge to analyze if predictions of text are correct. Children can *self-correct* by rereading a line and asking three important self-monitoring questions: *Does it make sense? Does it sound right? Does it look right?*

A pyramid of strategies to sustain meaning can be used to think about children's development of these strategies in shared reading as well as in guided and independent reading. The higher-level strategies are also taught in shared reading lessons and mini-lessons. Fountas and Pinnell (2001), Hindley (1996), and Taberski (2000) explain how to teach specific lessons on higher-level strategies.

Making connections is a very helpful strategy for students to learn in shared reading and transfer to their independent reading. Sometimes, even one word will trigger a connection for a child to another story. I remember a group of ELLs in kindergarten who were reading a book with me in a shared reading session that had *Stop!* on each page, as different characters yelled at a runaway milk truck. Two or three children said, "That's just like the Gingerbread Man. They yelled *Stop!* at him, too!"

Making inferences is difficult for ELLs if they fail to understand the subtlety of language or miss details in the text that guide readers toward understanding what the author meant. The meaning is often just under the surface but not explicitly stated, and ELLs may miss it in drawing conclusions and predicting what might happen.

Choosing which strategies to teach based on children's needs is important, but the format of any shared reading lesson for readers at all levels should have these higher-level strategies already built in:

★ Predicting outcomes of the story
★ Connecting to one's own life
★ Connecting to other books
★ Checking predictions during and after
★ Evaluating the text

Skills

Choosing which skills to teach during shared reading is part of the careful planning we undertake for each student based on assessment of his developmental levels in language and reading, grade-level

A chart for teaching the /h/ sound.

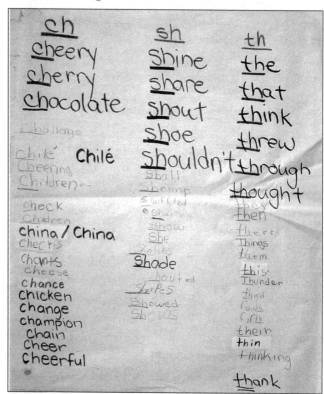

A chart for teaching the distinction between the /ch/, /sh/, and /th/ sounds.

TABLE 4.1 Problem English Sounds for Speakers of Other Languages

Native Language	Problem English Sounds
Spanish	b d dg h j m n ng r sh t th v w y z s-clusters end clusters
Vietnamese	a e k l ng p r sh s y l-clusters r-clusters
Chinese	b ch d dg f g j l m n ng o sh s th v z l-clusters r-clusters
Korean	b l o ow p r sh t th l-clusters r-clusters
Urdu	a a d e e f n ng s sh t th
Japanese	dg f h I l th oo r sh s v w shwa l-clusters r-clusters

This is not a complete list of languages. These are taken from The ESL Teacher's Book of Lists (1993) *by Jacqueline Kress. The Center for Applied Research in Education.*

equivalency, and the state English language development or English language proficiency standards (CDE 1999, TEA 1997, WIDA 2004). In general, these skills include phonemic awareness, distinguishing letters from words, learning English sound-symbol relationships, phonics, knowing regular spelling patterns and high-frequency words that cannot be sounded out phonetically, the textual significance of punctuation marks, basic and academic vocabulary, and syntax.

ELLs may have particular needs with regard to learning English sound-symbol relationships, depending on which language is the primary one. For instance, Spanish speakers who are literate in their native language will need to be taught that the pronunciation of the letters *a, e,* and *i* is different in Spanish and English, and how to pronounce the English sound of the letter *h,* which is silent in Spanish. (See chart on page 67.) The English /h/ can be approximated for them by referring to the Spanish sound of the letter *j,* which is pronounced /h/. For Chinese speakers, pronunciation of sounds like /b/, /ch/, /d/, /dj/, /f/, /g/, /j/, /l/, /m/, /n/, /ng/, /sh/, /s/, /th/, /v/, /z/, /l/ clusters, and /r/ clusters is likely to be difficult, whereas Korean speakers will have problems pronouncing /b/, /l/, /p/, /r/, /sh/, /t/, /th/, /l/ clusters, and /r/ clusters (Kress 1993). These difficulties arise not only from inability to shape mouth and tongue to produce unfamiliar sounds but also from inability to *hear* the distinctions among such sounds. Table 4.1 lists problem English sounds for six of the most highly used languages of our language learners. This is not an exhaustive list. There are many more languages used in our classrooms and too many to list here.

The language needs of our English language learners do not stop with the sounds of letters they have difficulty hearing, but rather that is only the tip of the iceberg. Our English language learners need to develop basic vocabulary as well as academic vocabulary, and they need to know how to use verb tenses and adjectives and pronouns, to name just a few of the specific lessons we could model in teaching the skills they need to develop as an English speaker. We need to also focus specific lessons on syntax or language structure, not just on phonics and phonemic awareness.

Punctuation conventions may differ in English and in other languages. For instance, quotation marks are not used in Spanish texts to indicate what is or has been said; rather, speech dashes are used for this purpose. If upper-grade students are literate in Spanish, the significance of quotation marks in English text would have to be specifically taught. The use of syntactical elements like pronouns, possessive adjectives, adverbs, objects, contractions, prepositions, plurals, and verb tenses also differs among languages and should be addressed via mini-lessons, primarily during shared reading time.

Part of planning for ELLs involves evaluating the composition of the class with respect to primary languages spoken, and researching the unique problems that may be associated with those (Bear et al. 2003). If a large part of the class consists of one primary language group, these kinds of skills can be taught within a shared reading lesson, on the second or third rereading of a text the children know well. (See chart on page 67.) Otherwise, if only one or two children speak a certain primary language, they must be taught individually. (See language mini-lessons taught during shared reading in Chapters 7 and 8.)

Discussion

Discussion is an important part of shared reading for English language learners. By engaging students through dialogue, connecting the learning to students' lives in order to help make meaning, and facilitating learning, including complex thinking, through joint activity among teachers and students, we can improve learning outcomes for ELLs (CREDE 2002). It is during discussion that higher-level thinking is encouraged and expected of all students. Discussion occurs before, during, and after the reading of the text, and a shared reading lesson is just as much about interacting with the text, commenting on it, predicting outcomes, sharing the favorite parts, and so on, as it is about reading the text aloud. The processing that goes on during the discussion of a text is critical for children to comprehend its meaning (Harvey and Goudvis 2000).

Leading discussions during shared reading takes time and patience. It can be difficult to get through a reading of a text when many children want to participate. They often go off on tangents, yet that shows they are thinking about the text and making connections to their own lives. It's worthwhile to slow down and allow them to share their observations even if they are a little off course because they are making meaning for themselves. In a primary classroom it may be hard to see where they are going with their responses, especially if their language production is limited. But we need to encourage their responses and try to understand the connections they are making. Then we can connect the responses back to the reading of the text and move on with the discussion and the reading. It's important, especially in upper-grade classrooms with large numbers of students, to ensure that beginning or even intermediate speakers have their share of opportunities to talk and participate in the discussion.

Discussion in shared reading helps build a sense of community and a supportive climate where the contributions of ELLs at all levels are recognized. This improves children's confidence as they are learning the language as well as learning to read.

They then take this new confidence to practice reading on their own in guided and independent reading and to discuss their thinking in small groups and literature circles.

Expecting Every Child to Participate

It is difficult to plan for differentiated instruction in the context of a shared reading lesson and expect all children to participate. It is natural to think of choosing one focus and teaching it to the whole class. Instead of striving to bring out the best of beginning, intermediate, and advanced speakers, teachers often just shoot for the middle and hope that silent children are learning through osmosis or picking up at least something.

However, research compels us to recognize that we are obligated to design every lesson with the best strategies in mind for ELLs at all levels of development, including using comprehensible input (Krashen 1996), total physical response (Krashen and Terrell 1983), being active in learning (Cummins 1994), and having high expectations for each child (Thomas and Collier 1999). We also have to expose ELLs to academic language, which they do not receive through basic communication (Cummins 2003). That doesn't mean we have numerous focuses but rather that we adapt what we are teaching to the various language levels so that each child can participate.

We cannot meet the needs of every child in every lesson, but we do shared reading every day. That means each day we try to reach those children who didn't participate the day before. We try to make beginning speakers feel comfortable to participate, accepting their yes/no responses or calling them up to interact with the text. We want both fluent readers and emergent readers to feel interested in a shared reading text. This isn't easy, but the wonderful books available for shared reading make the teacher's job more enjoyable. Children at all language and reading levels become engaged when we choose the right books (Gibbons 2002; Cambourne 1988; Fisher 1991; 1995). Through sharing rich literature, modeling what good readers do, and encouraging all children to join in, shared reading time is a significant opportunity within a balanced literacy program to encourage a love of reading that will hopefully last a lifetime.

GUIDED READING— READING BY CHILDREN

Guided reading is the time when children are in the role of readers yet have the teacher beside them to guide and support them. That guidance is critical to children's reading development. It is also critical that English language learners read for a purpose and that the language used in the text be meaningful to them. That is why it is important to choose appropriate books for guided reading that are both interesting and challenging for the readers. I find that guided reading is one of the most rewarding times of the day, as I see children try out new language skills and strategies as they successfully read unfamiliar books for the first time.

Guided reading is not round-robin reading where everyone takes a turn and reads a line aloud while everyone else waits. It's not choral reading where everyone reads the text aloud in unison. And it's not a lesson where the teacher reads to the children and the children repeat what she read. Rather, guided reading is a time when all children read by themselves with their own copies of a book with guidance from the teacher. Guided reading is a teacher-supported technique to help children gain their own meaning from a text they are reading by themselves silently or in a low voice. With her own copy of the text from the outset, a child can use her own strategies to discover the title, figure out unknown words, and discover the main idea of the fiction or nonfiction text she is reading. This is an opportunity for ELLs to expand academic vocabulary as they see new words in longer and more challenging texts.

A guided reading lesson has a set structure, with the important purpose of helping children comprehend more and more challenging texts on their own. There is an introduction, an orientation to the text, a first reading of the text, a possible rereading, and an ending discussion about what was learned. Also, a purpose is set for the lesson to help children work on both higher- and lower-level strategies to sustain and expand meaning while they are reading. During the guided reading lesson, the teacher skillfully scaffolds readers when they need support and otherwise lets them take on their own role as readers (Fountas and Pinnell 1996; 1999; *Reading in Junior Classes* 1985; *Reading for Life* 1996; Hornsby 2000).

Guided reading for ELLs should include all these components and, in addition, more discussion at each part of the lesson, so they can improve their language as well as their comprehension. The teacher should make sure that the children understand the discussion and the text at all times. She should use books with wonderful visuals, predictable text, and natural language. She should be aware of the children's language levels and gear her speech to those levels to ensure that the students will understand and be able to participate effectively in the discussion (Cummins 1989; 2003; Krashen 1981). At the beginning of the lesson, the teacher needs to tap into the children's background experience and spark their interest by asking them to look at the book and predict what the text will be about. We do that with native speakers, but ELLS need more time to think and to respond.

The teacher carefully sets the tone of the guided reading lesson to highlight the students' strengths rather than their weaknesses. For example, ELLs may substitute words they know and that make sense for words they don't know. One third-grader read, "She reads my e-mail *when* I'm asleep" instead of ". . . *while* I'm asleep" (*My Cousin Far Away*). This miscue did not change the meaning of the text, and the reader actually used a good strategy of substitution. Instead of focusing on the "error," the teacher can emphasize that the child made a good choice in reading the sentence to make sense and let it go. The teacher can also help her understand the word *while* if she doesn't know it, or, if she did know the word, can suggest that she use the strategy of checking the whole word, not just the beginning. Such positive interaction strengthens the strategies the child is using well and quickly teaches a new word or another strategy that she can add to her repertoire.

By praising them for what they did well while supplying new knowledge, we help ELLs read more effectively because we increase their confidence in their own reading abilities while at the same time challenge them to improve. They shouldn't feel threatened but, rather, encouraged to go on. Research has shown that paying attention to the children's affective filters is a critical component of building reading success in children (Krashen 1981). By providing opportunities for them to succeed and motivating them to take more risks with very little anxiety, we can help children become better readers. Thus the guided reading lesson for ELLs should be full of rich discussion and opportunities for success.

Guided reading is different from shared reading. The teacher's role in guided reading is that of a guide. As was mentioned, she does not read the book to or with the children but engages them in conversations about what would make sense in the text and what they can do to figure out the text on their own. Children do not need to know every word in the book before they read it. Once they have received some guidance from the teacher about the direction of the plot or the language pattern used, they need time to figure out the text on their own.

Guided reading is a valuable time for children

★ to try out new reading strategies
★ to work on comprehending the text
★ to try out new language patterns
★ to discuss with confidence new understandings about a text and new insights about themselves as readers

and for teachers

★ to diagnose children's reading and language levels
★ to instruct on the spot, when they see a need— either strategies, vocabulary, or language patterns appropriate to individual children's reading and language levels
★ to evaluate reading and language progress and plan for future instruction in read-aloud, shared reading, and guided reading

ELLs are trying to manage both their newly acquired English and their newly acquired reading strategies at the same time. The teacher carefully asks the right questions to make the child think; she highlights the right strategy or cueing system at the right time to help the child gain meaning. The trick is to do this without telling the child what the right word is, to be there next to the child, to be patient, to give him time to process information, and to allow him to figure out the word and meaning on his own.

Emergent readers are learning how to track from left to right, to touch each individual word while they read, to predict what the story may be about, and to bring in their background knowledge. They know that pictures can help them and that they can look at the beginning and ending letters of a word to decode it. Early readers know that they can reread a line to gain meaning and that the story should make sense. They know they can self-correct and use different cueing systems to cross-check by visually looking at letters in words and seeing if the words make sense and fit into the syntax of the sentence (Traill 1994; Goodman 1996; Clay 1991). Emergent and early readers use many of these elements; they just need help seeing the big picture. If they get stuck, the teacher prompts them to use another strategy or cueing system, to try to make sense of what they are reading, to understand the whole story, and to continue to sustain meaning while they read.

For transitional or early fluent readers, guided reading continues to be an important time to stretch and reach beyond their current levels and develop higher-level strategies to expand meaning while continuing to sustain meaning while reading (Fountas and Pinnell 2001). These readers need more time in guided reading sessions to expand upon their understanding of the text. Many children at the transitional, early fluency, and even fluency stages may seem to be able to read text well but have difficulty understanding the author's message or summarizing or analyzing what they have read. They also may have difficulty sustaining meaning in longer texts that they are reading at these levels. It is during a guided reading lesson for transitional- and fluency-level readers where children are grouped by strategy use and language development as well as reading level that their individual strengths can be celebrated and their needs can be met.

Guided reading is the time in the day when children are challenged to go beyond what they normally read on their own. "Come on, have a go," was what I often heard from New Zealand experts during my early training in guided reading. It was the same sort of prodding I heard from my father, who always challenged us to take the next step, to try a new sport, to climb a mountain, to not give up. That energy, support, and belief in us gave us confidence. I think we accomplished things or at least tried things that we otherwise wouldn't have.

I truly believe all children need that. They need to try something challenging and not give up. ELLs especially need this encouragement. They need us to give them extra time and support to figure out how to use the new language they are learning and make sense of the text they are reading.

As I have mentioned, it is critical to know ELLs' language proficiency levels before starting guided reading with them. If we are diagnosing their strengths and weaknesses and instructing to those, we must be able to distinguish between a lack of reading strategies and a lack of language skills. Students are only able to read based on the language functions and structures they have learned. Thus leading effective guided reading lessons with ELLs may be more challenging because we have to be constantly aware of what the children are able to do in reading based on their developmental English language proficiency (see Chapters 9–12 for more details on this).

We can highlight strategies that we have taught them in shared reading yet they are just starting to use independently, and we can point out strategies that they already know but have forgotten to use. We need to be attuned to the type of strategies they are trying to use to gain meaning and, if they are having trouble, to distinguish between a language issue and a literacy issue. We need to decide whether they are capable of using all three cueing systems to help themselves based on their language development as well as their strategy use.

Once children start to read by themselves in the lesson, we can sit back as observers, watching and listening to see who is reading well and who needs assistance. Then we move closer to each reader and help each child who needs it, not by reading unknown words for her but by asking guiding questions that will help her figure out the words on her own. This is the time to remind them to use their strategies when they get stuck and to try to move forward. We move from reader to reader quickly, though, because most emergent readers' books are only eight pages long, and early readers' books aren't much longer. Some children can read through them pretty fast, while others take more time and need more assistance. If a child reads the book very quickly, we can ask him to read it again while other children are finishing, or ask him to find his favorite page while he is waiting. Even fluent readers all read at different rates, so they can record information they learned on a strategy focus sheet while others are finishing in order to keep the group together so important discussion can occur after they have all read the text.

I don't believe that we should wait until children are fluent readers to start asking them to integrate the lower-level and higher-level strategies on their own. Although the focus of guided reading lessons is different for different stages of reading, we can naturally hit on both "sustaining meaning" strategies and "expanding meaning" strategies in the context of any guided reading session (to different degrees, depending on the readers). As emergent readers figure out words and use pictures or early readers cross-check or reread a line, we also want them to start thinking more deeply about the text:

Can they predict the ending before the last page?
Can they retell the most important idea of the book when they have finished a text?
Can they compare the text to other books they have read?
Can they explain why they think the author wrote the book?
Can they share what they have learned or how the story has touched them?

All this takes time to develop and discussion and practice. But it should be a part of even emergent readers' guided reading lessons in order for them to become proficient at it when they are fluent readers. Very young children can tell the main idea of a story if they have understood it, and they can make connections to other stories and to their lives if we encourage them to do so.

Often I see guided reading lessons where there is no discussion before or after the reading of the text: once they have read the book, children just put it back in their book box. This is a wasted opportunity to help them expand meaning, develop their language, and come to love reading for itself.

The most important role we can play in planning for and leading successful guided reading lessons is being "kidwatchers" (Yetta Goodman 1985). Observing each child's use of strategies and language both before and during the lesson is critical in planning guided reading lessons for all levels of readers (see Appendixes E4 and F3). We need to know how to assess the information we observe and how to then use that information to evaluate what we have planned for that child and what our goals should be in the future.

I take the time after each guided reading lesson to read with individual children, to help them if they need it, and to assess their progress to help plan for mini-lessons and other instruction. I might just spend five minutes with a child taking a running record and listening to his retelling, which also gives me lots of information about the child as a reader and a language user.

INDEPENDENT READING— READING BY CHILDREN

During guided reading time every day, while I meet with small groups of children, the rest of the children are reading independently or in literature circles. This allows them as much time as possible to read by themselves, which is just as important for ELLs as for native speakers. The more time children spend reading the better readers they become, especially in their second language. Krashen (2003) states, "There is overwhelming evidence that reading in a second language, especially free voluntary reading or pleasure reading, makes a powerful contribution to the development of academic proficiency in a second language."

For independent reading, children select books from their book boxes, the classroom library, the genre and author collections, or the read-aloud collection. They keep track of their reading through reading logs and reading journals. I confer with individual children about their reading choices and whatever they might want help with regarding choosing books, developing reading strategies, or picking goals for themselves as readers. I am always aware of their language development as they speak to me during a conference, and I take notes on their reading and language development on a reading conference sheet (see Appendix A2).

Often the most popular books that ELLs choose to read are books that were shared in read-alouds or shared reading. I encourage children to read Big Books again, and they often do so, with a friend and the pointer tracking along with the text on an easel. It is nice to see this still happening in fourth or fifth grade. Children might be lying on bean bag

Independent reading from book boxes.

chairs gazing up at a Big Book or reading independently in different corners on pillows.

The key is to have them engaged in their reading. Matching children to a good book, therefore, is important to their success as a reader. It not only should be at their independent reading level, but it has to be one that they are interested in reading and will enjoy. I sometimes spend a lot of time during a reading conference helping them pick a new book if they haven't found one in the library that they like. The better a teacher knows a child, the easier it is to help him find a book that he might enjoy.

In literature circles, the selection of the books to be read by the small group of children is also important to the success of the group. Literature circles take place during independent reading time, and often the children are so engaged in their literature circle book that they don't want to read any other book during that time. That's fine, the important thing is to have them excited about reading. I have seen literature circles fail, however, when the children did not like their choice of book. To avoid that, make sure that the children have previewed all of the books, understand the genres and the themes of the stories, and have the opportunity to decide which book they want to read, thus which literature circle they join. I usually provide the class with about five or six choices, accounting for a range of interests and reading levels. (Chapter 13 discusses literature circles in more detail.)

It is exciting to see children discuss and share their connections, their beliefs, their assumptions, and their favorite parts of the story regardless of their language and reading level. A good book seems to reach across all stages of development. Some teachers have their children run literature circles everyday, others do it two or three times week. The important discussion that takes place, however, should not take away from the children's independent reading time, regardless how many days they meet in groups. We can't forget that children still need time to read everyday in our classroom.

A BALANCED LITERACY SCHEDULE

With so many different children and lessons, how do we fit everything into our busy schedules? As I mentioned, I keep the To, With, and By model in mind. At the top of my planning sheet, I write the theme and subtheme we are working on (see Chapter 5), together with a unit of literary study like character analysis. Then under each area of To, With, and By, I organize the reading workshop so that all the necessary components of read-alouds, shared reading, guided reading, and independent reading, are included every day. Then I write in a column next to each of these the focus or the mini-lesson to be taught on specific strategies and skills and how it relates to the literary study. This is my guide and working document (Hornsby 1989). It seems as if I always need to change and add to it as the needs of the kids change daily.

Some teachers like to start their day with independent reading as the children first walk into the classroom, but I prefer to start with an opening or group meeting which includes the Daily News and then moves to the writing workshop (see Tables 4.2 and 4.3). Then there is a long reading workshop, into which I integrate content area reading where appropriate with the integration of teaching language functions and structures with reading strategies and skills. An easy transition from the writing workshop to the reading workshop for all grade levels is to have everyone join me on the rug for a read-aloud. I believe one can never read enough to children, so I do at least two organized read-alouds per day, the first one always a picture book, regardless of grade level. These picture books are wonderful to develop children's academic vocabulary and to provide children a model of a story well told and which are good examples to use in the writing workshop (Harwayne 1992). The book would be connected to the theme or genre study.

We then go into independent reading. Since they just saw me read to them in read-aloud, I want them to practice doing what I did. This is the time that used to be called DEAR—Drop Everything and Read—because that's what we all did. I would sit at my desk or on the couch reading a favorite book. I still enjoy doing this, and I think it is important for the children to see me reading in this way. The modeling that we do should really be designed to help children see *themselves* as readers, to realize that they don't always need to be read to but that they can also read by themselves.

TABLE 4.2 Balanced Literacy Morning Schedule for Primary Classrooms

8:15	**Opening**
5 minutes	*Shared Reading Activities*
	Morning Message—phonics in context
	Poetry box, Big Book, alphabet song
10 minutes	*Shared Writing Activities*
	Daily News

8:30	**Writing Workshop**
10 minutes	*Mini-lessons*
	Shared and modeled writing
40 minutes	*Independent Writing* (while teacher confers with individuals or small groups in writing and language development)
	Children compose writing or write in writer's
	notebooks, journals, buddy journals
	Write in variety of genres and forms
	Publish their work
	Meet in writing circles
10 minutes	*Sharing Time*
	Author's chair—sharing published pieces or work in progress

| 9:30–9:50 | **Recess** |

9:50	**Reading Workshop with Integrated Content Area Instruction**
15 minutes	*Read-Aloud*
	Teacher reads picture book
	Short mini-lesson
15 minutes	*Independent Reading* (while teacher confers with individuals or conducts small-group strategy or language lesssons)

10:20	**Regroup**
20 minutes	*Shared Reading*
	Mini-lessons with Big Book
	Focus on language patterns and reading strategies
45 minutes	*Guided Reading*
	Teacher meets with two guided reading groups
	Teacher takes at least one running record
	Some children many need small shared reading group
	*Independent Reading**
	Students read out of own book boxes
	Students read for and meet in literature circles
10 minutes	*Read-Aloud*
	Teacher reads from chapter book
	Integrates teaching of reading strategies
10 minutes	*Sharing Time*
	Sharing about a book that was read or suggest books
	Sharing about strategies used or how children see themselves as readers
	Sharing about new language or vocabulary learned

| 11:45–12:20 | **Lunch** |

* If centers are used, centers may include reading books from poetry boxes, Big Books, student-made Big Books, students' published stories, and wall print; reading along with tapes in listening center; working with pocket chart; using overhead projector to read; buddy reading; writing and illustrating responses to literature; language discussion group with flip charts.

TABLE 4.3 Balanced Literacy Morning Schedule for Upper-Grade Classrooms

8:15	**Opening—Group Meeting**
5 minutes	*Shared Reading*
	Morning Message, focus on language patterns
10 minutes	*Shared Writing*
	Daily News
	Language mini-lessons

8:30	**Writing Workshop**
10 minutes	Mini-lessons
	Shared and modeled writing
40 minutes	*Independent Writing* (while teacher confers with individuals or small groups
	in writing and language development)
	Children compose writing or write in writer's
	notebooks, journals, buddy journals
	Write in variety of genres and forms
	Publish their work
	Meet in writing circles
10 minutes	*Sharing Time*
	Author's chair—sharing published pieces or work in progress

9:30	**Reading Workshop with Integrated Content Area Instruction**
15 minutes	*Read-Aloud*
	Read picture book connected to theme or genre study
	Strategy and language function mini-lesson
20 minutes	*Independent Reading** (while teacher confers with individuals or conducts
	small-group strategy or language lessons)
	Individual reading, buddy reading
10 minutes	*Sharing Time*
	Sharing about books and reading strategies

| 10:15–10:35 | **Recess** |

20 minutes	*Shared Reading*
	Mini-lessons with Big Book or overhead projector
60 minutes	*Guided Reading*
	Teacher meets with two or three groups
	Teacher takes at least one running record
	Some children many need small shared reading lesson
	*Independent Reading** (students read out of a classroom collection, book boxes,
	or library or children read for and meet in literature circles)
20 minutes	*Read-Aloud*
	Read chapter book
	Integrate teaching of reading strategies
10 minutes	*Sharing Time*
	Sharing about a book that was read or suggest books
	Sharing about strategies used or how children see themselves as readers
	Sharing about content, genre, or new language patterns and vocabulary learned

| 12:25–1:00 | **Lunch** |

* If centers are used, centers may include reading books from genre collections, upper-grade content areas, thematic collections in science, history, social studies, mathematics; reading books from poetry boxes; reading Big Books, students' published stories, and wall print; reading along with tapes in listening center; using overhead projector to read; writing and illustrating responses to literature; using literature logs and literature journals; discussing content area vocabulary with flip charts and graphic organizers.

After I've started to read on my own and then see that everyone is settled and reading quietly, I get up and choose a few children to confer with that day. Or I might choose a small group of children who need extra assistance in developing reading strategies or language functions.

In an upper-grade classroom, we would then regroup after this first short independent reading time to have children share about their books, the strategies they used, or any connections they would like to make to content, genre or language functions they used. Since there is more time in the upper-grade schedule, I have two sharing times after each independent reading time. The cognitive and language development of English language learners is improved dramatically if they have time to share and interact (Tharp et al. 2000) so I try to provide as much time in my schedule as possible to allow them to process and dialogue the information. For primary children, I have one sharing time at the end of the reading workshop.

For both a primary and an upper-grade classroom, I also plan for a daily shared reading which I feel is one of the most important times of the day because of the interaction and the learning that I see go on in the lesson. Mini-lessons are planned based on language needs as well as reading strategy needs. Then the largest chunk of the reading block is the guided reading time, where the rest of the children are reading independently. Literature circles or reading centers may be options for children while the teacher is meeting with at least two different reading groups. This time allows for children to practice reading on their own the strategies and language patterns that I have taught them in read-aloud and shared reading.

I usually regroup the children again to read another book in a read-aloud, usually a chapter or section from a chapter book or novel. I try to integrate the teaching of reading strategies while I read and keep the same literary focus that I am highlighting in the other read-aloud as well. Then we end the workshop with a sharing time where all children have the opportunity to participate and share how they have constructed meaning that day during the reading block.

Many kindergarten teachers have unique schedules, such as half the children arrive early and then the other half of the children arrive late and stay late. I have been to more and more full-day kindergarten classrooms and dual immersion or biliteracy models. But there are also the traditional half-day kindergarten schedules sponsored by most states. Kindergarten teachers often complain, understandably, that they have even less time to fit everything in, yet have more demands on them. The schedule for the opening, writing workshop, and reading workshop for a half-day kindergarten would be the same as the primary with everything shortened just a bit—30 minutes for the writing workshop and one hour and 15 minutes for the reading workshop. The full-day kindergarten biliteracy schedule would spend all morning in Spanish, including math workshop, with a full English literacy block of one-and-one-half hours in the afternoon and another hour of PE, music, art, and extended science.

5

THEMATIC PLANNING

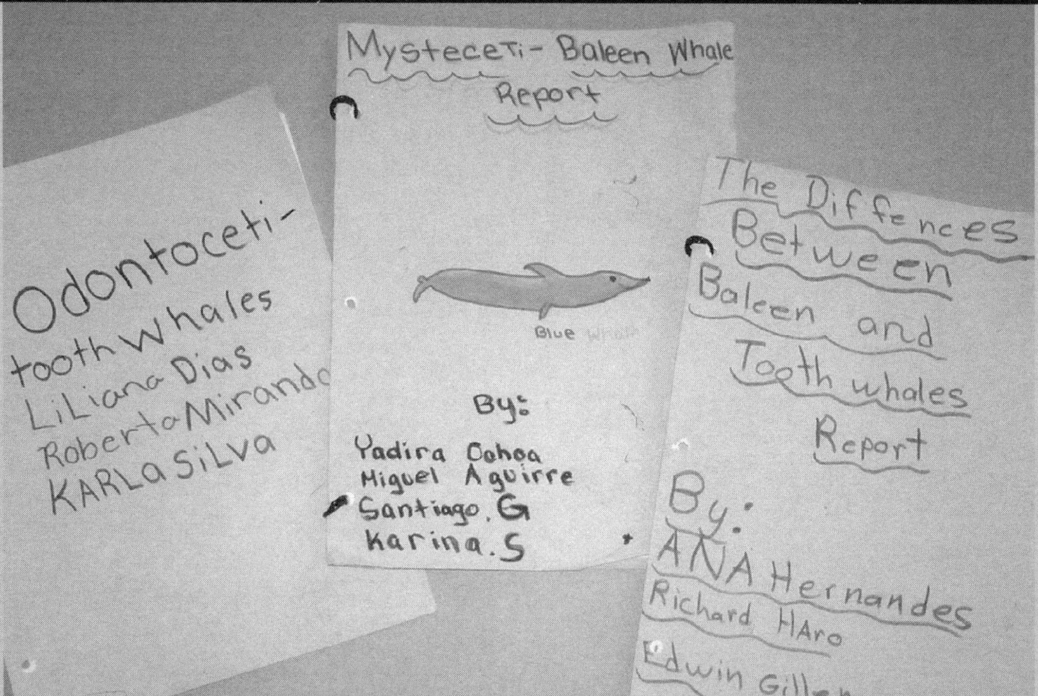

Mysteceti- Baleen Whale
Report

Odontoceti-
tooth Whales
Liliana Dias
Roberto Miranda
KARLa SiLVa

Blue Whale

By:
Yadira Ochoa
Miguel Aguirre
Santiago, G
Karina. S

The Differences
Between
Baleen and
Tooth whales
Report

By:
ANA Hernandes
Richard Haro

Edwin Gillen

The Art Lesson

My mother-in-law, Nelida, is an artist who has exhibited in galleries in Argentina, Brazil, Spain, and the United States. On one of her visits, when my twin daughters were in first grade, they couldn't wait to show her off to their class. "Why doesn't she come in and give an art lesson?" their teacher asked. Nelida was thrilled to be asked, but she was worried about the language barrier. "My granddaughters can barely understand me," she told me in Spanish. "How will the other children be able to?" I assured her that I would be there to translate and told her not to underestimate her granddaughters' Spanish—"they understand a lot more than you think." We arrived in the classroom with a large art book of Vincent Van Gogh's paintings; Nelida had decided to teach the children how to draw The Yellow House *with oil pastels. My girls, Francesca and Jackie, each grabbed one of her arms and sat down with her at the front of the room. Nelida began speaking, but before I could say the appropriate translation, Francesca and Jackie jumped right in to translate. They translated every word she said. They described the house in detail, how Van Gogh had tried to use it as a gathering place for artists, and why he had decided to paint this picture of the house. Nelida was amazed. We had never talked about the painting before. The girls had attended studio art classes and had had experience with shading and the blending of colors. But how could her granddaughters translate in such detail with their limited Spanish? "Was their translation accurate?" she asked me. I nodded yes. As Nelida moved to the board and started drawing on her chart paper, Francesca directed the children from her own seat on the colors Nelida was choosing, which ones they should use in their own pictures, and how to do proper shading. When the girls were done translating, and all the children had finished their drawings of* The Yellow House, *Nelida was clearly more impressed by her granddaughters' Spanish ability than their artistic ability. "They understand me!" she said with tears of joy in her eyes.*

Children's drawings of Van Gogh's *The Yellow House*.

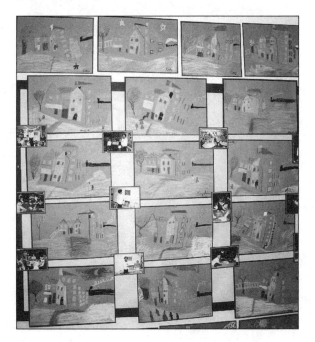

ilence does not mean that they don't understand. Many children understand more than they are willing to demonstrate. Each child has an individual comfort level and is motivated to communicate for different reasons. The affective filter is an important part of children's inclination to communicate. Many children have in-depth knowledge of certain areas, which allows them to comprehend new content in a second language. We should not assume that English language learners who do not participate in class discussions do not know anything or are not learning anything about a topic. Perhaps there are other factors. They may be beginning speakers who are unable to explain what they know because they are speaking only in one- or two-word phrases. They may be intermediate speakers who are embarrassed to make a mistake in front of their peers. They may be advanced speakers who do not participate because their culture dictates that, out of respect for their elders, they not offer comments unless called on specifically. We can only speculate why a child may not be participating. We shouldn't make negative assumptions but make a conscientious effort to talk to each child individually to figure out what he knows and how to make him comfortable to communicate. Some ELLs may be better in a small group, where they can share their knowledge in a less threatening way.

By tapping into what they do know in the primary language, we can deepen children's understanding in the second language. Concepts transfer to the new language. Francesca was able to easily translate the artistic techniques that her grandma was demonstrating because of her own artistic knowledge and ability. Her prior knowledge helped her comprehend what her grandmother was saying and by speaking in her primary language, rather than in her second language, she was able to demonstrate what she really knew about the subject. Concepts are not stored by language, so children do not need to learn them again (Cummins 1989; 2003). Rather, the concepts are stored in their underlying academic proficiency. Once a child knows how to mix colors, for example, she doesn't need to learn that again but only needs to learn the vocabulary in the new language to match that proficiency. Many children in our classrooms have in-depth knowledge of certain topics which allows them to comprehend better new content centered around the same theme while they are listening and reading in their second language. We need to take advantage of that background knowledge and use their primary language while we are teaching new concepts to our students. By acknowledging all of our children's background knowledge, we can learn which child is an expert in which topic and highlight their expertise as we build a community of learners.

In this chapter I show how to develop the language proficiency and literacy of English language learners through thematic planning and content area reading within a balanced reading program of Reading To, With, and By Children. By developing their vocabulary in the context of rich content and thematic units, by tapping into their prior knowledge in their first language, by using wonderful literature, and by utilizing lots of charting and visuals and graphic organizers, the language that our English language learners are hearing and reading becomes much more meaningful and comprehensible. While teaching reading strategies and language structures and content area thinking processes within a theme, we can have children use their language as a means to learn content instead of as separate subjects. Thus I stress the importance of integrating content into the literacy block and describe a thematic framework for planning toward this goal. I give examples of how to implement the framework for second-grade and fourth-grade classes and highlight the use of Spanish-English cognates because about 80 percent of ELLs in U.S. schools speak Spanish as a primary language (NCES 2002). And, as always, I emphasize the need to meet children at their individual language and reading levels in order to provide opportunities for them to grow and learn.

GUIDING QUESTIONS

What is the benefit to English language learners to teach thematically?

How can we integrate our content instruction into our literacy block and choose appropriate themes?

How can we make content more accessible to our English language learners?

What strategies are we teaching our English language learners to use while reading in the content areas?

continued

WHY THEMATIC PLANNING?

Thematic planning is definitely not easy, but the benefits for English language learners are dramatic. Comprehensible input increases when vocabulary is repeated naturally in related lessons within a theme or subtheme (Freeman and Freeman 2000). By relating language to content areas, an integrated thematic approach focuses on language used for a definite purpose rather than as a study in itself (Gibbons 2002). Children can use different functions of language like classifying, describing, comparing, and contrasting in the context of a common theme, which allows them to revisit language within the same topic as they go more into their thinking and learning processes. This allows them to read with and use their newly acquired English more effectively. Once they know more about a topic, they can continue to add on to their knowledge while at the same time learning new phrases and sentence structures that help develop their level of academic English. Content area reading becomes easier because they are already familiar with the theme. Krashen (2004) calls this narrow reading and makes the case that reading in the same topic helps ELLs acquire language efficiently. Instead of jumping from topic to topic, reading in one topic provides exposure to a large amount of unified syntax and vocabulary.

Another benefit of teaching thematically in a balanced reading program is setting up an environment where all children can participate at their developmental levels to a common understanding of concepts. By organizing the literacy block around a theme, children at diverse reading and language levels are able to participate in whole-group reading, read-alouds, and shared reading, and then read books at their instructional level in guided reading that relate to the theme the whole class is discussing. In small-group guided reading, literature circles, and independent reading, children can follow their interests while also improving reading strategies and language abilities. Small-group projects allow children with different levels of language proficiency to work together on a common theme.

For many years, teachers moved away from thematic planning for a variety of reasons: it became cumbersome trying to find enough theme literature at appropriate levels; the theme instead of content or standards seemed to drive the curriculum; teachers at every grade level seemed to pick the same theme, so there was a lot of repetition; and it was difficult to match the needs of individual children to what was planned for teaching within the theme. With careful long- and short-term planning and coordination with colleagues across grade levels, such obstacles shouldn't exist. Also, there is more high-quality literature today at various levels and topics than there was in the past. Thematic planning has become easier with Internet searches and emphasis on using good nonfiction as well as fiction texts at all grade levels, increased publication of thousands of guided reading texts on various topics and genres, and convenient tie-ins with recommended lists of literature from state frameworks in the content areas.

With the ebb and flow of changes in curriculum frameworks and teaching methods each year, it does seem difficult for teachers to decide what is the best way to organize their classrooms. But effective ESL instruction has never moved away from integrated thematic teaching. The ESL or ELD state adopted materials are, and have always been, linked to themes, and most newly adopted state reading materials have gone back to presenting and teaching materials in themes as well. Unfortunately, the thematic instruction for ELLs is often limited to thirty or forty-five minutes daily of ESL instruction by the classroom teacher or a pull-out program in which a different instructor, often only an instructional assistant, teaches the children. The theme the children investigate during this short time often does not correlate at all to the theme that the classroom teacher is using in reading block or content area instruction. And because of the pressures of state testing and the concern for improving literacy scores, many districts moved away from a focus on content area teaching.

Instead of looking at similarities between content area standards, English language arts standards, and English language development standards, and trying to integrate them, teachers tried to cover everything separately. For ELLs, going from one subject to the next in a disjointed way doesn't improve learning. Sometimes we don't take the time to look at how the thinking processes across subjects relate. It is important to realize that we use thinking processes like compare and contrast not only in a language and literacy context but also as social science and science processes. Providing ELLs with opportunities to use these thinking processes in different content areas within a theme allows them to build content and language knowledge in a unified way (Kucer, Silva, and Delgado-Larocco 1995).

Hopefully, by integrating content areas into literacy block, we will reverse a trend in many districts and schools that spend almost the whole day on reading, writing, and math with the other content areas taking a back seat. Perhaps more districts will go back to integrating curriculum and teaching standards in an integrated approach. It seems a natural response to meeting the many challenges that are asked of teachers. Especially for ELLs, integrating content into literacy block makes learning more meaningful, challenging, and comprehensible, and developing language and literacy across the curriculum is considered one of the five standards for effective pedagogy and student outcomes (Tharp et al. 2002). Daniels and Bizar (2004) include integrative units in their list of the seven basic structures to help create best practice classrooms. The others are reading-as-thinking, small-group activities, representing-to-learn, classroom workshops, authentic experiences, and reflective assessment.

This is not to say that I don't expect a block of time to be spent on hands-on science experiments or social studies or history research projects during the regular classroom day. Rather, content should be integrated not only because of the time issue but because academically it makes sense. What we read about in language block should relate to the science experiments being done that week. We integrate the content that we are studying by reviewing the content area standards, utilizing the literature lists available, and integrating the thinking processes used across all disciplines (Kucer, Silva, and Delgado-Larocco 1995). Some wonderful picture books are actually recommended by state frameworks in the content areas.

CHOOSING THEMES

Choosing a suitable theme is very important. The theme should be broad enough to allow for content area development as well as to encompass many subthemes, and it should allow for children's own research into topics that interest them but are also tied to the theme. I prefer to choose themes related to the content areas of science, history/social science (or social studies) first and then tie my English language arts and English language development standards into those themes. I also add in the arts when I can, usually with projects that relate to the theme.

A theme like Bears, for example, would be too limited. Although many primary-grade books have bears as characters, and teachers like to make connections to teddy bears, and many first-grade children do their animal reports on bears, the topic is not broad enough to allow in-depth discussions and continued study, nor even to be considered a theme.

On the other hand, a theme like Cultural Understanding is broad enough to encompass work at any grade level. Some of the subthemes to be explored would be differences among ethnic groups, problems that immigrants face, different customs, different holidays, different foods, overcoming prejudice and injustice, working side by side, taking pride in our own language and culture, and family trees. This theme ties in well with social studies. At every grade level, students can examine history, geography, customs, and family structures through the eyes of people from different ethnic groups and cultures. Biographies about people like Martin Luther King Jr. or Cesar Chavez are part of most history/social science curriculums and can be easily integrated into this theme with a focus on their cultural significance as well as their contributions to the nation. The best way to start any theme is with good literature. Reading it with children creates a community of readers and a common understanding that the class can build on (Harwayne 1992). Appendixes D2 and F2 list multicultural fiction and nonfiction books and guided reading books that lend themselves to discussion and research within this theme.

Although not everything all year has to be tied to a theme, I choose at least five content-inspired themes per year based on grade level and state con-

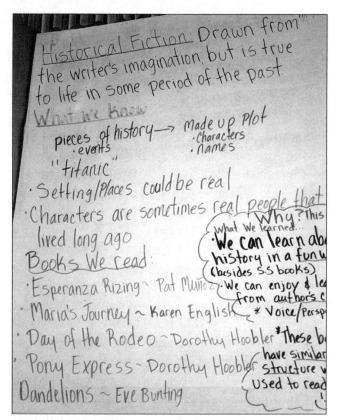

Wall chart for studying the genre of historical fiction.

books at their own reading levels within the same mystery series. As we investigated what makes a good mystery and did read-alouds and shared reading, I would encourage early readers to read the *Nate the Great* series, early fluent readers to read the *Cam Jansen* or *A to Z Mysteries* series, and fluent readers to read the *Boxcar Children* or *Encyclopedia Brown* series. The emphasis would be to model the same genre that the children are reading in independent reading.

Providing for children's projects to wind up the theme studies is also important. Such projects offer ELLs the chance to use language for authentic purposes (Herrell 1999). Working in small groups and discussing a project with their peers helps children develop their vocabulary and use it effectively. Project summaries could take the form of a group oral report with video support, a PowerPoint presentation, a written report, or artistic productions like a collage, painting, mural, or illustrated Big Book.

After choosing the themes to explore during the school year and coordinating with grade-level and cross-grade-level colleagues, I use a thematic planning framework that incorporates Reading To, With, and By children (Appendix C1) to organize the content and literacy objectives for a theme. Taking into account the students' reading and language levels as well as state standards, I record the content area concepts, literary units of study, and vocabulary to be taught, then list mini-lessons and book titles for read-alouds, shared reading, and guided reading. Independent reading books on the chosen theme will also be gathered and made available to children. (See examples on pages 89–90 and pages 92–93.)

tent area standards. The length of time spent on each varies based on interest, content area development, and children-initiated investigations. If one theme is especially appealing to a group of children, it often takes on a life of its own and spurs additional lessons and activities in response to the children's demands. At other times during the school year there are themes that all grades work on. During African American History Month, for example, I choose picture books, biographies, and historical fiction related to that theme.

Sometimes a literary genre itself might be the "theme," the organizing principle. If I notice that we haven't focused on the historical fiction or mystery genre through the content-based themes, for instance, I might plan units of study around these genres. Many children are also eager to read series books or books by the same author. As Krashen (2004) mentions in his case for narrow reading, the continuity such books offer is very motivating for readers in the early stages of language acquisition. They are familiar with the characters, the settings, and the vocabulary, which makes decoding easier, and they are eager to move on to the next related book. I might encourage children to read several

PLANNING FOR THEMATIC TEACHING

I have chosen the theme Learning About Oceanography as an example of how to plan thematically for a primary and an upper-grade classroom. Once the thematic planning framework is mapped out, the meat of the instruction fills in over time based on my knowledge of individual children. This overall framework helps me teach to the needs of my students while still covering content area and English language arts standards for the grade level.

For this theme, I webbed eight subthemes in a graphic web, which represent subjects that were explored with children at various grade levels. I also brainstormed about the theme and subthemes with teachers across grade levels because the content and the concepts to be taught spiral up through the grade levels. Such brainstorming often precedes the planning for a theme and should go on with the children. I wouldn't have time to explore all the topics in one classroom but would choose the ones that matched students' grade level, interests, and perhaps the books I had available to support the topics. Children could also independently do further research on topics of their choice.

It takes at least two weeks to cover any of the topics shown on the oceanography theme web, depending on children's age and interests. A colleague's fourth-grade class, composed almost entirely of ELLs, spent over a month just on Humanity's Effect on the Ocean. Students read books, newspaper articles, magazine stories, and Web sites, and did PowerPoint presentations on their small-groups research, which covered topics like overfishing the seas, the dangers of fishing nets for marine mammals, the dumping of trash into the ocean, the effects of nearby sewer and industrial plants on the sea, oil spills, urban runoff, and even the effect of large cruise ships on the ocean's environment. The principal was going on a cruise, and the students asked her to investigate for them how the cruise ship dumped its trash. When she returned, she described how the captain and crew had become very suspicious because of her keen interest in their waste disposal system and had wanted to take her off the ship at the next port because they thought she was a federal investigator. She had to tell them she was actually an investigator for a group of fourth-graders.

We might have a plan of where we want to take our students, but their interests and passions often take us in another direction. By having a framework and planning an overall structure with lessons and literature we want to use to encourage their literacy development, we can set the children up for success by giving them plenty of time in their independent reading and small-group work to explore their topics of interest within the theme. By providing a range of literature and resource materials at various developmental levels, we can set all children up for success regardless of their developmental language and reading levels.

After sketching out the thematic planning framework (see examples of this later in the chapter), I look at my collection of books and make sure that I have enough texts on the theme for all types of reading and reading levels. Locating the best literature is one of the most important tasks I have as an educator. I want the children to be engaged as they are learning, and the best way is for them to read exciting texts. We are lucky that there are such

Oceanography theme web.

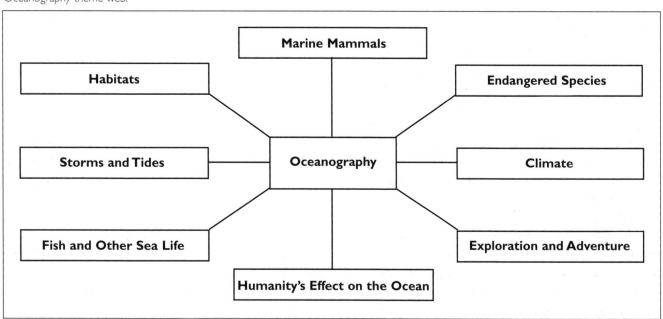

wonderful children's books available now, both fiction and nonfiction, and it is our job to locate them. With the help of the computer, the search is often very easy. I search for titles at the school and public libraries, on the Web, and on the state department of education's recommended book lists, use books from my own classroom library, and the leveled book room, and borrow books from my colleagues. Before I start planning the details of the unit, I gather all the appropriate books and other print resources to be used for read-alouds, shared reading, and guided reading. Appendix C3 lists books for the oceanography theme with those also available in Spanish highlighted. There are probably hundreds of other books that would fit this theme. What I have compiled, however, is the minimum number necessary to do justice to the theme for a month-long period including the high-volume demand of guided reading books. Note that some books can be used for both primary- and upper-grade readers without any problem. Some younger picture books are often interesting to older children who are just learning English, and some higher-level nonfiction narratives can be understood by children of all ages. Which books are used also depends on what I have already taught during the school year. Of course books are chosen for guided reading to match the developmental level of the child. Planning with the same theme and the same books might look very different later in the year, as children advance differentially their interests change and they are assigned to new groups. The classroom library should also have books in Spanish or their primary language that they can read independently.

Study within a unified theme builds children's vocabulary faster and more solidly because they have numerous opportunities to use it in reading and talking about the same topics (Freeman and Freeman 2002; Tharp et al. 2000). Each subtheme would have its own charts and graphic organizers connecting pertinent vocabulary and strategies and language functions to the topic (e.g., comparing and contrasting different types of sea animals or applying an understanding of cause and effect to analyze humanity's effect on the ocean). These wall charts and organizers serve as points of reference that children can always go back to and use in their own writing or reading. Venn diagrams, K-W-L charts, lists of adjectives, lists of comparison words,

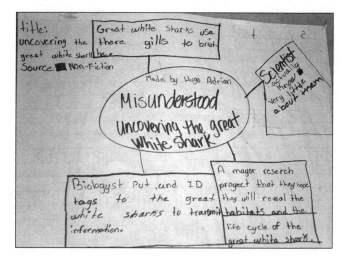

Web created by children during study of the oceanography theme.

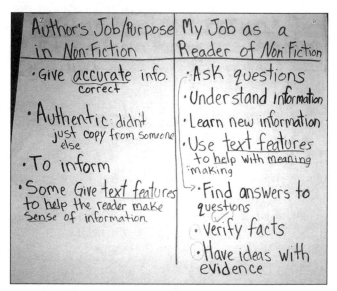

Chart describing nonfiction genre.

and children's own graphic webs should be posted around the room. Using erasable whiteboards loses the record of concepts and vocabulary that they are building throughout the theme. Charting is also used to teach the literacy focus for the unit and the language function or content area thinking processes. In the context of the thematic unit, children might have a mini-lesson on the difference between reading nonfiction and fiction, for example, and be able to refer back to posted charts describing these different genres when they need to.

BUILDING ACADEMIC LANGUAGE USING COGNATES

Another wonderful tool to use in teaching Spanish-speaking ELLs is Spanish-English cognates. The children may know words in their primary language that are almost identical to new words they are learning in English. Cognates give quicker access to new academic vocabulary. I keep lists of cognates as we start studying a theme or subtheme and then add them to the chart as we develop the theme. For example, if we were discussing the marine mammals subtheme of the Oceanography theme, the chart of cognates would show

marine	marino
biology	biología
ecosystem	ecosistema
mammals	mamíferos
cetaceans	cetáceos
dolphins	delfínes
animals	animales
crustaceans	crustáceos
penguins	pingüínos
sponges	esponjas

If we were discussing technology used in oceanography, such as echo-sounders, which are used to map the ocean floor, the cognate chart would show

technology	tecnología
abyss	abismo
echo-sounders	eco-sonidos
sedimentary	sedimentaria
rock	roca
submarine	submarino
canyon	cañón
scientists	científicos
discovery	descubrimiento
discovered	descubrió

Appendix C2 shows several other charts of cognates for the Oceanography theme. Appendix C3 shows lists of other Spanish-English cognates for other content areas, including language functions and higher-level thinking strategies used across the curriculum.

THEMATIC UNIT IN A SECOND-GRADE CLASSROOM

Now let's take a look at an example of thematic planning for a second-grade class. For a month-long thematic unit on oceanography, I chose two subthemes: *fish and other sea life*, and *habitats*, based on students' interests and grade level content standards.

Before starting the unit, I asked what the children already knew about the theme that they could express in either the primary language or in English, and began to build their background knowledge. We filled in a K-W-L chart (what I *k*now, *w*ant to know, and have *l*earned) reflecting all our common knowledge about the ocean (usually, at the second-grade level, there are a lot of similarities in what children know about the ocean). We filled in another K-W-L chart the next day, focusing on the narrower topic of sea life. These charts as well as the ones for the habitat subtheme stayed up for the duration of the theme study, and we added to them periodically as we worked through the theme. We also used other graphic organizers which stayed up in the room for reference. Sometimes the children's contributions to the K-W-L charts revealed interests that I hadn't considered, leading to additional paths for study.

A summary of the framework elements for *both* subthemes is on the next page. Fine-tuning comes with knowing your students.

The example thematic planning framework filled in on pages 89–90 is for the first two weeks, covering the first subtheme (sea life) and using fiction books to study character analysis. During the subsequent two weeks, the second subtheme (habitats) and nonfiction books are highlighted. Although in this example books for read-alouds and shared reading are all fiction, the children will still learn a lot about fish and other sea animals from the texts. The authors describe these characters' attributes, so we can ask, What did we learn about them as characters? as sea animals? How accurate is the literary depiction compared to the real-life forms? How can we find that out? The books for guided reading in this subtheme are mainly nonfiction. It is often difficult to match guided reading books to both theme and literary focus, so I try to relate them at least to theme.

The work on this subtheme comprises many ongoing small-group and whole-class projects, which can occur during the unit or as a culmination of the theme study. Comparison charts are used between subthemes and to synthesize new informa-

Theme. Oceanography.

Subthemes. Fish and other sea life; habitats.

Content Area. Science, with a tie-in from grade-level standards: ocean plants, animal life cycles, Earth has distinct properties and provides resources.

Content Area Concepts. (Tied to science standards.) There is a wide variety of sea life; fish and other sea life adapt to their surroundings, have unique ways to protect themselves, and live in varied ocean habitats.

Literacy Focus. (ELA and ELD standards.) Character analysis using fiction (two weeks); function of text features in nonfiction (two weeks).

Reading Strategies. (ELA and ELD standards.)

Emergent readers can be expected to predict the outcome of a story using pictures

Early readers, to cross-check using several strategies

Early fluent readers, to identify and summarize the main idea

Fluent readers, to analyze characters and synthesize information.

Language Functions and Structures. (ELD standards.)

Beginning speakers can be expected to name common nouns and use regular plurals

Early intermediate speakers, to describe characters using adjectives (colors, sizes) and the present progressive tense

Intermediate speakers, to infer and draw conclusions, and use correct sentence structure with adjectives

Early advanced speakers, to compare and contrast using correct descriptions

Advanced speakers, to use the irregular past tense and create new dialogue for characters.

Vocabulary Development and Word Skills. Types of fish, mammals, endangered species; habitats: reefs, kelp beds, ocean floor, different oceans; adjectives, cognates; blends, digraphs.

List of Books for Theme. Appendix C3 lists books on oceanography for Reading To, With, and By children. Big Books: *The Greedy Gray Octopus,* fiction; *Meet the Octopus,* nonfiction.

Mini-Lessons for Theme. Analyze main character, describe character (fiction), describe sea animals (nonfiction), summarize, use nonfiction features, compare and constrast.

tion learned, especially with new nonfiction books used in the second subtheme. Projects include

★ *Bookmaking.* The class or individual students make Big Books and small ones.

★ *Class Murals.* All children participate.

★ *Research Reports.* Individual and group reports on topics of interest, for instance, compare and contrast two sea animals and how they adapt to their environment.

★ *Invitations to Speakers.* Knowledgeable people are asked to come in and talk to the class; for instance, cetacean society volunteers; captains of fishing, commercial, or tourist boats; marine biologists; or aquarium docents.

★ *Field Trips.* Visit an aquarium, marine institute, beach, or marina.

THEMATIC UNIT IN A FOURTH-GRADE CLASSROOM

The planning for the oceanography theme for a fourth-grade classroom would be very similar to that for the primary-grade example, with two subthemes, marine mammals and exploration/adventure. The difference is in the content and the literary focuses. Once again, I would look to content areas—science, history/social science, English language arts, and English language development standards as well as knowledge of the students' individual needs to help guide my planning.

I start with K-W-L charts to tap into the students' knowledge, and encourage them to work in teams to do research projects based on questions they want answered. I group children of all lan-

Thematic Planning Framework

Grade Level __2__

Theme __Oceanography__ Time Frame __4 weeks total__

Subtheme __Fish and other sea life__ Time Frame __2 weeks__

Content Area __Science, English Language Arts__ Genre __Fiction__

Content Area Concepts (Content Focus) __Variety of sea animals; adaptation for__
Science or History/Social Science Standards __protection__

Unit of Study (Literary Focus) __Character analysis in fiction text; use of descriptive__
ELA and ELD Standards __language__

Vocabulary Development (Language Focus) __Sea animals; descriptive words; plural__
ELA and ELD Standards __nouns__

Reading To

Read-Aloud Books	Literary Focus and Reading Strategy	Language Focus and Language Pattern	Content Focus and Thinking Process	Teaching Group
Chapter Books: Dolphin in the Deep (F)	Character study Identify main idea	Descriptive language	Adaptation for protection; variety of sea life	Whole class
Picture Books: Swimmy (F) Rainbows of the Sea (F)	Character study	Compare and contrast Descriptive language	Compare and contrast	
The Rainbow Fish (F) One Tiny Turtle (F) Isla (F)	Character study Predict outcome Visualizing	Descriptive language Descriptive language Descriptive language	Describes	

Mini-Lessons	How to Record Information
Describing characters Comparing and contrasting characters Summarizing plot Visualizing with descriptive language Describing sea animals	Write on charts Venn diagrams Graphic organizers Draw pictures Charts, sentence strips

Continued on next page.

Reading With

Shared Reading Books	Literary Focus and Reading Strategy	Language Focus and Language Pattern	Content Focus and Thinking Process	Teaching Group
Big Books: The Greedy Gray Octopus Other:	Character development Predicting Making connections Print awareness	Descriptive words Using dialogue Sentence patterns	Types of sea life Food chain Compare and contrast Infers	Whole class

Mini-Lessons	How to Record Information
Analyzing main character	Write on charts
Cross-checking for meaning	Post-it notes, pointer
Predicting outcome	Chart predictions
Tracking text	Pointer
Learning nouns (sea animals)	Book and chart
Finding descriptive words	Book and chart
Using adjectives in sentences	Sentence strips
Reading dialogue	Write quotations
Comparing and contrasting	Venn diagram

Reading By

Guided Reading Books	Literary Focus and Reading Strategy	Language Focus and Language Pattern	Content Focus and Thinking Process	Teaching Group
Emergent: Fish Print At the Aquarium	Predicting outcome Using pictures Finding words	Adjectives Simple nouns	Fish body parts Different sea life	Small group
Early: Corals Crabs	Cross-checking for meaning Self-correcting Identifying main character	Plural nouns	Sea animals	Small group
Early Fluent: The Big Catch Sea Horses and Pipefish	Summarizing Identifying main idea	Using dialogue Past tense questions	Sea animals	Small group
Fluent: What's Under the Sea? Sam and Kim	Synthesizing information Analyzing characters	Descriptive phrases Conditional tense	Sea animals	Small group

Theme. Oceanography.

Subthemes. Marine mammals; exploration and adventure.

Content Area. Science, with a tie-in from grade-level standards: organisms need energy and matter to grow; food chains; properties of rocks (ocean floor); waves, wind, water, and ice shape Earth's surface.

Content Area Concepts. (Tied to science standards.) There is a wide variety of marine mammals; animals in the sea are part of a larger food chain; storms and ocean currents affect the Earth's surface; human beings explore ocean depths.

Literary Focus. (ELA and ELD standards.) Analyzing author's intent in fiction (two weeks); using nonfiction text features for research (two weeks).

Reading Strategies. (ELA and ELS standards.)

Hopefully, there are no *emergent* readers in this grade.

Early readers can be expected to predict and to cross-check using several strategies

Early fluent readers, to summarize the main idea and to self-correct

Fluent readers, to synthesize information and to analyze the author's intent.

Language Functions and Structures. (ELD standards.)

Beginning speakers can be expected to name common marine mammals and use regular plurals

Early intermediate speakers, to describe and to use negative statements and the present progressive tense

Intermediate speakers, to infer and to use possessive pronouns and ask questions in the future tense

Early advanced speakers, to synthesize information and to ask questions in the past tense

Advanced speakers, to use the irregular past tense and the conditional tense.

Vocabulary Development and Word Skills. (ELA and ELD standards.) Types of marine mammals, endangered species; ocean depths, ocean floor, different oceans, ships, scuba equipment; adjectives, comparison words, cognates; homograms, suffixes.

List of Books for Theme. Appendix C3 lists books on oceanography for Reading To, With, and By children. Big Books: *Cousteau,* nonfiction; *Whale Rap,* fiction and nonfiction.

Mini-Lessons for Theme. Use nonfiction text features for research, synthesize, ask questions, use adjectives and cognates, identify main idea, rereading for information.

---

guage levels and reading abilities together so that they can work cooperatively and learn from each other. I still pull homogeneous groups for guided reading and small-group instruction based on their instructional levels. In these content-based theme studies, I allow children to speak in the primary language if they wish because I want their thinking to continue to grow while their language is developing. If the child is an emergent or early intermediate speaker, I also accept written work in the primary language for the group project.

Upper-grade children are able not only to read for information in class and in the school library but also to research on the Internet. Also, there are many educational CDs or DVDs on varied topics, including oceanography. The focus of my planning is on books, of course, but we also use magazines, reference materials, and technology to learn about the content we are studying. I make sure that they also have plenty of books and resource material available to them in their primary language.

The example thematic planning framework filled in on pages 92–93 is for a two-week period, covering the first subtheme (marine mammals) and using nonfiction text features for research. A summary of the framework elements for *both* subthemes is shown above.

As I noted, after the books are chosen to match the theme, content, and literacy focus I want to teach, I fine-tune instruction to the individual needs of the students, planning for their developmental reading and language levels. If there is an early reader in fourth grade (reading at the first-grade level), I have to teach to that child's instruc-

Thematic Planning Framework

Grade Level __4__

Theme __Oceanography__   Time Frame __4 weeks__

Subtheme __Marine mammals__   Time Frame __2 weeks__

Content Area __Science, English Language Arts__   Genre __Nonfiction__

Content Area Concepts (Content Focus) __Variety of marine mammals; animals part of__
Science or History/Social Science Standards   __food chain__

Unit of Study (Literary Focus) __Using nonfiction text features for research__
ELA and ELD Standards

Vocabulary Development (Language Focus) __Marine mammals; endangered species;__
ELA and ELD Standards   __cognates; verb tense__

Reading To

Read-Aloud Books	Literary Focus and Reading Strategy	Language Focus and Language Pattern	Content Focus and Thinking Process	Teaching Group
Chapter Books: Island of the Blue Dolphins (F)	Author's intent	Cognates	Marine mammals Describe Ask questions Synthesize information	Whole class
Picture Books: Animal Safari: Sea Otters (NF) Sea Animals (NF) Sea Otters (NF)	Using table of contents, index Reading captions Descriptive language	Verb tense	Food chain Variety of marine mammals	

Mini-Lessons	How to Record Information
K-W-L chart Choosing topic to research Using table of contents Using index to find information Checking predictions	Graphic organizer Write on chart Use overhead projector Use overhead projector Charts

Continued on next page.

Reading With

Shared Reading Books	Literary Focus and Reading Strategy	Language Focus and Language Pattern	Content Focus and Thinking Process	Teaching Group
Big Books: The Whale Rap (rap song and nonfiction) Other:	Using text features Summarizing Drawing conclusions	Descriptive words Using cognates Sentence patterns	Types of marine mammals Food chain Synthesize information	Whole class

Mini-Lessons	How to Record Information
Using text features Drawing conclusions Cross-checking for meaning Predicting outcome Using descriptive language Learning nouns (marine mammals) Summarizing Using adjectives in sentences Using cognates to gain meaning	Book and pointer Write on chart Post-it notes, pointer Chart predictions Book and chart Book and chart Write on charts Sentence strips Chart words

Reading By

Guided Reading Books	Literary Focus and Reading Strategy	Language Focus and Language Pattern	Content Focus and Thinking Process	Teaching Group
Emergent: Whales in the Ocean Ocean Facts	Predicting outcome Using pictures Finding words	Present tense Simple nouns	Whales Animals in ocean Describe	Small group
Early: Dolphins (Capstone) Dolphins (Mondo)	Cross-checking for meaning Self-correcting Using nonfiction features	Past tense Simple cognates	Mammals Describe Infer	Small group
Early Fluent: Ocean Tides Ocean by the Lake	Summarizing Identifying main idea Comparing, contrasting Self-correcting	Dialogue within sentences Using lists of nouns	Sea animals adapt to tides Mammals Infer	Small group
Fluent: Whale Watching Shark! The Truth Behind the Terror	Synthesizing information Using nonfiction text features for research	Finding cognates Using perfect tense	Mammals Food chain Synthesize information	Small group

tional level and hope that I can improve his reading strategies as well as his language proficiency within small-group instruction. That is why I need guided reading books within the theme at all instructional levels. Ideally, all fourth-graders would be fluent readers, and their instructional level would be at grade level or above. Because that is almost never the case, I prepare for children who are still early or early fluent readers not only in guided reading, but also shared reading and read-aloud. If there are still emergent readers in this grade, who are just learning basic tracking or relying on pictures to get meaning, they should be getting all the special assistance I or other resources in the school can give them. Emergent books would be used at this grade level not for guided reading but to introduce new theme-related vocabulary to beginning speakers. Perhaps that would include immigrant children who have just arrived in the United States. Such beginning speakers should not be led through an emergent guided reading lesson if they already know how to read in the primary language. (See guided reading Chapters 9–12.)

During this study of oceanography I asked the upper-grade children to keep personal learning logs, in which they wrote during reading block, in order to keep track of research and to note plans for further reading and investigation. An excerpt from Ana's learning log follows. She was an intermediate speaker. Her first entry is in Spanish. Ana was not told in which language she should write, although the CD-ROM she used for research was in English. As the children kept their learning logs, they started to form groups based on their research interests. Readers and speakers at several developmental levels worked together. Since the primary language of those students was Spanish, the discussions moved back and forth between the two languages. Meaning making was evident, and if they couldn't understand someone in one language, they would switch to the other. (Spelling is Ana's.)

March 8
Ana: Las ballenas no son pescados por que los pescados tienen escamas. (*The whales aren't fish because fish have scales.*)

Richard: Y las ballenas tienen pelos y los pescados tienen escamas. (*And whales have hair and fish have scales.*)

March 9
Fihs and whales are different because fihs have scales. Whales are fat and healthy. Whales know when trouble is coming. I like whales because their soft, frienly, and smart. I want to see whales. Whales are really intelligen. Whales are mammals. Whales nure their young. Whales have hair and fish don't. Whales do not need air tank to breathe under water. When the water is cold they move to another ocean. Whales sing in the water.

March 10
The blue whale skeleton is very big. Is the biggest skeleton on earth. I like the blue whale because is very big and you can stuy a lot of it. The blue whales skeleton is really big. It has 33 m masterpiece. The skeleton of a blue whale hangs in the British museum.

March 11
The whales finger bones are very big. Their feet are big too. I like the whales fingers bones. Today whales still have hand like bones inside their flippers. Some also have the tiniest rmains of the hind legs, though these don't show on the outside of the body. To get the total picture baced on whale-bone clue.

March 15
We learn that the killer whale has teeth and it eats fish. Also eats whales bigger than it self. It could eat the biggest whale. That is the blue whale is the biggest whale. It also eat squid, penguins as well as seals, sea lions, and other mrmber of the dolphin family. A male can grow to over thirty feet and weight nine tons. Orcas are found in all of the worls oceans, from the poles to the tropics. They hunt for food in herds called pods. Yet they are usully gentle in captivity, and there is no record that an orca has ever caused a human death. They called killer whale orca because they perform in marine parks around the coutry.

The classroom had several computers, and children used them to write in their own files. They prepared oral presentations with video clips from CD-ROMS and laser discs that they displayed on TVs connected to the computer. The children controlled the computer to upload the video clips when needed. PowerPoint is commonly used to prepare formal presentations in classrooms because video clips can be pasted in easily. The computer should

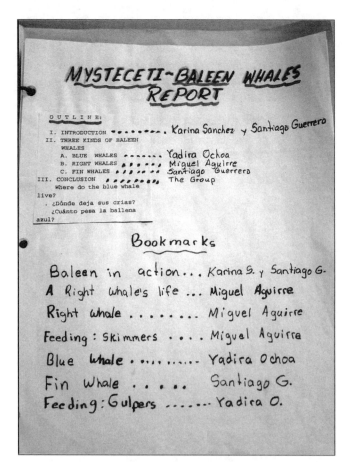

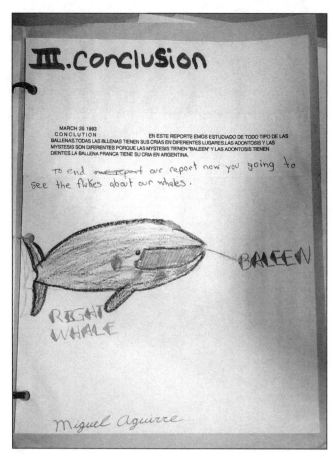

Children's reports using Spanish and English.

be connected to a large TV, or a projector should be used, so that the whole class can see and participate fully.

Projects to culminate the theme can include class books, art projects, or written reports. If the classroom has the technology, children could work on a group PowerPoint presentation or a written–oral report. I would require the report to be handed in written, with notes on how the children will orally present the information to the class, whether on charts, slides, or video clips.

I always ask for an oral presentation because speaking is an important part of the development of students' language. They need to practice using the academic language they have learned through the theme study. I would allow beginning and early intermediate speakers to share in the primary language but encourage them to use short English phrases with the support of visuals. They could also prepare articles for a class or group newspaper, having different members of the group work on news stories, features, and editorials, all relating to the theme or subtheme and to their individual inter-

ests or topics of investigation. They would also share orally how they wrote the articles, summarize them, or highlight the most important ideas. I would assess the children's speaking ability on a rubric (see O'Malley and Pierce [1996] for sample rubrics), and I would use the developmental checklists in Appendixes A3 and A4 to keep track of language patterns used.

The following are some topics that were presented for the oceanography theme:

Humanity's effect on the ocean
Power plants capturing sea animals
Water run-off from polluted creeks
Oil spills
Seals washed up on the beach
Sea gulls with plastic caught on their beaks
Exploring the oceans
Sinking of the *Titanic*
Shipwrecks
Buried treasures of the sea
Scuba diving for investigation
Difference between baleen and toothed whales

Are orcas really killers?
How dolphins communicate with humans
The singing whales
Life on a coral reef

Teaching thematically can be very productive, but just like anything, it takes reflection and time in order for it to be successful. Most important, it means knowing your students in order to shape instruction to their levels and interests. I think that is the essence of good teaching—making connections for children across subjects and engaging them in cognitive, language, and reading development.

Part III of the book discusses specific instruction through read-alouds and shared reading. The sample lessons are taken from a wide variety of classrooms.

6

READ-
ALOUDS

"Those Aren't Weeds!"

One of my favorite books to read aloud is Eve Bunting's A Day's Work. *Besides teaching the virtue of telling the truth, the story shares a wonderful experience of misunderstanding and trust. Francisco, a young boy, decides to accompany his grandfather—his abuelo—to look for work. His abuelo has just arrived in the country and doesn't speak any English. They stand in line with other day laborers, hoping to find a job for the day. To land an assignment, Francisco lies to a potential employer, saying they are gardeners. They work all day pulling out "weeds" from among the "flowers" planted on a hillside. At the end of the day, both Francisco and Abuelo were extremely satisfied with the work they had done even though they were tired, as they looked at the trash cans full of "weeds" they had pulled. Of course they were heartbroken when they found out that they had worked all day in vain. Because they really knew nothing about gardening, they had made a terrible mistake. "I can't believe it," says their employer at the end of the day. "You took out all the plants and left the weeds!" When* Abuelo *realizes that his grandson lied to get work, he scolds him: "We do not lie for work." He refuses their pay and promises to come back the next day to replant the uprooted "weeds," trusting the man to pay them after they completed all the work. The ending is upbeat. The employer tells Francisco, "The important things your grandfather knows already. And I can teach him gardening."*

Francisco and his grandfather were trying to be gardeners with no experience and no modeling at all. What might have happened if Francisco and his *abuelo* had had a bit more to go on—for instance, if the employer had said, "Pull out the yellow chickweed and save my young green ice plants" instead of assuming his workers knew what to do and leaving them to fend for themselves? Often we, too, assume that our students know more than they do, and we don't take the time to find out what they actually know and need help with. The employer acknowledged, "This is partly my fault. I should have stayed to get you started." But he was in a hurry to get off to another job. Often, we, too, are in a hurry to get on to another lesson and don't take the opportunity to teach what the children need at the moment.

In reading aloud a good book like *A Day's Work,* we can slow down and teach not only the lessons the author wants readers to learn but also those that we want to share, like how to enjoy a good book and what good readers do and what good speakers do as they are reading. Through modeling the joy of reading, we can show children how we stop and reflect, how we use language for different purposes, how we make connections to

our own lives, and how we are moved by certain parts of a book. We can also encourage children to respond, and choosing a good book like this one makes our job easier: children naturally want to respond to it. They want to make connections to their own lives, which is a critical part of any read-aloud and a necessity for deepening their comprehension. Some children make connections in their minds, others are more vocal, and still others need some nudging along and more modeling to show them how to do it.

In *Becoming a Nation of Readers* (1985), the Commission on Reading stated that the single most important factor in children's reading success is having people read aloud to them. Unfortunately many English language learners come from homes where no one reads to them in any language. That means our role as teachers in reading aloud to children is even more important. The Commission also stated, "There is no substitute for a teacher who reads children good stories. It whets the appetite of children for reading, and provides a model of skillful oral reading. It is a practice that should continue throughout the grades."

In this chapter I highlight the importance of having ELLs listen to and participate in at least two read-alouds per day (a picture book and a chapter book) in order to develop their speaking and reading ability, and to become aware of the rich range of literature that is available. This applies to all children from kindergarten through fifth grade. I discuss the importance of modeling higher level strategies, which helps improve their cognitive development. I also discuss the benefit of choosing to read multicultural literature for our diverse classrooms filled with children from all walks of life. The discussions that occur in our classrooms and the empathy, tolerance, understanding, acceptance and inclusion of those different than ourselves that happens by reading multicultural literature is wonderful to see and experience.

GUIDING QUESTIONS

What types of books should I choose to read to my English language learners from such diverse backgrounds?

What can we do to encourage all children to participate even with different reading and language levels?

How do I read aloud to my English language learners in my primary classrooms when their English level is so low? Can I use their home language?

How often should we stop during a read-aloud?

When is the best time to point out new vocabulary with a read-aloud?

What can we do to keep the children most engaged during a read-aloud?

CHOOSING READ-ALOUD BOOKS

When I choose books to read aloud, I first think of the pure enjoyment of reading. I want all children to enjoy reading for themselves, and I want to model for them far more exciting and challenging books than they could read on their own. For English language learners who may not have been read to in English at home, I still want to read books that will entice them to continue reading and books that are above their current language and reading levels.

Trelease (2001) talks about the importance of reading aloud books that are two years above the children's reading level and about the common mistake among parents and teachers who stop reading to children once they can read themselves. All children need to be read to—even college students. I remember one of my college English professors reading Shakespearean sonnets aloud to us. We enjoyed listening and understood the new genre much better when we heard an expert read it aloud. Reading sonnets was like reading a foreign language before I heard his oral reading. I often think of that when I read to ELLs. I try to read with the most expression and the best pronunciation and intonation I can to help listeners comprehend better and to make the reading exciting and interesting.

When I look at district or state reading lists, I think about the genres represented and about the two-year rule. Is this book at least two years above most of the children's reading level? And then, of course, I think, Will we all enjoy it? Trelease (2001) suggests that we read aloud chapter books that we may not traditionally think are for that grade level. For example, he recommends reading *Charlotte's Web* to kindergartners, not third graders, even though it is a "third-grade book." If most of my kindergartners are beginning speakers, however, and are just starting to hear English for the first time, that book would not be an appropriate choice. But I would still read them a chapter book, perhaps one from the beginning chapter book series *Henry and Mudge*, which is at the first-grade level and which would be about two years above the beginning language level of these children.

Since I need to read books that are at least two years above the reading level as well as the language level of the children, I might read *Esperanza Rising* to a class of third-graders if most are reading on grade level and if their language level is on track for their grade. If I have a class of fifth-graders with a lot of intermediate speakers and with many below grade level in reading, I might read that same book to them (even though it is a fifth-grade book) because it is actually about two years above their reading and language levels. Thus, when choosing books to read, we need to be cognizant of the language levels as well as the reading levels of our students.

Because of the range of speakers and readers in our classrooms, it is sometimes necessary to read different books to different groups of children. Sometimes I do an extra read-aloud to a group with a much higher language level or a much lower language level than the majority of the class. At least one daily read-aloud is always with the whole class, which I feel is extremely important for developing a community of readers (Harwayne 1999). But all children need to hear stories or nonfiction texts at their optimal levels of development and understanding, so I need to be flexible and make sure that they all have the opportunity to be read to above their reading and language levels. I might also ask an adult volunteer to read to some children in order to help me provide this rich reading environment in my classroom.

I find that reading a good picture book in one sitting allows all levels of ELLs to grasp story structure, plot, and character development. The illustrations play a vital role in this, and picture books of course have many beautiful ones, unlike chapter books, which have very few illustrations. I might read to younger students *Sheila Rae, the Brave* because of its expressive illustrations, often two per page to support the clear descriptive text. The book also is a wonderful character study of a child. The first line of the book sets up the whole plot: "Sheila Rae wasn't afraid of anything." For older children I might choose *Fly Away Home,* which has detailed illustrations to support the interesting story line of a homeless boy who lives in an airport with his dad. Bunting creates a simple description of a problem often difficult to describe to children by telling the story through the eyes of the child. This book creates a wonderful opportunity for discussion and allows older children at all language levels to see the hope that the main character still has that one day he will get out of his terrible situation. Appendix D2 includes a list of other Eve Bunting titles to use in an author study.

I also choose books connected with the theme or genre study on which we are focusing. For a unit on biography or California history, which is part of the California History/Social Science Framework, I might read *Harvesting Hope: The Story of Cesar Chavez.* I would focus on the literary elements of this picture book as well as the historical significance of Chavez's work. Once again, a picture book helps ELLs at all levels

access content that may be difficult for them otherwise. Also, by choosing nonfiction books, I can expose children to a variety of texts in a range of content areas with photographs or illustrations to support the content presented. In order to decide which books to choose, I would start with state standards or the curriculum frameworks, themes, and units of study that the grade-level teachers have designated, and select books to help me teach and cover those topics. Picture books include some related to math and science themes. And biographies of famous people, including sports stars, are always favorites.

I sometimes choose books just for the purpose of exposing ELLs to rich language—rhyming, alliterations, metaphors, or even just the sound of the language or phonemic awareness. I might choose *Tumble Bumble* for younger readers because of the rhyming and clever illustrations or *Hairs/Pelitos* for older children because of the metaphors Cisneros uses to describe the different types of hair of members of her family such as "My mother's hair, like bread . . . ." The bold colors in the illustrations are very inviting for all ages of children and help English language learners visualize the metaphors. If the children enjoyed this book, and if their English is at least at the intermediate level, I might read them chapters from Cisneros's novel *House on Mango Street,* which is where the picture book *Hairs/Pelitos* is taken from. Not all the chapters are appropriate for younger readers; the book is often used at the high school level. But the language is so descriptive that one can read sections slowly as poetry for children to hear. Since there are no illustrations, one can place the text on an overhead projector.

For ELLs and indeed all children, a familiar book that the teacher has read is like a good friend; they always want to go back and read it themselves. It is wonderful to see even kindergartners find a book we've read to them and try to read it almost word for word as we did. Then we can easily see that children are starting to love to read. The books we read aloud should be kept in a prominent, easily accessible place. Read-alouds should be planned with lots of care and should not just be something we do at odd times to quiet the children or fill time. They are an integral element of a balanced literacy block.

MAKING CONNECTIONS WITH MULTICULTURAL PICTURE BOOKS

One important strategy to help deepen children's understanding of text, and to see if they are really understanding what you are reading to them, is modeling for them how to make connections. Keene and Zimmermann (1997) and Harvey and Goudvis (2000) talk about having children make connections to their own lives, make connections to the text, and make connections to others. By modeling how to do this for the children in a read-aloud by thinking out loud, and then by having the children share their connections, I can help them enhance their own understanding. Other people call this building on background knowledge or schema, because the children are asked if they have had any experiences similar to the ones in the book. They use their own background or experience perhaps from another book they read to predict what might happen next or relate to why a character acts as he does.

A Day's Work is very effective with immigrant children and ELLs because they can make connections on a couple of levels. One is the difficulty that many of their families have in finding work, and another is that the children are often asked to be translators for the adults in their families and thus go to work with them. Most children I have shared this book with have had experiences similar to Francisco's and his *abuelo*'s. Or they have seen day laborers on the street. If not, they are still riveted by the descriptions that Bunting uses to help them make connections to their own lives and decisions that they have to make. I stop at various parts of the book to reflect thinking out loud and, if the children are ready, to accept their responses. I might stop at the following passage, for example:

"You and your grandfather in the back. Sixty dollars for the day."
Francisco nodded. His breath was coming fast. That much for a day's work? Mama would be so happy. Her job didn't pay much. There'd be extra food tonight, maybe *chorizos*.

After reading that, I would think aloud and wonder what I would buy if I received that much money. I would also ponder on the fact that it seems as if Francisco intends to use all the money for food, and how difficult it might be for a child his age to worry about getting food on the table. I would then look around at the children and see if they wanted to add any of their own reflections. Some might share similar experiences. Others would feel too shy or embarrassed to admit their poverty, especially if they are in a classroom with children from diverse social economic backgrounds. But I would accept any comments without soliciting them. If children want to share when I stop and reflect, great. But my purpose is not to ask them to respond each time I think aloud during the reading but rather to model for them how I make connections as a good reader. Asking for predictions helps children make connections, too, because they often predict what might occur in a book based on their own experiences. I might also model other strategies or the use of effective language while I read.

A read-aloud of a picture book or a chapter book should not take all day. The pacing should be natural, and the main purpose to share a good piece of literature. Yet, English language learners need time to talk as well. I try to encourage a dialogue mostly before and after the reading of the text. As the children share their reflections on the book and make connections to their own lives, their peers are able to learn more about them, and this creates a reading community.

A good multicultural book gives readers insight into the main character's particular culture, sphere of movement, and circumstances, but also highlights the challenges that character faces as a human being. Books that have characters of one particular ethnicity, for example, should appeal to members of other groups as well, even though their backgrounds may be very different from the protagonist's. If there is something in the book that they can grasp on to, that triggers a memory of a person, a place, or an experience similar to the one they are hearing about in the read-aloud, then they can come to realize that they have something in common with children from other backgrounds.

I had a wonderful experience reading aloud in a fifth-grade multicultural classroom as an invited guest. My friend asked me to come into her classroom to read my book *The Story of Doña Chila*. She said she had a mix of children, including many

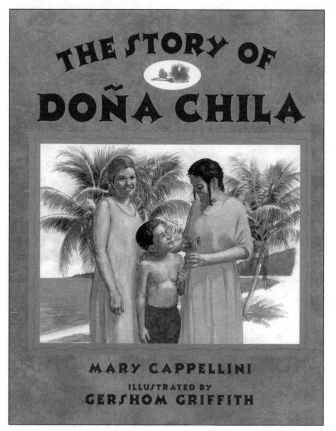

Cover of *The Story of Doña Chila.*

ELLs. There were four Hispanic girls who were bilingual, a boy from India who spoke Hindi fluently, two Iranian children who spoke Farsi and French, and three Chinese Americans. I asked if there were other nationalities, and the children cited Italian, British, German, or French ancestors, so I assumed the rest were European American. Interestingly, the Hispanic girls were quiet and didn't participate even though I introduced the book in both Spanish and English and told them I had lived in Argentina.

I was a little hesitant to read a picture book designed for second- to fourth-graders but hoped that even older children could enjoy a good story. I started by telling how I wrote the book, which is set on the Caribbean coast of Honduras. I told them that I had dedicated the book to a friend who had lived in Honduras while she was in the Peace Corps. And I told them the main character, Doña Chila, was a *curandera.*

A what? shouted a child.
A healer, I said.

Isn't that a witch doctor? asked another.
Not exactly. People in many countries, including ours, go to a healer to cure their illnesses.
My mother believes in homeopathic medicine. She goes to an acupuncturist, said an Anglo child.
Some people call healing "alternative medicine."
My mom takes lots of herbs and goes to a health store.

I explained that a *curandera* also used herbs and natural products to heal people and that many of our medicines come from plants. Just then one of the Hispanic girls, who had been quiet till now, volunteered, "My grandmother is a *curandera.*" Suddenly she became the expert, and the other children started asking her questions. I could see the pride in her face as she shared her family's experiences. The other Hispanic girls started speaking up now, too. They said their mothers had gone to *curanderas* in their homeland, Mexico, and here in the United States. I realized that their language ability was at an early advanced level and that their previous silence had not been due to low language level, as I had half assumed. Another girl, with a Norwegian mother and Mexican father, chimed in that her father also went to healers. The Hispanic girls nodded and smiled. The boy from India said his father was a doctor, not a healer. The Iranian child said his family also used herbs as medicine but went to Western doctors. One of the Chinese-American children said his family didn't trust doctors, and other children said their families went to regular doctors.

Since I was interested in the contrasting use of healers and Western doctors in the United States, I was thrilled that the book had elicited connections from so many children in this classroom. This read-aloud took longer perhaps than it should have, because I stopped several times to let students share their comments. But it was worth it to see the eagerness with which they engaged in the story.

The discussion that ensued with this rich multicultural mix of children even before I began reading the story was fascinating. It confirmed my belief in the importance of building a community of readers who realize that although we may have different ways of doing things, we also have much in common. The children in this class learned a lot about each other's backgrounds and different families' views and practices regarding medicine. And I learned again that we need to create opportunities for all children to feel comfortable participating in a discussion and that in order to understand children's language and cognitive abilities, we need to hear them speak. Appendix D2 lists many other multicultural books that will stimulate discussion and help children make connections to their own lives and the lives of others.

FOCUSING ON CHARACTER DEVELOPMENT WITH CHAPTER BOOKS

I once heard the children's book writer Lois Lowry talk about the importance of character development at a conference. She said that if a character does not go through some sort of change, if a character is not affected by events, or if a character does not proactively change the course of his or her situation, then there is no point in writing the story. We are drawn to a good story if we are touched by it somehow and feel empathy for the characters.

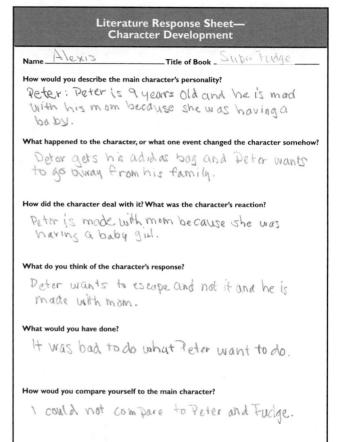

Student's literature response sheet about characters in *Superfudge*.

We can help children understand a story by looking at the personalities of the characters and how they change and develop. This can be mapped out on a wall chart as we are reading a chapter book or tracked in individual literature response journals. This charting is particularly helpful for beginning or early intermediate speakers.

We can also ask children how they feel about the characters' changes. They can reflect on what a character has had to go through, and what they themselves would do if they were in that character's position. This too can be recorded in literature response journals, shared in a class discussion, or recorded on a literature response sheet (Appendix D1). Often a class read-aloud lends itself wonderfully to such responding. During independent reading time, they may respond in their literature response journals, but I don't require it. Rather, I encourage them to respond just about once a week.

Since plot is so closely tied to character, I find it very difficult to discuss one without the other. Often teachers do whole units on plot and then separate units on character without making the con-

10/4 Island of the Blue Dolphins

I felt shockt.
Becus that story
Soned scary to be
left on a Island
all by your self.
I wod be sckard
if I got left on
a Iland all by my
self. I wod be sad
that some willd dogs
kill my little brother

Student's literature response journal entry about the main character's situation in *Island of the Blue Dolphins*.

nection between the two. Many chapter books have strong characters who have been affected by events with common themes to which we can all relate—the loss of a family member or dealing with prejudice or moving away from loved ones. They make us think: *What would we do if we were in the characters' positions?* By discussing how characters deal with the events in stories, by focusing on their point of view, we can encourage English language learners to compare how they would respond to such situations. These discussions improve their thinking and their use of English as well. As we accept all levels of response during a class discussion, we encourage participation and thinking, which are critical to their academic English development.

One book I have used very successfully to discuss character development with upper-grade children is *Esperanza Rising*. Esperanza's whole world is shattered the day her father is killed on their large ranch in Mexico, the day before her thirteenth birthday. She and her mother flee to California to escape her evil uncles and leave their privileged life behind to work as farmworkers, side by side with their previous servants. This is a wonderful story, which shows how a child can survive hardship and at the same time gives voice to poor immigrants who arrive in the United States as farmworkers. Many students respond to Esperanza's experiences by telling of their families' experiences as farmworkers or of having had to start over. I try to guide their discussion to focus on character development and how Esperanza changed from a child of despair to a child of "hope" (*esperanza*).

During the reading of the book, we make a wall chart of the events in Esperanza's life and how she responds to them. We describe her personality and how she slowly changes from being "selfish," as one child says, to "finally seeing what other people feel," as another puts it. The responses I get from children range from short phrases or one-word answers to complete sentences. As I write their responses on the chart, I always ask others to help children rephrase, or ask if they agree with what was said, in order to elicit as much language as possible. Many children criticize Esperanza:

"She's a brat."
"She's not nice."
"I don't like her."

This leads to heavy debate at times, as others give justifications for her actions:

"Her dad died."
"Give her a break."
"She lost everything."

Wall chart about character and events in *Esperanza Rising*—first half of the book.

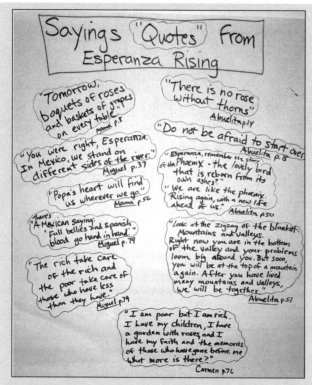
Wall chart with memorable sayings from *Esperanza Rising*.

"She had to move."
"How would you like it if you had to hide and escape like that?"
"I did."
"I left everything to come here."

When does all this discussion occur? Every day, after we have read a new part of the book. It isn't forced. Children are very interested in sharing their reactions to Esperanza's plight. Based on what they have heard in the read-aloud, they judge Esperanza and give their opinions on what type of person she is. They often infer from the book and back up their inferences with details from the text.

As we discuss Esperanza as a character and the children relate to events in the story and share their own stories, we notice that the author uses a lot of memorable sayings or metaphors throughout the book. For example, when Esperanza goes to her room with her friend Marisol after the funeral, they "held hands, and wept as one." I make a chart of some of these sayings, and the children reflect on what they might mean. (I write the page numbers next to the quotations so that the students can go back and revisit them.)

There is no rose without thorns.
Do not be afraid to start over.

Do you remember the phoenix, the lovely young bird that is reborn from its own ashes? We are like the phoenix . . . rising again, with a new life ahead of us.
Look at the zigzag of the blanket. Mountain and valley. Right now you are in the bottom of the valley and your problems loom big around you. But soon you are at the top of the mountain again. After you have lived many mountains and valleys, we will be together.
In Mexico we stand on different sides of the river.
The rich take care of the rich, and the poor take care of those who have less than they have.
I am poor but I am rich. I have my children. I have a garden with roses, and I have my faith and the memories of those who have gone before me. What more is there? [said by a poor "egg woman"]

The children are amazed that the author refers back to so many of these sayings in the last chapter of the book. "It's a circle," a child shouts, as others check out the sayings on the chart. Esperanza is described as rising on the *wings of the phoenix* and as realizing that *she had her family, a garden full of roses, her faith and the memories of those who had gone before her.* "She's like the egg woman," a child observes. Miguel and Esperanza are now *on the same side of the river.* "I think in California they can get married," says another. The children's favorite recap is when Esperanza says, *Do not be afraid to start over.* "Boy, she's changed!" exclaims a child. This sayings chart proves invaluable to the discussion and to the students' understanding of the text. It was not part of my initial planning, but I am sure glad we did it as part of the read-aloud session with this book.

Other good chapter books for the upper grades with strong character development tied to plot are *Island of the Blue Dolphins*, about a young Indian girl stranded on an island who survives numerous threats after losing her brother to the wolves; *Number the Stars*, about a girl in Nazi-controlled Denmark who courageously chooses to help save her Jewish friend; and *The Bridge to Terabithia*, in which a ten-year-old boy in rural Virginia becomes friends with a newcomer who subsequently meets an untimely death trying to reach their hideaway during a storm. For the primary grades I would suggest *The Key Collection*, which has the universal theme of the strong ties that exist between a grandparent and a young boy and how he deals with the loss of her companionship when she moves away. It is told through the eyes of a Chinese-American boy, yet written by an author, Andrea Cheng, who remembers missing her Hungarian grandmother. Appendix D2 lists other chapter books.

READING ALOUD CHAPTER BOOKS TO BEGINNING SPEAKERS IN THE PRIMARY GRADES

Many teachers unfortunately do not read aloud chapter books to beginning speakers in the primary grades. Perhaps they think that the children will not be able to handle it. We mustn't forget that many ELLs do not have the opportunity to hear a chapter book read at home. Beginning in kindergarten, we should always try to read to all children part of a chapter book every day regardless of their language level. The idea of reading a story over a few days and discussing the characters and the plot should not be lost to children because of their language level. We just need to adjust what and how we read aloud to these beginning speakers.

I would choose a short chapter book in English with a lot of illustrations to begin with and then choose longer books as their language develops. Numerous very short Early Readers or Ready-to-Read chapter books are available from most mainstream publishers.

If the teacher has time and is bilingual, I would also try to read higher-level chapter books in the primary language to foster cognitive development while ELLs are learning English. If the teacher does not speak the native language of most ELLs in the class, this would be a wonderful opportunity to ask a parent or community volunteer to come in and read to the children during literacy block. If there are many different primary languages in the classroom, I would focus on reading in the primary language of the majority of children who are beginning or early intermediate speakers. The rest would be able to understand and participate at a higher level of English, and it would not be as important to read to them in their primary language as for beginning speakers who are barely understanding academic English.

In one primary classroom where the majority of English language learners were native Spanish speakers, I read *Henry and Mudge and the Starry Night* in English and *Salven mi selva (Save My Rainforest)* in Spanish. The *Henry and Mudge* book, which has many illustrations, three chapters, and forty pages with only three or four lines of text on each page, took three days to read. It was perfect for my class of ELLs, a majority of whom were beginning and early intermediate speakers.

Salven mi selva was at the third-grade level with lovely illustrations, thirty-two pages, and forty lines of text per page. Every two pages were like a chapter in a chapter book, and the book took about three weeks to read. The discussion about the Spanish book was far more profound than the discussion about the English book, but the focus was the same in both—the analysis of characters and story plot. Although the themes of the two books are very different, they both have a little boy as the main character and show him interacting with his family and taking a hike to a new place.

Henry goes camping with his parents and his dog, Mudge. While reading *Henry and Mudge* to the children, I recorded their responses about the characters on a wall chart. Instead of focusing on one main character, we talked about all the characters, to elicit as much spoken language as possible. This story does not have as well developed a plot as longer books do, so it did not lead to as deep a discussion of the changes the characters go through, but there was still enough information for the wall chart.

Each day, after we had read a chapter, we paused and added descriptions to the chart while we discussed what we had learned about the characters. I wrote their responses in short phrases so that we could go back and read them again. Often the children inferred what the character felt based on the illustrations and the text. Sometimes their phrases came right from the text: they remembered them on their own, or we reread lines to refresh their memory.

Although the book was in the past tense, I wrote the short phrases in present tense because that was the tense the children were speaking in. Some children gave one-word responses in English; others responded in Spanish. When a child said *oso*, for example, I asked if someone could help us with

Henry and Mudge and the Starry Night

What do We Know About the Characters?

Henry's Mom
- Ch.1 - Was a Camp Fire Girl
- knows about Camping
- knows how to cook
- Ch.2 - likes to hike
- likes to camp
- Ch.3 - knows about stars
- loves to watch stars
- love's Henry's Dad

Henry's Dad
- Ch.1 - knows how to play guitar
- smiles
- Ch.2 - likes to walk
- loves to sing
- Ch.3 - is happy
- is funny
- loves Henry's mo

Henry
- Ch.1 - loves camping
- is excited
- is afraid of bears
- Ch.2 - likes to walk
- likes to climb
- likes to feed Mudge
- doesn't like Dad's Singing
- Ch.3 - is excited about seeing stars
- loves Mudge

Mudge
- Ch.1 - loves camping
- is excited too
- drools and yawns
- Ch.2 - loves to hike
- loves to smell
- loves to eat
- Ch.3 - loves to chew
- loves camping
- loves Henry

Wall chart about characters in *Henry and Mudge and the Starry Night*.

that in English; then another child said *bear*. "*Tiene miedo*," a child said, and I responded in English, "Yes, he's afraid of bears" and wrote that down. All language was accepted. The important part was that the children were understanding the story and grasping the concepts of character analysis. But at the same time, since the read-aloud was in English, I gave the new vocabulary in English in the context of the discussion. It is too difficult to try to guess ahead of time which words they may not know, so new vocabulary is taught in the context of a good story read to them above their reading level.

In *Salven mi selva*, Omar, saddened to hear that the last Mexican rainforest is being burned for farmland, takes a 1,400 km hiking trip, actually a protest march, with his father to the forest, stopping at the presidential palace along the way to persuade the president to stop the burning. Based on a true story, *Salven mi selva* enthralled the Mexican-American children. They came in from recess shouting, "*Selva, selva!*" and begging to read the book every day. They made posters like the one Omar carried on his march, which we put up on the wall. They wrote, "Save the Rainforest! ¡Salven mi selva!" We also predicted what Omar would do next. Would the presi-

dent listen to his plea? We had graphs and charts on the wall, and the children reflected on what they would do if they were in Omar's shoes.

As the children were developing their ability to speak in English, they were using higher-level thinking skills in Spanish. At the same time, I tried to get them to think, or at least listen, at this higher level in English, too. If the teacher does not speak the primary language and cannot entice a parent or community member to come in and read, he can still expose beginning or early intermediate speakers to short chapter books and focus on higher-level thinking skills.

STOPPING FOR UNDERSTANDING, PACING, AND FOCUS IN READ-ALOUDS

Children should be encouraged to tell us if they are having trouble understanding a read-aloud or a discussion. We need to set up an environment where making meaning is paramount and stop reading when necessary in order to clarify what is happening for children who are not following. We can't know that, however, unless children ask questions. Asking questions is a difficult skill, but it often shows that children are thinking and trying to figure out for themselves what is happening. As we read longer and more difficult texts, even known words may be confusing in longer sentences or a different context. Children should be allowed to stop the reading to ask for clarification of parts they don't understand. Once, while I was reading a *Harry Potter* book, a child raised her hand and said, "I don't get that." "OK," I said. "Let me read that tricky part again." Sometimes I just read a line again on my own initiative, modeling that even a good reader doesn't always get the author's meaning on the first try. But I rarely stop to explain words that I think students "need to know," nor do I ask, "Do you know this word?" Rather I pause after a complicated passage if I see some bewildered looks or if children ask me to explain.

I once observed a well-intentioned read-aloud go very poorly because of an overemphasis on questioning throughout the reading. A teacher was reading the book *Jouanah: A Hmong Cinderella.* On the board was a Venn diagram of Cinderella and this Hmong version. The teacher had set the scene nicely for the read-aloud, which seemed to be part of a unit on folktales in this fourth grade. What occurred, however, was that the teacher stopped so many times to ask questions, teach vocabulary, and check comprehension that the lovely story was lost.

As I mentioned earlier, stopping once or twice for prediction and clarification is fine, or stopping a few times very quickly to think aloud without interacting with the children is helpful. This still allows for a natural pacing, and the children can still hear the natural flow of the story. If, at the end of the reading, the discussion indicates that children missed some important parts of the story, the teacher can always go back and reread that part if necessary.

There are different focuses that we can highlight when we are reading aloud based on the expanding meaning strategies (see Appendix A7). Many, including making connections, analyzing the character, inferring, creating K-W-L charts, and self-questioning, were discussed in this chapter. Picking a focus for the read-aloud shouldn't distract the children from finding joy in the reading of a good story. Rather, it should complement the reading by helping children think more deeply about the story. By modeling good strategies and good discussion, the teacher models what good readers do independently and in literature circles, and this leads to better discussion in literature circles and better literature response journals when the children work independently. A focus on character development, for example, should also extend from read-alouds to shared reading and guided reading and then to independent reading. Books with good examples of useful focuses in read-alouds are Taberski (2000), Harwayne (1992), Fountas and Pinnell (2001), Keene and Zimmermann (1997), Harvey and Goudvis (2000), Miller (2002), and Sibberson and Szymusiak (2001).

USING RHYME AND RHYTHM AS A FOCUS IN READ-ALOUDS

There is no better way to have fun with English and help English language learners develop phonemic awareness than through poetry, song, and rhyming books. English has many sounds that other languages do not. Children who are learning English for the first time need to be exposed to these sounds and to the rich play of the language. Poetry, especially silly poetry, is a wonderful way to do that. I choose books written in rhyme or in poetic form instead of just reading a poem, however, because I feel that ELLs need to see illustrations to make sense of the text. Children who are trying to understand this new language often get lost in the silly text without pictures to help them place the text in some context. A good example is the first poem in the book *Dinosaur Dinner.* The illustration of the dinosaur dressed as a waiter with a black bow tie and a checkered tablecloth in its mouth makes the text "Tyrannosaurus Rex gobbled up the table 'cause they wouldn't pay their checks" comprehensible.

In *Counting Crocodiles,* a funny rhyming counting book, crocodiles cross the Sillabobble Sea with the clever monkey. The sounds of the language are a joy to hear, and because of the illustrations, the children are able to understand the patterns of words that were matched to rhyme but otherwise would never go together. From *Mrs. McNosh Hangs Up Her Wash* children can learn new vocabulary words—lamp, wreath, teeth—by looking at the pictures and at the same time hear the rhymes. In *Tumble Bumble* the huge illustrations overshadow the line or two of text on each page, and students are able to follow along as they see "A tiny bug went for a walk. He met a cat and stopped to talk." As the animals meet each character along the way, the children can see exactly what they are doing. A favorite page is, "They all began to dance a jig and bumped into a baby pig." Appendix D2 lists other books with poetry, rhyme, and rich language.

There has been a lot of research on the importance of phonemic awareness in learning to read and in listening to and being able to rhyme (Yopp 1988; Ayres 1998). Most state ELA and ELD or ELP standards and developmental checklists for beginning readers require that they be able to rhyme and hear rhyming words. But we may not realize that it is very difficult to rhyme in a second language. Native speakers can come up with a long list of rhymes for *pie,* for example, but until English language learners start to hear endings in words and realize that some words have the same ending sounds, and until they have a bank of words to draw on, which most five-year-old native speakers have, it is very difficult for them to rhyme. ELLs have not had the benefit of hearing rhyming stories like those by Dr. Seuss read to them in English for years. By hearing "One fish, two fish, red fish, blue fish" and seeing the illustrations, native speakers have internalized these English sounds from a very early age.

One of the best ways to highlight rhyming words in read-aloud books is to write them on charts and have children illustrate them or make books with them. English language learners will learn new vocabulary and how the words rhyme. Children-made illustrations also help with understanding rhyming books whose original illustrations might be too small or older books whose illustrations might not be as sophisticated or explanatory. An excellent read-aloud book for ELLs is *I Can't Said the Ant,* in which a kettle, a knife, a mop, a steak, a tray, a squash, and so on are characters who talk. These aren't nonsense words but items that ELLs would see in their own kitchens. Each item is sketched in color, so the children can see exactly what it is and learn the English word for it if they don't already know it, or match the English word to the word they know in their primary language. In a second-grade class I paired up children and had them work together on illustrating the item of their choice and writing what the item said in the book (see illustration below):

"Teapot broke," said the artichoke. "Is she dead?" asked the bread.
"Push her up," said the cup. "I can't," said the ant.

We then discussed the meanings of the quotations, for instance, "'A close scrape,' said the grape." Many were difficult for the beginning speakers, but through the class discussion most were able to understand the expressions. Because of the difficulty of the expressions for ELLs, this book is best used with intermediate speakers.

Students' illustrations of text from *I Can't Said the Ant.*

Students' illustrations of text from *I Can Fly*.

In one kindergarten class the children reillustrated the tiny classic Golden Book *I Can Fly*. After I had read it to the class, we made it into a Big Book and used it for shared reading. The children worked in pairs, and each pair illustrated one page of the book. Sometimes I ask children to illustrate other books we've read together just because they enjoyed them so much, and it is a wonderful way to integrate an art lesson with literacy. I do this with books that we have to return to the library but that they want to read over again.

I make charts of rhyming words, onsets, and rimes that we revisit throughout the day. When children find other words that rhyme, they can add them to the charts. Although I don't necessarily focus on this during read-aloud time, these rhyming books lead naturally to keeping track of such words and sounds. Thirty-seven rimes make up approximately five hundred primary-grade words that children encounter most in their reading. You can record these rimes on charts as you focus on them (Taberski 2000). Some teachers hang them from the ceiling. The photos illustrate this, and they also show how you can encourage your young children to write their own rimes. You can also see how one teacher used environmental print that the children

Wall charts of word families—or rhymes.

Wall chart of word families arranged by familiar places.

recognize, like fast-food restaurants and popular stores, to teach and record other words with the same rimes or in the same word family.

I try to keep read-alouds enjoyable and interesting and always choose a focus for them. By focusing on teaching language functions or patterns or higher-level thinking strategies while reading a good book, we can enhance ELLs' understanding and joy of reading. And by involving all levels of speakers in rich discussions of read-aloud books, we improve their language proficiency while creating a community of readers.

7 SHARED READING *with* PRIMARY-GRADE STUDENTS

"A House Is Coming"

My husband's cousins from Argentina were in California for a medical conference, and after the conference they drove north to visit San Francisco. As English language learners, they listened very carefully to conversations, trying to get the gist of what was being said and joining in when they could. They had reached a small beach town halfway up the state at about 2 a.m. and were looking for a place to stay. The streets were deserted, but all of a sudden they saw flashing lights coming at them. They thought it was the police and that they had done something wrong. But instead a car approached, its driver calling out, "A house is coming! A house is coming!"

As the car passed, they looked at each other and wondered, "Did we hear right?" They had no idea what to do. How could a house be coming? The driver kept waving at them to move over. Just then a huge truck with bright lights bore down on them, pulling a giant trailer with a two-story house sitting on top of it. The house took up the whole two lanes of the street. They pulled over just in time and watched in disbelief. Never had they seen a house moving down a street. Well, at least they hadn't misunderstood the English, they thought. A house really was coming!

A house is coming! Does that make sense even to a native speaker? How many people have actually seen a whole house being moved on a trailer? In Latin America house moving is pretty rare. That's why years later our cousins are still talking about their experience. It was not until they saw the reality with their own eyes that the sentence became comprehensible to them.

Shared reading is a time when reading becomes comprehensible to English language learners and so does the language. Children have the opportunity to see a large text in front of them, which an expert reader is modeling how to read, and then they can join in when they feel comfortable. The illustrations that go along with the text help them visualize right away something with which they might have had no experience. They then can add this new knowledge to their bank of experience. At the same time, as they listen to and watch the teacher read, and then participate in the reading, they absorb reading strategies and new patterns of language, and add those to their repertoire, too. Shared reading is a wonderful time for teachers to mentor eager readers and speakers of English, and scaffold their instruction, and it should be a central part of any balanced literacy program.

Shared reading is not new. It has been used in classrooms in the United States for over twenty years, and many books explain the use and benefits of shared reading (e.g., Holdaway 1979; Mooney 1990; Routman 2000; Fisher 1995; Parkes 2000; Taberski 2000). Also current research on effective teaching and student outcomes for English language learners highlight standards that make up the basis of shared reading lessons (CREDE 2002).

In this chapter I describe shared reading and how to plan for it with a balance of teaching higher- and lower-level strategies as well as langue functions and patterns. I provide an example of a primary-grade shared reading lesson including assessing children's reading and language proficiency, and in Chapter 8, an example of an upper-grade one that focuses on developing academic language.

GUIDING QUESTIONS

What are the important elements of an effective shared reading lesson?

How do I differentiate for lower-level speakers during shared reading?

How do I teach skills and strategies in a shared reading lesson?

What can I learn about the reading and oral language development of my ELLs in the context of a shared reading?

How can I keep track of what I learn and use it to plan instruction?

WHAT IS SHARED READING?

Shared reading is an extension of the bedtime story experience. It was developed by Don Holdaway (1979) after extensive research on how certain preschoolers learned to read on their own with no prior reading instruction except for what they might have absorbed from their parents' reading to them in a warm and nurturing environment. In the classroom during shared reading, the teacher reads a Big Book or an enlarged text with the children, and the children join in and read with the teacher when they feel comfortable. Just as at home with their favorite story, students chime in on their favorite parts of the book. Emergent readers and beginning English speakers think they are reading . . . and they are. Because many English language learners don't have this opportunity at home, it is especially important to provide it at school.

Some good reasons to do shared reading with ELLs are the following:

★ To encourage and foster children's love of reading.
★ To involve children; they join in almost at once.
★ To build a sense of community.
★ To model reading strategies.
★ To model natural language patterns.
★ To teach language skills.
★ To highlight fiction literary components like character development, plot, and author's intent.
★ To highlight nonfiction format elements.
★ To highlight different genres and writing styles.
★ To observe children and better grasp their language and literacy levels.

The lessons I highlight here are from demonstrations I did for classroom teachers who wanted to see shared reading modeled with their English language learners. When I go into a classroom to do a demonstration lesson with children I don't know, the most important piece of information the teacher can give me in order to make the lesson successful is the English language proficiency level of each child. This is done with a color-coded name tag worn by each child. Beginning speakers' tags have a symbol like a star. This allows me to interact with all the children easily, not just with the most talkative ones, and to encourage every child to participate at his ability level. Knowing his developmental language level up front, I know what I should expect from each child and can tap into the appropriate language level right away, as the classroom teacher would be able to do. Often the classroom teacher is surprised at how much language each child produces during my lesson. There could be many factors for that, but I think one of the most important ones is asking the children questions that I know they will be able to answer at their individual language levels.

Shared reading is with the whole class, but I expect each child to participate regardless of her language level. And I expect each child to produce language outcomes as well as reading outcomes based on her developmental language level. I have high expectations for each child, but I also want each child to enjoy the experience and to feel engaged in the lesson. That means I have to make each child feel welcome to participate. I also have to encourage each child to take responsibility for her learning. I want an early intermediate speaker to feel comfortable answering a question in a few words or in an incomplete sentence, and to show me that she can read short phrases or lines from the book, or identify and read rhyming words in the book. I expect an early advanced or advanced speaker to speak almost like a native speaker, answering open-ended questions in full detail and speaking in complete and correct sentences, as well as to read full sections of the text with me. See Appendixes E1 and E2 for expectations of language and reading outcomes for ELLs in a shared reading lesson.

Many beginning speakers need extra support to feel comfortable to participate and to help them understand what they are hearing and reading. They need real objects to hold and manipulate. I bring in props for these children—puppets, stuffed animals, or real objects like bird feathers and seashells, depending on the theme or content of the curriculum that we are exploring. Total physical response is an important part of helping beginning speakers learn language (Krashen and Terrell 1983). Having them use hand gestures, using gestures and facial expressions myself, and having them point to the Big Book or hold a prop—all these increase their participation, their understanding, and their learning.

My goal for the first reading of a shared reading text is to have the children enjoy the story, absorb reading strategies from the expert reading, and participate in the reading themselves. I want them to hear rich language and to discuss the story by sharing predictions, observations, and responses, which I record on a chart. That may seem like a lot, but all these things can occur naturally during the first reading if they are well planned. During the second or third reading of the shared reading text, I might focus on just one specific skill or strategy that needs to be modeled more in depth. In this kind of lesson reading, speaking, listening, and writing are integrated.

The Big Book I highlight here is *A Farm's Not a Farm*, about a couple who go to live on a farm but have no animals—what should they do? Starting with its title, the book encourages a lot of discussion. It is also cleverly designed to support emergent readers and beginning speakers: phrases or language patterns in boxes are placed on the page next to the picture they represent, almost like labels. The book also has bold-face and italic text and, most notably, different-color text for each of the two main characters when they are talking. Thus, it helps ELLs notice dialogue. The language patterns are predictable and repetitive and help ELLs use correct sentence structure, for instance, placing adjectives in the right place, using prepositions, and using the present progressive tense. The language patterns can easily be lifted from the page to use in a language study for students to copy and rewrite. I have used this book with all levels of ELLs at all grades from kindergarten to fourth.

PLANNING AND PREPARING FOR A SHARED READING LESSON

In planning a shared reading lesson, I first look at students' individual reading and language folders, and at my observations and notes from previous shared reading lessons (see the Assessment section later in this chapter). Then I try to find a Big Book that will match students' needs and interests. Next,

I fill in a focus sheet of outcomes (Appendix E1), a form designed to help teachers think about the language and reading outcomes they should expect from students with different English language proficiency levels during shared reading. The form is based on English language arts (ELA) and English language development (ELD) standards and on my knowledge of planning a shared reading lesson for English language learners. This primary focus sheet includes outcomes only for beginning, early intermediate, and intermediate speakers because those are the children who usually get lost in a whole-class discussion or group lesson (see higher levels included in the upper-grade focus sheet, Appendix E2). Because these students' language levels are not as high as those of their peers, it often happens that early advanced, advanced, and native speakers take over the discussion. The focus sheet reminds us to expect participation from lower-level speakers, too, who might make up 30 to 50 percent of any given class.

I also fill in a planning sheet (Appendix E3). This takes only about five or ten minutes but is very helpful to do each day because the children's needs change constantly. A planning sheet can be used for the first reading of a shared reading text or for later rereadings. A shared reading text is usually read more than once with the class, for instance, to teach mini-lessons on particular skills or just for children's enjoyment. This daily planning takes place within the context of thematic or long-term planning (see Chapter 5) and helps me refocus on how I will use a shared reading text and what to teach during a particular lesson.

The following is a summary of a planning sheet (see Appendix E3) for a first reading of *A Farm's Not a Farm*:

★ *Purpose of Reading.* I want the children to enjoy the story and appreciate a cleverly written plot. Also, to observe me modeling strategies: tracking, predicting, using pictures to understand, cross-checking; and to hear new sentence patterns. Also, to join in the reading and the discussion before, during, and after.

★ *Focus.* Predicting and checking predictions.

★ *Children's Needs.* This first-grade class has fourteen beginning to intermediate speakers

Shared Reading—Primary Grades
Focus Sheet of Outcomes for English Language Learners

Beginning to Intermediate Speakers

Thematic unit _Rural—Farm Life_

Mini-theme _Animals, Adjectives_

Shared reading material _A Farm's Not a Farm_

Features to Note in Text (examples):

Rhyming words: sty, by, buy

Plurals/words ending in s: pigs, cows, ducks

Places: hill, field, pond, house, barn, sty

Adjectives: color words; sizes; sleek, waddling

Verb tense: present progressive; past tense

Prepositions: in, on, behind

High-frequency words: a, not, are, there, in, man, the, said, they, were, and, went, so, some

Sounds: onomatopoeia, animal sounds

Text format: dialogue, different color text for speakers; bold

---

Expected language outcomes (examples)

Beginning speakers

One-word response __yes, no__

Regular plurals __pigs, cows, ducks__

Early intermediate speakers

Repeat simple sentence __There are cows in the field.__

Use present tense __I like cows.__

Intermediate speakers

Express understanding of text __They are going to buy animals.__

Possessive pronouns/subject-verb agreement __Their cat/They went__

Use past tense __They bought . . .__

Expected reading outcomes (examples)

Beginning speakers

Read aloud simple words in story __pigs, cows__

Early intermediate speakers

Identify and produce rhyming words __by, sty__

Intermediate speakers

Read simple vocabulary __strong gray donkey__

Read phrases, sentences independently __So they bought . . .__

All speakers

Tracking left to right __Have them use pointer sticks__

One-to-one correspondence __Mask words—children come up and point to words__

Outcomes based on performance standards from ELD Standards (California Department of Education)

Example of focus sheet of outcomes for shared reading in primary grades.

and only six early advanced and advanced speakers. They will need a lot of picture/text support and interactions with the text. Use puppets/stuffed animals to relate to text. Focus on title and story line to make sure they understand the problem and solution. Get more advanced speakers to share their language with beginning and intermediate speakers.

★ *Introduction.* Tap into children's background knowledge about a farm. Match stuffed animals to their predictions of animals. Use chart paper to record children's knowledge and predictions about the text. Set the scene using the picture on the cover. Introduce the title, and question the meaning. Chart more predictions about the text. Talk about the author and compare other books we've read by her.

★ *During Reading.* Use pointer stick to point to pictures and track text. Highlight the "labels" used in this book, and the different-color text to show which character is speaking. Use Post-it notes to cover up a few key words to help them predict and cross-check. Stop for predictions at natural pauses once or twice.

★ *After Reading.* Encourage responses about the text. Ask children to share their favorite parts, referring back to the text. Refer to chart to check their original predictions with the text.

★ *Possible Follow-Ups.* Reread as reader's theater. Class makes own version of Big Book. Use text to teach adjectives and language patterns.

There are definitely some classroom arrangements and materials necessary to have a successful shared reading experience. First is floor space and a warm, inviting corner of the room to sit. Another is an easel, or even better, two easels. I place the Big Book on one and chart paper on the other. If there is only one easel, chart paper should be mounted on a sturdy cardboard backing so that it can be moved off the easel yet always be visible when the children's predictions are written on it. Marking pens for charting and a pointer stick for tracking words in the Big Book are needed. Another necessity is Post-it notes, which I use to cover up words, check predictions, write words on, and move around between Big Book and the chart. They are great for working on language development and sentence structure: children can move around the notes with words written on them to figure out the order of

Setup for shared reading.

words in a sentence or the correct placement of adjectives. Props like puppets and stuffed animals are helpful for beginning speakers. Small books (and tapes) should be available for the children to reread the story during independent reading.

SHARED READING LESSON

Breaking the Ice

For a demonstration shared reading lesson in this classroom, I sat on a big chair with an easel next to it. All twenty first-graders were sitting on the carpet with their color-coded name tags on. Before starting the lesson, I scanned the name tags to see who the beginning speakers were. I said hello to most children individually and asked each one a brief question in order to listen to the oral response and to break the ice. How are you today? What is your favorite book? How old are you? Can you read my name tag? What do you like to read? Breaking the ice is important in beginning each new shared reading lesson, encouraging all children to share responses and feel comfortable to then participate in the reading.

I was able to get a quick overview of the group—where the beginning speakers were sitting, how many children were at each developmental speaking level, and whom I might want to focus on when I called on children to participate. There were three children whose name tags showed a star to mark them as beginning speakers; six early intermediate speakers; five intermediate speakers; three early advanced speakers; and three advanced or native speakers. I had puppets behind me, waiting for the opportunity to pull them out for the beginning speakers, and on the easel was the Big Book *A Farm's Not a Farm*.

Introduction

I began to engage the children in a discussion of predicting what the book might be about, focusing on their personal experiences, background knowledge of the topic, and inferences from the title of the book.

What do you see on the cover of the book?
What would you find on a farm?

Have any of you ever been on a farm?
If so, what was it like? Or where was it?
Where do you think these people are going?
Why do you think the book is called *A Farm's Not a Farm*?
What might this farm *not* have that other farms have?

The responses varied, but the intermediate, early advanced, and advanced speakers were the ones who were eager to answer and to have their ideas heard. I watched the beginning and early intermediate speakers as the others answered, and I was concerned about their lack of language outcomes. They didn't seem to feel comfortable answering the questions in the large group, and the questions themselves may have been a little difficult for them. So after a few more advanced speakers responded, I followed up each question and response with a short and direct question to the beginning or early intermediate speakers, encouraging them also to participate in the discussion. I wanted to make sure that they had an opportunity to speak.

For example, after an early advanced speaker had answered the question, "What can you find on a farm?" with "You find lots of horses on a farm," I asked two beginning speakers directly, "What else? ¿Que más?" "Pig," said one; "Cow," said the other. After an advanced speaker had answered the question, "Have you ever been to a farm or spent much time on a farm?" with "My grandmother has a farm in Mexico, and we go to visit her every year," I asked another beginning speaker, "What about you, José? Have you been to a farm?" "Yes," he answered with a smile. All these beginning speakers answered with what they were able to say at their developmental level. Although they were not able to speak even in short sentences, they were understanding and participating in the discussion, and their language output matched expected outcomes based on their language level. The early intermediate speakers were able to speak in short phrases, and their responses were also valued and encouraged. Keep in mind that ELLs at this level usually understand more than they can speak.

When I asked the children to predict what they would find on a farm, I recorded what they said on the chart paper as they responded. By charting their responses, I validated their language and at the same

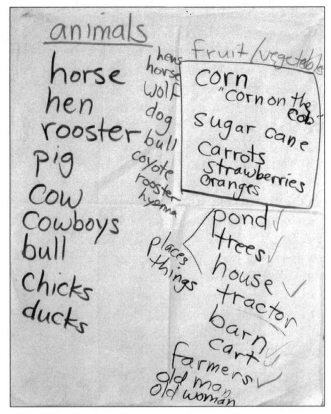

animals
horse
hen
rooster
pig
cow
cowboys
bull
chicks
ducks

hens
horse
wolf
dog
bull
coyote
rooster
hyena

fruit/vegetable
corn
"corn on the cob"
sugar cane
carrots
strawberries
oranges

places/things
pond ✓
trees ✓
house ✓
tractor ✓
barn ✓
cart ✓
farmers ✓
old man
old woman

Lists of animals.

time wrote down words for them to refer to later on, which is extremely important for children at the beginning stages of English language acquisition. Some beginning speakers can't hear or distinguish the words very clearly, but when the teacher writes them down and points to them, they are better able to understand what was said. This information—their predictions—was then available to refer back to as we checked predictions later, and their own words were available for them to rewrite the story.

Most children responded with animals. They also said *barn, house,* and *pond,* and *corn, carrots,* and *oranges,* among other things. While charting, I separated the words naturally into categories, keeping the animals in one column, places or things in another, and vegetables and crops in a third. As I categorized their responses, they were learning how to distinguish between different types of living and nonliving things. I didn't focus on it a lot at this time but thought I could revisit it at a later date. Their responses also allowed me to learn about their background knowledge and their depth of academic language or vocabulary, which helped in assessing their language levels and in planning for follow-up mini-lessons.

As I wrote their predictions of what they would find on a farm, I also pulled out a stuffed animal or puppet to match their words. For example, when a child said *horse,* I brought out my horse and lifted it up for all to see. I could see the three beginning speakers' faces light up. They could confirm their understanding of the words with concrete examples, so I gave the beginning speakers and a few of the early intermediate speakers the stuffed animals that matched their predictions and the animals in the book.

First Reading

During this first reading, while the children were enjoying a good story, I encouraged them also to focus on the strategies a good reader uses. I encouraged them to continue to predict and check their predictions. With my pointer stick, I pointed to the pictures as well as the words as we read the text together, showing students the importance of "reading" the pictures as well as the text. They also naturally learned to track because my pointer glided over the pages from left to right. As I mentioned, this book has special features that help ELLs. The text looks as if it were pasted right onto the pictures, labeling *a hill, a field, a pond, a house, a barn,* and *a sty.* This helps the children see the connection between the words and the illustrations. If children don't know what a barn is, they can learn it easily here because they can see a picture with the word directly on it. This also helps them to realize the importance of making the connection between picture and text.

The book uses dialogue and speech bubbles to show people speaking and thinking. So during the first reading I highlighted the different-color text for the different speakers, asking students who was speaking, which helped them follow the story line. The children quickly caught on that the old woman's words were in blue and the old man's words were in brown. This made it easy to point out the quotation marks, with which many ELLs are not familiar. The use of quotation marks was not a focus in this first reading but rather a quick aside to check that they knew who was speaking. I would come back to quotation marks later.

To help the children use the strategy of predicting and cross-checking, I covered up certain key words beforehand with Post-it notes. I only did this on a few very predictable words, which wouldn't stop the flow of the reading. The purpose of doing this on the first reading is to show them how naturally they can figure out a word by looking at the picture or the first letter or the context of the whole sentence. I have found that if I do this on the first reading, it is more powerful than on a second or third reading. I might cover up part of a rhyming word, like the *y* in *by* after they had read *sty,* or cover up the name of some animals they know and can see right in the picture, like *pigs.* As we read the text, the children say the word before I uncover it. When I do uncover it and we check their predictions, I say, *How did you know that?* And they tell me that they used the beginning letter and a rhyme or that they could tell by the picture and the description of the animal ("*some fat pink pigs*").

Checking the children's understanding of the text and the new vocabulary as we go through the first reading is important. For the beginning and early intermediate speakers who were holding stuffed animals, I checked their understanding by asking them to stand up when they saw the animal that they were holding on the page. "Oh, oh, oh," José shouted when he saw the donkey on the page, jumping up in excitement with the stuffed animal held up in the air.

Then I had them come up and touch the word that matched the animal. I was encouraging total physical response and tried to use as many hand gestures as I could, pointing to the pictures as well as the text. This could be done very naturally, without breaking the rhythm of the story, because there was a pause as every animal was introduced (the description of the animal was given with at least two adjectives). As we read the line slowly and with emphasis ("a strong gray donkey"), José had time to stand up, show his animal, and touch the word on the page. For the intermediate and early advanced speakers, I checked their understanding by asking them which character was speaking and which animals they thought the man and woman would buy.

Stopping for predictions on the first reading needs to be natural. Usually this happens only a couple of times during a story. This book has some very good spots to stop. Even after just the second page spread, there is a natural pause. When the children realized there were no animals on the farm, I asked, "What do you think they will do without animals?" One child said without hesitation, "They'll go to the zoo to find animals." We all laughed. You never know what children will say, and that is the joy of engaging children into making meaning for themselves and encouraging them to share. The discussion quickly included the types of animals one would find on a farm versus a zoo. But when we turned the page, the children laughed to see that the man and woman went to an animal market. They thought that was so interesting and funny.

I encourage children to read along with me even on the first reading. Sometimes a book has a very repetitive pattern that they pick up on right away. This book is very predictable because of the pictures and the story line, but some children prefer just to sit back and enjoy the story on the first reading, which is okay. But I think it is important for them to join in when they can, as soon as possible, so that they see themselves as readers too. That is another reason that stopping for predictions is important: to have children read the line that naturally follows. This book also has some wonderful onomatopoeia. After I pointed to the first animal noise, of a goat on a hill *maaing, maaing,* for example, I asked them to say it. Then they read every other animal sound with me, as if the animal were really making the noise. It was wonderful to watch the beginning speakers especially become so involved with sounding out these animal noises as I pointed to the words.

As we were going through the first reading, I found that even the better speakers had trouble with some of the adjectives the author used. We had to stop to define what *waddling, sleek,* and *frisky* meant. We looked at the context of the sentence and tried to get descriptions from the children of what they knew about the words or what they thought the words meant. It took a lot of creativity to help everyone understand what the adjectives meant.

For the phrase "and some waddling white ducks," Maritza said, "Ducks waddle."

"Yeah, like this," said Joachin, who took it upon himself to stand up and waddle like a duck.

"Oh" said Mayra.

We then looked at the picture again and saw how it appeared that the ducks were all "waddling down the path."

For the phrase, "some sleek brown cows," Crystal said, "That's like *slick*."

"Or *slippery*," said Mario.

"*Soft*," said Ivan.

"Like this?" I asked. I had on a silk skirt and showed them how it was shiny and silky and kind of slippery. Unfortunately, that meant I had half the class touching my "sleek, silky, slippery, soft skirt." But it worked. I compared the coat of the cow to the silk material of my skirt, and Esmeralda said, "My *abuela's* cow feels silky like your skirt."

For the phrase, "and some frisky black goats," Monica said, "*Frisky* is like *jumpy*."

"They like jumping," said Jackie.

"Goats bites things," said Adrian.

"Yeah, they always in trouble," said Tony.

"Are they playful?" I asked.

"They takes my hat," said Jennifer.

"They funny," said Mayra.

"One took food out of my hand," said Jessica.

"Sounds like they are mischievous . . . *travieso* . . . and playful," I said.

"Like this," said Marco, making his stuffed animal jump up and down and onto some kids.

Discussion

A discussion, even if it is short, is always warranted after reading a text. The children are so excited about the story, they want to share their feelings and opinions. In this lesson the children started to talk about the story and its ending right after we finished the last page.

"What about a dog?" asked Jessica.

"Yeah, a farm's not a farm without a dog," said Crystal.

"Do you agree with Jessica and Crystal, Juan?" I asked.

"I like dogs," said Juan.

"I like cats," said Kaila.

"So, does that mean you think a farm should also have a dog as well as a cat?" I asked.

"Yes," many children shouted.

"What else should a farm have?" I asked.

"A horse," said Cesar.

"And some chicks," said Monica.

"I like when they go to animal store," said Irma.

"Yeah, that was funny," said Mario.

"I liked when the animals were making all the noises," said Tony.

"Cows are so loud," said Esmeralda.

"I can moo like a cow," said Jackie.

Of course, a few children started to moo.

While the children were discussing animals that were in the book and ones that were not, we referred to the list of predictions on the chart paper, which was still on the easel. The children were able to check very quickly which animals they had thought might be in the book and which ones had actually appeared in the story. Some children seemed disappointed that their animal had not appeared. This led to their wanting to write their own book, which was a wonderful idea to follow their interest and help develop their language. Many children wanted to share their favorite parts, so we turned back to different pages of the book, highlighting their favorite parts. I asked Adrian and Mayra to just read a phrase because they were early intermediate speakers, but I asked Jennifer and Tony to read a short sentence because they were intermediate speakers. I expected the early advanced and advanced speakers to read more complex sentences.

Children's reading aloud to the class was not the main point. But in the context of the discussion it was natural and supportive to have the children read their favorite parts, especially the beginning speakers because they often feel proud that they can read. It is best not to let this discussion wear on too long yet to allow lively talk.

Second Reading

Often a text like this warrants another reading right away because the children say, "Let's read that again!" If I have time, I often just say, "Okay, let's read it again. But this time . . . ," and suggest how we could reread the text differently the second time. This book lends itself nicely to a modified reader's theater because of the different-color text, which is easy for the children to distinguish, and the bold text, which makes the reading very easy to follow. The children can see their parts highlighted without your having to retype them or give a lot of explanations. I usually ask the boys to read the old man's part, which is in brown, and the girls to read the old woman's part, which is in blue, and I read the narrator's part. Then everyone joins in when the text is in bold print, specifically on the animal sounds.

Using a reader's theater format or choral reading for a second reading of a text can motivate the children and give English language learners at all levels a chance to practice reading orally in a comfortable and nonthreatening setting.

A second reading does not have to be in reader's theater format. This book just happens to lend itself to that. Often just closing the book and reopening it inspires the children to join in the rereading. Joining in a shared reading experience scaffolds children's reading and helps them see themselves in the role of reader. If the book is not one that most of the children enjoyed, I don't take the time or energy to reread it.

Assessment

Before I revisit a text, usually the next day, I jot down on a form (Appendix E4) notes on what I observed during the first reading about each child's reading and language development. This information helps me plan for future mini-lessons and decide how (and whether) I want to use this text again. My observations have a lot to do with how the children participated. And I keep their language levels in mind when I assess their output during the lesson. Questions I keep in mind while watching children in a shared reading lesson are

---

How did they react to the text?
Did they join in on the reading?
Did they join in on the discussion?
What did I notice about their reading strategies?
What did I notice about their language functions?
Did the children's language output match their
    language levels?

Although it seems difficult to lead a lesson and observe the children at the same time, it is an absolutely critical part of effective teaching. For it is through these observations that I am able to reflect and plan for the next lesson. In this case, I was pleasantly surprised at how almost all the children participated in the reading and discussion. A couple of shy children chose to sit back and watch more than speak, but I called on them to add to the discussion, and they did answer according to their language levels.

I don't always get notes on everyone, but each day I try to add to the notes by focusing on children I didn't write about the day before. When I revisit the text, I try to involve children who weren't engaged the day before or who didn't produce enough language for me to see how they were doing. To make assessments quicker, I have the sheets prepared ahead of time with the children's names at their developmental levels.

Besides their developmental language levels, I also keep in mind their developmental reading levels, which I know from the checklists that I have been keeping on them. When I write down comments, I take notes on their reading output as well. I might notice whether a child is now able to follow my tracking when she couldn't before, or whether a child can identify words and letters. I might comment about their use of graphophonics to help them check a prediction, or whether a child is able to read individual words.

Based on these notes, I can plan for future mini-lessons. These notes are transferred to the children's individual reading and language folders, where there are notes from other times when I have observed them, such as guided reading, reading conferences, independent reading, and read-alouds. I can transfer information to their folders when I am meeting with them individually. I can pull my observation sheet from the shared reading lesson and show them what I observed they were able to do that day, and compare that to what I see them do while they read independently.

It is important to have a class roster with the children listed by language levels to plan for and reflect on a shared reading lesson. This helps me keep track of all the children and reminds me to focus so that none of them gets lost in the shared reading group. I can also cross-reference and make sure that I am observing all the children in different reading and language situations. Copies of this roster are printed out on the observation and notes form for easy use.

Shared Reading
Observations and Notes from a Lesson

Date 11/3   **Big Book** A Farm's Not a Farm   **Which Reading** first

Language Level	Language Output/Participation	Reading Output
Beginning		
Marco	Participated, one- or two-word responses, followed along	Rereading some individual words
Elizabeth	Seemed interested, one- or two-word responses	Read the labels in text
Jose	Quiet but participated with stuffed animal	Pointed at words, followed tracking
Early Intermediate		
Adrian	Spoke in short sentences	Found words
Ivan	Didn't participate much	
Irma	Said a long complete sentence, seemed chatty; perhaps higher level?	Read short lines and tracked fine
Cesar	Spoke in short phrases	Predicted
Kaila	Said one short correct sentence	Found words
Mayra	Spoke in short sentences	
Intermediate		
Jennifer	Participated nicely even though her sentences were incorrect	Could read sentences from text
Jackie	Made personal connections and comparisons, used present progressive	Read along fine
Tony	Participated freely, good syntax	Read sentences from text with no problem
Juan	Reluctant to talk	
Maritza	Used correct form of verb	
Early Advanced		
Mario	Enjoyed the reading, discussion	Found lines in text
Crystal	Good verbal interactions	Lifted title and used it in reading
Monica	Answered questions, used comparisons	
Advanced		
Jessica	Participated throughout with great sentences and thought	Read page of the text very well
Esmeralda	Good personal connections	Reads great
Joachin	Jokester, helped beginning speakers	

Example of observations and notes from a shared reading lesson.

MINI-LESSONS

All children, whether primary or upper grade, need a balance of mini-lessons on higher- and lower-level strategies, literary elements of fiction and nonfiction, and language functions and patterns to develop as readers and language users. This balance is necessary to cover the requirements of the ELD and the ELA content standards. My observations of the students throughout reading block play a vital role in deciding the types of mini-lessons I need to plan.

Following is a partial list of the types of mini-lessons to think about while planning a successful and balanced shared reading program for ELLs:

Higher-Level Strategies

Literary Elements   *Expanding Meaning*
Fiction
★ character development   ★ inferring
★ concept of time   ★ summarizing
★ problem/solution   ★ analyzing
★ plot development   ★ author's purpose

Nonfiction
★ table of contents   ★ comparing/
★ glossary   contrasting
★ index   ★ connecting
★ headings   ★ reflecting
★ captions   ★ evaluating
★ reading graphics

Word/Language Study—Functions and Patterns

★ parts of words   ★ sentence structure
★ adjective placement   ★ asking questions
★ contractions   ★ answering questions
★ word endings   ★ making statements
★ verb tenses   ★ using dialogue

Lower-Level Strategies

Print Awareness   *Sustaining Meaning*
★ tracking   ★ solving words
★ pointing to words   ★ monitoring
★ return sweep   ★ predicting
★ noticing spaces   ★ self-correcting
★ following the text   ★ rereading a sentence
★ using illustrations   ★ cross-checking

A number of books provide a wealth of information on mini-lessons for shared reading in literary elements and reading strategies for primary and upper-grade children (e.g., Parkes 2000; Taberski 2000; Fountas and Pinnell 2001; Routman 2000). English language learners also need direct instruction in English language patterns and structures. Language mini-lessons should be included in the second or third rereading of a familiar Big Book.

There are a variety of language mini-lessons one could do with *A Farm's Not a Farm*, depending on the needs of the children. I have used it to teach prepositions because it so nicely shows the placement of the animals—on the field, in the barn—and to teach the present progressive tense because the animals are mooing, heehawing, and so on. I have used this book to focus on changing tenses, for instance, into the past tense. Asking questions is an important and difficult language skill, and this book has some good examples of questions. Often the books the children like best have predictable patterns, like this one does, or rhythm or lyrical phrases that they enjoy repeating and rereading. Writing some of the lines from the text on chart paper provides an enjoyable and natural way to interact with the language. I always try to pull out interesting text that helps me focus on a set skill or sentence structure.

As I mentioned, in planning language mini-lessons it is critical to know the language needs of the students first, and then to look closely at the text to see if it can be used to teach to them. It is easy to evaluate the usefulness of a text in one sitting once we know what we are looking for. If we know, for example, that many students in the class need to work on the past tense, it will be clear right away whether the book is good for that. If not, could it be used to teach another skill or strategy? When we take time to observe children and analyze the text, planning becomes easier.

After the shared reading of *A Farm's Not a Farm* with the class mentioned earlier, I noticed that all the ELLs from early intermediate speakers on up needed to work on adjectives and adjective placement, particularly since in their primary languages adjectives are placed differently. The beginning speakers did not need to focus on that structure yet but could still find some benefit from any language lesson.

Post-it notes were very useful in this mini-lesson. The children could move words around without worrying if they put them in the wrong place, because they could easily be moved again. They held the adjectives in their hands and put them into phrases in correct order. I tried to get as many children involved as possible; some came up and helped me write; others helped classmates find the correct placement for the adjectives. They were all engaged, interacting with the text and each other, and developing their language through interactions with a text they enjoyed.

Mini-Lesson on Adjective Placement

We reread the book until we got to the text "What shall we buy? asked the old man" and lifted that line onto chart paper as the focus for the mini-lesson. First I wrote, without punctuation, *What shall we buy asked the old man,* and after discussion students added the punctuation. Then each child answered the question by naming animals: *donkey, pigs, cow, ducks.* I wrote these words on Post-it notes and stuck them on the chart. Then I wrote *So they bought* and drew four underscore blanks for words.

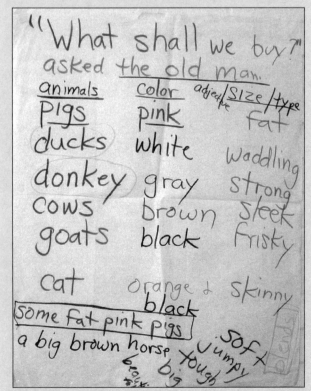

Adjectives in category columns for a mini-lesson on adjective placement.

_____ _____ _____ _____

What did they buy first? I asked.
A donkey.
Good. What color was the donkey?
Gray.

I wrote their answers on different-sized Post-its with pens to match the color (I outlined the word *white*): *gray, pink, brown, white.* Then I asked someone to come up, find the word *gray*, and place it in correct order on the underscore blanks. Maritza looked at the book on the easel and placed the Post-it with *gray* in order on the line, and Miguel did the same, placing the *donkey* Post-it after gray.

_____ _____ gray donkey

How else did the author describe the donkey besides gray?
Strong.
Yes. Where would you put the word "strong" in this phrase?

Adrian came up and placed the *strong* Post-it in the correct place.

_____ strong gray donkey

What is strong and gray?
A donkey! everyone shouted.

I wrote *a* and *some* on Post-its, and Mayra placed the Post-it with *a* to complete the phrase.

a strong gray donkey

We read the phrase again, emphasizing the type of donkey—the adjectives that described it—and then went through other phrases in the same way: I wrote adjectives on Post-it notes, and the children consulted the book on the easel and moved the Post-its around on the chart to put the adjectives in the right place.

some	fat	pink	pigs
some	waddling	white	ducks
a	sleek	brown	cow
some	Frisky	black	goats

The children could see the different kinds of words lined up, and this ordered placement helped them see the pattern in the phrases. We reread the phrases, and they naturally wanted to add to the list: *a furious red bull, a big yellow dog* (which we saved for another day, when they were going to make their own version of the book). The author had not provided a color for the cat, so the children added colors: *a skinny orange and black cat.* They were very proud of that and wanted to write the author to ask her to add it to her book.

My planning for this mini-lesson and third reading of *A Farm's Not a Farm* was done on the same planning sheet (Appendix E3) used for the first reading. This sheet does not take long to fill out but is very useful for responding flexibly to children's needs as they come up rather than sticking to a preplanned lesson that might have meant something the previous Friday but is out-of-date today.

★ *Purpose of Reading.* I want the children to enjoy revisiting the story and appreciate well-written lines of text. Also, to read new sentence patterns with me, identify descriptive words, use the pictures to help understand, and engage in discussion before, during, and after the lesson.

★ *Focus.* Identifying adjectives and correct adjective placement.

★ *Children's Needs.* All students in this first-grade class need to improve their knowledge of adjectives and how to use them in sentences. Beginning speakers can learn new color adjectives; early intermediate speakers, other adjectives; intermediate speakers, putting two adjectives together with a noun in a short phrase; early advanced and advanced speakers, correct sentence structure with adjectives in place. All need picture/text support.

★ *Introduction.* Talk about problem of the story: no animals on the farm. Set the purpose of revisiting: to talk about descriptive words and how they are used in a sentence. Record children's knowledge of adjectives on chart paper.

★ *During Reading.* On chart, write, "What shall we buy?" Discuss types of animals to buy,

with the adjectives from the book. Record nouns (animal names), color words, size, or other descriptive words in separate columns. Make blank lines on chart for children to place Post-its in correct order.

★ *After Reading.* Encourage children to come up with their own adjectives. Record on Post-its and place on chart paper. List other animal names and make new descriptive phrases using nouns and new adjectives.

★ *Possible Follow-Ups.* Use newly created text to make a class book on other animals they could buy. Make a wall chart categorizing types of adjectives, with children adding words they find in their reading.

Mini-Lesson on Forming Questions

Another first-grade class in Santa Ana, which also had a majority of ELLs, spent a lot of time in shared reading. They read and reread their favorite books and wrote their own renditions, and the teacher did a lot of charting of their language right in front of them. What she noticed in the context of their discussions was that the children had difficulty asking and answering questions correctly. This is a very difficult skill even for fluent English speakers, so she decided to do a mini-lesson during shared reading time based on what she had observed. They were studying animals and had read a lot of animal books, but she decided to go with the children's language instead of using the language from a text.

The children had been fascinated with frogs. Ever since José had brought a frog in from the playground one day, they had done almost everything except dissect a frog. They had become experts on frogs. They had turned their investigation of frogs into a unit of study. They had read, and the children had checked out from the library, many books on frogs. So she told them that they were going to make a question-and-answer book on frogs for the other first-grade class to read, titled Frogs Can . . . . Thus she gave the children a purpose and an audience for their writing, to write a book for their friends, and through that meaningful task she wanted them to gain the knowledge of how to form questions correctly. Actually, that was her whole purpose for creating this new book—the children needed to develop their language.

She led them in a shared discussion, which became a shared writing, with all the children helping to form correct questions. They thought of crazy and funny questions to ask about frogs, which they knew weren't right, so that they could also show off their knowledge and teach their friends about frogs. Here are some of their questions, which the teacher wrote on a chart after they had collectively formed them. The answers were then written by individual students in different-color pens. The shared writing thus became interactive writing as well.

Do frogs eat pizza?
No! Frogs eat ants, flies, worms.
Are frogs magenta?
No! Frogs are green.
Can frogs fly?
No! Frogs leap.
Do frogs sleep in soft beds in the winter?
No! Frogs sleep under the mud.
Can a frog drink water from a glass?
No! Frogs drink from their skin.

The teacher then took the sentences from the chart, asked the children to illustrate them, and helped the class make them into a book. Each set of question and answer had its own page and illustration. The book was so successful and popular that they did a follow-up book titled *Children Can . . . .*

MAKING A CLASS BIG BOOK

Making a class Big Book is nothing new, but it is a practice in our busy classrooms that many of us have gotten away from. This event—and I call it an event rather than an activity for a reason—is really valuable in building class community and, more important, in developing the language of the children. Making a book is a shared activity that all children can participate in, whether in small groups with numerous books or the whole class with one book. A rendition of a text, an elaboration of a text, or a takeoff on a text is made. There are many benefits for developing readers and language users

in making a class book. The act of creating a new story based on a text's plot or using the same language pattern and just doing a "copy change" by changing the nouns or verbs to create a new rendition of the story is a wonderful exercise in using language for a real purpose. It allows English language learners to play with language and still have the support of the language patterns or story structure in a text. It also allows children to go back and reread the story they have created, which is based on a familiar topic, story, or sentence pattern. For beginning speakers, even a simple picture book in both languages based on the theme being studied can be helpful for developing academic language.

I have been in classrooms where children have created their own version of *A Farm's Not a Farm* using the same story line but substituting different animals that might be on a farm. For example, one first-grade classroom created a version in which a grandpa and a grandma bought an old brown horse, some little yellow chicks, and some soft spotted rabbits. A third-grade class came up with the same story structure but a totally different setting. They named their book *An Ocean's Not an Ocean* and filled it with sea creatures like a large blue whale, some tiny pink shrimp, some sleek gray seals, an enormous black shark, some playful gray dolphins, and a beautiful orange seahorse.

Many books describe how to make class Big Books and illustrate and bind them. I encourage teachers to chart all the children's writing in a shared lesson before having them start to illustrate and put the book together. I truly believe it is in the shared experience of creating the text, of playing with the language, of listening to sentence patterns that children learn from their peers and take ownership of the text and of the new creation. They then feel they were part of a process and are proud to show it off.

Once the book is completed, it can be read in independent reading, and shown in other classrooms and the community. It can be read to the librarian, the principal, a buddy class, or families, to firemen or at the senior center. If the book just sits on the shelf and the children don't have the opportunity to reread it often, the benefit of making it is diminished. All children need an audience for their stories. And the more they read the book, the more they practice reading and using their newly acquired language.

Class-made book.

CHOOSING TEXTS FOR SHARED READING

Class-made books, class poems, or famous poems are good texts for shared reading. These can be written out on a large chart or professionally printed on large cards or flip charts. Schools that have state-adopted materials for ELLs have such charts. Also many publishers have produced strategy charts with short texts for shared reading. Wall charts can be reread in a shared reading. The Daily News (see Chapter 1), brainstorming charts, or graphic organizers that have been developed in thematic units or read-aloud lessons can be revisited in a shared reading lesson to teach certain strategies or skills.

It is still my preference to choose Big Books for a shared reading lesson, because they naturally draw children with their illustrations or story lines and model for children how to read a whole book. Chapter 8 discusses how to choose books for shared reading, including nonfiction books for the primary grades, while also discussing the benefit of using shared reading with upper-grade English language learners. Appendix E5 provides shared reading book lists and other resources for shared reading.

8 SHARED READING *with* UPPER-GRADE STUDENTS

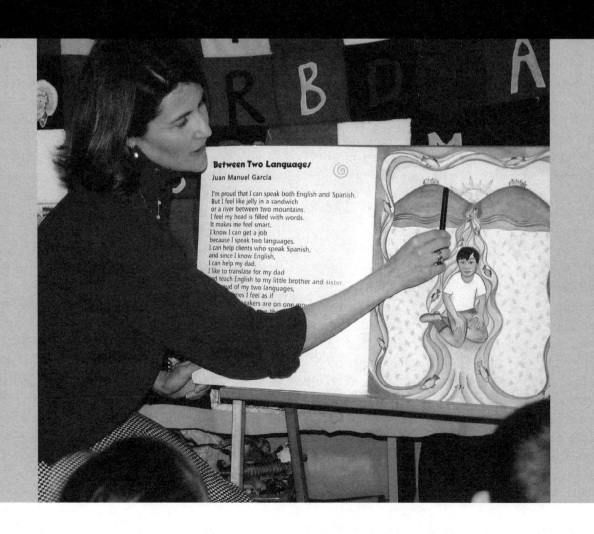

Between Two Languages
Juan Manuel García

I'm proud that I can speak both English and Spanish.
But I feel like jelly in a sandwich
or a river between two mountains.
I feel my head is filled with words.
It makes me feel smart.
I know I can get a job
because I speak two languages.
I can help clients who speak Spanish,
and since I know English,
I can help my dad.
I like to translate for my dad
and teach English to my little brother and sister.
I'm proud of my two languages,
but sometimes I feel as if
English speakers are on one mou...

"Let Your Hair Down"

My husband and I are good friends with a couple whose background is similar to ours. One is an immigrant, one a native citizen. Sandra is from Mexico and Mark is originally from Cincinnati. She came here as an adult, as my husband did, but she didn't know anyone when she arrived. She had to learn a new language as well as new customs on her own. Even after she became fluent in English, she recalls, there were times when she didn't understand everything. Sandra and Mark used to go out a lot with his friends, and she always got very dressed up for the occasion in a dress and high heels. She always wore her long beautiful hair coiled up on her head. She seemed conservative to her husband's friends who were not quite as formal. They all liked to have a good time together, but Sandra did not participate as fully as the others in the fun. They were constantly getting up to dance to the music, or sing along to songs at the bar, and Sandra would just watch. They tried to encourage her to participate, but she declined. She continued going out with them, and she enjoyed herself, but her husband's friends still nagged at her to join in more with the fun. One night, one of them said to her: "Oh, Sandra, why don't you let your hair down!" She stared at them in disbelief. She couldn't understand why they wanted her to let her hair down. She always wore it up! She almost broke into tears when she finally worked up the courage to say, "I like my hair up!" Everyone stared at her in silence until they all burst into laughter. "Oh, Sandra, we like your hair up too. That's not what we meant." They then explained what it really means to "Let your hair down." And Sandra still laughs about it to this day.

How many English language learners don't fully understand English idioms or the nuances of a second language? As children begin reading more difficult texts, the language they encounter is much more advanced and sophisticated. Shared reading is a good time to expose older children to language and genres with which they may not have had experience. Just because they have gone beyond the primary grades does not mean they are too old to read a Big Book or do not require help in sustaining meaning while learning higher-level strategies like summarizing, inferring, and analyzing.

Older ELLs may have broader conceptual knowledge, and a wider speaking and reading vocabulary in the first language, than primary-grade children do. We need to build on this prior knowledge as they are learning English. And since upper-grade children have so much more content area reading to contend with each day, shared reading texts should be chosen to tie in with the theme currently being studied so that the vocabulary and concepts learned in shared reading can be put to good use in other daily activities like writing.

During shared reading, the teacher scaffolds developing readers and language learners as they climb the ladder of literacy. Upper-grade children are not necessarily expected to read text on their own during shared reading; the teacher still demonstrates good reading strategies and appropriate language use with longer texts containing more difficult academic language so that older ELLs can be successful in trying these out on their own in guided reading, literature circles, and independent reading.

In this chapter I use a nonfiction text to model a shared reading lesson with upper-grade English language learners. I emphasize the importance of discussion in improving their critical thinking and higher-level strategies and helping them sustain meaning while reading a text with challenging vocabulary. I show how to use cognates and the elements of nonfiction texts to deepen understanding of the academic language and major concepts presented in the book. And I discuss how to choose appropriate Big Books for ELLs of all ages regardless of grade level.

PLANNING AND PREPARING FOR A SHARED READING LESSON WITH UPPER-GRADE CHILDREN

The Big Book I highlight here is *Bringing Water to People,* and the theme is Geographic Regions. One reason I chose this book is that it relates specifically to the history of California (where I live and work) and lends itself to meeting the standards of geographic literacy that are outlined in the History–Social Science Framework for California Public Schools (2001). It focuses on cause and effect by showing how people in three different geographic regions—California, Bali, and Machu Picchu—solved a common problem: how to bring water to where it was needed. The children can learn from the book that the building of three distinct but equally ingenious irrigation systems helped transform whole regions that otherwise wouldn't have survived. They can also compare and contrast the regions.

The California children to whom I taught the demonstration lesson in this chapter were fourth- and fifth-graders in a summer literacy institute, and they were very interested in this book because of the section on the California Aqueduct, which is part of the State Water Project. But I have used this book with children in Texas, Illinois, and other states, and they too found it interesting because the three irrigation systems described in the book are architectural and engineering wonders. Most children are curious regardless of where they live or what language they speak.

This book has the elements of a good nonfiction text, such as photographs and captions, maps, charts, and bold print to indicate words defined in the glossary. ELLs are greatly helped by such visuals, although they may still not be able to access all the information in the text through them. Often we assume that older children have already learned how to read nonfiction text with skill; this is usually not the case. The elements built into a nonfiction book are there not only to break up long text passages and make the format more attractive, but also to ease comprehension for readers by giving them several ways of accessing the detailed content of the book. Inexperienced readers must be explicitly guided in how to use these elements to their advantage to gain meaning, but these elements should be taught in the context of reading the text, not as an end in themselves.

Each nonfiction book has its own elements, and some have more than others. In addition to the visual elements just mentioned, *Bringing Water to People* has page numbers, a table of contents listing the page numbers of sections, and a glossary with page numbers of the words defined. It is likely that the use of all the elements cannot be thoroughly discussed in one lesson, although all might be touched on during a lesson. Clearly, learning to use the table of contents and understanding the relation between bold-print words and the glossary are critical in helping children find information that they want to explore. What that information is can be elicited from the students and listed on a K-W-W-L chart.

The lesson is done with the whole class regardless of class size or the children's reading or language levels. All children are expected to participate in the meaning-making process and to respond with language at their developmental and comfort levels. So I need to be aware of the language levels of all the children in the class and what kind of responses to expect at each level, and to accept all types of speech from one word to full sentences. I therefore fill in a focus sheet of language and reading outcomes (Appendix E2) before the lesson. To this focus sheet for the upper grades I have added expected outcomes for early advanced speakers because many upper-grade children are early advanced speakers, though still not close to the levels of proficiency or fluency in speaking and reading of native speakers of their age.

Beginning to Early Advanced Speakers

Thematic unit _Geographic Regions_

Mini-theme _Life Necessities; Features of Nonfiction_

Shared reading material _Bringing Water to People_

Features to Note in Text (examples):

Cognates: Spanish—decide, irrigation, canal, tunnel, pipe, aqueduct, collect, use, system

Plurals/words ending in s: systems, canals, tunnels, plants, rivers

Prepositions: in, by, to, from

Verb tense: present, present progressive, past

High-frequency words: many; introduce by stages

Text format: table of contents, bold, captions, chapter heads, glossary, photos, maps, diagrams

---

Expected language outcomes (examples)

Beginning speakers
One-word response _yes, no_
Regular plurals _common nouns: canals, tunnels_

Early intermediate speakers
Repeat simple sentence _There is water in the canal._
Use present tense _We need water._

Intermediate speakers
Express understanding of text _They are bringing water to people._
Possessive pronouns/subject-verb agreement _They wash_
Use past tense _They built_

Early advanced speakers
Speak in complete sentences _The aqueduct is a big canal that brings water to people._
Ask questions in past tense _How did they build the aqueduct?_

Expected reading outcomes (examples)

Beginning speakers
Read aloud simple words in story _water, land, what_

Early intermediate speakers
Identify subject, read short phrases _water, body needs water_

Intermediate speakers
Read simple vocabulary _drink, animals, people_
Read phrases, sentences independently _Bringing water to a place where it is needed is called irrigation._

Early advanced speakers
Read captions and glossary easily _aqueduct: big canal that carries a large amount of water p. 13_
State main idea, finds supporting details _The State Water Project brings water to people._

Outcomes based on performance standards from ELD Standards (California Department of Education)

Example of focus sheet of outcomes for shared reading in upper grades.

The lesson format for a shared reading with upper-grade children is the same as for primary-grade children with perhaps a bit more shared writing. I scribe more of the children's predictions, interests, and hopes for what they want to get out of the reading. I continue to chart predictions or new language when it helps gain meaning. Older ELLs can usually read and understand written language better, and thus they are able to handle more information written down in front of them without picture-text match, because they have had more years in school to acquire the language and to work on literacy. Many older children might also be educated in their primary language and can comprehend language better when it is written down than by just listening to it orally. (Of course, some newcomers are illiterate in their primary language.) Many children are visual learners, and the class discussion might not make as much sense to them as to other students. For these learners, when words or concepts are written down in front of them, the language becomes more comprehensible (Krashen 1981; 2003). The language written down in the context of the lesson can then be referred to again as they are reading other books and working on other inquiries within the same theme. It is important to display the charts around the room and not use a whiteboard that will be erased.

The discussion before, during, and after a shared reading lesson is a vital part of the language and literacy development of upper-grade ELLs. It helps them focus on meaning making. The sample lesson has a lot of discussion as we analyze a nonfiction text. By validating children's prior knowledge and accepting contributions regardless of language output, the teacher can help upper-grade students make connections and deepen their understanding of the text.

The following is a summary of a planning sheet (Appendix E3) for a first reading of *Bringing Water to People* within the thematic unit Geographic Regions based on the questions and concerns from teachers in the summer literacy institute on doing shared reading with their older children. The teachers were most concerned with helping children comprehend more detailed text while still understanding the main idea.

★ *Purpose of Reading.* I want the children to comprehend the main ideas of this nonfiction text by understanding the detailed information in each paragraph and section. Also, to learn to use the nonfiction text as a resource for finding answers to their inquiries.

★ *Focus.* Using the elements of a nonfiction text to help them gain meaning: table of contents, glossary, bold print, maps, illustrations, and captions. Rereading to locate and clarify information by moving back and forth among the elements of the text.

★ *Children's Needs.* This special summer class for ELLs reading below grade level has twenty-three fourth- and fifth-graders, reading at levels from emergent to fluent. They have difficulty sustaining meaning while reading more challenging texts; early fluent and fluent readers need strategies to understand nonfiction texts and develop the ability to reread and dig deeper for meaning. As speakers, they need support in understanding the academic vocabulary used in these texts. There are one beginning, five early intermediate, eight intermediate, seven early advanced, and two advanced speakers in this class. Many are Spanish-speaking ELLs.

★ *Introduction.* Discuss cover of book and what title means. Chart children's responses. Make K-W-W-L chart, record children's responses to what they know, what they want to know, where they can find information, and leave space for "what we learned." Use illustrations to help students, especially early intermediate speakers.

★ *During Reading.* Orient children to elements of nonfiction text, starting with table of contents. Have children decide how they want to read the text to find answers to their questions. Follow children's lead in choosing what to research, highlighting elements that give information. Use Post-its and charts to record vocabulary and new learning. Have children reread paragraphs silently to verify their understanding of the text. Show how to use nonfiction elements to clarify meaning by flipping back and forth between them (e.g., bold-print words and glossary).

- ★ *After Reading.* Use Post-its to organize the new language and to answer the questions on K-W-W-L chart. Fill in section on "what we learned."
- ★ *Possible Follow-Ups.* Reread book to do further research. Compare/contrast three irrigation systems. Use text to teach cognates and sentence structure.

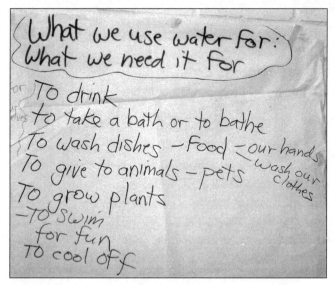

Chart of children's responses during a shared reading of *Bringing Water to People.*

SHARED READING LESSON

Introduction

I asked the children to sit up close to me on the floor so as to involve all of them in the shared reading experience. I put the Big Book on the easel with chart paper behind and had pens, Post-it notes, and other props ready to use, including a globe and previous books they had read. I began the lesson by connecting to the book they had read with the classroom teacher the day before, *Postcards from the Planets.* We talked about the postcards they had made and where the postcards were sent from: space. I then asked if *Bringing Water to People* takes place in space, and they answered, "No, here on Earth." Then I tried to tap into their background knowledge about the new book's subject, asking them to share their knowledge with me rather than telling them what the book is about.

What is the title of the book?
Bringing Water to People.
What do we use water for?
To drink.
Yes. Anything else?

I wrote on the chart paper, What do we use water for? and started to list the children's responses: to drink, to take a bath or to bathe.

What do we need on the end of "bath" to make it "bathe"?
An *e.*
Good. What else do we need water for?
To wash dishes, food
To give to animals, pets
To grow plants
Why do you think we need to bring water to some people?

They don't have any.
They can't get it themselves.
It's too hot.

I also wanted to set the scene (the environment or types of climate mentioned in the text), and I used the globe as well as their knowledge about arid places. We discussed briefly what they had learned about planets from reading the previous book: some are very hot, like Mercury; some have no water, like Mars; and some have moons, like the Earth. One child commented: "The Moon has no water, too." I lifted up the globe to see if they knew what planet it represented, and they all shouted: "Earth." We then found California and Mexico on the globe, and I asked, "Where do we get our water from?"

Although many hands shot up, and "the rain" was heard from many of the children, I suggested that we do a K-W-W-L chart: what we *know,* what we *want* to know, *where* we can find the information, and what we *learned.* I wrote K-W-W-L on the chart paper and explained it for the beginning and early intermediate speakers. I wanted to be sure everyone would participate. Then I started charting their questions. Instead of starting with "what we know," we started with "what we want to know." I did this because I thought the topic of water could be so large that they might not get to how we bring water to people, which is the focus of the book. Also, since I had modeled the question, What do we use water for? I wanted them to continue with their own questions.

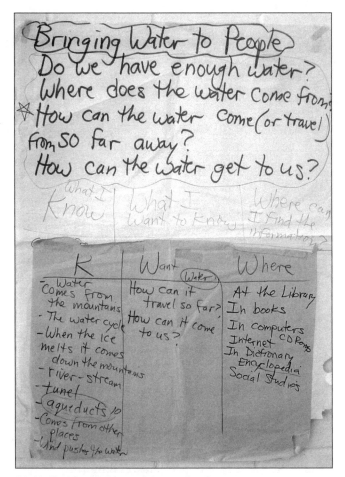

K-W-W-L chart for *Bringing Water to People.*

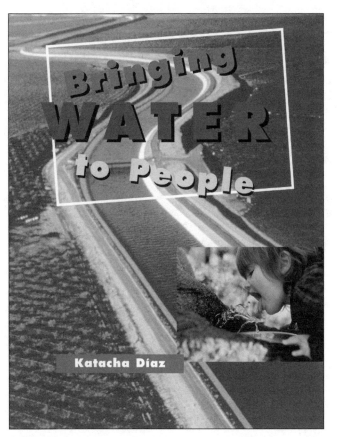

Cover of *Bringing Water to People.*

Do we have enough water?
Where does the water come from?
How can the water travel so far?

I prompted to rephrase the last question:

How can it travel and come to . . .
Us!
Good—How can the water get to us?

Once their questions were listed on the chart and we understood what the interests of the class were, I charted what they knew about the subject. Their questions formed a basis for their inquiry and research as we read the text.

Bringing Water to People is a complicated book with information comparing three irrigation systems in three parts of the world, but I hadn't introduced that yet. They had only looked at the cover of the book, which has a small picture of a child drinking from a water fountain overlaid on a full-

cover photo of the California Aqueduct. I don't think most adults, let alone children who are English language learners, would recognize that the cover picture shows the California Aqueduct. Yet I wanted to gauge the children's language and knowledge before I introduced the information in the text. That way I could make natural connections if their language and knowledge had similarities to the language and the information in the text. That built confidence and showed that I valued all the children's language and contributions. Their charted words could be used later to check their predictions with the text. It also gave me an opportunity to assess their language before, during, and after the reading. I charted their responses under "What we know" on the K-W-W-L chart.

Does anyone have answers to any of the questions about water?
Comes from water cycle.
When the ice melts, it comes down the mountain.
What does it turn into?
Water.
Yes. And it goes into . . .

Pipes.
Are there always pipes up in the mountains?
 Where does the water fall into when it melts?
Tunnels.
Are tunnels natural?

I continued to chart all these words: *pipes, tunnels,* and so on.

What else do you have in the mountains?
Streams.
Yes. There are streams.
Aqueduct.
Wow, what is that?
It brings us water.
Let's write that word down. Did I spell it right?

We check the spelling in the book.

Where do you think one of the largest aqueducts is?
California.
It is in California.

These children knew much more about bringing water to people then I had expected. I was surprised that one child, Areceli, knew about the California Aqueduct. I wondered if her family had discussed the aqueduct, or if she had driven up the central part of California and seen the aqueduct, which is hundreds of miles long or maybe she is originally from the central valley or had seen it traveling. Or perhaps she could just tell from the cover photograph that we were going to talk about the aqueduct. Other children also came up with some difficult vocabulary that we were going to encounter in the text. By tapping into their prior knowledge and language base rather than preteaching vocabulary, children can make their own connections which will help them while reading. New academic vocabulary is then discussed in the context of the text. I also learned much more about these children's language and knowledge then I would have if I had just told them we were going to read about aqueducts and different ways that water travels to people. Many children already had the academic vocabulary necessary to be successful with the text.

After the charting of "what we know," I wanted to narrow the focus of our reading. I wanted them to realize that we didn't need to start at the beginning and read to the end of a nonfiction book. Rather, they could use the text as a resource to find the answers to their questions. I asked them to prioritize the questions they wanted to research. Marcus said his number one question was, "How can the water came to us?" I accepted his language and reread it correctly. Then I asked if everyone agreed, and we decided to start there.

Before we opened the text, I asked,

Where can we find this information if it is not in this book?
The library.
In books.
In computers.
CD-ROMs.
Internet.
In the dictionary.
In social studies books.

I charted and commented on each response, asking whether we had time to use any of these resources now, if we had the resources in the room, or if we could use them in independent reading time. Many children were eager to go to the Internet and the library before we even read the text.

Orientation to Nonfiction

A nonfiction text very often needs an orientation. Because it has many elements that a fiction text usually does not, like a table of contents, a glossary, maps, and charts, it is important to give the children an overview of how to read the text using these elements. They need to be shown how to navigate through the text, turning the pages back and forth, searching for information, and using elements like the picture captions to gain meaning. I wouldn't spend too long orienting in this way because the elements can be explored while reading the text. However, I would choose one or two to highlight. In this orientation I focused on the title page and the table of contents.

During the orientation we can fine-tune the options for reading the text based on the interaction with the children. They should be taking an active part in deciding what the class will read in a nonfiction book on the first reading. *Bringing*

Water to People is too long to read in one sitting, so the teacher and the children should make joint decisions on what to tackle each day. Although the teacher might have a plan in mind on what to cover, often the children go in a different direction. As long as the teacher can still instruct and teach the strategies she was hoping to, how to get there doesn't really matter. We need to be flexible and let the children set their own purpose for their reading. The children had come up with their own questions, and now they would decide what part of the book to read first.

We turned to the title page, and everyone laughed seeing the child under the water. "He's taking a shower!" yelled Mario. "He playing," said Esperanza, and I responded, "You're right, it does look like he is playing in the water." I modeled correct grammar in a natural way and then engaged them in a quick discussion of swimming and playing in the water. I accepted all levels of responses and modeled complete sentences as appropriate, without explicitly correcting their speech. We talked about how the title page often gives us clues about the book. We then turned to the table of contents and read the first line: "Why do we need water?" I turned to the chart we made when we talked about what we use water for and asked if we should add "to swim" and "to play." They all said yes, so I added these. We then reread the questions on the K-W-W-L chart and thought about the main question: How can water come to us? We looked at the table of contents to see where that question might be answered and read the lines "How do people get water in California?" "How do people get water in Bali?" "How do people get water in Machu Picchu?"

I asked if they knew where any of those areas were and suggested we locate them on the globe: "We've already found California. Can anyone find Bali? It's in Indonesia. Have any of you heard of Indonesia from the news?" I was relating to current events, which I thought some of them might have watched on TV. No one knew much about Bali or could find it on the globe, so I helped them and pointed to it. I then asked if they knew where Machu Picchu was. I told them I had been there and that it was in Peru. José came up and found it on the globe. He said his mother was from Peru. Then I asked, "Where can we find information on these three different parts of the world?" The children looked at the open page of the table of contents and answered, "Page 10 for California, page 18 for Bali, and page 24 for Machu Picchu." They were reading the table of contents and using it for information.

Then I asked, "What do you want to read about first?" "California," they all called out. "Okay, let's read how people get water in California." We turned directly to page 10, and I reminded them that we didn't have to read a nonfiction text from the beginning like fiction.

First Reading

As we read the text, the children joined in with me when they could. I also wanted them to reread and dissect the paragraphs to make sure they understood what we were reading—to tell me what they had learned from each paragraph, what was its main idea, and whether they could find support for that idea with a line from the text. Often children read a line aloud but do not fully understand its meaning.

Before researching *how* people in California get water, we talked about why they might need water brought to them. One child asked, "Don't they have water?" I encouraged them to think about that question. We read aloud the paragraphs on pages 10 and 11, looked at the map and photographs, and read the captions. As we read the pages together I took the role of discussion leader and asked questions that would guide their learning. I was persistent in having them reread the text to find information and to verify their statements.

What is one thing you learned about California?
There are more people here than anywhere.
Good. Can you find that line in the text?

We went back and found the line, and revisited the paragraph to get the main idea.

What will happen to our water supply? Will we have enough water?
It will go.
We won't have enough water.
What do we know about California? It says it is a land of contrasts. What does that mean?

Hot/cold opposites.
Water in the north, desert in the south.
Where do we live?
The south.
That's right. What is our climate like?
Dry.
Desert.
What happens in the north? Why do they have more water?
It rains.
Yes. Let's go back to the text and find that.

We reread the paragraph for information.

How do we get our water in the south?
[No response]
Does the text answer our question here?
No.
What should we do?
Keep reading.

We then talked about some of the vocabulary they had come up with before the reading, like *tunnel*. We looked at these words on the chart, and I asked the children to look for them in the text. Were any of the words in bold print? What would it mean if they were? How could they figure out new words if they didn't know the meaning? My focus was still on having the children gain meaning within a paragraph of text. I hoped to teach them to figure out key academic vocabulary within the context of the supportive format of this nonfiction text, and if not, how to use the resources provided, like the glossary, to help them. By teaching them how to use the format and elements of the book, I would be helping them read this nonfiction text with skill.

"What is the State Water Project?" I asked. The children were reading the Big Book text on page 12 while I skimmed over it with my finger. When I received no response, I asked,

What is the key word?
Irrigation system.
Yes. What does that mean?
[No response]
If we don't know what that means, what can we do?

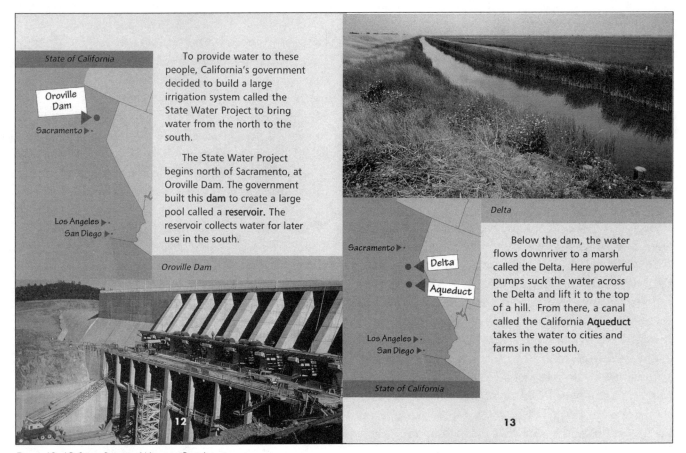

To provide water to these people, California's government decided to build a large irrigation system called the State Water Project to bring water from the north to the south.

The State Water Project begins north of Sacramento, at Oroville Dam. The government built this **dam** to create a large pool called a **reservoir**. The reservoir collects water for later use in the south.

Oroville Dam

Below the dam, the water flows downriver to a marsh called the Delta. Here powerful pumps suck the water across the Delta and lift it to the top of a hill. From there, a canal called the California **Aqueduct** takes the water to cities and farms in the south.

Pages 12–13 from *Bringing Water to People.*

Look in glossary.

Yes, we could do that. Does this book have a glossary?

Yes, it does.

I placed a Post-it on page 12 so we could go back to our place later. We turned to the glossary, found the word *irrigation,* and read the definition: "system that brings water to a place where it's needed."

We need water in California.

You're right. The definition also lists page 8 as a reference. Did we read page 8?

No, we skipped it.

We went right to page 10, didn't we? Okay, let's go to page 8.

We read the paragraph containing the bold-print word *irrigation* and looked at the picture of people working in fields with lots of water. We wrote down *irrigation* and discussed what it meant. We read the next paragraph to find the word about how water is brought to people who need it. "Through canals," said Areceli. "Yes, canals, just as in Spanish, *canales,*" I said.

As I mentioned, we need to model for ELLs how to understand new vocabulary in context and use what they already know in the primary language to help them. Many English words, especially academic ones, have Greek and Latin roots, and if the primary language originates from Latin, as Spanish does, we can take advantage of cognates—words in the two languages with the same ancestral roots and with similar spellings and similar meanings—to ease children's grasp of English vocabulary. Because the primary language of many ELLs in this class was Spanish, during this first reading I started a Spanish-English cognate chart. Each time we noticed a cognate word, we added it to the chart for future reference. There were twenty cognates in approximately 100 words of text from pages 12–14. By drawing on their knowledge in their primary language and using cognates to make connections provides ELLs with an academic advantage while reading higher-level content (Cummins 2002, 2003; Bear et al. 2003). See Appendixes C2 and C3 for more lists of cognates.

Areceli was an early advanced speaker, so she was able to read the English word *canals* easily. But

canal	canal	state	estado
tunnel	túnel	project	proyecto
irrigation	irrigación	north	norte
system	sistema	pumps	bombas
aqueduct	acueducto	create	crear
government	gobierno	collect	colectar
provide	proveer	decided	decidió
use	uso	miles	millas
pipe	pípa	millions	millones
lines	líneas	gallons	galones
valley	valle		

Chart of English-Spanish cognates from *Bringing Water to People.*

by restating the word in Spanish, I helped children at a lower level of proficiency understand it. I did not have to explain what it meant because they already had the concept in the primary language.

"Do you think they use canals in California?" I asked. Several children said yes. "Let's go back to page 12 now," I said, "and see if we have a better idea of what the State Water Project is."

We read the next few pages with interest, and the children seemed to be more focused on the description of this enormous irrigation system. They noticed that there were a lot of bold-print words in the paragraphs. We talked about these in context and used the glossary to check our understanding. When we looked at *reservoir,* for example, we went back to the glossary and read, "a very large pool built to hold water for later use." I asked the children if they had seen any reservoirs, trying to help them make connections to their own experiences. I also mentioned that the two cities in our school district have hidden reservoirs or reserves of water—*reservas de agua*—using another English-Spanish cognate to help them. We tried to find *aqueduct* in the text because it was one of the words we had written on our K-W-W-L chart. I asked if anyone could find it in Big Book text. Lucia came up and pointed to the word, on page 13. I rewrote the word on a Post-it note, and I gave it to a child to hold. We then read the paragraphs about aqueducts, checking to see if Areceli's description of an aqueduct was accurate and learning more details about it. We wrote them in the "what we learned" section of the K-W-W-L chart and also wrote a couple of other statements about the State Water Project.

During the discussion of the California Aqueduct, I wrote the most important words—*aqueduct, reservoir, irrigation, dam, canal, pumps, pipelines*—on Post-its and gave them to children at different language proficiency levels to hold. They were now holding in their hands the main concepts of how the irrigation system functions and most words were cognates.

After we finished reading the section on the California Aqueduct, I wanted to check the children's comprehension of the main concepts. This comprehension check was done in a very nonthreatening way. Because all levels of speakers had Post-it notes with the key vocabulary, they could all take part in the meaning-making process. As we reviewed the components of the State Water Project and the purpose for it—bringing water where it is needed—the children came up and pasted their Post-its on a chart, always referring to the Big Book in front of us.

"Who has the word *canal*?" I asked. Diane brought up her Post-it with the word *canal* and pasted it on a blank chart. "Who has the word *aqueduct*?" Mario placed his Post-it under *canal*.

"What do we use to pump the water over the mountains?" The Post-it with *pumps* was added to the chart. José brought up *pipelines* and placed it under *pumps*. Next came Marcela with *dam*. "What's after *dam*? On the other side." "A reservoir," said Miguel. "Yes. Who has *reservoir*?" Miguel had it, and he pasted it on the chart.

Why do we build dams and canals and aqueducts?
To bring water.
Yes. Why do we have all of these things? [I was trying to elicit another word.]
To irrigate.
Yes. What does "irrigate" mean?
To bring water to places.
Yes. And this book talks about bringing water to people in different ways. Does anyone have the word "irrigate"?
I have "irrigation." (The Post-it was added to the chart.)
What is the large irrigation system in California called?
The State Water Project.

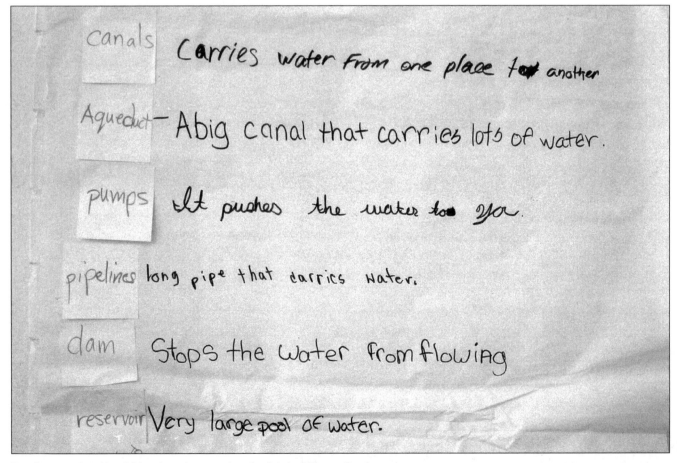

Post-it notes placed by children in order on a chart for *Bringing Water to People*.

Reflections with the Children

Once all the Post-its with the key vocabulary words had been pasted on the chart, the children had learned the words pretty solidly through rereading the text and through discussion. When we looked at the words and at the text, however, we realized that we had learned a lot but hadn't read much of the book. I reflected with the children how we had focused on the irrigation system in California. I suggested that perhaps the next day they could focus on the irrigation system in Bali or in Peru with their classroom teacher. They seemed excited about reading more in the book and learning about the other irrigation systems. José was interested in having his friends read about his mother's country, Peru.

We looked at the "what we learned" section of the K-W-W-L chart and added to it. Monitoring their own learning by adding to the *L* section helps children be conscious of what they've learned and is an important strategy for ELLs (Cummins 2001). The children were eager to share their new knowledge about reservoirs, dams, and irrigation systems. After adding the new statements of "what we learned," I asked the children to reflect on the strategies they had used to gain this information. They responded with the following strategies, and together we phrased them into complete sentences. Many early intermediate and intermediate speakers participated as readily as the early advanced speakers. Even though they weren't speaking in complete sentences, their ideas were valued and most children understood what they wanted to say.

Strategies with a Nonfiction Text

★ We looked up words in the glossary.
★ We reread the paragraph to help us gain meaning.
★ We used the pictures.
★ We used the captions.
★ We used our background knowledge, about Planet Earth, about water, and about what we use water for.
★ We thought about what we were reading so it would make sense.
★ We looked for information.
★ We asked questions.
★ We wrote down our own information.
★ We looked at the text and the chart to help clarify our ideas.

I recorded the strategies on a chart so they could review them and reuse them as they read on in the book. The classroom teacher could reinforce these strategies or add to them during subsequent readings of this book or other nonfiction texts.

Assessment and Evaluation of the Lesson

As before, observations and notes from a shared reading lesson (Appendix E4) could be filled out for the children in this class and placed in their individual reading and language folders. For example, the teachers watching the demonstration lesson had taken notes on the children during the lesson on the observation sheet. Together we picked one child at each developmental stage of English language proficiency and made the observations on the next page collectively.

Reflections on the Lesson

Self-reflection is always an important tool in teaching (Routman, 1994, 2000). It helps us fine-tune our techniques and it helps us understand and analyze our effects on the children we are teaching. It also allows us to better understand the needs of the children and what we can do to help them improve. When I do demonstration lessons with numerous teachers or work in a coaching model with just one or two teachers, I always make time for us to reflect on the lesson.

Some of the teachers' comments were:

Post-its! What a great tool.
You highlighted important words. I liked the way you wrote those down and brought them out from the text for them to see and focus on.
You brought out through the discussion what irrigation systems are, what they are used for, and how they work by constantly going back to the text and using the key words. An otherwise difficult task.
It's so important to use their background knowledge. I like the way you tapped into that.
I like the way you went right into the middle of the book. You skipped the beginning and went right into the meat of the book.

Language Level	Language Output/Participation	Reading Output
Early Intermediate Mario	Spoke in phrases, short sentences, not always correct; interested in participating	Understood concepts, main idea
Intermediate José	Followed conversation well, knew topic, answered questions in short statements	Reread text, found key words
Early Advanced Areceli	Surprised us with her knowledge—knew *irrigate, aqueduct*; shy, responded briefly but always with right word or answer	Knew how to find information while reading
Advanced Joaquín	Spoke in complete sentences, used a comparison, could summarize what he learned	Showed command of English

Observations of children at each stage of language development during shared reading lesson.

You went right into what the children wanted to know.

You spent a lot of time on the cover, on the introduction, which helped them get prepared to read the text. I usually just read the title and move right into reading the book.

You used their skills of comparing and contrasting, you sequentially developed the system of bringing water by pulling back from them the words on the stickies, one by one, and placing them in order to see how they relate to each other. That helped the children understand the whole irrigation system.

You involved all children, calling on them by name and encouraging all of them to share.

I like the way you validated their language, by using cognates to help them.

My goal for this lesson, which I felt I had made a good start on, had been to guide the children to comprehend the rather complex details in each paragraph of this nonfiction book and how to use the book's elements to their advantage for gaining meaning. This book had lots of new academic vocabulary and content, and I modeled various strategies for improving their comprehension while reading, such as relying on background knowledge, rereading, and moving back and forth between the pages to seek information. Fluent readers use numerous strategies simultaneously as they read (Keene and Zimmermann 1997). The interactive discussion throughout the lesson and expecting every child, regardless of language level, to partici-

pate were critical for getting children to learn. The children were actively working with me and figuring out the concepts in the text for themselves. Scribing their language on charts for visual learning and later use was also important.

Revisiting the Text

After the demonstration lesson, the classroom teacher used *Bringing Water to People* in several shared reading sessions over the next ten days, and the children revisited the book during independent reading time. They were so interested in the content that they reread passages and compared details of the three irrigation systems.

The students also made wall maps and word charts, and defined each of the terms on Post-its notes in their own words. They reread the small book versions of *Bringing Water to People* during independent reading time. The children also worked in cooperative groups to further clarify, classify, and analyze the effects of living in different parts of the world, and how people developed irrigation systems with the types of technology, machinery, and expertise available to them. They used charts, Venn diagrams, and illustrations to demonstrate their findings. They also researched the topic further, visiting the library and writing in depth about the subject, trying to answer their inquiries.

In the context of rereading the text and doing further investigations, the classroom teacher was able to focus on numerous reading strategies and language functions. She also worked on the children's language patterns by using the key words and the original Post-it notes from the first lesson (see chart on page 142). They used the words to label the maps they drew of California and where the Aqueduct was. Some of the children drew their own detailed plans of how to build the Aqueduct; others drew plans of how the water came from the mountains to the kitchen sink. All of this activity was just on the California section of the book. Other groups used the language they had learned to draw plans of the Machu Picchu and Bali irrigation systems. The teacher realized that it was very easy to go back to the Big Book and teach spinoff lessons on new strategies and language, and to spark the children's curiosity into investigating and reading more.

SHARED READING IN SMALL GROUPS

At times I have used shared reading with small groups of upper-grade ELLs (and even primary children) who need extra support in their reading or language development. But a small-group shared reading experience should *not* preclude a child from participating in shared reading with the whole group. It is critical that all children participate with the whole class every day in a shared reading lesson. This encourages speech from all levels of children and validates what everybody has to say regardless of their language level. It also sets up an environment and a community of shared expertise where no one feels left out of learning something new or reading a good book. And it shows native or advanced speakers that just because a child may not be as advanced in English language proficiency as they are does not mean that the child is not as advanced in knowledge of the content being studied. Very often a lower-level speaker has an opportunity to shine or share his knowledge with the whole group if the teacher asks questions that encourage him to answer at his developmental level.

In an upper-grade classroom with a wide range of speakers, children with lower levels of English sometimes are eclipsed by higher-level speakers even if they know the subject or are more knowledgeable about it than the advanced speakers. Therefore it is not appropriate to pull a child for a small-group extra lesson if it will take away from her ability to participate with the whole group. If the child is getting extra help from another teacher or an instructional assistant, do not take the child away during shared reading time. Rather, if the child does have an instructional assistant, it is more appropriate to ask that assistant to help her in the primary language before or during a whole-group lesson than to pull her out for special instruction. For example, the assistant could preview the teacher's lesson in the child's primary language so that the child could understand the context better and be prepared to participate at her level with the rest of the class (see Chapter 1).

I might pull a small group (or ask a qualified instructional assistant to pull a group) when there are lower-level English speakers or readers who could benefit from rereading a text with a special focus in mind. For instance, I might have a few children who have just entered the class and who are not literate in their primary language or in English. These children might not be ready for guided reading. They might need a lot of shared reading and modeling of what good readers do before they can read even partly independently. I might choose to read the same book in the small group that I shared with the whole class, or I might read a different book that is geared to primary-age children but that has appeal for older readers.

CHOOSING TEXTS FOR SHARED READING (FOR PRIMARY AND UPPER GRADES)

Many types of texts can serve for shared reading, for instance, a chapter from a novel; a section from a nonfiction book; or an excerpt from a newspaper or magazine article; the principal's newsletter; a history textbook; or a cooking recipe. Any printed material can be used for shared reading by enlarging it and placing it on an overhead. (It is not recommended to have students looking at individual copies of a text during a shared reading lesson because all should participate together with one text.) But strategies like those described in the shared reading lesson with *Bringing Water to*

People—going back and forth between pages of text and the glossary, for instance—are too hard to demonstrate with an overhead projector, because only one page at a time can be shown and it is difficult to emulate what one would do with an actual book. Children often don't see how the pages that are taken on and off the overhead are connected.

As I mentioned previously, I prefer to choose Big Books for shared reading because they have expressive illustrations and well-written text, look and feel like "real" books, and are written to suit particular levels or ages of speakers or readers. Big Books today, from numerous publishers, cover all genres and topics—fiction, nonfiction, science, math, history, biography, the arts, poetry, fables, and others. Appendix E5 has lists of Big Books and other resources for shared reading. Big Books were first designed in New Zealand through the work of Don Holdaway (1979) and others. Back then, teachers carefully enlarged their favorite books themselves, often drawing their own illustrations or having children do so. We are lucky today to have professionally published Big Books with detailed story lines, interesting characters, colorful illustrations, beautiful photographs, a wealth of facts and information—rich models to share with children at all grade levels, in all genres and content areas, both in English and Spanish. Some of the favorite Big Books I've heard primary-grade children read or sing along with are *Mrs. Wishy-Washy, My Dog,* and *Crocodile Beat.* It's also nice to walk into upper-grade classrooms and see childen working together to figure out riddles, solve problems, and learn new information from Big Books like *The Cat on the Chimney, Which Is Which?,* and *Skeleton.*

Nonfiction Big Books for Primary Grades

One of my favorite Big Books is *I Spy,* a nonfiction text for primary-grade children that starts with the rhyme, "I spy with my little eye the eyes of an animal looking at me." On every page it has two or three clues about the animal below cut-out holes showing its eyes. At the bottom of the page is a box enclosing the words "What can it be? It starts with ————." Each page has a different letter corresponding to the first letter of the animal's name. This book has great rhymes and interesting facts about animals, and it encourages children to use the three cueing systems to figure out the puzzle. They can use picture clues, sentence clues, and letter clues, which correspond to the semantic, syntactic, and graphophonic cueing systems, to find the answers. Children are so motivated that they start to make all sorts of predictions, which I capture on charts or Post-it notes. This validates their predictions, gets everyone involved in the reading, and hooks each of them into trying to check their predictions.

One group of second-graders was so excited about predicting that I wrote their predictions on Post-its and stuck them right on the pages of the book that had the clues. I covered up the letter the animal's name started with. For an animal with the best eyesight, the children guessed owl, eagle, and hawk. They noticed on page 6 that the child's hairband had a bird on it, something that many adult readers do not notice. They also noticed that her collar looked like feathers. "Must be a bird!" someone exclaimed. So, as they were checking their predictions, they were pleased to find that all the animals were birds, and most of the class agreed on the three predicted options. But before I turned the page, I revealed the letter *V.*

They then looked at their predictions and realized that although they seemed to make sense, they didn't work. What animal or bird starts with a *V*? For most English language learners, that is difficult. No one could make a different prediction. When I turned the page, "Vulture!" someone shouted, and I wasn't sure if he had recognized the animal or read the word. I smiled and read, "I spy the eyes of . . . a vulture." Then they read with me the interesting science facts about the vulture. In a speech bubble, the vulture says, "I can see a mouse from 1 mile above the ground." And, of course, the discussion led into comparing our eyesight with that of vultures.

This book provoked wonderful questions from the children and spurred their interest in learning more about animals. We charted their questions, which they investigated later. How can vultures see so far away? How far can an eagle see? How far can a human see? Can an owl see as well as an ostrich?

On each page we also did a K-W-L chart: what do you *know* about the animal? What do you *want* to know? What have you *learned*? The children were fascinated by the information they learned and by what certain children already knew. Charting the information and looking at the wonderful visuals in the book involved all the children regardless of language level, and all learned new information, because the input was comprehensible for them.

I have used this book with first- to fourth-graders, and it has been good for teaching strategies as well as keeping their interest. The younger learners and beginning speakers were interested in the rhyming words and noticed that even the beginning letters of the animals' names rhymed: *t, v, c, b, g,* and with *me*. Other recommended nonfiction Big Books for primary-grade children are *Is This a Monster?*, *Which Is Which?*, *Creatures Features*, and *Skeleton*. Appendix E5 lists more titles.

Nonfiction Big Books for Upper Grades

Another of my favorite books for English language learners is *The Cat on the Chimney: Solving Problems with Technology*, which is part of the Realization Technology series for upper-grade children. This nonfiction text presents children with real problems that they have to solve. The problems are clever and could really happen, for instance, the cat is on the chimney and is afraid to come down, or your friend dropped your key down the drain and you can't reach it, or on a field trip to the zoo you dropped four things in a pond but you only have time to save one of them and your decision on which to save has environmental costs as well as monetary ones. The book gives a page of suggestions for materials that could be used to solve the problem. Each problem together with the technology needed to solve it is on a two-page spread. This enables the teacher to read one problem at a time with the children.

The book encourages children to think. It also encourages them to work together and talk out solutions, with everyone having to share and refine their ideas. And it encourages children to read for information and to use their language for real purposes. All of these are proven components of a well-planned program for developing the language and literacy of ELLs (Gibbons 2002). There are no right

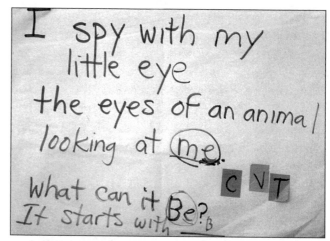

Chart highlighting rhymes in *I Spy.*

answers, and there are many ways to solve the problem stated in the book. But the solutions need to be rational, and they must work. The whole class can work together on a solution, or after having read the problem and analyzed the pictures and text carefully with the whole class, children can break into small groups with ELLs at various language levels in each group. The Big Book can be left on the easel as a reference. When each group has devised a solution, it can share the plan with the whole class. Then even livelier discussions ensue as the groups compare and contrast their plans.

Other recommended nonfiction Big Books for upper-grade children are *The Paper Skyscraper*, *Which Is Which?*, and *Alone in the Desert*. Appendix E5 lists more titles.

Choosing from a Variety of Genres

We need to introduce children to a variety of genres. If we choose to focus on a different genre each month as a "theme," for example, I would use books of that genre for shared reading, read-aloud, and guided reading during that month, and encourage children to read books of that genre sometimes during independent reading time. I would need to choose good representatives of that genre in order to teach the children how to read it.

Narratives

These books should have interesting story lines with predictable endings but still have the three *R*'s—rhyme, rhythm, and repetition, which help ELLs hear sounds and patterns in language and make the book fun to read. A classic for primary grades is *Greedy Cat* by Joy Cowley. The repetitive pattern is, *"Mom went shopping and bought some ———. Along came greedy cat. He looked in the shopping bag. Gobble, gobble gobble, and that was the end of that."* Joy Cowley has written hundreds of Big Books, and most are wonderful. Anything written by her is worth getting, especially *Mrs. Wishy-Washy* and *Grandpa, Grandpa*. The family theme works very well with ELLs because so many of them live with extended family or have close ties to their grandparents.

For upper-grade children, *Judge for a Day* is a wonderful story about a child that has to judge Hispanic foods in an international cooking contest at school. He is afraid that all Hispanic foods are too hot and tries to build up his courage to taste them, thus the repetitive line, *"This food won't be too hot. I think I'll like it quite a lot."* Then, when he finds out that each food is different, he repeats the line as he eats each food: *"I thought all Hispanic foods were hot. What a surprise! ——— it's not."*

Fables and Folktales for Upper Grades

Fables are good for teaching higher-level thinking, especially analyzing and understanding the main idea. Since they are usually short, it is easy to read a fable with children and focus on higher-level strategies in one shared reading lesson. I recommend *A Book of Fables,* which has eight fables in it. Most English language learners have strong oral traditions, and although they may not have heard these fables before, they might have heard a variation of them in their primary language or might be able to compare and contrast them to fables from their homeland.

Folktales are also an important genre in literature and wonderful to share with ELLs because they come from all countries around the world. Many children can relate to the folktales because they have heard similar ones from their families in oral retellings. *Folk Tales: A Short Anthology* contains five folktales with large text, so the children can follow along with it in shared reading. Another fine Big Book is *The Crying Mountain: A Mexican Legend.* This is a retelling of a famous legend about the two mountains outside of Mexico City, Popocatepetl and Ixtaccihuatl. It is a beautiful and tragic love story and has been passed down through generations through numerous retellings. Most Hispanic children, especially Mexican Americans, relate to this book.

Poetry

The teaching of poetry has become popular in elementary schools, and many books are published on how to teach children to write their own poetry. There are also many compilations of famous poems, including Big Books. Collections of multicultural poems have also become more prevalent. One of my favorites is called *Catch Me the Moon, Daddy.* It has a variety of poems from around the world, which are lovely to read with all children. The photographs are spectacular, so the book can be used with primary- and upper-grade children.

I Am of Two Places is a book of Hispanic children's poems, a product of a unit on writing poetry with third-, fourth-, and fifth-graders. They were asked to write poems to express their feelings about their immigrant experience. The poems that were selected for publication, "Divided Heart," by Lorena Lozada; "Between Two Languages," by Juan Manuel García; "I Am of Two Places," by Jimmy Vásquez; "I'm a Teacher," by Verónica Valdez; and "Feeling Proud," by José L. Aguayo, represent the feelings of children who have ties to both the United States and their Latin American countries. All the poems were written in English and Spanish by the children, and there is a Spanish version of the book, *Soy de dos Lugares.* Every time I use the book with a group of children, they come up to me afterwards sharing their own stories, writing them down, feeling motivated to write their own poetry. By studying the text together, teachers can help children see how the children featured in the book wrote their poems. There are photographs and mini-biographies of the poets.

Historical Nonfiction, Primary Sources, Biographies

History is a component of national and state standards. Many states, including California, have history/social science state frameworks rather than social studies, and history can be taught within thematic units or tied into the language block. There are many Big Books to help English language learners read these content area texts in a comfortable and supportive setting. This allows them to access the core curriculum. There are Big Book compilations of original documents that can be utilized to study certain eras, with explanations for teachers on how to use them. I have found that these books are appropriate only for grades 3 and up, but one that is extremely interesting is *Primary Sources in Early American History.* It includes documents from the voyage of the *Mayflower* in 1620, and the teacher can show children how to analyze them.

Biographies are also an important genre for children to study in the context of a history/social science or social studies theme. A Big Book biography is *The Story of Sitting Bull,* another one is *Cousteau.* The timelines provided place the real person in the context of history. By reading it with the whole class, ELLs are supported in reading a genre with which they may have little experience.

Appendix E5 lists Big Books in all these genres.

9

GUIDED READING GROUPS AND BOOKS

Pray for Vacations

One Saturday night my husband and I received an urgent plea for help from our parish priest just as we were going out to dinner. He needed his homily translated for the three Spanish masses he was to say the next day, and his usual translator was gone for the weekend. Would we translate it? Reluctantly we went to the rectory on the way to the dinner party and picked up the four-page typed speech. The theme for that Sunday was Vocations.

As we read the homily over dinner, we all started laughing. Throughout the English version of his homily, which his secretary had typed, he asked the congregation to pray for Vacations. What a novel idea, we thought. Why not pray for vacations—we all deserve them! This became the moral question for the evening: Should we do a literal translation, "pray for vacations (vacaciones)," just as the typescript said, which would cause him much embarrassment in church or should we do the noble thing and correct it to say what the priest (probably) intended: "pray for vocations (vocaciones)"? We talked a bit about how one vowel could make such a difference. We knew in English he would catch his typo, but although we know he reads well in Spanish, we weren't sure he would catch the error. In the end, we did the right thing. We knew we'd have to go on a long vacation if we didn't!

How many of our students read a text without stopping to see if what they read makes sense? How many children recognize their miscues? Reading is a very complex process, but its main purpose should be to construct meaning. How can we as educators help our students construct meaning while they are reading? What strategies can we teach them to become more effective readers?

We can help children become better readers by having them read on their own with guidance and support from us. In a small group, with just a few children, a teacher has the opportunity to tailor instruction to each reader as he tries out new language and new strategies for the first time. Guided reading is an important part of our daily instruction when children try out the strategies they have learned in shared reading and read-alouds. It is their time to practice with us by their side, helping them listen for and catch their own errors. It is also a time when higher-level strategies are used and when children are stretched to learn academic language as they gain a deeper understanding of the text.

A lot has been written on guided reading (e.g., Fountas and Pinnell 1996; 1999; 2001; Hornsby 2000; *Reading in Junior Classes* 1985; *Reading for Life* 1996), but in these next few chapters I hope to shed light on how to approach guided reading with English language learners. Forming groups and choosing appropriate texts for guided reading with ELLs are more complex than with native speakers, because it is not only a child's developmental reading level that must be assessed but also his English language proficiency level and concept development in the primary language. It is critical to look at both the language and literacy needs of each child when we are planning for and leading a guided reading lesson with ELLs. This chapter addresses forming guided reading groups with children at different language and reading levels; looking at the three cueing systems and how to effectively assess ELLs' ability to sustain meaning through miscue analysis; choosing books to develop vocabulary and to match language and reading levels; understanding the three book-leveling systems and how they correlate to grade level; using book rooms to best advantage; and managing groups in the weekly schedule.

How can we use guided reading to help our English language learners?

How do I form guided reading groups with so many different levels of speakers and readers in my classroom?

How do I differentiate a reading problem from a language problem?

What do I do when these students are lacking so much vocabulary?

What types of books do I choose for my English language learners?

What are the leveling systems that I should use for my guided reading books and how do they relate to the grade level standards?

How can I manage my guided reading groups when I have so many?

BUILDING CONFIDENCE

A guided reading lesson should provide enough support to make an ELL feel confident to take on new challenges. Unlike independent reading, when the child is reading totally by himself, guided reading still allows an expert to keep a careful eye on the child while he is trying desperately to put all of his strategies to use and to utilize the new language he has acquired while tackling a new text.

You might equate a guiding reading lesson to a lesson on riding a bike without training wheels. The child listened to you read in read-aloud, has practiced reading with you in shared reading, has been learning new strategies and skills to help him become a better reader, and has had time to try out his strategies and skills in reading with books at his independent level or books on tape. And he has been acquiring his new language and practicing it in the context of this literary environment. Just as a child has been practicing his bike riding skills and strategies for a while with his training wheels on, following you down the street and watching what the expert does, now both the reader and the bike rider are ready for the next challenge.

Plus, you are there to help him succeed, to help him comprehend what he is reading. You are there to point out what strategy he should use as he gets stuck, or help him with the language structure he is comfortable using, just as you probably once ran next to your own child or younger sibling when he was learning to ride a bike to give him guidance and support. Your hand was on the child's seat, holding him up, as he struggled for the first time, trying to put everything together: turning the pedals fast enough to keep a forward motion, holding the handle bars straight so as not to swerve into the parked cars, and looking forward and trying to keep balanced while doing everything so as not to fall off the bike. And you were there, running tirelessly alongside.

With gentle help from you, a hand when needed, suggestions on what to do, both the bike rider and the reader become successful. And, oh the joy that comes to the child's face when he knows that he can do it! Look at me! I'm riding by myself! Look at me! I'm reading on my own!

Choosing a book that a child has never seen before and helping her feel successful at reading and understanding the text is the challenge and joy of guided reading for the teacher. And when, after a fifteen- or twenty-minute lesson with a new book, the child holds up the book and says, "I can read this!" it is like magic. Guided reading holds that kind of magic for children.

FORMING GUIDING READING GROUPS

Not all English language learners are alike, yet I often see ELLs lumped together because they make up only a handful or so in a class or grade level at some schools. Other schools have whole populations of ELLs and yet still see them as a group rather than as individuals. Just as with all children, we need to know each ELL's individual needs in order to help them become literate. The subtleties in grouping ELLs appropriately for guided reading are somewhat difficult to master. A child with a lower language level than another student may actually be able to read at a higher reading level. And a child communicating at a higher language level than her peers may not have the strategies to read at a higher reading level. We need to remember, also, that ELLs' having a lower language level than native speakers is not a reason to exclude them from guided reading lessons but an opportunity to help them based on what they know.

	Josue	Crystal	Jessica
English language proficiency (ELP) level	*Early intermediate* speaks in short sentences	*Intermediate* speaks in complete sentences	*Early advanced* speaks almost like a native speaker
Developmental reading assessment (DRA) level	(10–12)	(2–4)	(6–8)
Developmental reading stage (DRS)	*Early* strategy use is high; cross-checks; self-corrects	*Emergent* knows book has meaning; tracks left to right; uses pictures to help	*Early* starting to cross-check using three cueing systems
Primary language	Strong support at home; reads at early fluent stage in Spanish	Some support at home, but not in reading; Spanish reading not tested	No support at home; older siblings speak English

Josue, Crystal, Jessica

To group ELLs for guided reading, we start by analyzing the information we have on them to see if two or more of them match to form a group. As an example, I look at three children with three different language levels and three different reading levels in the chart above. See Tables 2.1 and 2.3 in Chapter 2 for details on these levels; and Chapter 2 and Table 9.1 for information on DRA, a formal developmental reading assessment and book-leveling system (Beaver 1997).

Could these children be grouped together for guided reading? Ideally, all would have the same reading and language levels and thus fit logically into the same group. But this doesn't happen very often. Usually, there are many different children with many different needs, and trying to create completely matching groups might result in over ten reading groups for a class of twenty, or more for a class of thirty, so that clearly isn't feasible. The groups therefore need to be flexible, and we need to try out different children with different books to see if there is a good match, and we need to constantly assess their language and strategy use.

If I had to choose, I would group Josue and Jessica together because they are both at the early stage of reading development and using similar strategies while they read. Although Josue is able to read a little higher-level text, Jessica's stronger English language level could help carry her in a group discussion of the text. Also, there really is not

that much difference between a level 8 or a level 10 text, and we might need to provide a choice of books in bands of texts levels, as mentioned in Hornsby's book *A Closer Look at Guided Reading* (2000). The one problem I might have with grouping these students is the discrepancy in their language levels. I would need to carefully choose a text that Josue would be able to handle based on his developmental use of grammatical structures and yet continue to challenge him to improve his reading level. I would also need to carefully watch Jessica as I select a more challenging text for both of them.

The Three Cueing Systems

While assessing students and planning for their instruction, we should note whether they are tapping into the three cueing systems to sustain meaning as they read: the semantic ("Does it make sense?"), the syntactic ("Does it sound right?"), and the graphophonic ("Does it look right?"). If a child's basic knowledge of the three cueing systems in English is not developed, she will have a difficult time sustaining meaning through the reading strategies of sampling, predicting, checking, confirming, and self-correcting. (For details on the three cueing systems, see Clay 1979; 1991; *Reading for Life* 1996; Traill 1994; and Chapter 4 of this book.)

How many students keep on reading when they make a mistake? or make substitutions that don't make sense? or become great decoders but have no idea of what they've just read? Many native speakers have these same bad reading habits, but ELLs are at a double disadvantage if we do not develop their language, which has a direct correlation to their reading development (Cambourne 1988; Krashen 1996). When we ask ELLs "Did that make sense?" or "Did that sound right?" and they don't know because of their lack of English, we will have a more difficult time helping them use these cueing systems effectively. Unless we help ELLs develop their semantic, syntactic, and graphophonic knowledge, they will not be able to understand what they read.

Does It Look Right?

The child may not know if it looks right because she does not have a developed knowledge of English sounds and spelling. This child would have difficulty sampling information from the page. Crystal, for example, although she is at the intermediate language level, has not mastered understanding of English phonics and can't use that to help her figure out unknown words and check predictions. She still has trouble with many consonants and consonant blends and endings.

Does It Sound Right?

The child may not know if it sounds right because his knowledge of English syntax is not developed. This child would have difficulty self-correcting effectively. Josue, for example, although he uses strong strategies because of his strong literacy level in his primary language, which has transferred to his English reading, cannot use knowledge of English language to help him while he reads because his language level is still too low. He is just beginning to speak in short sentences, and his knowledge of grammatical structure is not developed enough to know whether something sounds right even though he rereads to check. Reading "That he is" instead of "There he is" may sound right to him.

Does It Make Sense?

The child may not know if it makes sense because her background knowledge in the subject or knowledge of vocabulary and grammar is not developed enough. This child would have difficulty predicting, confirming, and self-correcting, or recognizing a miscue or how to correct it. Jessica, for example, although she is at the early advanced language stage and speaks almost like a native speaker, has not mastered English completely. She often comes upon new vocabulary that she tries to sound out but substitutes words that are not correct and has trouble knowing whether they make sense.

ANALYZING MISCUES

One way to look closely at a child's ability to utilize the three cueing systems and sustain meaning is to take a running record (Clay 1979; 1991). However, if we use running records with English language learners just to record a score on the reading percentage without looking at the miscues, we might get an inaccurate view of what a child is capable of reading. We must analyze a child's miscues very closely in order to figure out what type of text he needs. Often the type of book we choose will have a huge effect on a child's ability to progress in reading. Choosing a book with appropriate vocabulary and background information the child is familiar with will help him succeed in guided reading. Sometimes we don't know, though, until we try out a book whether the book is appropriate for the child. Sometimes the language used in the book is not appropriate for the reader but not because he is not able to read at that developmental level. By looking closely at the reading strategies the child is using as well as the child's language level, we will be better able to analyze the child's miscues and match him with the right text.

Nathan

Let's look at a running record to help us understand the connection between analyzing miscues and understanding a child's developmental needs. Nathan is an intermediate speaker, like Crystal, and an early reader, like Josue, but he uses different reading strategies than Josue does. For the purpose of analyzing the strategies he is using and to give a flavor of his use of the three cueing systems, I show here just a part of his running record. By looking closely at these few lines of the text and analyzing his miscues, we can see what his strengths are and what he needs to work on.

Nathan was a second-grader and the only ELL in his class. His teacher worked with him one-on-

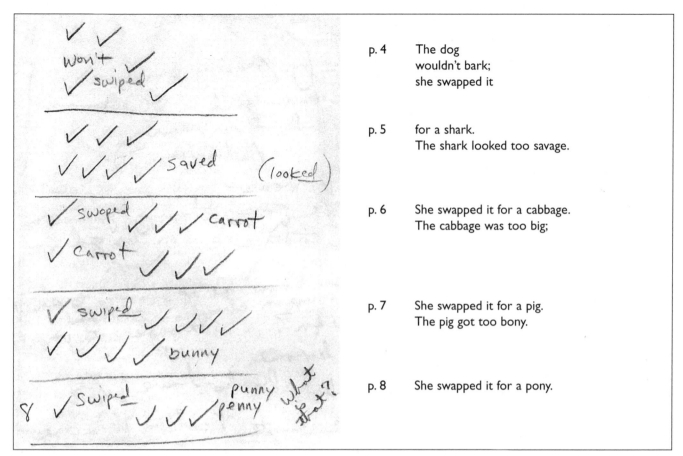

p. 4	The dog wouldn't bark; she swapped it
p. 5	for a shark. The shark looked too savage.
p. 6	She swapped it for a cabbage. The cabbage was too big;
p. 7	She swapped it for a pig. The pig got too bony.
p. 8	She swapped it for a pony.

A part of Nathan's running record on *Poor Old Polly.*

one as often as she could and tried to integrate him into a guided reading group in her classroom. She asked me to do a running record to help her assess his reading ability. She chose *Poor Old Polly*, a Reading Recovery or intervention level 10 (see Table 9.1). Nathan had never read the book. The text has strong picture support with one to three lines of print per page. The repetitive pattern and point of the story is that Old Polly keeps swapping things for other things because they aren't acceptable in some way.

By looking closely at the types of miscues Nathan made and noting the coding of those miscues, we can see that Nathan was using his knowledge of graphophonics to help him (Wilde 2000; Clay 1979). All his substitutions visually looked close to the word: *wouldn't/won't, swapped/swiped.* And if he didn't know a word, like *cabbage*, he replaced it with *carrot*, also a vegetable and starting with *c*, even though it didn't match the picture. He used the contraction *won't* instead of *wouldn't* because it is a more common tense for his language development. Both miscues made sense and didn't detract from his understanding of the story. The

running record also shows his use of the syntactic cueing system because words were replaced with the correct parts of speech. He had trouble with *swapped* on each page, saying either *swip-ed* or *swop-ed.* He was trying to find a word that sounded right but couldn't. It seems he had heard *swiped* before, so went back to that one. Although the meaning slightly changed, his substitution was grammatically correct (it was a verb and in the past tense), even though he pronounced the *ed* as a separate syllable, a very common practice for ELLs.

Nathan's knowledge of reading seemed to be that a word has to match visually even if it doesn't make sense. He tried to pull out a word in his vocabulary to fit the visual pattern. That can be seen in his substitutions for *bony* and *pony*. I thought he would say *horse* for *pony* because I knew *horse* was in his vocabulary. But he knew the printed word started with *p* and ended with *y*, and *horse* doesn't look anything like that. He may have made the connection to *bony* also ending with *y* and tried to find a rhyming word. While he was reading the text, he kept looking at the pictures and back at the words. He even tried to slowly pronounce a word and hesitated when he wasn't sure. But he never went back to reread. Rather, he figured it out in his head, with some wait time, but then said it and didn't go back. I could see by the look on his face that he knew *punny* didn't make sense, but he didn't have the correct word for it. After the running record was done, I went back again to the page with *pony* and asked him, pointing to the picture, "Do you know another word for this?" And he said right away, "Horse."

What did we learn about Nathan as a reader and language user from this brief encounter with this text? And what can we say about matching this text to this child? Nathan did not have the background knowledge to be successful with this text, so he could not use his semantic cueing system to help him, even with the support pictures. The pictures were not a help because he didn't have *savage, cabbage, bony,* and *pony* in his vocabulary. His retelling of the story was actually pretty good, but he didn't have the vocabulary to effectively understand this text, which is rather silly and without a strong story line. He was speaking at the intermediate level. Although he was speaking in complete sentences, they weren't always grammatically correct. For example, while describing his little brother to me, he said, "My brother have three years old." He did show appropriate reading strategies for a strong early reader. Although I didn't hear any rereading, I could tell he was thinking in his head and was using his three cueing systems to cross-check. They just weren't developed enough to deal with this particular text.

So what are our options for Nathan? I chose another book. I went to the school's book room and chose *Sleepy Bear,* another early text, Reading Recovery level 8, and he read it with 100 percent accuracy. That told me he needed to be challenged more, not given a lower text. So I choose *Red Socks and Yellow Socks,* Reading Recovery level 12, and he read it with 94 percent accuracy at his instructional level. Interestingly, the book also had the word *swapped* in it, which we had discussed beforehand, and he had no trouble with the word and the vocabulary in this text, even though it was on a higher level than *Poor Old Polly.* Perhaps, therefore, we can assume that the language patterns and vocabulary in *Poor Old Polly* were not appropriate for Nathan as an intermediate speaker. His

difficulty was in the lack of language development, not only in his reading strategies. That book was not a good choice for Nathan. He needed a book with a stronger story line, which he could make sense of, like *Red Socks and Yellow Socks* and *Sleepy Bear. Poor Old Polly* might work well for another ELL. But we have to analyze carefully why a particular book did not work well with a particular child, and not assume that it is a problem with the child's developmental reading level without analyzing the child's miscues and looking closely at the text itself.

It is in the context of the balanced literacy program that we can help English language learners like Nathan, Josue, Crystal, and Jessica develop their use of all three cueing systems, especially in shared reading and shared writing. But it is in guided reading that they can practice what they are taught. And it is in guided reading that we can get a closer look at how they are doing developmentally and how we can help them further develop. We need to take a close look at each child's language development and literacy development during and after each lesson. We can use developmental checklists (Appendix A) for reading and language development to help us keep track of each child's progress. We can also record the information we have observed during a guided reading lesson on record sheets of the group (Appendix F3) (see Fountas and Pinnell 1999). But I would put the running records of the children and any observations from the group record sheet right into their individual reading and language folders. By reviewing their folders during conferences with them, we can keep a continual watch on their reading and language needs, which then helps us plan for effective instruction. The observations that I make during guided reading lessons drive my instruction during the rest of the balanced literacy program.

CHOOSING BOOKS TO DEVELOP VOCABULARY

Nathan came across several words that he did not know. This is true for most ELLs while they are reading. We don't always need to choose books whose vocabulary the children are familiar with. It would be very difficult to know who is familiar with which words before one goes into a guided reading lesson. Instead of screening out books that we think they might not understand, we can use books with strong story lines or familiar themes and help them add new vocabulary to their bank of words (Freeman and Freeman 2002; Cambourne 1988). Exposing children to new vocabulary in the context of reading a story and themes they are familiar with is a very effective way to build their academic vocabulary. By having them look at the pictures, validating their knowledge of words in the primary language, and using books with sentence patterns that are appropriate for their levels of language development, we can help develop the vocabulary that they need.

Example of an Emergent Reader

I go back now to Mayra's classroom to share an example of helping primary-grade children add new vocabulary to their bank of words. I observed a guided reading lesson at the beginning of the school year. The teacher was using an intervention level 2 book, *A Friend for Me,* with a small group of ELLs. The story and pattern is about a girl who is showing her dog all the things she has for it: a bed for you, a collar for you, and so on, until the end, which shows a picture of the girl hugging the dog and "a friend for me." The children in the group were familiar with taking care of dogs, but they often didn't have the exact word for the item the girl was showing her dog in the pictures on each page.

Mayra was one of the children who didn't have the exact vocabulary. She was in first grade at the time and an emergent reader with an early intermediate English language level. She was very engaged in the text and was following along with the teacher's introduction and orientation of the book. Although there was strong picture support, Mayra didn't know the words to match the pictures. When they got to the page that said, "a collar for you," the teacher pointed to the collar and asked, "Mayra, what is this?" Mayra looked at the picture and put her hands around her own neck and said, "For around the neck." She didn't know the word *collar* in English, but she knew what it was used for. She also didn't know the word *leash,* but she pointed to the picture of the "red thing" and said, "For you to walk dog."

Mayra's teacher validated her knowledge, and they discussed whether Mayra or anyone else had

ever walked a dog. Most of the children in the group did not have dogs of their own. The teacher realized that not knowing the English name for the item did not prevent Mayra or the others from understanding or enjoying the text. She then gave them the correct word, *leash,* after they had tried unsuccessfully to sound it out. They tried to sound out *collar* also, but found it very hard to do. The teacher knew that these words would have been part of a native speaker's oral vocabulary. The native speaker wouldn't have to sound it out; by just looking at the picture, she would be able to figure it out and find the word *collar* or *leash* on the page. Since Mayra and the other children did not know the word, the teacher gave it to them, and thus they were able to say it and learn it in context.

These children expanded their academic vocabulary during the guided reading lesson by learning the words in English for concepts they already knew in the primary language. The pictures of course helped them understand the words' meaning. And the new words were cemented into their vocabulary by the time the lesson was over. By being introduced to the words during the orientation of the text, by learning them in context, by locating the words on the page and touching them, they were able to read them on their own during rereading of the text. Mayra had read the book three times before the lesson was over and had learned vocabulary words that she could now use in discussions about dogs.

Some teachers might have given up if the children didn't know the vocabulary. But since the children knew the concepts in the primary language and were interested in the story line and content of the book, they were not frustrated. Mayra, for example, was thrilled with the subject of the book because she loved dogs. She was excited to learn the words *leash* and *collar,* and she was proud to be able to find the words in the text and reread them on her own. She also showed that she used the pictures to help her figure out the new vocabulary, and the sentence pattern of the text helped her use the new words in a sentence that made sense to her.

Example of an Early Fluent Reader

Another example of using a guided reading lesson to help develop children's vocabulary is a demonstration lesson I did with a group of fourth-graders reading at second-grade reading level. This was one of the lowest reading groups in the class, composed of 95 percent ELLs, all Spanish-speaking in the border town of San Ysidro. I used my book *The Big Catch*, which is at Reading Recovery or intervention level 24. The lesson was designed to teach specific strategies that they needed to work on, but the issue of new vocabulary came up throughout the lesson. Often, they had the concepts and vocabulary in the primary language, but not the specific vocabulary in English. They discovered the words they needed by themselves, however, through the illustrations and cognates, and by searching for the words and using them in context.

During the introduction, I engaged them in a dialogue to tap into their background experience with fishing and to elicit their predictions of what they thought might happen in the story and why they thought the title was *The Big Catch*. Two of the children had never fished before, but one of the boys had gone fishing a lot with his father. I started chart-

ing some of their sharing and vocabulary related to *The Big Catch* on a small graphic organizer next to me as we all sat on the floor. Juan tried to describe how to catch fish, including using a fishing rod and bait, the word for which he knew in Spanish but not in English. We accepted his approximation and listed the Spanish word. Maria was also sharing what she thought the boy might catch, including *fish* and *cangrejo* (*crab*). Surprisingly, none of the other children in the group knew the English word *crab* either. Instead of telling her, I wrote the word in Spanish and told her that perhaps she might find the word in English while she was reading. Both Maria and Juan planned on looking for those words in the text and were motivated to find them.

Maria's face lit up when she came across the word *crab*. "A crab, a crab. Here it is!" she blurted out while the others were reading silently. She saw the picture first on page 8. "Oh," she said, and searched the text on pages 8 and 9 until she found the word *crab*. She was thrilled. Then, on her own, she wrote the word *crab* on her focus sheet. I took

Michael started to climb up the rocks and,
since the tide was so low, he began to notice things
that he had never seen before.

He saw something crawling on the rocks.
He followed it and found it was a crab.
Very carefully, he trapped it and brought it to his dad.

8

9

Two pages from *The Big Catch*.

the time right then, while the other children were reading, to ask her what Michael did with the crab. I wasn't sure if she knew what *trapped* meant. She said, "He caught it and took it to his dad." She obviously understood the meaning, but I had her find the words on page 9 that told her this. She pointed to *trapped*, which she had difficulty pronouncing, and *brought*, which she was able to pronounce a little easier. "Yes, he trapped it," I replied. "How do you think he did that?" "Very carefully, because the crab has pinchers," said Maria, while she made gestures with her fingers of claws opening and closing. We both laughed, "You're right!" I said, and then we discussed how much it would hurt if a crab did pinch you.

A guided reading lesson does often take longer with ELLs because they are discovering new vocabulary along the way. It's also because an author often chooses different words to say the same thing to create variety and to make the book more interesting (but not necessarily easier for new language users). For instance, on page 13 of *The Big Catch*, I said the same thing as on page 9 but used the word *grabbed* instead of *trapped*: when Michael found a starfish, "He grabbed it and took it to his dad." Maria didn't have any trouble with this sentence, but she was challenged by, "As he poked around . . . ." We looked at the picture, and I asked what Michael was doing with his hand. I also used the same word in a different context to see if she had any knowledge of it. "Has anyone ever poked you?" I asked, and poked her lightly on the arm. "Oh, yes," said Maria. Then we compared that to Michael's poking around in the tide pool and touching the starfish.

Juan never found the word *bait* because, as he discovered, Michael and his dad never talked about "what they used to catch the fish," so I gave him that word later. But the motivation for trying to locate new words while he was reading was evident; he stopped numerous times and pointed out new words to me: "Patience. Teacher, that's like *paciencia* in Spanish." As I've mentioned, cognates are a powerful tool for ELLs who are fluent readers in languages that share roots with English (see Appendixes C2 and C3).

We need to have patience when using new texts with ELLs while they are developing their vocabu-

lary, but we don't have to stop and investigate the fine points of every word. Does it really matter whether Michael *caught, trapped,* or *grabbed* a sea animal? From a writer's perspective, it is always critical to find the exact word; in that context there is definitely a difference between *trap* and *grab*. So, if the goal of the lesson is to analyze the author's choice of words, then we do need to examine the subtlety in the language and perhaps teach children how to use it in their own writing. But in a lesson to help ELLs sustain meaning while reading, such subtleties would take a back seat.

ELLs need to be exposed to natural language patterns and appropriate vocabulary, which will build the language base they are developing. We shouldn't disqualify a book because we think it has too many new words. Rather, we should choose guided reading texts that will help children expand their vocabulary, and teach the new words through questioning and tapping into prior knowledge, always in context. ELLs need that exposure in order to catch up with their native-speaking peers. Smith (1994) writes that teaching vocabulary words by a list is much too slow and that children need to read as much and as widely as possible to learn new vocabulary. They need to develop a bank of vocabulary in the context of reading lots of fiction and content area books that are well written (Allington 2001; Cummins 2003).

Some teachers prefer guided reading texts that are built around high-frequency words. The thinking is that students can practice reading them and feel success because they see them over and over in the same text. I don't disagree with this premise but believe we are doing our students a disservice if we do not also expose them to books with natural language patterns, interesting story lines, and a rich vocabulary. It is necessary to strike a balance between presenting challenging vocabulary and knowing when the volume of new words becomes too daunting. This is a difficult balance, but I think we should err on the side of challenging rather than easy, and work hard to ensure that the children are comfortable with the topic and context before starting to read the text. Learning the specific vocabulary will come.

Building background knowledge and language is very helpful when introducing new guided reading books. This can be done in the introduction and the orientation of the text. If we are able to choose guided reading texts that relate to the current thematic unit, much of the background knowledge may already have been developed. The children may have their own background knowledge or experience about the topic, and we can accept their primary language as they start making connections to the new books. They might remember some of the same vocabulary or topics from other books they have read, or they might make connections to the print-rich classroom environment that is developed in the context of the balanced literacy program. Children might see words in their new guided reading books that are on wall charts in the room, or they may have developed the concepts to understand the topic because of prior investigations they have done in the classroom.

CHOOSING BOOKS TO MATCH CHILDREN

When a text seems too difficult for a child, we need to differentiate between a language problem and a strategy use problem, analyze the child's miscues, and make a rational decision as to whether the reading level is too high or whether the child would do better in another book at the same level with more appropriate language structures or vocabulary.

I have found that teachers are more likely than not to keep ELLs in books that are too easy for them. When they see a problem, like verb tense, they tend to automatically go down a level instead of considering another book at the same level, perhaps because they haven't taken the time to examine various books at different levels to evaluate how their characteristics might best match children's language and reading levels.

Guided reading books are supposed to be challenging. If children could read a book independently, they wouldn't need the teacher to guide them through it. Although some authors (e.g., Fountas and Pinnell 1996; Hornsby 2000) recommend erring on the side of easy rather than challenging, I don't favor that approach. We need to challenge English language learners and yet be positive in doing so. Otherwise, they will always lag behind.

We need to be aware of children's ability to use the three cueing systems to sustain meaning. They may have strategies to gain meaning, like cross-checking and rereading, but still not be able to make sense of what they are reading because of a lack of syntactic knowledge or background knowledge, for example. Then books at various levels should be examined, and chosen based on what we know about the children as readers and language users. Often this fine-tuning of book selection occurs after we have used a book for a guided reading lesson and are reevaluating whether it was appropriate for certain children, or perhaps why it was not. The following page has some questions to consider.

When a child has difficulty with a text, teachers often assume the level is too high without closely examining the book. But the difficulty may be with the book itself. We should always examine a variety of texts at each reading level in order to evaluate whether the level really is too difficult for a child or whether the style of writing or illustrations in a particular text are what make it difficult for ELLs. By choosing a different book they may be successful.

We should select the best possible materials for guided reading. The books should have the best illustrations, natural language patterns, the topics should be interesting and exciting, and our students should see themselves in the books. Do the books invite the children to come back? Do they want to read them again, or read more books by the same author? Do *I* want to read the book? If I am bored with the story line or the illustrations, I won't choose that book. If I don't like it, I'm sure my students won't. I want them to get excited about reading, and good books will make that happen, even the small guided reading books.

LEVELED TEXTS AND GRADE LEVEL CORRELATION

When guided reading books first came out and teachers began to build up their own leveled libraries, they would often spend hours leveling the texts based on Barbara Peterson's (2001) leveling characteristics in order to make sure they were providing children with the right level of text. Today, there are at least three well-known leveling systems relating guided reading books to children's developmental reading levels. Table 9.1 shows the correla-

ELL's Ability to Use Semantic Cues

Does the child

have sufficient background knowledge to help her with this text?

recognize what the pictures represent?

know vocabulary in the primary language but not in English?

have the English vocabulary to describe what is in the pictures?

If not, should I *go down one level*?

Or, could the child have more success with another book *at the same reading level*?

How can I shape instruction in other parts of the program to increase the child's English vocabulary development?

How can I expose her to more content and experiences in English?

Suggestions to Develop Semantics

★ Teach thematically
★ Read aloud daily
★ Integrate content
★ Expose them to rich literature, fiction, and nonfiction picture books
★ Use graphic organizers
★ Chart cognates
★ Build on own experiences
★ Bring the world into the classroom

ELL's Ability to Use Syntactic Cues

Does the child have sufficient knowledge of English language structure to help him with this text?

Are the structures in this book—especially verb tense—too advanced for his proficiency level? If so, should I *go down one level*?

Or, could the child have more success with another book *at the same reading level*?

What can I do in shared reading, shared writing, or other parts of the program to develop his grasp of English language structure?

Am I keeping track of his syntax and grammar development?

Am I focusing on language study as well as word study?

Suggestions to Develop Syntax

★ Plan language mini-lessons using a Big Book from shared reading
★ Daily News
★ Write patterns from speech and texts
★ Read poems
★ Study placement of words in sentences

ELL's Ability to Use Graphophonic Cues

Does the child

have sufficient knowledge of English sound-symbol relations to help her with this text?

know how to use spelling patterns and word families to help her decode unknown text?

recognize chunks in words?

Are the words or phonetic patterns in this book particularly difficult for ELLs?

If so, should I *go down one level*?

Or, could the child have more success with another book *at the same reading level*?

How can I shape instruction in other parts of the program to increase the child's knowledge of sound-symbol relations, word families, and spelling patterns?

Suggestions to Develop Graphophonics

★ Teach alphabet
★ Songs
★ Charts/poems
★ Phonemic awareness
★ Phonics in context
★ Charts of rimes (onsets)
★ Word families
★ Daily News/Morning Message

TABLE 9.1 Leveling Correlation Chart

Grade Level	Developmental Stages of Reading	DRA Level	Guided Reading Level	Intervention Level
Kindergarten	Emergent	A 1 2	A B	1–4
Grade 1 (Beginning)	Emergent / Early	3 4 6–8	C D E	5–8
Grade 1 (Midyear)	Early	10 12	F G	9–12
Grade 1 (End of year)	Early / Early Fluent (Transitional)	14 16	H I	13–16
Grade 2	Early Fluent (Transitional) / Fluent	18–20 24–28	J–K L–M	17–20 21–24
Grade 3	Early Fluent (Transitional) / Fluent	30 34–38	N O–P	
Grade 4	Fluent	40	Q–R	
Grade 5	Fluent	44	S–T	

tions between these systems as well as grade-level equivalency. I refer to intervention level based on the well-known Reading Recovery leveling system, with guided reading level based on the leveling system by Fountas and Pinnell and developmental reading assessment (DRA) level based on the leveling system developed by Joetta Beaver.

Most guided reading books published today are already leveled in all three of these systems (by teachers who are familiar with them). To find the level of a certain title, one simply goes to the publisher's Web site and looks for the correlation and leveling charts and finds books leveled by all three. Fountas and Pinnell have published large lists of books that are leveled in their system, and it is easy for teachers to look up some of the titles in the Fountas and Pinnell books (1996; 1999; 2001; 2002). (Not all guided reading books are included.) Appendix C4 has a leveled list of guided reading books tied to the theme of oceanography.

It is useful for teachers to understand the leveling process even though most books are already leveled. Barbara Peterson (2001) discusses the nuances of comparing different levels of books based on the characteristics of these levels. This clarifies how texts can be both supportive and challenging for emergent and early readers. I use a text evaluation sheet (Appendix F1) to help plan how to use a particular guided reading text with children at certain language and reading levels.

Of course, leveling systems are subjective, so there is always room for improvement. If teachers find that certain books don't seem to be leveled appropriately, they can make adjustments themselves and let the publisher know, so that the level can be reviewed and changed.

USING BOOK ROOMS EFFECTIVELY

In order to run an effective guided reading program within a balanced literacy program, teachers have to have a large selection of books and know how to choose books to match children's needs. That usually means that unless the school has endless amounts of funds available to purchase guided reading books for each classroom, there is a schoolwide book room used by all the teachers to share guided reading books. Often, that book room is the key to the success of the guided reading program.

Many schools have set up wonderful book rooms that function very well and that the teachers use successfully. But in schools that have not had great success with book rooms I have seen a common problem: teachers are not using the room effectively because they do not know the books and are not sure of the leveling system in place. There can be a lot of reasons that this occurs, but often the room is not set up in a manner easy to understand, teachers are not trained in how to use the room, and teachers have not been given time to read the books.

Usually one or two people have set up the room, and no one else has taken ownership. The teachers come into this beautifully set up room containing boxes of books labeled with some strange numeric or alphabetic system, and they don't know how to choose books. They haven't had the time to get to know the books, and they just start picking from boxes without really reading the titles or understanding the levels. They get back to the classroom and realize that the book they have chosen is not appropriate; then they go back and choose again, often more than once. Through trial and error, they often take months to start feeling comfortable using the book room. That can be months lost for children who are in need of just the right text to help take them instructionally to their next level of development.

Once most of the teachers start to use the book room, another common problem is that they don't understand the correlations of reading levels and grade level, so they often are not aware of how they should be advancing through levels in the book room as the year progresses. I have seen very bright children stay at the same developmental level all year because the book room had such a large collection of books at that level and the teacher just kept pulling out the next book.

What's important isn't the quantity of books that the child reads at one level but how the child can move through increasingly higher levels of books. Some children take giant leaps in their development, and their teachers should be matching with giant leaps through levels of books in the book room. It is just like going to the library. We would not expect a child to read all the books but only those he is interested in or that match his developmental level at the time. Next year or even next month he will naturally want to read different books with different challenges.

How do we know that a child is ready to take these big leaps? Because we are doing ongoing assessment, both with running records and by observing the child in guided reading lessons or reading conferences. Sometimes, we just know the minute the child starts to read a text that the book we chose is much too easy. If the child can read it independently, there is no reason to use it for a guided reading lesson. Then, of course, it's back to the book room to choose a higher-level text. That is where it is critical to be able to know quickly where in the book room one can find a more challenging text or a text with a topic the child will be interested in.

The most important thing in setting up a schoolwide book room is to set up a system that all the teachers understand and are trained in. It doesn't matter if it is color-coded, alphabetic, or numeric, but teachers need to know exactly how the different levels of books are indicated and how they correlate to grade level. If a book is well below the child's grade level, for example, the teachers should know that and realize how far they have to stretch the child in books that year to catch him up to grade level, if possible.

I have seen teachers pick books for children, especially ELLs, and think that the children were doing fine. Yet they didn't realize that the books they were choosing were over a year below grade level. Perhaps that was truly where the children were able to read, but the teacher should know how the developmental level correlates to where the children are expected to be at grade level, so that she can work to try to catch them up to their grade level peers.

An effective teacher knows at which levels her children are and what she needs to do to help them progress. Mayra's teacher knew that by the end of first grade Mayra and the rest of the first-graders

A teacher's classroom collection of leveled guided reading books for instruction.

Individual book boxes for independent reading.

Leveled books in buckets for children's independent reading.

were expected to be at DRA level 16 to be reading at grade level. She is hoping that they will all get there. She knows some will not, and some will surpass it. And she knows that some children will get there sooner than others. Throughout the year she plans her instruction based on the changing needs

of her students. She takes running records daily on two or three children and keeps track of their reading development, language development, and strategy use in their reading and language assessment notebooks. She then draws from her large collection of leveled guided reading books. Besides her large collection of guided reading texts by instructional level, which she keeps for instructional use in guided reading groups, she has books in buckets by levels for children to choose for independent reading and individual book boxes for each child as well.

It is critical for teachers to take the time to read through the texts, not just pick them up right before the guided reading lesson begins. I have observed guided reading lessons where the teacher knew the children's instructional levels and chose books at those levels but hadn't read the book carefully ahead of time. That lack of planning became evident in emergent or early guided reading lessons if there was a tricky part that the teacher hadn't noticed; children struggled with the text unnecessarily. Children rely heavily on the orientation of the text by the teacher and also on supports in the text, like repetition or pictures. For early fluent and fluent readers, we need to know the purpose for choosing a book, like matching a strategy children need to work on or matching a literary focus the class has been working on. If the teacher does not read the book ahead of time, she will not know how to use it effectively to help children in the guided reading lesson.

MANAGING GROUPS

Primary Grades

ELLs come with a wide range of backgrounds in primary languages and English language proficiency. Therefore, the language and reading development of each child must be analyzed individually. Then we have to make decisions on how to group children for guided reading based on language level, literacy level, and strategy use. The groups will change continually.

Although the groups are fluid, one still needs to keep track of the individual progress of children on a developmental continuum. Table 9.2 shows how Mayra's teacher grouped children for guided read-

ing in November and February when Mayra was in second grade. The eighteen children in this class, predominantly emergent and early readers (see Table 9.1), were initially divided into six groups. Jonathon was in a group by himself at the beginning of the year because of his language level (beginner) and reading level (2). He needed daily instruction from the teacher. Because he was the only one in the group, the teacher took only ten to fifteen minutes to lead him through a guided reading lesson each day. But those minutes paid off. By February, Jonathon had caught up to reading group level 8, which helped his confidence as well as his skills. He would now regularly participate in small-group discussion and benefit from that instruction with his peers.

Each child needs instruction to move forward, and that means sometimes there is just one child in a group, and sometimes there are three guided reading groups per day instead of two. Two guided reading groups per day is ideal for the teacher, but since the emergent and early books are short, a third group can be fitted in if necessary. (Early fluent and fluent guided reading lessons take longer,

Children reading from book boxes.

TABLE 9.2A Guided Reading Groups Schedule—November and February

Monday	Tuesday	Wednesday	Thursday	Friday
November—Six Groups				
Level 2*	Level 2*	Level 2*	Level 2*	Level 2*
Level 4	Level 10	Level 4	Level 10	Level 22
Level 14	Level 18	Level 22	Level 14	Level 18
February—Five Groups				
Level 8	Level 14	Level 8	Level 14	Level 8
Level 18	Level 20	Level 24	Level 18	Level 20

Note: *Levels are DRA. *One child in group.*

TABLE 9.2B Guided Reading Groups—November and February

		November—Six Groups		February—Five Groups	
Grade	*Primary Language*	*ELP Levels*	*DRA Levels*	*Change in Group*	*DRA Levels*
1	Jonathon (Spanish)	(B)	Level 2		
				Jonathon (EI)	Level 8
1	Kailey (Spanish)	(I)	Level 4		Level 8
1	Lisa (Korean)	(EA)	Level 4		Level 8
1	Janty (Lithuanian)	(A)	Level 4		Level 8
1	Barbara (English)	(A)	Level 4		
				Barbara	Level 14
1	Alexa (Spanish)	(I)	Level 10		Level 14
1	Brian (English)	(A)	Level 10		Level 14
1	Kameron (Vietnamese)	(I)	Level 10		Level 14
1	Jazmine (Spanish)	(A)	Level 10		
				Jazmine	Level 18
2	Mayra (Spanish)	(I)	Level 14		Level 18
2	Sunday (Spanish)	(I)	Level 14		Level 18
2	Diego (Spanish)	(EI)	Level 14	Diego (I)	Level 18
2	Pauline (Spanish)	(EA)	Level 14		
				Pauline	Level 20
2	Katrina (Spanish)	(EA)	Level 18		Level 20
2	Joseph (Korean)	(EA)	Level 18		Level 20
2	Darlene (English)	(A)	Level 18		
				Darlene	Level 24
2	Sara (English)	(A)	Level 22		Level 24
2	Tim (English)	(A)	Level 22		Level 24

Notes: *Primary languages and English language proficiency levels are shown in parentheses. English language proficiency levels that did not change between November and February are not shown.*

Levels are DRA. In November first-graders are at levels 2, 4, and 10, and second-graders are at levels 14, 18, and 22. In February first-graders are at levels 8 and 14 except Jazmine at level 18, and second graders are at levels 18, 20, and 24.

and there wouldn't be time to fit in three instruction groups per day.) In February, the level 24 group met with the teacher only once per week, and the level 8 group met with her three times per week. The number of meetings per week for the groups could vary, but at the time the teacher felt the level 8 group needed more help. She also wanted to keep extra attention on Jonathon. The level 24 group was reading a chapter book during guided reading and meeting two or three times per week on their own while she was engaged with other guided reading groups.

What were the rest of the children doing while the teacher worked with guided reading groups? They were reading independently—out of buckets of leveled books they had read before with the teacher and out of their individual independent reading book boxes. Some were working on reading response sheets while others, like the level 24 group, were meeting in literature circles.

Upper Grades

One of the challenges of managing guided reading groups with early fluent and fluent readers is that the range of strategy use and language development seems to broaden. In one classroom there could be twenty different reading groups if one were actually able ever to plan for that many. To meet such varied needs, planning has to be done almost daily. The teacher in such a classroom needs to group carefully to help children in their individual development. Groups need to be flexible because children need to develop many different higher-level strategies but not all at the same time. An observant teacher knows how to plan for the full range of children in the class. For example, there might be three or four children who aren't necessarily reading at the same levels, but close enough to group them because they all need help summarizing.

Teachers often group for reading levels rather than strategies, and this is understandable if they have students at many language levels as well as reading levels. Some classrooms today have constant streams of new children coming in, often with no English and low literacy levels. Some schools have hired resource teachers through Title I to help at their schools, especially in the upper grades, where classes are larger and the range of reading levels is wider.

One classroom I worked in, in an inner-city school in San Diego, had thirty fourth-graders, all Spanish-speaking English language learners, with the support of a resource teacher. Even so, scheduling guided reading groups was challenging. The children's English language levels ranged from early intermediate to advanced. All the children were reading below grade level, although only two were reading way below (end of first grade, beginning of

second). The rest were at different reading levels that correlated to the middle of second grade to the end of third.

The teacher had grouped the children into six different guided reading groups. She met with two per day, and the resource teacher met with two other groups three days per week (see Table 9.3). Schools with resource teachers or literacy coaches are able to use these extra teachers effectively to help with ongoing instruction. Many teachers are not so lucky, however; their schools do not have extra support staff. They have to teach all the guided reading groups themselves. The children will then not have the opportunity to read in a guided reading group as often, because one teacher can still only meet with two groups per day. It is possible to teach a third group in a shortened lesson, only ten or fifteen minutes. But at the early fluent and fluent reading stages, a successful guided reading lesson takes about thirty minutes. The children learn much more in a longer lesson, where they can go into depth with higher-level strategies and deeper discussion, which helps ELLs develop cognitive thinking skills and academic language (Saunders and Goldenberg 1999).

The teacher met with the lowest group, level 18, every day (see Table 9.3). She felt they needed more support because they were reading the farthest behind grade level. The level 24 group met four times per week, with the help of the resource teacher, because it also was very far behind. The groups at levels 28, 30, and 34 each met twice per week, with either the teacher or the resource teacher, and the level 38 group met only once per week. The individual reading levels of the children in a group were all close to the group level.

This grouping based on reading level was pretty much set for weeks at a time, although some children did move in and out of groups. But because the classroom teacher had a resource teacher coming in to help, there wasn't as much flexibility because they both planned for their own groups. Except for the level 24 group, which they shared, they planned separately. Ideally, they talked daily, but this wasn't always possible. They did switch groups after a period of time so that the classroom teacher could work with all her students. Each teacher also took observations and notes on the children, which they shared as they had time.

TABLE 9.3A Guided Reading Groups Schedule—Teacher and Resource Teacher

Monday	Tuesday	Wednesday	Thursday	Friday
Teacher				
Level 18	Level 18	Level 18	Level 18	Level 18
Level 34	Level 30	Level 34	Level 30	Level 24
Resource Teacher				
Level 24	Level 24	Level 24		
Level 28	Level 38	Level 28		

Note: *Levels are DRA.*

TABLE 9.3B Guided Reading Groups—Teacher and Resource Teacher

Level 18	Level 24	Level 28	Level 30	Level 34	Level 38
Alberto (EI)	Jesse (I)	Liliana (I)	Angela (A)	Joseph (I)	Angel H. (EA)
Veronica (EI)	Diana (I)	Angel Z. (I)	Nidia (I)	Yaneli (I)	Vicky (I)
	Denise (EI)	Esmeralda (EI)	Kevin (I)	Oscar (EA)	Rubyette (A)
	Eric (EI)	Yuridia (I)	Laura (I)	Eduardo (I)	Melissa (I)
	Isabel (I)		Lizbeth (I)	Jazmin (I)	John (EA)
			Cristian (I)		Cecilia (EA)
			Jessica (EA)		Juan (I)

Notes: *Levels are DRA. The primary language of all children in this fourth-grade class is Spanish. English language proficiency levels are shown in parentheses.*

Table 9.4 shows how I would group the children in this class for guided reading if there were no resource teacher. After meeting with the classroom teacher, I helped her develop a plan in case she lost the assistance of the resource teacher. Without a resource teacher to help, she would not be able to see the groups as often as she would like and still have time for a balanced literacy program. There are five groups, and here, too, they would not meet for equal amounts of time with the teacher. The lower two groups, at levels 18–24 and 24–28, would meet more frequently—three times per week. The higher groups would meet only once or twice per week, each getting a turn at meeting once or meeting twice over a three-week rotation.

In regrouping from six to five groups, I would combine children with a wider range of reading levels in order to meet their language needs which often affected their strategy use. Attention to their English language levels within their reading levels can be seen in the table especially for the two

groups at levels 30–38. The children in the 30–38[A] group, at the intermediate language level, needed to work on analyzing text and understanding the author's intent. Their lower language level sometimes impeded their ability to catch text subtleties and infer underlying meaning, so they needed to focus on learning in context the meaning of complex phrases and words with multiple meanings. The children in the 30–38[B] group, mostly at the early advanced language level, needed help synthesizing information from various sources or parts of the text to gain meaning. There is an intermediate speaker in the group that has the same strategy needs even though her language is lower.

I would also pull children out of these groups periodically into groups studying other specific strategies, for instance, summarizing. So, the groups would be flexible. My notes from guided reading lessons, individual conferences, and shared reading help me make informed decisions on which children need to be called out for different pur-

TABLE 9.4A Guided Reading Groups Schedule—Teacher Only

Monday	Tuesday	Wednesday	Thursday	Friday
Levels 18–24	Levels 18–24	Levels 24–28	Levels 18–24	Levels 24–28
Levels 30–38[A]	Levels 24–28	Levels 30–38 [B]	Levels 28–30	Levels 28–30

Note: *Levels are DRA.*

TABLE 9.4B Guided Reading Groups—Teacher Only

Levels 18–24	Levels 24–28	Levels 28–30	Levels 30–38[A]	Levels 30–38[B]
Alberto (EI)	Jesse (I)	Yuridia (I)	Cristian (I)	Angela (A)
Veronica (EI)	Diana (I)	Nidia (I)	Joseph (I)	Angel H. (EA)
Denise (EI)	Isabel (I)	Kevin (I)	Juan (I)	Oscar (EA)
Eric (EI)	Liliana (I)	Laura (I)	Eduardo (I)	Rubyette (A)
	Angel Z. (I)	Lizbeth (I)	Jazmin (I)	Jessica (EA)
	Esmeralda (EI)		Melissa (I)	Yaneli (I)
			Vicky (I)	Cecilia (EA)
				John (EA)

Notes: *Levels are DRA. The primary language of all children in this fourth-grade class is Spanish. English language proficiency levels are shown in parentheses.*

poses. The students learn to expect being called out for groups with different children at different times. I set out a plan for the week, but children are often switched during that week if there is a need to do so. Flexibility is the key, and record keeping of whom the teacher has worked with, and for what purpose, is essential. Usually, though, in the upper grades there are so many children in a class that it is easier to get to know them and plan for their needs if they can be kept in the same groups for at least two weeks.

10

GUIDED READING *with* EMERGENT READERS

A Room for Three

When my sister, a friend, and I traveled in Spain one summer, I acted as translator for everything from ordering meals and reserving rooms to answering anyone who spoke to us in Spanish. I had spent a semester studying in Valencia and was pretty fluent in that language. But as we traveled on to France, I prepared to cede my translator's role to our friend, who had studied French for a year in the United States. As we reached our first small French hotel, our friend froze and was unable to speak to the innkeeper. I took her French-English dictionary and, feeling quite proud of myself, read out a line from the "short guide for tourists": "I want a room for three." The innkeeper gave me a horrified look. Then I kept reading, "With a bathroom, please." He stared at me blankly. "With a window, please." Assailed by my atrocious accent, he suppressed a laugh and asked, "Do you want one room or three?" Surprisingly, I understood him, so why didn't he understand me!? I read the line from the book again, "I want one room for three," but just to be on the safe side I raised a finger in the air to indicate one. Somehow, through great forbearance on his part, we managed to get a key. And for some reason the incident did not destroy our confidence in our ability to "read" our way through France communicating our basic needs.

This anecdote points up that language levels and reading levels don't necessarily correlate. I could "read" anything, but I sure couldn't speak French. As mentioned earlier, an English language learner who is a beginning English speaker may be capable of using better reading strategies than a child who is speaking at a more advanced level. It is essential to assess both the language level and the reading level of each student in order to plan for instruction to meet individual needs.

If a child has already learned to read in the primary language, it is much easier to teach him to read in English because the concepts and the reading strategies will transfer. But most ELLs are learning to read at the same time they are learning to speak English, so the job for the students and the teacher is harder. That doesn't mean it can't be done. We just have to look very closely at a child's literacy and language development and spend extra time developing both. How we build on the language patterns and reading strategies that students are (or are not) using has great impact on their success. This chapter provides sample guided reading lessons with ELLs who are, and who are not, receiving instruction in the primary language. It also considers book selection for guided reading.

GUIDING QUESTIONS

What does an emergent guided reading lesson look like?

What are the reading strategies that emergent readers use and do they correlate to their language level?

How can we really decide a child's reading level if her language is just beginning?

When are English language learners ready for guided reading?

Are some students early or early fluent readers in their primary language and yet not even emergent readers in English?

The next page shows the format of a guided reading lesson for both emergent and early readers. The lesson is, of course, preceded by planning and followed by evaluation with running records taken on children. A guided reading lesson for emergent and early readers takes about fifteen to twenty minutes, and usually there are about four children in the group.

Session is fifteen to twenty minutes with four readers in the group

Introduction. Teacher leads students in a discussion about the book by looking at the cover and by drawing on each child's personal experiences and background. Vocabulary that they will need to know in the book is introduced through the discussion by tapping into their prior knowledge.

Guide Students Through an Orientation. Teacher orients students through the first viewing of the text from the title page on, guiding them to use all of their cueing systems. She asks students to look at the pictures, find words in the text, predict what might be happening, and ask leading questions that are carefully formed to solicit the vocabulary that they need to be successful at reading each page on their own.

Students Read the Text by Themselves. After teacher guides students through the text the first time, she asks them to close the book and go back to the beginning to read it now by themselves. Students read the book individually, out loud, so that the teacher can see and hear what strategies the students are using as they read the text by themselves. Teacher may decide to sit in closer to one or two students during the reading in order to help individual students with specific questions to have them help themselves. Teacher may also observe the group and take notes on individual readers.

Discussion. After students' individual reading of the text, teacher leads them in a brief discussion of their personal reactions to the text. Individual responses and interpretations of the text are essential. This brief discussion gets students thinking about their own responses that they may like to pursue later. It is also a time to share strategies that they used to help themselves.

Students Reread the Text. Often there is time within the guided reading session to have students turn to a partner and reread the text one-on-one. If there is no more time available, students can take the text back with them and read to each other in their independent reading time. They can learn a lot by listening to each other read, by helping each other, and by sharing the text.

Students Respond to the Text. There are numerous responses that students can make to a text. Often a short discussion led by the teacher will motivate students to come up with their own written, oral, or artistic response to a text. Still, the best response to a book is to read it again. This response should not only be accepted, but should also be validated as perhaps the only response a student wants to make to that particular text.

GUIDED READING LESSON WITH EMERGENT READERS RECEIVING INSTRUCTION IN ENGLISH ONLY

In order to use guided reading effectively with emergent readers, I believe, ELLs need to have at least early intermediate language proficiency, which means that they should be responding with more than one or two words or yes/no as beginning English speakers do. (Because of strong picture support, though, some beginning speakers with strong reading strategies are able to do fine.

Also, books at Reading Recovery (RR) levels 1–4 are very helpful for building beginning speakers' vocabulary and basic sentence structure during language development time and small shared reading group instruction.)

Laura, Bryon, and Cristofer were all emergent readers and early intermediate speakers at the end of kindergarten. They were participating in a summer school program in Costa Mesa for English language learners which doubled as a literacy institute for teachers. They had been in school since the beginning of the year but, unlike many of their peers, were just beginning to show signs of what emergent readers can do. They were native Spanish speakers with no primary language support at school, and their families were not literate in the primary language. They had no models to read to them at home. Their classroom teacher during the institute noted that they seemed to need extra support in book-handling skills and developing their knowledge of sound-symbol relationships. They had had extensive work in shared reading and in following along with little books in the listening center, but the teacher wasn't sure if they had much experience with guided reading. She wasn't sure if they could do it, so she asked me to do a demonstration lesson with them, and invited other primary teachers in to watch.

We chose *Green Footprints,* an intervention level 6 book for strong emergent readers (see Table 9.1). It uses prepositional phrases, which is a skill beginning speakers master, and the pictures match the text, so we thought it would be supportive. There are two lines of text, however, with four lines on the last page, so we thought it would provide enough challenge for them.

Introduction

The introduction is a very important part of the guided reading lesson for emergent readers. This is the time when the teacher sets the scene for what the children are going to discover in the text, taps into their prior knowledge, and gets them thinking what the book could be about. Eliciting from the children in a natural way the same language that they will find in the text is also an important goal when working with English language learners. Instead of front-loading them with words all at once, the teacher draws attention to pertinent vocabulary through careful questioning, designed to have the children come up with the words themselves.

I began with a question regarding a prior book they had read.

Did you like the story "Who Sank the Boat?"
Yes.
Bryon: I like the mouse.
I liked him, too.

Then, looking at the cover picture, we speculated what the new book might be about. I did not tell

Written by Connie Kehoe • Illustrated by Terry Denton

Cover of *Green Footprints.*

them the title. I tried my best not to say "footprints" before they did. I wanted to see what language they could come up with by themselves.

Today we're going to read a new story, but before we do, let's look at the cover. What do you see in the picture? What is all over the floor?

I pointed at the floor shown on the cover of my book, and they looked at their own book covers. I accepted their responses, whether in English or Spanish, whether grammatically correct or not, and modeled new vocabulary in complete sentences.

Bryon: Feet marks.
Yes, those are called footprints.
Laura: Huellas.
Yes, they are "huellas" [Spanish for footprints]. Your feet make prints or "huellas" when you walk. Have you ever seen your own footprints in the sand when you were at the beach?
Bryon: Yes.

Q *What if I don't speak the child's primary language?*

Even if we don't speak the children's primary language, we can still encourage and accept any response in any language, especially if we see that the child knows the concept. Usually there is a child in the group who can translate what another child has said in the primary language. Bryon and Laura knew what footprints were; they just didn't have the correct English word.

Where do you think these footprints go?
Laura: On the floor.
Yes, these footprints are on the floor, going across the floor.

I walked my fingers across the cover, over to the kids, and up their arms, to show how something might go across. I try to use total physical response when needed to increase comprehension.

Who do you think would make these footprints? Maybe a mouse?
Bryon: A cat.
Cristofer: A dog.
Good. What else might make them?
Bryon: Maybe a rabbit.
Yes, maybe a rabbit. What color are these footprints?
Laura: Green.
Can you find the word "green" on the cover? [All pointed to the word.] *What else do you see? Let's cover up part of the word to see "foot." Can you find "foot"?*

They all placed their fingers over the word prints *on the covers of their books to leave* foot *uncovered.*

Good. What does that say?
Foot.
Now take your fingers off the other part of the word. What does that say? [No answer] *Can you say "prints"?*
Prints.
Good. Now look at "foot" and "prints" together. Can you slide your finger over the word and read "footprints"?

They all read it. Then I threw in a quick aside that footprints *is a compound word. I did this only because others in the class were examining compound words, and I wanted to show these children that they had found one.*

Bryon: Green footprints.
Yes, that is the title of the book—"Green Footprints." Are footprints usually green?

No.
How would you get them to be green?
Laura: The grass.
Bryon: Maybe the grass.

Q *Why don't you just tell them the title and tell them what the book is about?*

I accept and confirm students' contributions, but I don't tell them the title or what the book is about because I want them to discover for themselves, to make their own meaning. Just as a fluent reader would read the book independently, I am training them to figure out for themselves what they need to do to read a text. I am also setting a purpose for their reading. Rather than telling them how footprints would get to be green, I want to tap into their prior knowledge and get them to think. The picture on the title page gives much more information about how the footprints got to be green. I hope that, using picture clues and their collective language, the students will help themselves to figure out the story on their own.

Before moving on to the orientation, we read the author's and illustrator's names, Connie Kehoe and Terry Denton—difficult even for me; if they were simpler, more common names, I might ask the students to attempt them on their own.

Orientation

Once we turn to the title page, the orientation of the text begins. This is the time students walk through the text with the teacher, making predictions as they look at the pictures, touching words as they confirm their predictions. The orientation tends to be longer for ELLs because the group really needs to discuss what is happening in the pictures, and the teacher needs to make sure the students know and understand the vocabulary in the book. The teacher also reminds them of reading strategies they will need to use to be successful in reading the text.

Now I wanted to see if they had the vocabulary to predict how the footprints got green and where the footprints would go.

Where are these footprints that you see in the picture? Are they at the beach?
Laura: The kitchen.
How can you tell they are in the kitchen?
Laura: The floor.
Yes, those tiles look like they may be part of a kitchen floor. What else do you see in the kitchen?
Bryon: Maybe a sink.
Yes, maybe a sink. Here it is. Now, turn to the title page. What do you see? [Title page shows a pot of green paint, brushes, and a child's painting with some green footprints going over it.]
Bryon: Paint.
You're right. There is paint. Where does it come from?
Bryon: A boy painting.
Could be a boy. What do you think was his favorite color?
Green.
Maybe a boy painted and went away. Then what do you think happened?

I was surprised that none of the children responded. I knew they could make the connection, but I thought perhaps my question had been too difficult or that I had phrased it wrong. So I decided to let the pictures make the connection for them.

Let's go back to the cover.

As soon as we turned back to the cover, the connection was made.

Laura: Went in the paint.
Who went in the paint?
Bryon: Cat or dog in the paint.
Good. Let's turn to page 2. What do you see in the picture? [Child's painting, footprints going over it and under the bed]
Cristofer: Footprints.
Yes. Let's find the word "footprints" again. [All point to the word in their own books.] *Where did the footprints go?*
Bryon: The bed.
Yes, they went under the bed. Can you find the word "under" on the page? [All point to the word.]

On page 3, Cristofer pointed and said, "Boy."

Yes, it does look like a boy. What is it?

Cristofer didn't answer, but Laura did.

Doll.
Do you have a doll, Laura?

Green footprints
under the bed.

2

Green footprints
across the doll's head.

3

Wall chart about character and events in *Green Footprints*.

Laura: Yes.
Can you find the word "doll"? [All point to the word.]
Laura: Face.

At this time, I was hoping to use their language as well as their literacy skills to help them as we moved through the text. I wanted them not only to look at the pictures but also to find the words on each page and touch them in order to read them. If they didn't already have the vocabulary, they were learning it in context with the help of the pictures and my guided questions, and matching the oral language to the written words.

Q *Do you give them the vocabulary if they don't have it?*

If individual students in the group don't know the vocabulary, I prefer them to hear it from each other, not just from me. For instance, Cristofer had described the doll as "boy," using a word in his known vocabulary that he felt fit (to his credit, it did look like a boy doll). But he learned a new word, *doll*, when Laura said it, and he was then able to find the new word in the text. Children should naturally learn from each other in a group, especially during the orientation discussion. After the orientation, they are on their own to try out strategies and new language.

The students seemed engaged in the text and were excited to read on to figure out what would happen and where the footprints would go. Laura continued the interaction.

Face. That makes sense. The footprints could be on the doll's face. But what letter does "face" start with?
Laura: F.
What letter do you see here [in the word head]?
Laura: H.
What sound does that make?
Bryon: Ha.
Good. So what word could it be?
Laura: Head.

Q *When do you have them use their knowledge of phonics in the orientation?*

Emergent readers and early intermediate speakers need to check to see if the language they use is the same language the author has chosen for the book. A word they say might make sense in the context of the pictures but not match the word in the written text. They need to use their knowledge of sound-symbol relationship to help them check and confirm their predictions. In this lesson, I modeled how the students could use their knowledge of phonics—*face, head*—to help themselves while reading by checking their predictions.

When we got to the last page of the book during the orientation, I asked what had made all those green footprints. "A cat," they all said. "That's right," I said. "Bryon, you knew that all along, didn't you?" I confirmed his prediction, and he smiled, proud in front of his peers. All of them were pleased that they had figured out who had made those footprints. I then asked if they would like to read the book by themselves. "Yes," they all shouted.

Q *What about comprehension for emergent readers?*

While using the strategies of checking, predicting, looking at the pictures, and noticing sound-symbol relations, comprehension should always be the main goal. If the children don't understand the main point of the story—that an animal had tracked paint all over the house—then there is no point in continuing to read. It is through the discussion, the guiding questions that we ask, that we can check the children's understanding. Often it is hard to tell, with children who are just speaking in short phrases, whether they understand. But we must be patient and confident that we can help the children gain meaning and figure out the text on their own.

Student Reading

If the orientation was effective, and if the book was chosen appropriately, the children should be able to read the book on their own. My task now is to observe and instruct if necessary.

I ask the children to spread out on the floor so that each has space to read aloud individually and so that I can move over to sit next to any one of them to listen in and help if needed. I then pick up my own copy of the book and begin to read silently. This signals that everyone reads on their own. As the children read aloud, I take mental notes on their strategy use and language levels, trying to decipher if they need more help in language or reading development. After the lesson, I write the notes down on anecdotal record sheets (Appendix F3) and checklists (Appendix A).

I want the children to feel comfortable as readers, to have the opportunity to read by themselves yet still within the safety of a small group and knowing they have teacher support. My goal is for each child to ignore the others and get lost in his own reading. Early intermediate speakers are often reluctant to read aloud.

Q *What do you do if kids start to choral read?*

Sometimes they start chiming in with each other, which can become (undesirable) choral reading. I usually start reading aloud—cover and title page—and pause at the author and illustrator names so that some readers move on ahead of me and others wait. Then I stop reading and move close to one child, encouraging others to read on their own. This usually works for me to stop any choral reading. If at any time choral reading does pick up again, I move next to a different reader to break it up. If that doesn't work, I let it go. It might mean that these ELLs need much more support and confidence to read on their own and that their peers help them gain that confidence.

Some educators (e.g., Hornsby 2000) encourage silent reading during a guided reading lesson. I find, however, that I can help English language learners who might be emergent and early readers more effectively when I hear how they are reading because they are also learning the language. I often move quickly over to a child who I hear is making the same mistake over and over again on every page. A timely suggestion can help her read the word or sentence correctly; then she can put that new learning into practice immediately. When students read aloud, I feel better able to manage the group and to move promptly to where I am needed. With more advanced speakers and fluent readers, silent reading during guided reading time is appropriate, but I still make time to move close to individual children while they read so that I can listen to them and monitor how they are doing.

When the children started reading, I moved closer to Bryon first. He was tracking the lines and reading fine. Then he got stuck on *stopped*. I prompted him.

What did the animal do?
Stepping.
Yes, he could be stepping. "Green footprints stepping for a drink." Does that make sense? Do you see the animal stepping right now for a drink?
No.
What did the animal have to do to get a drink?
St . . . stop.
Yes. Look at the whole word. [Together we read stopped.] Now read it again. Does that make sense?
Yes.
Good. The animal already stopped and took a drink. Where do you think the animal goes now? Why don't you read on to find out.

I was aware that because of his early intermediate language level, Bryon did not have the past tense yet and naturally used a word in the present progressive tense that was visually close to the word in the text. He was able to read the correct word with me, though, and then to repeat it himself. I gently suggested that because the animal was not in the picture, the scene was not taking place now but had already happened.

Cristofer had the same problem with *stopped*. He at least used the correct word, just the wrong tense. With a reminder to look at the picture and to check the letters, using graphophonics, he was able to correct himself.

You said "stopping." Does that make sense? Is the animal still there?
No.
So it has already happened. Do you see "-ing" at the end of the word? [Cristofer looked at stopped and pointed to the ending.]
No.
So, what does it say? The animal already . . . there.
Stopped.
Good. Now, can you reread that line? Don't forget to look closely at the words to check yourself.

Is the children's language level appropriate for this text?

Both Bryon and Cristofer reread the line "stopped for a drink" fine, and Laura read it on her own. Sometimes, if a child is not ready to talk in the past tense, it is difficult for him even to repeat the word. If this is the case, then focusing on the word won't help the child, and choosing a different book at the same level, or a book at a lower level, would be appropriate. All three children in this group, however, were able to focus on the word and read it, even though they were early intermediate speakers and speaking in the present and present progressive tenses. Reading the past tense might have been a stretch for them given their language ability, but they rose to the challenge and showed that they were on their way to becoming intermediate speakers.

Guided reading is a time to challenge children to try out new strategies and language patterns. But if the text is too difficult, it is appropriate to choose a different one. It is a matter of judgment. I always try to err on the side of challenging rather than easy in order to expose ELLs to as many words and language patterns as they can handle because they are often behind their grade-level peers.

While Bryon and Laura finished, I noticed Cristofer didn't seem to be progressing. I turned to Bryon and said, "Can you and Laura be partners and read the book again together? Cristofer and I can be partners." Then I said to Laura, "Is that okay? Why don't you read it first and Bryon can help you if you need it" and to Bryon, "But don't tell her the word; try to see what she can do to figure out the word by herself."

Encouraging faster readers to read the story again creates more time to listen to and guide slower readers, who may not be struggling but often just need more time to work through the text. Also, it suggests indirectly that a faster reader isn't necessarily a better reader. Pairing up students to reread the text gives them a chance to practice it again. Since emergent texts are only about eight pages long, this doesn't take much time. And the benefit of keeping the group together rather than letting faster readers go back to their seats is that when everyone finishes, all can discuss the text together.

While Laura and Bryon were rereading the book, I turned my attention to Cristofer, who seemed to be waiting for me to read with him, not having the confidence to continue reading himself. With some minor support, he finished reading the rest of the book while I listened. The last page shows a girl with green footprints on her clothes holding a cat with green-covered paws. "Where are the footprints on the girl?" I asked Cristofer. "On her shirt, on her pants." "Would you like that?" I asked. "No!" he said, and laughed. Cristofer did a fine job reading that text, even though he had been so hesitant to start reading on his own. It occurred to me that he had few opportunities to have an adult sit next to him and listen to him read. He needed more confidence, and more guidance and prompting while he was becoming an independent reader. By moving to sit next to different children during guided reading, the teacher can give the necessary push at the right times.

Discussion

As each child finishes reading the text, I ask a quick question to elicit a response to the book, to establish a connection, thus hopefully predisposing the child, even if he is a reluctant speaker, to take part in the group discussion. My primary goal is to encourage children's love of reading, and I try to keep their interest by asking them for their reactions to the text, not by drilling them on what it is about. Hopefully they will all want to read it again. During the group discussion, after children have shared what they liked about the book or what their favorite parts were, the teacher can reach deeper, asking, for instance, about inferences they may have gathered or what strategies they used to help themselves while reading.

Why is the discussion so important after the reading?

The discussion that follows the students' first independent reading of a book is critical for deepening their understanding of the text and for assessing their comprehension and language level. We can note their higher-level thinking skills and which strategies they need to help them improve comprehension. Can they infer, evaluate, analyze, make connections? These small books for emergent readers do not have in-depth plot structures, but there is usually a funny twist or joke at the end that could be analyzed. It is important to have the children reflect on what they read, so that they can learn this is what expert readers do.

How many of you liked this story? [All raised their hands, with big grins on their faces.] *What was your favorite page?*
Laura: On baby doll's head. [She pointed to the picture.]

I decided on the spot to write this down because I felt that emphasizing the language pattern would enhance the children's learning. They could look at this chart of prepositional phrases later as a reference for writing their own sentences. When we become aware, through responses in the discussion, that the children would benefit from certain language being written down, we should do it. But I don't as a rule take the time to chart students' responses during the short guided reading lessons for emergent readers because that is not the purpose of the lessons and there often is not enough time.

Let me write down what Laura said. I'll use the green pen. Why do you like this page, Laura?
It is face.

I remembered that when she had first read the page, she had said *face*, then changed her response with my guidance. *Face* seemed to be firmly in her vocabulary, so I validated her response but reminded her of the strategy she had used to read the actual word on the page, *head*.

Yes, that is the face. I liked the way you looked at the beginning letter to figure out that it said "head." That was a good strategy. This was my favorite page, too, because I thought of my daughters, who love dolls.

Green Footprints . . .
under the bed   across the floor
on baby doll's head out of the door
in the sink   up the tree

Chart of prepositions from *Green Footprints*.

Bryon: Out of the door and up the tree. [I wrote this down.]
Why did you like it? Why was it your favorite page?
Bryon: The cat go out of the door and up.
Cristofer: In the sink. [I wrote this down.]
Yes, he stepped in the sink. Why did you like this page?
Cristofer: He step in sink.

Bryon and Cristofer were only giving me short phrases of what they saw in the pictures, not sharing why they liked them. Were they able to? I wondered. Or maybe they're just not used to being asked for their reasons for choosing something.

Would you like to have your cat step in the sink while you are washing the dishes?
Cristofer [laughing]: No!

Follow-up

The best follow-up could be just rereading the text through buddy reading or independent reading, especially because ELLs need practice reading for fluency. If they haven't had time within the lesson for buddy or partner reading, this is a very good follow-up. They could also write their responses to the book in their reading response journals. For emergent readers, that usually means drawing a picture about their favorite page and perhaps writing a short sentence about it.

Often, a good follow-up for emergent readers is to have the children write variations on the repetitive pattern of the text by changing a word or two. This is very helpful for ELLs to practice correct sentence structure and build vocabulary.

In this follow-up, I asked, "If you were going to write another place that the footprints go, where would that be?" and "Would you like to use green footprints or another color?" We reread the prepositional phrases on the chart, and I underlined the prepositions. Laura chose *red* and *on the chair*. With a red pen, I wrote *on the chair* directly on her paper and said, "Okay, you can take this paper and draw red footprints on the chair." Bryon chose *brown* and *out the window*. Cristofer took a little longer to decide:

Orange.

Are your footprints going to go on, out, up, or in?

In.

Okay, where will they go?

The sink.

That was already in the book. Where else could they go? In the bathtub? In the trash can?

In the trash can.

I would not always assign a written follow-up to guided reading, however, because during that time we really want the children to be reading, and we don't want them to think that reading always comes with an assigned task.

Q *Do you do word work in your guided reading lesson?*

Sometimes during a guided reading lesson it becomes evident that certain children need more help with word recognition or a particular language pattern or reading strategy. Some teachers do "word work" during or at the end of a guided reading lesson. If I can naturally fit in five minutes to focus on vocabulary or a language pattern, I do that (as I did with compound words during the introduction of *Green Footprints*). But I prefer to give such particular instruction in mini-lessons outside of guided reading, to children from the class who need it, or even to the whole class in shared reading or writing workshop. The chart of prepositional phrases from this guided reading lesson went up on the wall and became a class resource. Children kept track of prepositional phrases they read in books and recorded them on the same chart during the week. Phrases that they created on their own were also added to the chart and used in writing.

ELLs need as much time as possible to process, discuss, and relate to the text they are reading in guided reading. There often isn't enough time in these short lessons to work on isolated "word work" or language patterns as well.

Evaluation

After each lesson it is important to evaluate the children's use of reading strategies, whether the book was appropriate for them, and what mini-les-

sons should be planned to support their language and literacy development. At first it might seem that these early intermediate students didn't produce enough speech to evaluate them; higher-level speakers would be able to explain better what they are thinking or what they know. But we can still observe the reading strategies the children used.

The teachers that were observing the lesson and I evaluated the children's reading and language use together. As a group we decided that these children were using reading strategies appropriate to emergent readers: they were tracking, finding words they knew in the text, using the pictures to gain meaning, using graphophonics to help themselves, and predicting what the text would be about (see emergent checklist in Appendix A5). They used vocabulary and language patterns that they heard in the orientation while reading the text on their own. Individually, Laura was the strongest reader and needed little help from me. She made one miscue, *face* for *head*, but corrected herself easily. Bryon seemed the most verbal, speaking almost in complete sentences, and he too read the book confidently. Cristofer, although hesitant and not confident as a speaker or reader, did fine when I was next to him. The problems with *stopped* were not surprising for early intermediate speakers with no mastery of the past tense, but both boys were able to read the word with guidance. Many teachers thought they were almost intermediate speakers (see developmental language checklist in Appendix A3).

I didn't bother to take a running record on these children. Once I had guided them, they were able to reread the book on their own with no miscues (and would be able to add it to their independent reading book boxes). For the purposes of guided reading, I felt, the book was too easy for them. The goal of guided reading is to challenge readers to read more difficult texts at their instructional level, ones they couldn't read on their own without guidance. If they are unable to read a book after receiving guidance, then we could judge it too challenging and pick an easier book.

We need to be careful not to underestimate early intermediate speakers' understanding just because their responses are short. We need to expect language outcomes to match their language level but still validate their successful reading of these emergent texts. If we have received no response, we might try rephrasing our questions using a different key word that they can latch onto for meaning. I once heard a teacher ask a beginning speaker and emergent reader, "How many children do you see in the picture?" She waited and waited, and there was no response. "Can you count them?" she asked. The student pointed to each child in the picture and counted them perfectly: "One, two, three, four—four!"

GUIDED READING LESSON WITH EMERGENT READERS RECEIVING INSTRUCTION IN ENGLISH AND SPANISH

If a child is speaking English at an early intermediate level and reading Spanish at an early fluent level, then at what level could she be expected to read effectively in English? Checking Tables 2.1 and 2.2, which list language patterns used at each developmental level of language proficiency, and Table 2.3, which shows reading strategies used at each developmental reading level, we can conclude that the child may be able to read a guided reading text at a strong early level. (As mentioned, beginning speakers are not really ready to benefit from guided reading lessons.)

Often there is a large discrepancy between perceived reading levels in Spanish and English because teachers have not looked carefully at students' strategy use and language level, and have underestimated the abilities of ELLs. We know that reading strategies transfer from the primary language to English. If a child has the necessary cross-checking strategies to be an early reader in Spanish, and a minimum of an early intermediate speaking proficiency, she is ready to be challenged in English reading. A fluent Spanish reader will have an even easier time transferring her strategies to use in English reading.

One summer I was working with a group of bilingual teachers in San Diego. I was asked to help with guided reading instruction for ELLs who had wide discrepancies in their Spanish and English reading levels. This group of four children had just finished first grade, and I was told they had a beginning or early intermediate language level and were reading Spanish at intervention level 18 and English

at intervention level 2–3 (an emergent level correlating with kindergarten; see Table 9.1). I doubted that these children would be that low in their language proficiency after two years of instruction in English language development, so perhaps they were newcomers, at a very beginning level of English speech, although I hadn't been told that. If their language proficiency really was that low, they would need more direct language instruction—new academic vocabulary, new sound-symbol connections—before starting to read in English. But if their language proficiency level was higher than the teachers thought, then what was the reason for the wide discrepancy in Spanish and English reading levels? Wouldn't reading strategies that an early fluent reader used in Spanish transfer to English?

Planning

The purpose I set for this demonstration guided reading lesson was for the teachers to accurately assess the children's English reading developmental levels as well as their English language proficiency levels. Were they transferring to English reading any of the higher-level strategies that they used as early fluent readers of Spanish? Based on their strategy use in English, what would be the correct level of guided reading text? I asked the teachers watching to help assess the children and provided them with a guided reading observation form (Appendix F3) to take notes on their strategy use and their language patterns.

To present a bit of a challenge (as I thought), I chose a level 4 text, *Fish Print*, which I wrote and photographed. Mayra, Alex, José, and Margarita each received their own copies of the book.

Introduction

The children had never met me before, so I introduced myself, pointing to my nametag and then to my name on the book cover. "Who wrote this?" I asked. They all looked at the cover, looked up at me with big smiles, and blurted out, "You."

"What grade are you going into?" I asked.

"Second grade," they all answered.

"So are my twin daughters. Do you know what twins are?"

"Two," said Margarita.

Cover of *Fish Print*.

"Yes, twins are two people born at the same time." I confirmed her answer and modeled a complete sentence. We looked at the cover picture again and I had them guess which two of the three girls in the photograph were mine. I shared that I had taken the picture when the girls were in kindergarten. They all seemed engaged and interested in the girls as well as in the book.

My introductory questions went first toward what they saw in the cover photograph. Besides the three girls, they noticed the fish right away. Mayra, Margarita, and José almost at once read "Fish Print." Well, that told me right away that they didn't need me to help them read the title. Normally, I would guide children to figure out the title with questions like, What is on the table? What are the girls holding? Can you find the words in the title? and How would you make a fish print? I rarely read the title outright because I want even emergent readers to see the importance of predicting what the book may be about by using the cover picture to help and then looking at the title to see if it matches the predictions.

Since I wanted to tap into the children's background knowledge and experiences, I tried to gain information about their experience with fish, with color words, with making a print, with painting, and so on. The discussion moved pretty slowly. I wasn't sure of their speaking ability because they weren't sharing a lot. Perhaps they were shy or nervous to have so many teachers watching them. I had to question and redirect often to get them to respond. José revealed some interest in the fish, so I pried further.

"Have you ever seen a fish? Have you ever caught a fish?" I thought I was setting him up for success by asking him questions that required only a yes/no answer.

"No," he responded, "but I went fishing. I touched one."

Wow, I thought. I wasn't as much interested in his fishing as in his full-sentence response, which is a language skill of intermediate speakers (see Table 2.1). None of the other children had seen a real fish or gone fishing, but they had all read *Rainbow Fish*, and Mayra and José said it was their favorite book. So they were making connections to their own experiences.

I also asked them what they would need to make a fish print. We looked at the title page, which shows a fish, brushes, and five cups with different-color paints. In an emergent text the title page is designed to help readers learn more about the story before they even start reading it. We need to capitalize on these picture clues and have children make predictions that will help them as they read the story. They noticed the paint and brushes, and they knew all the colors. Margarita said, "The fish has scales over its body." Another full sentence! Another intermediate speaker!

Orientation

During the orientation of the text, it became very clear that they didn't need me to help guide them through this book. Because of the strong picture support, they figured out the repetitive sentence pattern: *Paint the mouth orange. Paint the eye green* and so on. I did ask some questions to remind them to use the pictures and the text in unison: "Look at the picture to see what color she uses to paint the fish now. Can you find that color word in the text? What part of the fish does she paint now? Can you find that word in the text?"

Student Reading

I sat back and watched as they started reading the text aloud on their own. They didn't even look at me but went through the text very quickly. They were so good at checking their predictions and

Paint the tail pink.

Press the paper.

6

7

Two pages from *Fish Print*.

reading the text that they even adapted easily to the pattern change on page 7: *Press the paper*. Mayra first said, "Push the paper" and then reread the line correctly. She not only cross-checked by looking at the picture and the word but also self-corrected, both strategies that early readers use.

They had finished the book in less than a minute. I thought about having them read it again to see if there was anything else I could learn, but decided not to. There really would have been no point in it. The book was too easy for them. None of them made any miscues. Mayra self-corrected, but she was the only one who even needed to. As they read aloud, I could hear how effortlessly they did it. Because the book was so easy for them, it was hard for me to learn much about their language levels and what strategies they needed to work on.

Discussion

I hoped to learn more about their language levels during the discussion. "What was your favorite page," I asked. Most of them chose pages based on their favorite colors. I pressed further: "Why did you like that page?" but they could only say the color word. Then I thought, Is their language really as developed as I thought? Asking students why they like something is to push for more than language; it seeks to find out whether they are developing their thinking abilities and expanding meaning by having to explain their answer.

In response to my *why* question, José pointed at the "pink" page and said, "Because it looks like a rainbow." He related that to his favorite book, *The Rainbow Fish*. This demonstrated that he could make a connection to another book and explain his reason for choosing that color. He also showed strong sentence structure.

Margarita's response threw me for a moment. Pointing at the page that said *Paint the eye green,* she said, "I like plants." I rapidly tried to figure out why she would say that, then saw that the color on that page was green.

"Oh. Plants are green. Is green your favorite color?" I asked.

"Yes, I love green plants," she said.

Wow, I thought again. She had made a wonderful connection that I wouldn't have understood if I hadn't made the analogy and pried a little further. She showed a strong use of language that went beyond basic communication.

In response to my question about his favorite color, Alex said, "Blue," and when I asked why, he just looked at me. I waited a few seconds, then tried to think of something to help him express himself. I noticed that his shirt collar was blue. "Is blue your favorite color because your shirt has blue on it?" He continued to look at me blankly. I smiled and waited. Then he said, "I like blue because the sky is blue." What a stunning response!

"Yes, the sky is blue. I love to look at the blue sky," I said.

"I do, too," he said with a big smile.

This reminded me of the importance of giving children, especially English language learners, enough wait time to allow them to process. We need to make them feel comfortable, give them time to interact with us, and listen carefully to their responses. Often we are pleasantly surprised by how much our students know.

Follow-up

I asked the children what they would like to write about as a response to this book. Mayra and José chose to write about a rainbow fish, relating back to their favorite book. I asked them to write about the colors they would paint on their fish and perhaps to use those colors in an illustration. Alex said he would write about why he liked blue—the sky is blue. Margarita wanted to write about liking green plants. It is not surprising that they wanted to write about what they had shared in the group, because it was comfortable for them and they felt proud of what they had shared.

The best response is often just rereading the book, but in this case, since the book was too easy for them, that would not have been appropriate.

Evaluation

The lesson met the purpose I had set for it. It made the teachers think and reevaluate what they knew about these children. It clarified that these ELLs had higher levels of English language proficiency and made stronger use of reading strategies than had been thought. Their strong strategy use did indeed transfer from the primary language to English. They didn't need to track, they cross-checked using the pictures, they read high-frequency words and sentences with ease, and they used not only beginning letters but letter clusters to self-correct (*push/press*). They could speak in full sentences. They were at least intermediate speakers and at least early readers in English, probably almost early advanced and early fluent. Guided reading texts at intervention level 10 or 12 would be appropriate to start.

How did it happen that their language and reading levels had been misdiagnosed? One reason could be that the children displayed minimal lan-guage output, so the teachers assumed that their language level was low and compared that to a low reading level without also looking at reading strategies. Depending on the types of questions I asked, I got everything from blank stares to one-word responses to full sentences. Questioning techniques are critical in influencing the types of responses children give, especially if students are not yet comfortable with their surroundings.

We need to assess the language proficiency and reading development of individual ELLs closely and on an ongoing basis in order to place them correctly in English reading, and not assume that children reading fluently in the primary language have to start at very beginning levels of English reading. Knowing the skills and strategies that are used at each developmental stage of speaking and reading (see Tables 2.1–2.3 and Appendixes A3–A7), and comparing children's output with those, is essential.

Here, an emergent-level book, *Fish Print*, was inadvertently mismatched with children who turned out to be very strong early or early fluent readers. This can happen in classrooms, and often does. Then we just have to realize that we chose the wrong text and try to pick a more challenging one next time. Sometimes, if we are lucky, we might have two alternative books picked out and can use the more challenging one with the group right away. If not, we just have to say to the children they are such good readers that the book is too easy for them, and the next time we come together, they'll have a more challenging text to read.

CHOOSING TEXTS FOR EMERGENT READERS

Emergent-level texts have supports built into them to help readers, and a book can be evaluated according to how well it does this. (See text features form on next page.) The pictures and text must match exactly because emergent readers rely heavily on picture clues to gain meaning. In *Fish Print*, for example, only one color paint was shown on each page, and it matched the color word on that page. Also, on each page a child is shown painting the exact fish body part described by the word on that page: *mouth, eye,* and so on. The teacher then

Guided Reading—Text Features Form

Title I Wash

Author/Illustrator Mary Cappellini/Adrian Heke - photographer

Genre nonfiction   **Series** First Stories - Pacific Learning

Stage emergent   **Intervention Level** 2

Number of Running Words 35

Supports
Repetitive pattern - only one word change per page
Pictures match text
Large photograph of object/noun on each page

Challenges
The last page says "little" sister instead of "baby" sister. Most kids see the picture and say baby and then have to self-correct.

Interesting Features
Photographs of little girl and baby on last page are great. Cute ending.
Uses objects that are very common or familiar.

Sentence Structure
(including verb tense)

I wash my _____ .

Vocabulary and Theme
Child's play objects - duck, doll, dishes
Washing - dishes/hands and feet and face

High-Frequency Words

I, my, little

Phonics Features

l/y (my)   w/sh (wash)   f = face, feet   d = doll, duck

Punctuation

Period at end of every line.

Example of text evaluation.

guides students to notice the correspondence between picture and text, and to use them in unison to help themselves read (some children don't make this connection on their own). It is important to have emergent readers point to and touch a word that the teacher wants them to focus on. That way, when they are reading on their own, they will notice and remember the words that the teacher helped them locate.

Books for emergent readers should also have repetitive patterns and be predictable. Children should be able to use their background experiences to predict the ending of a very short book because the elements in the story are familiar to them. The best guided reading books at this level also have funny endings that turn on a play on words or the repetitive pattern. In *The Scarecrow,* for example, the scarecrow scared the pigs, the horses, and the sheep, but he didn't "scare the crows." Or, in *I Wash,* a girl washes a cup, a plate, "my hands," "my face," and finally, "my little sister." Both these books use vocabulary and life experiences that are familiar to most children. Even if readers have not seen a real scarecrow or lived on a farm, they have probably seen a picture of one and understand the concept "scare-crow," or "scare-birds" (Spanish, *espantapárajos*).

If the children understand the concept but lack the specific English vocabulary to read the book on their own, this would be okay unless it was the text on every page. If they knew none of the animal names in *The Scarecrow,* where these are the only words that change on each page, the book would not be appropriate. But perhaps it could be used in a small shared reading group to teach beginning speakers vocabulary (see next section). Or, in *Spots,* the children may know the Spanish word *corbata* but not its English translation, *tie*; then I would have them sound it out or just give them the English word. But if they also don't know *dress* and other items of clothing, they need to work on vocabulary for the clothes category before reading that book. Thematic planning (see Chapter 5) helps develop academic vocabulary and builds background knowledge. And if they know the basic vocabulary but have trouble with the sentence pattern *This dress has spots. This tie has spots* and so on, perhaps their language proficiency is too low to be successful with that book.

In choosing a book for guided reading, I am more concerned with the children's level of concept development—their understanding of what is happening in the story—than with their specific vocabulary. If they know the concepts and the vocabulary in the primary language, they can quickly learn the English equivalents. We shouldn't fear having children learn new words as they are reading the text. Guided reading books should stretch children to learn new vocabulary and try out new strategies.

USING EMERGENT-LEVEL BOOKS FOR BEGINNING SPEAKERS

Often I use emergent-level books with children who are beginning speakers, and who aren't really ready for a true guided reading lesson, for the sole purpose of developing their vocabulary. I call this a small-group shared reading lesson. I lead them on an extended walk through the text, and we just repeat the words that match the pictures. Many of these children might be newcomers and need the vocabulary development. Others might be young children who have never held books in their hands, and this helps them point to the pictures, turn the pages, and learn vocabulary along the way. I feel this is a much better way to integrate oral English language development with literacy instruction than just holding up pictures from magazines or picture files. While reading emergent texts with even just one word per page, children feel like readers. They learn about book-handling skills, the natural progression of story lines, and the rhythms of English language patterns while they are developing new vocabulary, including high-frequency words.

One example of an emergent text that has wonderful photographs and a strong natural language pattern is *Shells*. The pattern text on each page . . . *This is a snail shell. This is a turtle shell. This is a peanut shell.* . . . is printed under a photograph of the shell's exterior, and on the facing page are a photograph of the animal or plant in its natural setting and a smaller photograph of the inside of the shell (see next page). A table on the last page lists all the shells according to the category Plant or Animal. This book would fit well into a class thematic study of these topics.

This is a turtle shell.

Two pages from *Shells.*

When I worked with ELLs who were underperforming in the classroom, I led them in typical guided reading lessons using books at their instructional levels and in separate mini-lessons using emergent-level books to focus on set vocabulary or language patterns. I have also used the Spanish, Portuguese, or Cantonese versions of emergent-level books to teach vocabulary to English speakers who are studying those languages. A friend of mine, a parish priest who was trying to learn Spanish to address his Spanish-speaking parishioners, borrowed over a hundred of my Spanish guided reading texts at the emergent and early levels. He was an early intermediate speaker in Spanish and knew most of the vocabulary, but the books helped him develop his sentence structure.

A large selection of guided reading books is published every year. Because children need to read so many of these books during the year and have a wide range of developmental levels, I would advise buying whole series of such books, including multicultural ones (see Appendix F2). Buying series sets is economical, and it is not efficient to evaluate each title before buying it. Then the sets can be taken apart and placed by level in boxes in the classroom or in the school's book room. Each title should be evaluated for its supports and challenges before using it in a lesson because some titles in a series will be better than others (Appendix F1 provides a blank text evaluation form).

11

GUIDED READING *with* EARLY READERS

Miss Viola Swamp

One year, while I was teaching a bilingual Spanish-English third grade, I planned a surprise for the class on Halloween. I read to them Miss Nelson Is Missing, *about a sweet third-grade teacher whose students were behaving terribly. (I was hoping my class would see the parallels.) She decided to trick them, and she pretended she was sick so that she could come back as her own substitute, a mean witch named Miss Viola Swamp. So, on Halloween morning I came to school as Miss Viola Swamp. I dressed exactly as she did in the book. I wore a black curly wig and hat, striped knee socks, a black dress, and big black shoes. Just to make sure the children knew who I was, I pinned a big sign to my dress:* Miss Viola Swamp. *My entrance was superb. The librarian went in first, telling the class I was absent and that they were going to have a substitute. "Where is the substitute?" they asked in Spanish. "I'm sure she's coming," she said. Just then, I walked in the door and banged on the wall with a yardstick.*

"Sit down!" I yelled in English. "I'm Miss Viola Swamp."

There were shrieks of terror from a few children, some were in awe, some in disbelief, and some suspected it was me. But I wasn't prepared for the response from Salvador. He was traumatized. He retreated into the corner crying and refused to come out. When I went closer to him, he started screaming. I was speaking only in English, trying to keep up my disguise. The librarian came over and spoke Spanish to him and took him out of the classroom. She comforted him and then explained all about our customs here. Salvador had just arrived that week from his war-torn country, El Salvador. They don't celebrate Halloween there. She explained about Halloween. She told him that Miss Viola Swamp, the mean English-speaking witch, was really me, his Spanish-speaking teacher. He took a while to calm down, and it's no wonder. His father had lost his family members in the war. Also, everything was new to Salvador here. He had just started to warm up to me the day before, although he was still pretty silent in the classroom.

After some time he came back to the room and kept staring at me. I just winked at him and smiled, but I never gave up pretending I was Miss Viola Swamp, not even the next day when I came back dressed normally. Actually, I never told them. Students came back the following year and still asked if I was Miss Viola Swamp. But Salvador knew. It was our little secret. He still looked leery, though, and was glad I was back to normal the next day.

Many of our English language learners are recent immigrants from war-torn countries all over the globe. These children are not only dealing with personal tragedies but also trying to adjust to a new country, new customs, and a new language. In planning my Halloween surprise, I hadn't thought of what effect it might have on such children. I hadn't taken the time to provide them with enough background knowledge for them to be comfortable with one more new challenge that they had to adjust to.

ELLs often feel overwhelmed trying to adjust to a new culture and learning to read and speak English at the same time. It becomes a daunting and tiring task. New words come at them so quickly. They might know what individual words mean but can lose the meaning in a conversation or a story if they aren't given enough support to help make the learning comprehensible.

Early readers are starting to use many more reading strategies than they did as emergent readers. But they are also facing new challenges with longer texts and less picture support to sustain meaning. Teachers may feel that children lack the vocabulary necessary to read more difficult texts, and they tend to choose guided reading books at a lower, less challenging level because the vocabulary is easier. As I've mentioned, though, I lean toward challenging rather than easy. Lowering the reading level for children just because they are developing their vocabulary is not appropriate. Research has shown that significant gains in word knowledge can be made after just one exposure to an unknown word in context (Nagy, Herman, and Anderson 1985).

This chapter provides two sample guided reading lessons, one with upper-grade ELLs who are reading below grade level and receiving instruction in English only, and the other with ELLs who are receiving instruction in Spanish and English, and who are fluent readers in their primary language and early readers in English. I discuss the importance of miscue analysis and of analyzing the language patterns in a text. The chapter also considers guided reading book selection for early readers, including older ones.

GUIDING QUESTIONS

What are the reading strategies that early readers use, and do they correlate to their language level?

How much of the vocabulary of the book do they need to know in order to be successful in the guided reading lesson?

How is the early guided reading lesson different from an emergent guided reading lesson?

What can I do to monitor their comprehension during the guided reading lesson?

How can I have time to assess both their reading strategies and their language level?

When are they ready to read in English guided reading?

GUIDED READING LESSON WITH EARLY READERS RECEIVING INSTRUCTION IN ENGLISH ONLY

A guided reading lesson with early readers has a similar format to one with emergent readers: introduction, orientation, student reading, discussion, rereading, and follow-up (see Chapter 10). And the important observations of what the children are using as far as language patterns and reading strategies can be recorded on Appendix F3.

The group for this demonstration guided reading lesson comprised three children at the end of third grade who were, according to their classroom teacher, speaking at an intermediate level and reading at a very early level—perhaps level 6. The teacher and I compared several texts at levels 6 through 10 and decided on *Dad Didn't Mind at All*, an intervention level 10 book for strong early readers at the first-grade level (see Table 9.1). She thought the story of a dad who takes his kids camping would appeal to these upper-grade children. As I often did, I silently wondered whether their language and reading levels were really as low as diagnosed. We filled out the guided reading text features form on *Dad Didn't Mind at All* on the next page to see the supports and challenges the text holds for the readers.

Introduction

Norma, Jannette, and Bryan sat on the floor, and each received their own copy of *Dad Didn't Mind at All*. Just like emergent readers, early readers need a strong introduction to tap into their prior knowledge as a basis for predicting what the book will be about.

After we had introduced ourselves, I asked about the types of books they would usually choose for independent reading.

I hear you like to read. What books do you like to read?
Bryan: About basketball.

We had a quick discussion of his favorite basketball stars, but the girls didn't seem interested in sports.

Besides sports, what other fun things do you all like to do?
Jannette: Ride my bike.
Norma: Play with my sister.
Well, let's see what the people in this book like to do.
What do you see on the cover of the book?
Norma: Dad and his children.
Yes. What is Dad doing? Where are they going?
Jannette: Camping.
Have you ever been camping, Jannette?
Jannette: No, but my sister's going.
Is she going with a group of people? with a camp?
Jannette: With students.

Guided Reading—Text Features Form

Title Dad Didn't Mind at All

Author/Illustrator Ngarangi Naden / Martin Bailey—illustrator

Genre fiction   **Series** Literacy 2000 - Rigby

Stage early   **Intervention Level** 10

Number of Running Words 141

Supports
Repetitive patterns throughout   Day of the week - pattern
Pictures tell the story
Sentences placed in same position on each page

Challenges
Pictures don't match the text exactly
Use of past tense, contractions - couldn't, didn't
Some difficult vocabulary - light/baked/tore/prickles

Interesting Features

Speech bubbles
Funny saying becomes clever ending "Dad didn't mind at all"

Sentence Structure
(including verb tense)   Past tense   Some sentences with two clauses
  Prepositional phrases   One simple sentence on each page with contractions
                      "Dad didn't mind at all"

Vocabulary and Theme

Camping - tent, light the fire, cold baked beans

High-Frequency Words
at, we, the, on, it, was, for a

Phonics Features
we: we, Wednesday, was, went, want
ing: camping, raining, fishing (thing)
a: day (Sunday, Monday, Tuesday, etc.), played, rained/raining

Punctuation
Periods, commas, contractions

A text evaluation of Dad Didn't Mind at All.

What about you, Bryan? Norma? Have you ever gone camping? Do you know what they do when they go camping? [All shook their heads no.]
Well, we'll learn a lot about camping today. Let's look at the pictures to help us. What do they have in their arms? What do they need to bring camping?
Bryan: Sleeping bag.

Instead of saying the word myself, I wanted to see if they had the word *tent* in their vocabulary.

Yes. Why do they need a sleeping bag? Are they going to sleep in a house?
Jannette: A tent.

Q *What have we learned so far about the children's language?*

Bryan is speaking in short phrases or one- or two-word responses. Jannette seems to have more language and speaks in complete sentences but seemed to prefer to answer in short phrases if not pried. She used a contraction with the present progressive tense. Norma is speaking in short phrases. She knows how to use possessive adjectives. She responds with yes/no.

However, the discussion so far hadn't really provided enough information to assess the children. It also had not prepared the children with enough background knowledge to predict what would happen in the book and to read it successfully.

I continued trying to tap into their prior experiences to see if these could somehow be connected with camping. It appeared that they knew more about it than they had let on at first. Jannette knew that they would sleep in a tent outside on the ground. Bryan knew that they could go camping in the mountains, and he mentioned the local mountain, Big Bear, which triggered Jannette to recall that her sister was going camping there. Norma didn't add much to the discussion; she just seemed to be listening. The other two seemed engaged but were still only talking in short phrases.

What do you think they will find in the mountains on their camping trip?

Jannette: Bears.
Oh, they might find a bear. Sometimes there are bodies of water up in the mountains. What would you call those?
Jannette: Lakes.
What could you do if you go to a lake?
Bryan: Fish.
Oh, do you see anything in the cover picture that they could use for fishing?
Norma: Yes. Look [points to fishing pole].
Oh, you're right. That's a fishing pole. It's all stuffed in the car. Do you think their mom is going to go camping with them?
Norma: No.
She's probably glad to stay home alone and have time to herself. [All laugh.]

Since we had gained some new knowledge from looking at the cover picture, I thought it was time to tackle the title, which is an English expression. I wasn't sure they understood it even if they could read it. I felt it was important to discuss it and then think about all the things that could happen when people go camping.

What do you think the title of this book is?
Jannette: Dad Didn't Mind at All.

Bryan and Norma chimed in with Jannette, but I wasn't sure they could read it.

That's right. Can we read that again? [All read the title aloud.] What does that mean?
Jannette: He didn't care.

I tried to use both *care* and *mind* in a question to help the children hear how they were used.

Do you think he would care about anything? Do you think he would mind if something spilled on him?
Norma: No.
What do you think might happen while they are going camping? What do you think Dad's response will be?
Jannette: Ants might get on the food.
Maybe. How will Dad respond?
Jannette: Dad won't mind.
What else might happen? [No response] They're going to go fishing. Do you think they are going to catch any fish?
Bryan: Yes.

Jannette added that they might see a bear. I knew there was nothing in the book about a bear, but there was about the weather.

What type of weather do you think they are expecting while they go camping?
Norma: Warm.
It might be warm.

Q *What else have we learned about the children's language?*

Bryan is still only responding with one or two words. He seems to have more language but doesn't seem to want to produce it. Jannette has a strong sense of sentence structure and answers questions like a native speaker, without hesitation although not always in complete sentences. She uses plurals and contractions easily as well as the conditional tense. Norma is also still responding with one- or two-word answers. It's hard to tell her language level.

Orientation

Now I wanted to see what kind of reading strategies the children were using to gain meaning from the text. We noted the author's and illustrator's names, then looked at the pictures on the title page and the first few pages of the book to predict what might happen.

What are they doing? [title page]
Norma: They're driving.
Jannette: They're singing.
How do you know they're singing?

Two pages from *Dad Didn't Mind at All.*

Jannette: These things [points to musical notes]. *Do you know what those are called? They're called notes. Musical notes. Look at the kids in the car* [pages 2, 3]. *Do they look very happy?*
No.
There are some speech bubbles. Do you know what they might be saying?
Jannette: "Are we almost there?" "How much longer?"

Jannette understood all my questions and read the text easily. I asked what time of year it was. Bryan answered right away: summer. He was able to scan the text, read for the answer, and answer quickly.

What do you see in the background? It's blue. What is it?
Norma: The sky.
It could be the sky. Look closer, down below in the picture.
Jannette: It's a lake.
Can you find the word "lake"? [I wanted to see if Norma could find it.]
Jannette: Here [pointing at the word]. [Norma and Billy also pointed at it.]
How long did it take them to get to the lake? Can you find that in the book?
Jannette: A day.
Let's look at the line that tells us that.

I wanted to see if they had the strategy of searching the text for information and whether they could reread the text on their own. They all pointed to the line *It took us all day to get there.* Norma and Janette read aloud, "All day."

Do you think Dad cared? What was the title of the book?
Dad Didn't Mind at All.

We turned the pages, *On Monday . . . , On Tuesday . . . ,* the children using the pictures to predict, finding matching words, and scanning for the repetitive line, which they all said with emphasis every time it came up.

What day is it now?
Monday.
What is happening?

On Wednesday,
we couldn't light the fire.
We had cold baked beans
for breakfast, lunch and dinner.

Dad didn't mind at all.

Two pages from *Dad Didn't Mind at All.*

It's raining.
Look at the tent. What is happening inside the tent?
It's dripping.
What about Dad? What did he think.
Dad didn't mind at all!
What else did you notice about Dad and the kids?
Bryan: He was sleeping.
Jannette: The kids were awake.
What did the kids do all day?
Jannette: They played cards.
Is Dad awake?
Jannette and Bryan: No, he's still asleep.
He didn't mind, did he?
Jannette: No, he didn't mind.
What do you think will happen on Wednesday? [pages 8, 9]
Norma: Eat.
Yes, it looks like they are going to eat. Do you think the kids look very happy about the food?
No.

I wanted the children to infer why something is happening, to understand cause and effect. These are higher-level strategies they would need in order to become more fluent readers. These pages had some difficult words, *couldn't light,* and unless they used these strategies together with the pictures, it would be hard for them to just sound out the words and make meaning on their own.

Oh, look at their faces. What did they have to eat?
Jannette: Beans.
Yes, they had beans. How were the beans?
Jannette: They weren't cooked.
Why weren't they cooked? [No response] *Was there a fire? Could they light the fire?*

Jannette: No.
Do you think they lit the fire? What do you notice in the picture? A lot of what?
Jannette: There was a lot of wood.
Is it burned, Norma?
Norma: No.
Why not?
Jannette: Maybe they didn't have matches.
Maybe. Or maybe Dad wasn't very good at getting the fire . . . [waiting for the word]
Jannette: Started.
What happened the previous days?
Norma: Rained.
Yes, it did rain. So what happened to the wood?
Bryan: It got wet.
Good. Let's read this line: "On Wednesday . . ." [I stopped to let them finish the line.]
"We couldn't light the fire."
So they ate . . . ?
"Cold baked beans."
Do you think Dad minded?
No.

I asked when they ate those cold beans; Jannette said for lunch, Norma said for dinner, and Bryan said for breakfast. Then I asked them to find the words in the text, and they all found them easily. On the Thursday page, I guided them to think out another cause and effect sequence.

What do you think happened while they were fishing?
Norma: They were sad.
Why do you think they're sad, Norma?
Norma: They're sad.
Yes, they may look sad. I like the way you are looking at the picture and thinking. Why do you think they look sad?
Norma: Um . . . Dad is sleeping.
Let's go into the text and find out why they are sad.
Jannette: Because they didn't catch any fish.
Can you all find where it says that? "We . . ." [I paused to let them finish the line.]
"We didn't catch a fish."
How would you feel if you didn't catch a fish?
Norma: Sad.
I would be, too. What about your dad? Would he mind if he didn't catch a fish?
Jannette: My dad would mind.
Bryan: Mine, too!

I noticed the children had made a miscue, reading *fish* for *thing* in the line *We didn't catch a thing*. On the next page they read *ripped* instead of *tore*. Neither of these miscues changed the meaning. I could choose to ignore the miscues or help them self-correct. I took advantage of a teachable moment to help them go back, compare the beginning letters of the miscued words, and use their knowledge of graphophonics to read correctly. Continuing with the orientation, we took note of their predictions so far and discussed what would happen on the last day of the trip.

Well, what happens on the last day? Oh, this is something that Jannette said might happen.
Jannette: "On Saturday, we found ants in the food."
Just what you predicted. What do the kids say?
"Oh, Dad, we want to go home!"
What do you think Dad says?
Dad didn't mind at all!

We laughed, and I asked, "Did you like the book?" They all said yes and talked about the great way the author had used the repetitive line for a funny ending. It was hard to tell at the end whether they were reading the line or had memorized it after so much repetition.

Q *What else do we know about the children now?*

Language patterns and vocabulary used: Bryan answers in short responses. He isn't participating as much as Jannette and Norma but seems capable. Jannette speaks in complete sentences. She makes very few errors and sounds like a native speaker, using contractions and conditional tense. Norma speaks in short sentences and phrases. She uses adjectives and some contractions.

Reading strategies: Bryan uses pictures and text to gain meaning. He cross-checks and finds unknown words. Jannette finds information accurately in the text. She reads for meaning, cross checks, and infers. Norma uses the text and the pictures to help her. She predicts and uses background knowledge. (Use Appendix F3.)

The introduction and orientation took about ten minutes. Because of the classroom teacher's esti-

mate of their language level (intermediate), I didn't want to make any assumptions. I went over every page, made sure they knew what the text was about, and highlighted reading strategies in order to set them up for success when they read the book on their own. What we learned through the discussion, however, is that the assumptions of the children's language levels were not correct. I have found that if more time is spent during the introduction and orientation, less time needs to be spent helping children during their first independent reading. This is also a good time to assess language in the context of meaning making. With ELLs, language development is an important key to their reading success, even with these early texts.

Student Reading

We reviewed the strategies they would need to use in reading on their own:

★ Think what would make sense.
★ Use your background knowledge.
★ Use the pictures to help you.
★ Reread a word or line to sustain meaning.
★ Use your knowledge of graphophonics to check your predictions.

Now my role was to listen to the children read aloud on their own and to guide them if needed. Otherwise, I sat back, listened, and took mental notes on my observations. As they each started to read aloud, I moved to sit next to Bryan first. He read, "It *look* us all day to get there." I asked, "Does that make sense?" He self-corrected immediately: "It *took* all day . . . ." Then he read the rest of the page and continued, so I moved on to Norma.

Norma did fine until she got to *breakfast*. "We had cold baked beans for br . . . break . . . br . . . ." I asked, "Can you think of what meal of the day that is?" "Breakfast," she said right away, then read the line and continued without any miscues. (By the time Norma was on page 6, Jannette had already finished reading the sixteen-page book, so I suggested she find her favorite page. She began flipping through the pages.) On the fishing page, Norma read, "We didn't catch *anything*" instead of ". . . *a thing*." The miscue made sense, but I reminded her

Helping a student in guided reading.

to look closely at the text and to reread. (Now Norma was on page 8, and Bryan was done. I hadn't heard him having any trouble, so I suggested he find his favorite page, too. I noticed that Jannette was rereading the whole book quietly.) On the Friday page, Norma read, "Thursday." I reminded her again to look closely at the text, and she finished very nicely.

Discussion and Follow-up

Just as in an emergent guided reading lesson, a discussion and follow-up is important for English language learners. The children were still laughing about all the things Dad had slept through and the children put up with before Dad finally decided that he "didn't mind at all" to go home. They liked the repetitive pattern the author had used. Bryan liked the part when ants get in the food, though that had never happened to him. Norma said that had happened to her once at a picnic. Her favorite page was when Dad and the children had to eat cold baked beans. Jannette's favorite page was when Dad tore his jeans picking berries: "He didn't care. He was just picking berries." I said he was quite an easy-going dad; he gets rained on, he tears his jeans, and he doesn't care. "Is your dad like that?" I asked. "No!" said Jannette, and they all laughed again.

For a follow-up I asked them if they could create their own adventures of something that had happened while a dad and his children went camping. After some discussion, they went off to write

about their ideas: maybe the car gets stuck in the mud (Jannette); maybe a bear came into the camp (Norma); maybe they fell into the water while fishing (Bryan). They wanted to add the repetitive line to their new versions. I suggested they might want to change it to *Mom didn't mind at all*. Jannette nixed that train of thought. "My mom wouldn't go camping!" she said.

Evaluation

Norma

Norma was speaking in short phrases and sentences, and used adjectives and some contractions. Her reading strategies included using the pictures to help her, finding matching words in the text, predicting, and using background knowledge. She made a few miscues, but those did not change the meaning. How would Norma score on a running record with this text? She actually scored very high, 96 percent, on a running record after the lesson. It was a seen text, but that doesn't invalidate it. ELLs often tend to score relatively poorly with running records. They have a tendency to replace words in the text with others that don't affect the meaning and to not self-correct. Often teachers look at this as an error rather than seeing that the child was trying to make meaning. It is critical to analyze miscues carefully (Wilde 2000; Goodman 1996).

This book was appropriate, even a little easy, for Norma based on her language level and strategy use. Although she was only an intermediate speaker, she was able to take part in the discussion and knew what the text was about. Her reading strategies were those of a strong early reader. I would try her out in another text at level 12 or 14 depending on the language patterns and topic of the book.

Bryan

Bryan read much more quickly than Norma and was a strong early reader. He cross-checked, used pictures and text to gain meaning, and scanned for unknown words. I had to slow him down because he made a miscue that didn't make sense and kept on reading. Once I pointed it out, he knew his mistake right away and self-corrected. During other guided reading lessons, he would need to be slowed down every once in a while to make sure of his meaning making. I didn't do a running record with Bryan after the lesson (I usually only do one, on the child I'm most concerned about or haven't learned enough about), but it was clear he could handle a more challenging book. I would definitely choose at least a level 14 text for him, but one about sports or other nonfiction topic he might be interested in. He hadn't shown much interest in this book about camping, and perhaps that is why he hadn't participated much in the discussions. His language level was higher than Norma's, probably early advanced, and a book closer to his interests might encourage him to speak more.

Jannette

Jannette was definitely misplaced in this group. Her English language level was advanced, close to a native speaker's. She used complete sentences, contractions, and the conditional tense, and made very few errors. She read the text almost effortlessly and used strategies that fluent readers use. Besides cross-checking and finding information accurately in the text, she inferred and thought beyond the text to why events occurred and what else might happen. Because the text was too easy for her, it was difficult to assess all that she could do. She should be placed in a fluent guided reading group and started at least at level 22 (which is still only a second-grade level; see Table 9.1). I would use the checklist for expanding meaning (Appendix A7) to monitor closely what she needs to do to become a fluent reader. She might want to try chapter books. I would also determine her interests and pick a series of books to match, and possibly place her in a literature circle with other children in the class.

GUIDED READING LESSON WITH EARLY READERS RECEIVING INSTRUCTION IN ENGLISH AND SPANISH

A school in San Ysidro, California, with a biliteracy strand and an overall goal of raising the English test scores of ELLs asked me to teach a demonstration English guided reading lesson while I was consulting at the school. The group for this lesson comprised four second-graders who had arrived from Mexico at the beginning of the year. They were flu-

ent readers at intervention level 24 in Spanish and estimated to be at an early intermediate English language proficiency level. I asked the classroom teacher to select a text based on what she knew about the children as English speakers and readers. She chose *Pets*, an early text at intervention level 9 with supportive pictures, only a couple of lines per page, and a subject familiar and interesting to most children.

I knew the text well, so I asked her if she was sure she wanted to use it, and she said yes. My hesitation came from the fact that the book is written in the past tense, which children only start to use at the intermediate language level. I didn't say this, however, but decided to go along with it, partly to see whether the children were actually speaking at the diagnosed language level of early intermediate. If so, I knew I would have to work hard to get them to use the past tense, if they could, while reading this text.

Pets has a predictable pattern. On each page the boy acquires a new pet but loses it in some way. The book also has rhymes: *I had a frog. It jumped out of its bowl. I had a mouse. It ran back to its hole.* Rhymes can be supportive, but rhyming in a second language is not easy and therefore not supportive for English language learners. The book's vocabulary is accessible to early readers because of the pictures, although it includes some challenging words like *hutch*, which even native speakers may not know if they don't have a rabbit. The pictures illustrate an action word, or verb, on each page: *jumped, ran, ate, got out of, flew.* But one could argue that they do not clearly match the past-tense verbs (*I had a parrot. It flew out the door.*) because the pets are still shown in the pictures (one could read, *I had a parrot. It was flying out the door.*). What difference does it make? Well, if the children are ready for the past tense, this book would work perfectly for them. But if they are not yet ready to use the past tense, the book would be more difficult than it looks. And this is just what happened.

One of the teacher's tasks in a guided reading lesson is to set the students up with the proper background and vocabulary that they need to read the text on their own. I don't believe in reading the first few pages for them, so I guide them with skilled questions to figure out the title and predict the story by themselves.

| I had a fish. It ate too much. | I had a rabbit. It got out of its hutch. |
| I had a parrot. It flew out the door. | I *wanted* a dog . . . |

A few pages from *Pets*.

Can you say *flew*?" They still couldn't repeat those lines. I almost laughed. They so clearly demonstrated their developmental language stage (see Table 2.2). Yet the children weren't bothered a bit. They were understanding the story fine and responding to my prodding appropriately. I am sure they understood the concept of the past; their English was just not developed enough to use that tense effectively.

Q *Were these children ready for guided reading in English and for this level of text?*

I would say yes. The concepts they had learned in the primary language were transferring to their reading in English. They were using effective reading strategies that strong early readers use: using the pictures to help themselves, cross-checking for meaning, rereading, and trying to self-correct. They were making meaning, their retelling was great, and they were engaged in the discussion. They just didn't have the grammatical structures in English to read this book accurately.

Q *Was the reading level of this particular text too difficult for this group?*

Based on strict running records, yes. But based on their miscues, which were primarily syntactical errors, I would say no. There are many other books at the same instructional reading level that do not use the past tense and thus would be more appropriate for these children. These students did not need more help with reading strategies. They needed help with language development. It would be the teacher's job to help them develop their syntax—strengthen their sentence structure and use of the past tense—in the context of the balanced reading program, for instance, through focused lessons during shared reading. Pets would be an appropriate intervention level 9 book to use with intermediate speakers. This points up the importance of carefully evaluating ELLs' language development when assessing their reading abilities and selecting guided reading books.

We started the lesson by looking at the cover picture, which shows a boy at a pet store with a tadpole in a jar. Behind him in cages are rabbits, kittens, and a puppy. Then we talked about the title page, which showed a bowl containing a tadpole sprouting legs, and the first page, where a full-grown frog is shown jumping out of the bowl. Without telling them what happened, I tried to elicit language from all of them. I asked all questions in the past tense to encourage them to use the same tense they would need to read this book: Did you ever have a pet? What happened to your pet? Where was the boy? What did he choose from the pet store? What happened to the tadpole when he took it home? What did the frog do?

The children followed the progression on each page easily and were speaking in short phrases and sentences, as early intermediate speakers do. But they had difficulty on each page with the past tense. No matter how hard I tried to prompt them to speak in the past tense, they couldn't do it; all their answers were in the present tense. "Yes, the mouse runs, but look here, he *ran* back to the hole. Can you find the word *ran*?" I said. "Yes, the parrot does fly, but he already *flew* out the door. Look at the picture. It already happened.

Books at the same reading level as *Pets* but written in the present tense are *Grandma's Memories, Paper Patchwork, When Jose Hits That Ball, Sleepy Bear,* and *The Water Boatman,* and many others can be found in publishers' lists. As mentioned, it is important to evaluate each book carefully before using it in a guided reading lesson.

CHOOSING TEXTS FOR EARLY READERS

Just as emergent readers do, early readers need support as they are developing their reading strategies: pictures that illustrate and match the text, repetitive patterns, a predictable story line. Not every line needs to be repetitive, but one line out of four on a page, for example, helps early readers as they read longer, more challenging texts. Perhaps most important for ELLs is to be exposed to natural language and new and interesting vocabulary. High-frequency words are important, and books that are written to teach them are fine for readers who need the practice, but they are not conducive to developing ELLs' vocabulary, especially if that is all the text they will be exposed to.

The illustrations should be by a variety of illustrators, not all the same design or color scheme. Photographs should be bright and exciting, and stimulate children's interest in reading the book or investigating the topic further. One criterion for choosing a guided reading book is, Does the teacher like it? Is the story interesting? Is it funny or does it have great characters? If we don't like a book, it is unlikely most children will. Our goal is to get children hooked on books. Do the kids like it? Some may not have opportunities at home to read, and this may be the first time they hold their own books

in their hands. So it is important to choose appealing guided reading books. Appendix F2 lists many of the guided reading series that are helpful for ELLs as well as multicultural guided reading books. Among the latter, one of my favorites for early readers is *My Special Job,* which has rich illustrations showing the love in a Hispanic family.

CHOOSING TEXTS FOR OLDER EARLY READERS

Unfortunately there are many fourth- and fifth-graders who are reading at first-grade level. We should be careful not to choose texts that seem too young for them. For instance, *Dad Didn't Mind at All* is appropriate for older readers, but many texts for early readers have themes that are too young or pictures showing very young children. Luckily, there are many new series of guided reading texts that are designed to interest older readers who are reading below grade level (see Appendix F2). I have also found that nonfiction texts, say, about animals or sports, are ageless and appeal to young and older readers alike. One example is *Ready, Steady, Jump!* which shows how a jumping spider jumps from one leaf to another to spin a web. The photographs are beautiful, but the text is very limited (it is only intervention level 6). *My Cousin Far Away* has limited text on each page, but the children in the photographs look like they could be fifth- or sixth-graders, and they talk about topics that would interest older children, like snow boarding and boogie boarding.

12 GUIDED READING *with* EARLY FLUENT *and* FLUENT READERS

"Reading" the Newspaper

When I traveled to Spain for my junior year abroad, I had already taken eight years of Spanish and definitely considered myself a fluent reader. One of my passions was reading the newspaper, so every morning in Valencia I picked up El Páis, *the national newspaper of Spain. But as I made my way through the pages, I found I had no idea of what the articles were about. Even though I could recognize and pronounce the words easily enough, I knew nothing about Spain—its government, its politics, the issues and concerns facing its citizens, its sports heroes, and its national fiestas. I had no background knowledge to make my reading comprehensible. I also couldn't catch many of the idioms and expressions in the more informally written stories. I felt lost and discouraged, and the newspapers began to pile up unread. I brought them all home with me, though, and years later as a bilingual teacher I enjoyed sharing them with students, reliving my time in Spain. By then, after having made several more visits to Spain and gained some adult perspectives on the world, I was able to understand what the articles were about. They were memoirs rather than fresh news by then, but at least I could finally put them in context and understand them. I could truly read them.*

How many fluent readers in our classrooms have no idea what they are reading? As English language learners become more fluent readers in English, they can figure out words on their own, and they often sound like they can read just about anything. But because they are reading longer and more difficult texts, they sometimes lose track of the overall meaning of what they read. As ELLs start to read chapter books with more complicated plots and nonfiction texts packed with new information, they have more of a challenge than native speakers do because often they don't have the necessary background knowledge and specialized academic vocabulary to understand the texts. It is our job to help ELLs develop their higher-level comprehension strategies and engage them in deeper discussions of the text while they are becoming more fluent readers.

Sometimes a child reading at a lower fluency level actually has better higher-level strategies than his peers. Some children have trouble with word attack skills but are good at pinpointing the author's purpose or the main idea of a story. Other children might be good decoders and read quickly but not be able to tell the main idea or summarize the plot. When stopped and asked about what they are reading, they have no idea. There is little evidence that decoding skills lead to long-term growth in reading comprehension (Cummins 2003; Allington 2001). It is essential, therefore, in the context of a fluent guided reading lesson, that we take the time to slow down readers by having discussions not only before and after entire readings but also between sections. This helps children see the importance of checking for meaning while they are reading, not just after they have finished (Harvey and Goudvis 2000). Good readers continually self-question to check meaning. They stop themselves when something doesn't make sense or when they aren't sure of what they've just read. Unfortunately, some ELLs are more concerned with sounding out words and pronouncing them correctly than checking to see whether they understand what they are reading. They usually just keep on reading. Where do they get this from? Is it because they have picked up a skewed impression in the classroom of what constitutes a good reader? We need to emphasize clearly what good readers really do: try to gain meaning by using various higher-level strategies. Hopefully we can send the message that meaning making is paramount for success in reading.

Figuring out new words in context is an important focus for guided reading lessons, but there are other focuses that we should highlight as well. These include comparing and contrasting, finding the main idea, finding the author's intent, differentiating between fact and opinion, inferring, analyzing information, summarizing text, and synthesizing information (Harvey and Goudvis 2000; Fountas and Pinnell 2001; Routman 2000; Keene and Zimmermann 1997). This chapter discusses how to form groups and choose a focus for guided reading lessons with fluent readers and how to teach higher-level strategies using both fiction and nonfiction texts.

GUIDING QUESTIONS

How do I choose a focus for the fluent guided reading group?

How do I keep the groups fluid instead of stagnant?

What is the best way to lead a fluent guided reading lesson for English language learners?

How much time should I spend teaching vocabulary in the lesson?

How can I tell if they really understand what they read?

What are we doing to keep track of the expanding and sustaining meaning strategies children are using?

How can I assess the children's language level as well as their reading strategies they use?

CHOOSING A FOCUS AND FORMING GROUPS

The groups I form vary week by week and are based on the strengths and needs of the children. My ongoing assessments of the students' language and reading development are made by observing them in daily activities like other guided reading lessons, shared reading, read-alouds, and reading conferences. The records for each child, such as checklists of strategies to expand meaning (Appendix A7), are stored in their reading and language assessment folders (see Chapter 2), and I consult these to help me in my planning. During the current lesson I also observe the children's language and reading development to evaluate what they might need in future lessons, and later add these notes (Appendix F3) to the folders.

Although fluent readers may be reading at the same developmental level, they have very different needs. Some may be expert at reading fiction and have difficulty reading nonfiction. Others may be able to summarize well but can't analyze or infer to get at the core meaning. So one day I might choose inferring as the focus and form a guided reading group comprising several children in the class who need to practice that strategy. The next day I might gather one or two of these same children together with others into a group with a different focus like analyzing the main idea. The texts are chosen to enable children to practice the focus strategy. In these shifting groups that are formed with a set purpose in mind, the text might be a little too easy for one or two readers, but that is okay because the primary focus of the lesson is to help them work on a higher-level strategy that they need to develop.

A guided reading lesson with early fluent and fluent readers is very similar to a lesson for early readers; it is designed to guide children to learn and practice the strategies they need to become successful independent readers. An important difference, however, is that the focus of the lesson is one higher-level strategy to expand meaning rather than several lower-level strategies to sustain meaning. If some children at this reading level still are not using "fix-up strategies" (Tovani 2000) like cross-checking or rereading lines, one complete lesson could focus on these sustaining-meaning strategies.

Children need to work, read, and discuss with peers having a range of abilities. This not only helps build a community of learners but lets children see that they all have different strengths and weaknesses. There is nothing more devastating for children than to be pigeonholed in reading groups with the same four or five children all year or half-year. Unfortunately, I see this in many classrooms. Perhaps teachers feel it is easier to plan if the groups stay the same: the children are reading at a certain level, and they can be moved along together to the next level. But, as mentioned, children advance in different skills at different rates. They have individual peaks and valleys in language and reading development during the course of a year. They need to be given the opportunity to mingle and mix with a range of readers and English speakers who are also moving in this ebb and flow of literacy development. Organizing and managing guided reading groups flexibly, based on different focuses and

How to Lead a Fluent Guided Reading Session

To Prepare:

Planning and Grouping

Group the students based on similar strategy or language needs.

Decide which one higher-level strategy should be taught based on their individual needs.

Choose the book that will best help them use that strategy while reading either fiction or nonfiction.

Choose a focus sheet for students to use in the lesson.

To Begin:

Introduction and Orientation

Lead the students in an introduction of the text, tapping into their background knowledge.

Use graphic organizations to chart predictions and highlight focus.

Orient them to the book and have them look at the elements of the book, especially if it is nonfiction.

Review the strategy that they will practice using while reading.

During Reading:

Guide Students to Read Independently

Guide the students through the text with a set purpose, with students reading a few pages or a section at a time silently.

If some of the students finish reading the section sooner than the others, have them use their focus sheet to write down their findings based on the purpose for their reading.

Individual Instruction Observations

While the students are reading silently, sit up close to one reader at a time to listen to her/him read and to help if needed.

Take notes on individual students on strategies and language used.

Discussion:

Share Findings During the Lesson

Have the students discuss what they found or learned after they read sections of the text depending on the focus and strategy being highlighted.

Discuss the Text at the End of the Lesson

Include all students in the discussion, to compare their findings, and to help individuals broaden their own comprehension after their reading.

Follow-up:

Continue Reading or Reread

Continue reading the book if group hasn't finished or reread sections of the text.

Further Research

Do further research on the topic or use the strategy with another book.

---

learning needs, is admittedly more complex, but it can be done (see Chapter 9).

Early fluent and fluent readers are already reading independently, so there can be more than four children in a group as long as each child has her own copy of the book and all the children take part in the discussions. The lessons tend to take thirty minutes rather than twenty. Ample discussion is particularly important for fluent readers, allowing them to process new vocabulary, clarify meaning, and reach deeper levels of understanding by sharing information with their peers. (It also prepares them to take part in literature circles; see Chapter 13.) The lesson should provide many opportunities not only to practice reading strategies but also to discuss them in the group. Each child might also be provided with a focus sheet to record her findings, for instance, figuring out new words (Appendix F4), main idea (Appendix F5), learning log (Appendix F6), questioning and monitoring learning with a K-W-L chart (Appendix F7), facts or opinions (Appendix F8), inferring (Appendix F9), and author's intent (Appendix F10). By setting a short goal of reading a few pages at a time or researching something specific in the text, we keep the children together in the group lesson yet provide time for each to read silently at her own pace. Then, in the periodic discussions, they talk about what they have read so far. Those who read faster than others can record their findings on the focus sheet.

Although the format of a guided reading lesson for fluent readers with an introduction and orientation, student reading, and discussion is similar to the lessons for lower-level readers (see Chapters 10 and 11), the teacher's role in leading the lesson and the readers' responsibilities are different.

GUIDED READING LESSON WITH EARLY FLUENT AND FLUENT READERS

Choosing the Focus and the Text

The children in this demonstration lesson were four ELLs in a fourth- and fifth-grade combination class who were reading below grade level, although they were all early advanced speakers and fluent readers who read at an average rate. The classroom teacher was concerned with the children's comprehension level because of their poor retellings of the texts they read. She was also concerned with the children's ability to deal with difficult vocabulary in new texts, primarily in nonfiction, and thought that they needed to learn more strategies to help themselves while reading.

Often English language learners have difficulty with new academic vocabulary because they do not have the strategies necessary to gain meaning, and thus meaning breaks down. We decided, therefore, to focus on strategies to learn and enrich vocabu-

lary in context. We chose the nonfiction text *Storm Trackers,* which has some very technical language yet has supports to help readers learn the vocabulary. The book has a glossary, and the words included in the glossary are bolded throughout the text. Although there are no chapter headings or captions, the photographs are a wonderful source of information to help the children figure out the new vocabulary.

The book is about a class of children in Virginia who have their own weather station on the school roof and who study weather and track storms. They received a grant from Channel 4 in Washington for a permanent weather station, and they use it to do research and to provide information on the local weather to the meteorologist at the channel. The instruments on the weather station are connected by cables to their computers in the classroom, and they also use technology to analyze the data and transmit information to Channel 4 daily. The fact that these are older children with a responsible and unusual project makes this book very interesting for upper-grade readers.

Before starting the lesson, I had prepared a focus sheet on figuring out new words (Appendix F4), but the teacher stated she didn't always have time to prepare a focus sheet, so I gave the children blank pages on clipboards.

Introduction

We introduced ourselves, and I outlined for the children the strategies they should use for figuring out new vocabulary:

★ How is the word used in the context of the sentence?
★ Think what you already know about the word.
★ Reread the line and the paragraph with the new word in mind.
★ Use photographs to discover new information.
★ Use the glossary.
★ Find the word in another place in the text and compare.
★ Try to paraphrase the meaning of the word.

Gabriela, Nayeli, David, and Ivonne had read a lot of other nonfiction texts about storms and had

Cover of *Storm Trackers*.

David: Read.
Nayeli and Gabriela: Study.
David: Work.

I enjoyed their simple responses, but encouraged them to flip through the photographs to see if they could find out what the children in the book would need to be expert weather trackers. "Would they need information?" I asked. The children said they would need maps and computers. "Where do you think they get their information? I prodded. "From books," they responded. I was surprised they hadn't come up with any other response and wondered whether they understood that the large photograph on page 5 illustrated the main idea of the text, which is that the storm trackers use a weather station to help them study weather. We turned to page 5, and I asked, "What might this be? Have you ever seen something like this before?" Then I asked if any labels in the photograph looked familiar and had each choose one instrument that was labeled there.

David: Weather vane.
Gabriela: Thermometer.
Ivonne: Rain gauge.
Nayeli: Anemometer.

I asked them to write the words down on their papers and to write something about them. I wanted to see if they already knew about these instruments.

Are these words instruments?
David: No.
Really. What are instruments? What do you think these instruments do? Why are they in the book?

The children didn't respond to these questions, so I realized that they knew very little even though they had read the words fine. David said, "Because it's about weather and storms." So I asked David what a weather vane does, but he couldn't provide me with any information. Gabriela had chosen *thermometer*, and when I asked her what the instrument does, she responded, "Checks temperature." I asked Ivonne what she thought a rain gauge does, and she said, "Follows the rain." Nayeli said,

watched the weather report on TV. It seemed as if they would have a lot of background information that would help them understand *Storm Trackers*. I asked them questions like, What do you think the book will be about? Who are the people on the front cover? What else do you see on the cover? How do you know it's a weather map? Can you share what you heard on TV about the weather in our area or about the storms in Mexico last night? Do you have any experiences to share about being in a storm or hurricane? While listening to their responses, I wrote key words on a chart (*storm, hurricane, flooding in Mexico, trackers*)—something I don't usually do with emergent or early readers but that is very effective for fluent readers because it helps them focus on important ideas while reading and helps ELLs in the discussion if their English language level is not as high as their peers'. We talked about tracking, following the weather, and what they thought the children in the cover picture would do. "Talk about weather," said Nayeli. I confirmed her prediction and said that the children in this book are expert weather trackers.

What do they have to do to be expert weather trackers?

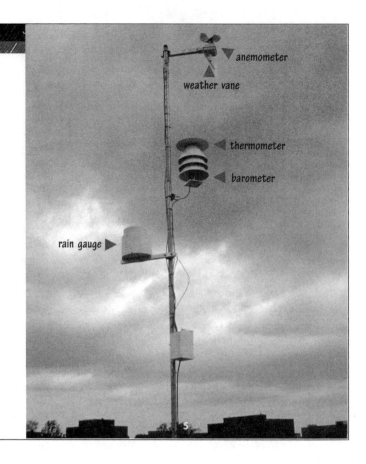

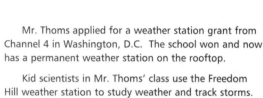

Mr. Thoms applied for a weather station grant from Channel 4 in Washington, D.C. The school won and now has a permanent weather station on the rooftop.

Kid scientists in Mr. Thoms' class use the Freedom Hill weather station to study weather and track storms. It has special instruments to measure wind speed and direction, light, air pressure, temperature, humidity, rainfall, and more.

The **anemometer** measures wind speed, and the **weather vane** shows wind direction. A **thermometer** records the high and low temperatures for each day. The **barometer** shows air pressure, and the **rain gauge** measures the amount of rainfall.

A weather station pictured in *Storm Trackers*.

"Anemometer will turn if there is a lot of wind. It goes around and spins." I then asked, "Can anyone help David? What do you think the weather vane does?" The girls had no trouble answering, "Tell you which way the wind is going." I charted each of the responses.

I learned that these children had trouble with open-ended questions, but when I asked specific questions regarding the vocabulary, the girls came up with some pretty good answers. It was difficult for me to tell yet if they had searched and found the main words in bold print—if they had, they did a good job of paraphrasing—or if they had thought about each instrument as they looked at the picture, or if they had had prior experience with instruments like a thermometer. David didn't seem to have tried any of these strategies and seemed to have trouble reading for information and discovering the meaning of new vocabulary.

What do these things do? They give you . . . .
Ivonne: Information.
Good. These are instruments, and they give you information.

I wrote that down on the chart.

Orientation

"Let's start reading," I said, "and each of you can check for your instrument to see if you are correct in your definition or see if you can learn anything else about the word you chose." In this way, I gave them a purpose for their reading. I asked them to write down what they found out about the words from the text. I also told them to look in the glossary to check their predictions and see whether the glossary gave more information than they could find in the text. We talked about the use of the glossary, and I pointed out that all the words in bold print were in the glossary. I also asked them to read the first paragraph on page 4 to see what all these instruments together are called. Ivonne read, "A permanent . . . ," and they all read, "Weather station." We went back to the first page to help them focus on why these children had a weather station at their school. We talked about specific information they could get from that page: the number of students, the teacher's name, the location of the school. Then we looked at a map to find Virginia and its location relative to California, where we lived. We talked about how the children in the book got their weather station—from a grant—and about their being "real scientists." I encouraged the children in the group to think of themselves as scientists, too, and asked them to write *scientist* on their papers. They, too, were going to do research, as real scientists do. They also wrote what they thought the word *research* meant and checked their predictions in the glossary. I told them they were going to collect information on words that were new and tricky for them. First each would research her own word. Then, if they finished, they could also find out about *barometer*, which no one had chosen. I suggested they write down any other word that they would like to research.

Reading and Discussion

I asked the children to read up to page 9 (out of 24) and to write anything they learned about the words they were researching on their papers. They all started reading silently.

I sat next to Nayeli first and listened to her read aloud. She was reading beautifully, and I told her so. Then I had her go back and look at the word *humidity*. I encouraged her to find out what it means and to look in the glossary if she couldn't figure it out on her own. I listened to Ivonne next. She was reading fluently with no problems. She came across *rain gauge*, and I asked, "Does it mean the same as what we wrote down?" She said no. So I asked her to write down what she had learned about the rain gauge.

David had already finished reading to page 9 and was sitting quietly. He had written down definitions of *weather vane* and *barometer*. I told him he was doing great, and that he could continue reading. Nayeli was also reading very well. She came across *anemometer*, and I asked what the book says about that instrument. "It measures wind speed," she responded. I asked her if that is what we had written down, and she said no. So I asked her to write down what she had learned about that word.

As a group, we discussed what we had learned from reading those pages of the text. We went back and compared their predictions, which I had charted, with what they had found out while reading the text. Ivonne shared that she had said the rain gauge "follows the rain," but now she knew it "measures the amount of rain." We looked at the photograph, and they thought it looked like a bucket and wondered how full it was. I asked, "If we want to know more about the rain gauge, where else might we look?" Gabriela said, "Encyclopedia." I said, "Maybe, but what about in this book?" I reminded them of the glossary, and we looked up the word together.

We also looked up *barometer* and wrote down what they learned on the chart: that it is an instrument that measures air pressure. We compared what they had predicted to what they had learned from the text. The discussion included David's discovery of what a weather vane does and Nayeli's finding that an anemometer measures wind speed. We also talked about questions they had from their reading or about words they had had difficulty with. Nayeli shared her difficulty with *humidity* and observed that it wasn't in the glossary. We talked about the word *humid*. Gabriela said, "It means hot," and Ivonne said, "It's sticky when it is humid." I added that the air feels heavy when it's humid. "What instrument measures humidity?," I asked. Since I got no response, I had to paraphrase my question: "What instrument measures the amount of water in the air? or tells you how heavy the air is? to tell you whether it will rain?" Gabriela said, "The barometer." We talked about what they had done to figure out words—the strategies they had used.

"I looked at the context first."

"I read the sentences."

"I reread and read on to see if I can gain any new information in the book. Then I looked in the glossary."

I encouraged them to use these same strategies as they continued reading. They read the next section of the book to page 17. I asked them to write down any other words they had difficulty with or anything they learned about their new words.

Once again I listened to individual children read aloud. Since they were reading so well, I had the opportunity to ask them challenging questions about the new vocabulary they had encountered in order to help them think deeper about what they were reading and to see if they comprehended the text. After they finished reading that section, some of the words we discussed were *data logger, meteorologist, equator,* and *simulation.* With my guidance, Nayeli looked up the word in the glossary because she hadn't been able to figure it out in context. But once she read the glossary meaning, she added her own knowledge ("It is a line.") and synthesized this with the glossary definition, "earth's middle."

Although David read faster than the others and "finished" his task first, he still had trouble figuring out words in context. (He thought a meteorologist was an instrument.) The others in the group helped him with the strategies necessary to be more successful during the discussion. Nayeli, for example, pointed out that *his* in the sentence with *meteorologist* showed that this was a person, not an instrument. Ivonne told him there were clues in the sentences. They also pointed out the glossary definition to him, since he hadn't used that strategy either. Guided reading is a small-group activity, and children are able to learn from each other, not just from me. I find the discussion during and after the reading is the most valuable part of a fluent guided reading lesson for ELLs.

Follow-up

I told the children they could take the books back to their seats and continue reading. They seemed pleased. I asked them to predict before reading what they thought would happen in the hurricane simulation the children in the book were building, and to compare how they gathered information to decide if it was a hurricane with how they gathered daily weather station information from the data logger and computers. Which information did the group think would be more accurate? I also reminded them to use strategies to figure out unknown words and add them to their vocabulary.

Not every book demands a follow-up, but follow-ups are beneficial because we don't always get to finish reading the whole text or get back to that guided reading group right away. If the children are interested in the book, it is easy to do a follow-up: just continue what the group was already doing in the lesson. Sometimes I ask the children to put their

focus notes on my desk after they finish the book. Other times I ask them to place them in their reading and language folders. They can then take them out the next time we meet, or share their findings with me in a conference. Or they might just want to finish reading the text and practice the strategies without recording anything on paper.

Evaluation

I filled in a guided reading observation sheet (Appendix F3), which would serve as an informal assessment and help the classroom teacher plan for future lessons with these children (see next page).

Ivonne needs more language experience to help develop her sentence structure. She should have lots of opportunity in small groups to discuss books and share ideas because this will help build her confidence. She needs more shared reading demonstrations of sentence patterns from texts or Big Books. And she can read along with books on tape, which will help develop her language proficiency.

David should be placed in a guided reading group to work more on his comprehension skills. He needs to slow down to help him check for understanding of what he is reading and to focus on inferring. Mini-lessons in read-alouds on inferring and figuring out words in context would help. He would also benefit from participating in literature circles, which would help him focus on comprehending the text in order to share his findings with his peers.

Gabriela and Nayeli both used effective strategies to figure out words, so they could try out these same strategies on higher-level texts. Their language level also seemed very high. They could perhaps work on synthesizing information or summarizing the text in other guided reading lessons. They should also spend time sharing their findings in literature circles. They would be good models for other children, but they need to be continually challenged to catch up with their English-speaking peers.

FIGURING OUT NEW WORDS AND USING GLOSSARIES

I encourage children to try to figure out new words on their own first, even if a book has a glossary, by

Guided Reading Group Observation Sheet

Guided Reading Group <u>Fluent readers, focus on vocabulary</u>   **Date** <u>9/18</u>
Title of Book <u>Storm Trackers by Katasha Diaz</u>   **Level** <u>_____</u>

Name of Child	Overall Comments	Language Patterns and Vocabulary Used	Reading Strategies Used
Gabriela	Found information in the text to answer questions. Was engaged in the lesson.	English level seems higher than her peers'. Used grammatically correct sentences.	Paraphrased definitions very easily.
Nayeli	Connected to her own life. Made leaps from one thing to another.	Said words like "anemometer" with no problem. Used "equator," higher-level vocabulary and sentences.	Wrote down words to check later. Used context to figure out meaning. Used other strategies - syntax, pictures, thinking what makes sense - to figure out the word.
David	Always offered information. Willing to participate in the discussion, yet his responses were brief.	Spoke in short phrases but had no problem with grammar. He "read" difficult vocabulary and seemed to have a high oral language level, even though brief.	Finished reading quickly but seemed to have difficulty comprehending what he read, especially difficult vocabulary.
Ivonne	Comprehension seemed deeper than ability to express. Engaged, involved in reading.	Sentence structure not as developed. Used simple sentences.	Used good strategies. Read well. Used context, read on, reread, made connections, and could paraphrase.

Example of a guided reading observation sheet.

When the morpho butterfly flies, it shows its brilliant blue wings, but when it lands, it seems to vanish. The underside of each wing blends perfectly with dead leaves.

5 SURVIVAL IN THE RAIN FOREST

HIDE AND SEEK

There are insects everywhere in the rain forest, but sometimes it's hard to see them. To hide from predators, many use **camouflage**. They have bodies that look like leaves, lichens, or twigs.

Many of the hunters of the rain forest, like the jaguar and ocelet, also use camouflage. Their spotted brown, yellow, and black coats match the patterns of light and shade on the forest floor. This helps them creep up on their prey unnoticed.

This katydid looks like a leaf – it even has small holes to look as if insects have nibbled it.

The green chameleon is suited to life in the canopy. It moves very slowly and is hard to see among the foliage.

Pages from *The Living Rain Forest*.

using strategies like thinking about how a word is used in context, using their background knowledge and the pictures, and thinking about any other way a word has been used. They can use a focus sheet (Appendix F4) to help them. They write down words they have trouble with and what they know about the words, anything the words remind them of, or how they might have heard them used before. The word *vegetation* in *The Living Rain Forest,* for example, reminded a child, Luciana, of vegetables, and *equator* reminded her of Ecuador. Then they look again at the text and think what the words might mean in context. Luciana made the leap to "a line" for equator. When I asked why she thought it was a line, she said she had looked at a map in the book and had seen a line labeled equator. This child seemed to know that in a nonfiction text the photographs, maps, or charts are an important source of information. Next, the children write sentences from the text that contain the words, and we dis-

cuss them. Often in this process children do not choose the same words, and their descriptions of different words and how they interpreted them enrich the group discussion. When one child is sharing, all the others turn to that page, and they all benefit from discussing new (or perhaps familiar) academic vocabulary.

On the focus sheet the children have starred words if they appeared in boldface in the text, indicating that the words are in the glossary. ELLs benefit greatly from glossaries, but we have to teach them how to use glossaries effectively. The function of a glossary is to help readers learn the meaning of words while reading if they have not been able to figure them out in context. Words that are critical to understanding the text are the ones usually boldfaced. If they do understand a word's meaning, there is no point in looking it up in the glossary unless they want to check their understanding. Glossaries should not be used to have children

Fluent Guided Reading Focus Sheet— Figuring out New Words

Name __Luciana__

Title of Book __The Living Rain Forest__   Genre __Nonficition__

Author __Nic Bishop__

New Words or Phrases	What I Know About the Words	What I Think They Mean	How They Are Used
humid*	hot	hot	rain forests grow in places that are humid
surface	surface of a table	on top	Rain forests cover part of earth's surface
equtor*	Ecuador	a line	The ground is covered with rotting vegetation
vegetation*	reminds me of vegatables	vegtables	
uderstory	below-underneath	the ground floor	The middle layer is the under-story.
canopy	umbrella	covers something	The canopy is where the tree tops finally reach the sun light.
species*	special	special ani-mals	There is twice as many specie liveing on the canopy.
camouflage*	army clothes	to hide	To hide from preditors many use camouflage

* words listed in Glossary

Luciana's focus sheet for figuring out new words in *The Living Rain Forest*.

review vocabulary before they read the text nor as a quiz for them to pass after they have read the text. Most authors include a glossary when they feel there is enough specialized vocabulary that readers would benefit from a more detailed description of certain words.

In this lesson, after discussing the words the children had written down on their focus sheets, we checked the definitions in the glossary to see if the predictions were correct. Some children noticed that most of their words were not in the glossary, and this led to a discussion of the limitations of a glossary and how one cannot always rely on it to figure out new words. Luciana was excited to discover a description of equator in the glossary as "an imaginary line that goes through the middle of the earth." She inferred that Ecuador must be in the middle of the earth and wondered what other countries were also on the equator. I suggested she find an atlas or use a better map to help her locate other countries with rain forests on the equator. After the lesson, that is what she did with a partner.

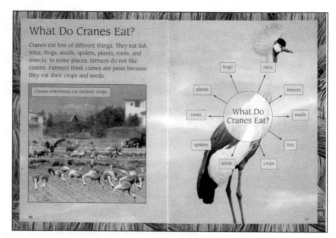

Pages from *Cranes*.

LESSONS WITH OTHER FOCUSES

Summarizing and Finding the Main Idea

Summarizing and finding the main idea are essential comprehension strategies. Often children read fluently, but when they are asked to summarize a page or tell the main idea of a passage, they have lots of difficulty. ELLs often lose track of the bigger picture as they try to absorb so much new information in longer, more complex texts. Guided reading lessons provide the perfect opportunity to slow these readers down and guide them to break the text into chunks to analyze and summarize what they are reading. I often choose nonfiction texts for lessons with this focus because children get lost in the many details, but fiction books also call for summarizing and understanding the main idea.

The children in this third-grade class used the focus sheet for finding the main idea (Appendix F5) in two different guided reading lessons, with texts related to the same theme but of different genres. *Cranes* is a nonfiction book, and *Dance My Dance* is a fictional account of why cranes dance. Many teachers use the fiction and nonfiction books that

are paired by publishers to facilitate discussion on the same theme across genres (see Appendix F2).

In the lesson on *Cranes*, I found that some children copied sentences directly from the text to list the main idea and supporting details on the focus sheet. That was fine because the sentence structure was quite simple and there wasn't a lot of room for paraphrasing. Also, one child, Melissa, who was an intermediate speaker, felt more comfortable taking down the information right from the text. In the lesson on *Dance My Dance,* another child, Alex, did a good job of finding the main idea and supporting details, writing some down, and sharing others orally (for lack of time in the lesson). Having practiced these strategies on short, double-page sections of this book, the children were later able to use them on longer sections in other guided reading lessons and while reading independently. Both Melissa and Alex finished reading the books and filling out their focus sheets after the lesson (see next two pages).

Learning New Information

Children often need help organizing all the new information they are learning about a topic as they read. Using a learning log (Appendix F6), they can focus on important details and vocabulary. Before I guided a group of ELLs through *Whale Watching,* a nonfiction narrative, we filled in a K-W-L chart (Appendix F7). I told them their learning logs would help them check if "what we know" about gray whales is correct and to see if any of their questions ("what we want to know") were answered in the text. When they had finished

Fluent Guided Reading Focus Sheet— Main Idea

Name Melissa

Title of Book Cranes   **Genre** Nonfiction

Author Sally Cole

Main Idea of Chapters/Paragraphs Supporting Details from Text	Heading/Page
All cranes are tall birds with large, strong wings. Some cranes are 6ft. tall. All cranes are over 3ft. tall. Cranes have long legs, necks, and beaks.	What Do Cranes Look Like? p.4
Cranes live on grasslands, in marshes, and in swamps by rivers and lakes. They use their long legs to wade in marshes and swamps. They stomp their feet to make insects come out of marshes and swamps to eat them. Cranes that live in cold places fly to warmer places during the winter. They use their large, strong wings to fly high in the sky. Some fly way above the Himalayan Mountains. Cranes live on five continents.	How and Where Do Cranes Live? p.6 Introduction p.2
Cranes eat a lot of things. They eat fish, frogs, insects, crops, snails, and mice. They eat spiders, seeds, roots, and plants. They eat farmers' crops.	What Do Cranes Eat? p.10

Melissa's focus sheet for finding the main idea in *Cranes*.

Fluent Guided Reading Focus Sheet— Main Idea

Name Alex

Title of Book Dance my Dance   **Genre** fiction

Author Ned Osakawa

Main Idea of Chapters/Paragraphs Supporting Details from Text	Heading/Page
A flock of Japanese cranes lived by a big lake. They stood all day. They looked for food. One day they saw a sign. They read the sign: Bird Olympics	p. 2-3
The cranes were excited to enter all the events. Life was boring by the lake. They wanted to win all the prizes. They got ready for the Bird Olympics. They thought they would win.	p. 4-5
Birds from all sizes came from far and near. There were chickens, geese, ducks, crows, hawks, and many others including penguins and cranes.	p. 6
Flying—The cranes wings weren't mad for flying fast and they came in last. They flapped there wings, but they couldn't keep up with the other birds	p. 8-9
Running—The crane's legs weren't made for running fast and they lost the race. They moved thier skinny legs, but they weren't fast enough.	p. 10-11
Swimming—The crane's feet and legs weren't made for swimming fast, and they lost. They paddled thier legs and feet as fast as they could but it wasn't fast enough.	p. 12-13
Dancing—The cranes were the best dancers of all the birds and won the prize. They sayd in time to the music and glided gracefully across the floor. The other birds weren't fast. From then on Japanes cranes danced at the lake end	p. 14-15

Alex's focus sheet for finding the main idea in *Dance My Dance*.

Fluent Guided Reading Focus Sheet— Learning Log

Name __Jessica__

Title of Book __Whale Watching__   Genre __Nonfiction narrative__

Author __Mary Cappellini__

What I Learned About the Topic and Vocabulary That Helped Me	Chapter/Page
Gray whales swim from Alaska to Mexico for three months to have their babies	p. 3
They travel close to shore. They swim just below the surface.	p. 6
Fluke - tail, whale's footprint They move it up and down, and it makes a big, flat circle	p. 6
Whales breathe - blowhole When whales breathe, they blow air and water from their blowholes.	p. 9
Barnacles Little animals that look like rocks are barnacles that grow on the whale's back. These barnacles are only found on gray whales	p. 13
Breaching - whale jumps out of the water.	p. 14
Diving - gray whales make two or three shallow dives. They make a deeper dive and stay underwater almost 10 minutes.	p. 14

Jessica's learning log about *Whale Watching*.

But look!
Her back looks strange.
It looks like there are rocks
on her back!

Oh! I know what they are!
They're barnacles!
They're little animals
that grow on gray whales.
They look like the barnacles
that grow on piers.
But these ones are the kind
that only grow on gray whales.

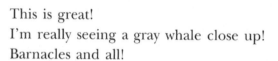

This is great!
I'm really seeing a gray whale close up!
Barnacles and all!

12

13

Pages from *Whale Watching.*

reading, I said, they could add the new information ("what we learned") to the last column of the K-W-L chart.

A learning log is also helpful to children when they do research. I find that this focus sheet is used most successfully with nonfiction texts, but it could also be used to keep track of what has been learned about a character, for example, or to keep track of the clues in a detective novel.

Keeping track of new information helps children synthesize by adding new knowledge to what they already know. It is often difficult for children to synthesize while they are reading. Synthesizing is very important, however, because students need to figure out which information is important, which information they should add to their knowledge base, and which information they should just leave behind (Harvey and Goudvis 2000). They can help each other do this by keeping track of important ideas and vocabulary and then discussing these with peers in a small group.

Facts or Opinions

Distinguishing between fact and opinion is an important strategy for all readers yet a difficult one to learn and one that can be especially tricky for

English language learners. Often children believe everything they read, and ELLs are just trying to make sense of the text, so trying to decide if something is fact or opinion can be challenging. In factual articles, for example, the author often shows his slant or prejudice, and it is important for the readers to be aware of this. One teacher at a school I was consulting at in Los Angeles County in a third- and fourth-grade combination class noticed that many of her students had difficulty distinguishing fact from opinion when they were reading articles from magazines and newspapers and even the history textbook. We therefore chose the focus of understanding the difference between fact and opinion for a demonstration guided reading lesson in order to help fluent readers gain a better understanding of what they were reading.

We chose *Canoe Diary* because it provides a lot of facts about animals in the wild and also lets readers look closely at the writer's choice of words as he shares his personal experiences on the canoe trip. The author's voice truly comes through, revealing his opinions throughout the text. We wanted to see if the students could distinguish between fact and opinion and if their level of language proficiency influenced their ability to distinguish between the two. The children in the group were intermediate

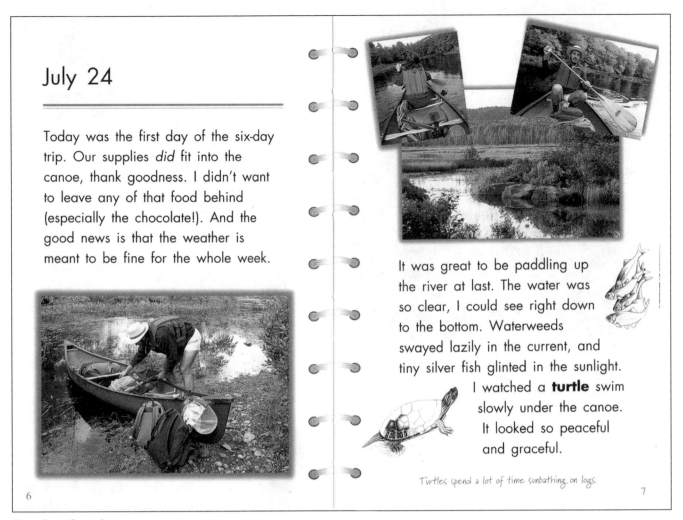

July 24

Today was the first day of the six-day trip. Our supplies *did* fit into the canoe, thank goodness. I didn't want to leave any of that food behind (especially the chocolate!). And the good news is that the weather is meant to be fine for the whole week.

It was great to be paddling up the river at last. The water was so clear, I could see right down to the bottom. Waterweeds swayed lazily in the current, and tiny silver fish glinted in the sunlight. I watched a **turtle** swim slowly under the canoe. It looked so peaceful and graceful.

Turtles spend a lot of time sunbathing on logs.

6

7

Pages from *Canoe Diary.*

and early advanced speakers, and most of them were reading pretty close to grade level. The text is at third-grade reading level (level N). Most of the children were third-graders.

In the introduction we talked about the difference between fact and opinion and looked at the front cover, the back page blurb, and the photographs. I elicited the children's experiences with canoes, camping, river trips, and plants and animals. A couple of children had been camping, and only one had been in a canoe, but many of them had been to a river. Right away they focused on the animal names on the back cover, yet none of them knew what a moose, a loon, or a muskrat was. The photographs in the text riveted their attention: "There's the moose!" "Here's the loon!" "Wow, look at that snake!" I asked them to look at the index of animals, and they found that the muskrat was described on page 21. Instead of reading the book from start to finish, I said, they could go right

to the page and find information on the animal they were interested in. Their job, I reminded them, was to distinguish fact from opinion.

We then read the first few pages of *Canoe Diary* together, giving them a taste of the author's voice. They read the entries dated July 21 and July 24 silently and listed on the focus sheet (Appendix F8) a fact and an opinion from each. After we had shared in the group whether what they found were facts or author's opinions, they used the text to research the animals they were most interested in. By allowing them to choose their own topics, they were motivated to read and find out information, and by sharing in the group they benefited from learning much more information than each could have learned by herself.

When one of the children shared his findings, we all turned to the same page and discussed whether we agreed that the statement was a fact or the author's opinion. We realized that the children's language level was not a hindrance to their ability to understand the concept of fact or opinion. The format of the text helped substantially because most of the pages have the animal names in bold-face type with a small drawing and a short high-lighted paragraph about each animal. Many of the sentences are very short, so the children often copied them directly onto the focus sheet in the fact or opinion column. The shared oral discussion was the most important part of the lesson.

Some of the children read more slowly and didn't write down as much as others. But they still shared in the discussion. The focus sheet is designed to help children focus on the purpose of the lesson, but it is not meant to require children to spend the whole time writing when they should be reading and discussing. If some students finish reading faster than others, they can write down their findings. Or, as a follow-up they can take the sheet back to their seats and continue reading and researching.

I rarely finish a guided reading book for fluent readers in one session. The strategy we are working on and the group discussion are more important than finishing the book. I then have a choice of choosing that book for another guided reading lesson or choosing a new book and focus for the next lesson while leaving students to finish the old book on their own. I tend to choose the latter but not always. Sometimes the children want to come back and share their individual findings with the group. Sometimes I encourage them to discuss the book with partners as they continue their investigation. If they are well trained in literature circles, that is a worthwhile extension of the guided reading lesson. The following writing samples are from two children who worked together after the lesson to try to continue distinguishing fact from opinion. The teacher noticed from their writing that they still needed work on this strategy and would revisit it.

DISTINGUISHING BETWEEN FICTION AND NONFICTION

Many children in the upper grades still have trouble distinguishing between fiction and nonfiction. Even with units of study on different genres, it seems they still get confused. Because some ELLs don't have access to libraries or books at home,

Students' focus sheets for fact or opinion in *Canoe Diary*.

they may not read a variety of fiction and nonfiction books. I try to choose books for this focus, therefore, that have a combination of fiction and nonfiction within them. As I mentioned, there are paired fiction-nonfiction sets available today that could be read in different lessons and compared in the discussions. But I still think it is valuable in one guided reading lesson to help children put their knowledge of different genres to use by trying to decipher the genres used by the author in one text.

A book I enjoy using with fluent readers is *The Land of the Dragons,* which has a combination of fiction and nonfiction within it. It is difficult for readers to catch the difference between the legend at the beginning and the author's experiences on the island of Komodo, where Komodo dragons live. The book starts with the author's dialogue with his daughter about a carving of a dragon from Indonesia, and moves right into a legend about how dragons came to be on the island, and then moves back to a dialogue about real dragons (large lizards) that live on the island today. There are supportive photographs and descriptions throughout, even accompanying the legend, so the children have trouble perceiving what is real and not real. It is amazing to hear how many children think that the dragons of storybooks are real. This book always gets the same response whenever I use it: fascination with the real Komodo dragons yet a belief in flying dragons from the time of castles and princesses, with difficulty distinguishing between the two.

One group of fourth-graders in San Ysidro, California, had just such reactions. I started with a discussion of the title, which led to a group K-W-L chart on dragons:

Dragons—What I Know

"They throw fire from their mouth."
"They fly."
"They have sharp teeth."
"They're green."
"Sharp nails and a long tail"
"The tail has an arrow-point."
"They're like dinosaurs."
"Don't like water."

They seemed to know a lot about dragons from storybooks. "Are dragons real?" I asked. They looked

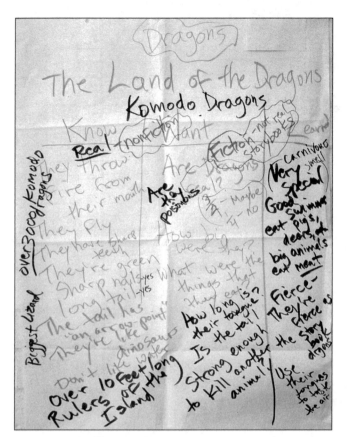

K-W-L chart for *The Land of the Dragons.*

at me, grinned, and looked uncertainly around; most of them said maybe. One child said no. Their only questions before we opened the book were How big are dragons? and What do they eat?

We wrote those questions on the K-W-L chart. They still hadn't answered my question of whether dragons are real. I purposely did not call their attention to the back cover, which states, "Komodo dragons are the world's biggest lizard, and are just as fierce as the dragons you read about in storybooks." I wanted to see if they could figure this out themselves. The author's daughter, featured in the book, doubted if dragons were real.

I asked them to read the first chapter on their own to see if any of their questions were answered or to see if they had any more questions. Once they read past the legend and realized that real dragons lived on Komodo, they added these questions to the K-W-L chart regarding the Komodo dragons: Are they poisonous? How long is their tongue? Is the tail strong enough to kill another animal? I used different-colored pens to distinguish between the predictions we had originally written down on the chart and information the children gathered on their focus sheets.

Name _Manuel_

Title of Book _____ **Genre** _Fiction/Nonfiction_

Author _The Land of Dragons_

What I Learned About the Topic and Vocabulary That Helped Me	Chapter/Page
I learned that theres type of dragons that are real.	Pg 1-9 chapter 1
I learned that komodo Dragons eat almost any type of animals, They are good swimmers. They are very big. That they have forked toonges. that looked like fire and are yellow.	chapter 2 Pg 10-16
How much time do the eggs take to hatch?	chapter 4-5 29-33 pg pg 17-28

Student's focus sheet for fiction or nonfiction in *The Land of the Dragons.*

Name __Jocelyn__

Title of Book __The Land Of The Dragons__ Genre __nonfiction and fiction__

Author _____

What I Learned About the Topic and Vocabulary That Helped Me	Chapter/Page
I learned that they had red eyes. They are ten feet long.	Ch.1 Pg.1-9
Comodo Dragons are canivors. They are also good swimmers so you would have to be carefull when you got in the water. They yellow forked tounges.	Ch.2 Pg.10-15
Comoda Dragons fight for mates. When one is defeated, Another will hold it down and scratch it twice. They like to live in holes. After they lay eggs they look alot thiner.	Ch.3 Pg16-18

Student's focus sheet for fiction or nonfiction in *The Land of the Dragons.*

We talked about the difference between real and make-believe. They still had trouble understanding that the book's beginning legend about a crippled boy who turned into a crippled dragon was not real. I told them that they were now going to read true information about the Komodo dragons and asked them to keep track of that in a learning log (Appendix F6). Often I give children a K-W-L focus sheet to record their research (Appendix F7), but since this book is a little more complicated, I chose to use a learning log so they could just write down what they learned. I said we would confirm what they wrote down about Komodo dragons.

I stopped their silent reading after about ten minutes in order to discuss their findings and check their understanding of the text. Then they went back to reading silently again. Each time we talked about the difference between the dragons in storybooks and the Komodo dragons. The children found the two references in the book where the author made the distinction. One included the line from the back cover, so we turned to it and read it together. The other reference talked about the Komodo dragons being like "the fire-breathing dragons in storybooks" with "flickering" tongues and watching over a "buried treasure." "That's their eggs," shouted Jocelyn. Then they all started to realize that the dragons in legends were not real but still similar to real dragons.

We checked the group K-W-L chart to confirm their new knowledge. They realized that the only things they had predicted correctly were that Komodo dragons have sharp teeth, sharp nails, and a long tail. Komodo dragons don't fly and they are good swimmers. "Watch out," said Carolyn. "I'm never going swimming again," said Juan. I assured them, however, that Komodo Island is very far away and that there aren't any Komodo dragons off the coast of California.

Other Strategies

There are many other strategies that could be highlighted in guided reading lessons for fluent readers, such as inferring (Appendix F9) and author's intent (Appendix F10). It is important to remember that what we teach in shared reading the children can practice in guided reading with our guidance. Then they can truly put these strategies to work while they read independently and in literature circles.

13 INDEPENDENT READING AND LITERATURE CIRCLES

It's All Greek to Me

When I was in college, I always dreaded the courses I had to take outside my major, especially in the sciences. Once, sitting in a large lecture hall trying to take notes on a biology lecture by a professor who spoke rather rapidly, although it was in English, I understood very little—it was all Greek to me! When I looked over at a Puerto Rican friend of mine who was sitting next to me, I saw he was keeping up with the professor's pace—by jotting down notes in Spanish. Here I was, a native speaker barely able to understand the lecture in English, and there he was, not only understanding it in English but at the same time translating it into his primary language. (True, he had a strong background in science.) When I asked him later why he had taken the notes in Spanish, he said, "I couldn't write fast enough in English." What mattered was that he had the conceptual background to understand the lecture; the language it was delivered in was immaterial to him.

Comprehension is the key to learning, regardless of language. Even for advanced speakers and fluent readers of English, higher-level thinking may come easier in the primary language. My friend, in this difficult situation, used his native language to his advantage. When we want the focus of English language learners' reading and book discussions to be meaning making, which language they think or speak in to achieve this is secondary. Many ELLs reading in English understand much more than they are able to explain. We hope, of course, that ELLs will improve their English language ability enough not to routinely rely on the primary language to express their comprehension, and we know that one of the best ways to improve it is for them to read more books in English. The more time they have to read, the better readers they become and the more academic vocabulary they develop (Krashen 2003; Shin 2001; Allington 2001; Cummins 2003). Continuing to read books in the primary language after they have learned English does not interfere with their English language development (Krashen 2003). Independent reading is therefore something we have to make time for in our classrooms—it is an important part of a balanced literacy program.

A large selection of books for independent reading should be easily accessible in a well-organized classroom library to all children, whatever their reading and language levels, in leveled collections, category collections, theme and genre collections, author collections, series collections, and if possible in primary languages other than English. Young readers often need help in choosing books that will interest them and that they can succeed with, and this guidance can be offered through book talks, book reviews, or conferences.

Also important is to encourage children to discuss and respond to what they are reading. If they are engaged in discussion about their reading—in conferences, buddy reading, small-group lessons, literature circles—they will deepen their understanding and learn that comprehension is paramount. They can retell a story to an adult, share a story with their peers, or respond to their reading in a response journal in English or their primary language. The discussion that takes place in a literature circle, or book club, encourages some ELLs to take more risks using their new language and to participate much more than they would feel comfortable doing in larger-group settings. As teachers, we are not privileged to hear all the discussions that go on in literature circles, nor do we need to. Yet if we listened in, we would hear ELLs naturally negotiating between their two languages, using a little of both to describe their reactions to the chosen book.

In this chapter I discuss the importance of managing an independent reading time for your English language learners, including helping them select appropriate books out of a well-planned classroom library, using their own book boxes, and participating in rich dialogue and discussions in literature circles or book clubs.

GUIDING CHILDREN TO SELECT BOOKS FOR INDEPENDENT READING

Children learn to read by reading. Even after much research showing the importance of having children read (Smith 1988; Allington 2001; Krashen 2003), many people think English language learners are not ready to read independently in English because they are at lower levels of language proficiency. But if we agree with the conditions of learning (Cambourne 1988), then children need to practice what they are learning. That means we have to guide children to find books that they can read at their independent reading levels. For a beginning speaker who is barely producing one or two words, a chapter book would not be a good choice, but neither would a board book designed for babies. If a student already knows how to read in the primary language, he can transfer his reading strategies and be able to read a higher-level English book than a child who is illiterate in the primary language.

We need to match students with a good book based on the child's interests, age, language level, and reading level. Although independent reading books are self-selected, children need guidance and direction. To help them make good choices, they need someone who knows their individual reading and language levels to recommend the best authors and the best titles. ELLs in particular need a lot of guidance choosing books because of limited exposure to English books in their homes. If a book is too hard, a child might spend half an hour just flip-

A child gets help choosing a book for independent reading.

ping through the pages, or if it is too easy, he might just reread it because it is less work; or he might not be able to find a book to read and spend independent reading time dillydallying.

In a fifth-grade classroom in San Diego, I noticed one child lingering near the classroom library while everyone else started reading during independent reading time. When I approached the child, I noticed he had on a Padres t-shirt. I asked him if he liked baseball, and he said yes. During our brief discussion, he told me his dad didn't know how to play baseball, but loved it. His family spoke only Korean at home. Although I knew he was an English language learner, I wasn't sure of his reading level. He was gravitating toward the picture books, so I assumed he was reading below fifth-grade level. I luckily found *Baseball Saved Us,* which describes how baseball brought hope to the Japanese American boys in the internment camps. He seemed pleased with the selection. We opened a page and he read it to me with interest without any trouble. I also looked for *Willie Wins,* about a Filipino boy who gets teased after striking out in Little League, but I couldn't find it in the teacher's library. I told him about it and suggested we check in the school or public library.

I noticed that the teacher did not have a designated sports section or tub of sports books in the library, and I thought I would suggest her to do so. Looking through her chapter books, I didn't see any with a baseball theme or at a lower level for him. I did know, though, that she had some shorter chapter books that were set aside for guided reading for readers reading below grade level, but with high interest level. She had some *Toocool* books and *Boyz Rule!* books (see Appendix F2). We went through the titles and found *Baseball's Best,* a chapter book at the second-grade level, and numerous other sports titles about soccer, ice hockey, basketball and other sports. Although the teacher might want to save these for guided reading, it is critical that we use all the resources in our classroom to find books to match the interest and readability level of each child for independent reading.

In order to find a "just right" book for children to read, some people suggest giving students a "five-word" guideline for choosing independent reading books, that is, if there are five words on the page that a child does not know, the book is likely too difficult and the child should look for something else. But, for English language learners especially, I prefer to use an "I don't get it" guideline; that is, if they get lost on a page, try strategies to help themselves, and still don't get it, then the book is likely not right for them. There are often more than five words on a page that ELLs have difficulty with, but they still understand the point of the story or haven't lost the meaning. If children find a book that they "don't get" but still would like to read, I ask them to put it into their individual book boxes, and I will help them find a way to read it later. They might have a buddy, or perhaps an adult volunteer, who could read it to them. I might also read it with a child during her conference time, even if this means reading it over several conferences if it is a long book. Or, I might read the book aloud to the whole class.

Placing a good book in a child's hands that is close to her appropriate level gives her confidence as a reader. Having children reread small books and Big Books they are already comfortable with, having them follow along with audiotapes, or having them do "light reading" like magazines, comics,

Children choose books for independent reading.

and picture books is important, too, for ELLs who might be struggling with reading (Routman 2002).

Book talks are a great help in interesting children in particular books. Throughout the year, with a variety of titles from different genres, teachers tell students about a favorite book, why they like it, and why they think others will like it. Or they review new books that come into the classroom library. They don't give away the ending but encourage children to pick up the book and read it themselves. Children practice reviewing books themselves by reading the blurbs on the back cover, listening to the teacher give book talks, writing reviews in their response journals, and sharing their recommendations with peers.

One review from a first-grader recommended a book in this way: "It has mysteries, excitement, thrills and chills and sometimes heart-touching parts" (quoted in Goodman, Bird, and Goodman 1991). The editor remarked, "I don't know what book [this] first-grade student was reviewing, but I intend to find out and read it myself." Children should always be this excited about books they have read. Book talks by students inspire other children to read the book and also give speakers a chance to use their new language for an authentic purpose. The language function of recommending will be useful in many other situations and helps English language learners develop their oral fluency.

Teachers or family volunteers can videotape or audiotape children's book reviews. Some teachers keep one tape on each child and record the book reviews the child does throughout the year. This is a good opportunity to record the progress of English language learners. It is also a wonderful gift to give families at the end of the year or to place in the child's portfolio.

When we show interest in a book a child has read, we model how to think and talk about it. We have opportunity to do this while we confer with children during the first independent reading time (see Chapter 4 for reading schedule).

What did you read?
Did you like it? Why?
What was your favorite part?
What do you think about the main character?
Did the book remind you of anything in your own life?
What do you think about the author's style of writing?
Did you like the topic?

We also want to get feedback on whether the book's topic and level felt right to them in order to recommend further choices:

Was the book hard to read, or just right?
Are there parts you didn't understand?
Do you need any help?
Would you like help picking another book?
Would you like to read another book by the same author?
Would you like to read another book in this series?
Did you like reading a story, or would you like to try a book with facts?

Reading conferences are a wonderful time to also take notes on what you've learned about the reader in order to plan for further instruction (see Chapter 14 on individual instruction).

ASSEMBLING A CLASSROOM LIBRARY FOR INDEPENDENT READING

It is clear, even to the untrained eye, whether a classroom has a good library. A classroom library is

Part of the classroom library.

essential to the reading success of children (Routman 2002). Do the books in the library take up at least one wall or one large corner? If not, there are not enough books.

Luckily, there are thousands of books in every school—in the classrooms, the library, the book room, or teachers' personal collections—to enable a teacher to put a good book in every child's hands. Picture books, books on tape, small books, Big Books, leveled collections, poems and poetry charts, theme collections, author collections, genre collections, award-winning books—all should be part of the classroom library from kindergarten through the upper grades.

The books should be displayed so as to entice readers to take them off the shelf. Especially in the lower grades, books should be displayed in clearly labeled tubs or baskets so children can easily see them and browse through them. The books should be organized by topics, authors, genres, series, and if possible, by primary language if there are many ELLs in the classroom with one primary language like Spanish.

Picture books should be a large part of the library regardless of the ages of the children. These books often address problems and topics appropriate for all ages (see Appendix D2). Books with multicultural illustrations and themes are good for teaching diversity. A substantial percentage of the books in the upper grades should be chapter books and nonfiction. Upper-grade ELLs reading below grade level tend to choose nonfiction texts. They also tend to choose books with characters from TV shows, like Arthur or Rugrats, even though the themes may seem young. Perhaps it is because they watch a lot of TV at home, so the characters are familiar to them and reading about them is at their comfort level. But it is our job to introduce them to book characters in series books that they can also become familiar with, like Nate the Great, Cam Jansen, Flat Stanley, or Amber Brown (see Appendix G1). Studies have shown that children reading below grade level read more if series fiction books and other high-interest books including comics are readily available to them (Krashen 1999). Series books are popular with both beginning readers and fluent readers (e.g., Harry Potter).

Many publishers provide tapes with all their books for in-class reading, including books for older children (see Appendixes E5 and F2). Older children at all stages of English language proficiency can benefit from reading along with a tape, especially because few ELLs have the benefit of models reading to them at home.

The following books discuss suggestions for books and how to set up a classroom library: Routman 2002; Sibberson and Szymusiak 2001; Fountas and Pinnell 2002; Harvey and Goudvis 2000; Taberski 2000; Dorn, French, and Jones 1998.

SCHEDULING AND MANAGING INDEPENDENT READING TIME

As shown in Tables 4.1, 4.2, 4.3, and 4.4 during reading workshop, when I am conferring with students or meeting with small groups for guided reading or mini-lessons, the rest of the children are reading independently. This should start in kindergarten. Children at a very young age can explore texts, pick them up, start to read. Besides just reading books, I have always tried to set up learning environments where the whole focus is literacy and children see the time when they are working on their own not as unfocused activity time but rather as learning time where the goal is to read or write. Even in kindergarten, children can read menus and write recipes or shopping lists for the kitchen area, for example (see Diller 2003 for more information on literacy centers). I have to trust the children to take responsibility, and when I do that, they successfully take on their role as readers.

Nothing motivates children to read more than to be able to pick up a book and see themselves as readers. One year I had thirty-five first-graders who all thought of themselves as readers. Wherever I was in the room during reading workshop, I could look around and see everyone reading. Yesenia, a child who was thought to belong in special ed because she couldn't sit still, was sitting in a rocking chair, moving back and forth and reading for half an hour at a time. José, Miguel, and Mario were sitting on the floor in a corner reading their favorite books to each other. Ivonne was reading a book I had read to the class during read-aloud, and others were reading Big Books we had used in

Reading small books for independent reading.

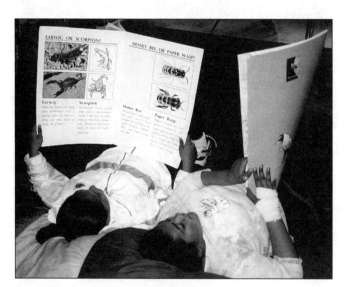

Reading Big Books for independent reading.

shared reading. Four or five children were listening to books on tape. Others were scattered in bean bag chairs, couches, or their seats reading books from their individual book boxes.

There was no way I could keep up with what every child was reading every day that year. They kept their own reading logs, which listed all the books they had read and the genres. They also responded in response journals, some with a picture, others with sentences. I didn't set up literacy centers per se but rather offered them the chance to read different types of books in different areas of the room. There are books, however, that discuss setting up literacy centers for children, especially for primary classrooms (e.g., Diller 2003; Dorn, French, and Jones 1998; Fisher 1995).

Independent Reading Log

Date	Title	Fiction	Non-fiction
3/8	My Camera	X	
3/8	Baby Animals		X
3/9	So THaT'S What I+ is!		X
3/9	the PuPPy	X	
3/10	Have you Got Everything colin?	X	
3/10	Ears		X
3/10	HeLP!	X	
3/11	Where IS curly?	X	
3/11	Animal Homes		X
3/11	Special Places	X	
3/12	My Plant		X
3/12	Boomers Big Surprise	✓	

Independent reading log.

If I want to meet with guided reading groups every day during independent reading time, in the primary grades I only have time for two or three conferences per day, in the extra-short independent time, so in a small class I could confer with each child every couple of weeks and in a large class less often. In the upper grades, since the reading workshop is somewhat longer, I might have time for three or four conferences per day. My interactions with individual students during guided reading also offer some of the benefits of conferences as I listen to a child read, discuss the text, help him with strategies, and take notes. But in separate conferences I can focus on a child's independent reading and help her make good choices while she is looking for books in the classroom library.

Individual book boxes are a wonderful way for children, especially in the lower grades, to keep track of their own independent reading books. Book boxes contain

Self-selected books
Books they have read
Guided reading books they have read
Books they want to read but can't read alone
Books they want to read with a buddy
Books the teacher has selected to challenge them
Books that the teacher or a friend thought they would like
Books that match the class thematic study

Where do all these books come from? They come from the classroom library or from the school book room. This means that books which go into the book boxes need to be returned eventually and the boxes replenished. For upper grades, it is the classroom library rather than the individual book boxes that the children rely on for their independent reading, although some children may still have their own private selections. The classroom library is also the focus for the primary grades, but individual book boxes are helpful for kindergartners and first-graders to keep their own books easily accessible.

LITERATURE CIRCLES

Literature circles are a natural outgrowth of independent reading. Students can respond to their independent reading in personal journals, but reading or responding by oneself is not the whole satisfaction one can get out of reading a book. Most people, children and adults alike, seek the extended satisfaction of sharing their insights and opinions about books with their peers, as millions of adults do in book clubs throughout the United States. Oprah Winfrey's nationally televised book club is often credited with boosting the popularity of this activity, and many children have heard of a relative or teacher who takes part in a book club. Thanks to books describing the use of literature circles in the classroom (e.g., Daniels 1994; 2002; Peterson and Eeds 1990; Short and Pierce 1990), literature circles have become a formal part of many teachers' literacy programs.

Children's literature circles are heterogeneous, composed of English language learners and native speakers of diverse cultures and at various reading and language levels who have agreed on a book they would like to read and discuss. They get together to have "grand conversations" about books (Peterson and Eeds 1990). This format was endorsed as "one of the best classroom practices" by the National Council of Teachers of English and International Reading Association in *Standards for the English Language Arts*. In these book discussions or dialogues (Daniels 2002; Peterson and Eeds 1990), children construct meaning naturally by listening and responding to others, and sharing their opinions and experiences in relation to a text.

With the diversity in our multicultural classrooms, cross-cultural learning becomes a natural occurrence (Samway, Whang, and Pippitt 1995). Engaging in literature circles, students come to appreciate their peers' different strengths and backgrounds. This breaks down barriers in the classroom community. For instance, one group of fifth-grade girls from different cultures learned that each of them had experienced moving to a new school or a new place. They shared how hard it had been, and seemed to gain a new respect for each other after having talked about these common experiences.

Children are very capable of taking part in literature circles by themselves, and ELLs often use both the primary language and English to express themselves in such settings. This is okay because the foremost purpose of such groups is independent meaning making.

As I mentioned earlier, by allowing children to simulate what they read in their primary language actually increases their cognitive development (Freeman and Freeman 2000). So when you talk about setting up literature circles, the dialogue is what should be encouraged, regardless of the language.

Managing Literature Circles

Literature circles meet, preferably daily, during the hour set aside for independent reading time while the teacher is meeting with guided reading groups. Daniels (2002) suggests that students meet in literature circles a couple of times per week, but I feel discussion is so important, especially for ELLs at the upper grades, that it should take place every day to achieve its greatest benefit. During this period, not all children are engaged in literature circles at the same time. Some may not have joined ongoing groups but may do so later, when new groups form. A literature circle may be formed when one or more children have read or heard about a book they want to discuss and request the teacher to add this to the wall chart of literature circles in progress. Interested in the new addition, other children sign up to join that discussion group or book club.

A different way of forming literature circles would be for the teacher to present a selection of books to the whole class and ask them all to choose titles from among them, or for the teacher to ask the whole class at a certain time to suggest for literature circles books they have read or heard about, share a brief description of the book, and then to list these choices on a wall chart. Children could then choose to join the group of their choice. On occasion, if the teacher perceives that a child often chooses a book that is way too difficult or joins a group just because of friendships, she could encourage the child to join a different group in order to reap the benefits of participating more fully in a shared discussion which are: deeper comprehension, appreciation for others' viewpoints and experiences, and confidence as a speaker and reader.

Once the books are chosen and children have signed up for the groups that will discuss particular books, they can sign up for specific roles (with accompanying role sheets) to take in starting the group discussion, for example, the *connector*, who speaks of connections he has found in this book to his own life or another book; the *literary luminary*, who highlights for the others an interesting, funny, or exciting part of the story; the *summarizer*, who summarizes key points or the main idea; the *discussion director*, who asks open-ended questions (Daniels 1994; 2002).

There are numerous other roles, like *artful artist*, that Daniels lists in his book as a guide for teachers and students, including roles specifically for nonfiction titles. But he warns about an over-reliance on role sheets: "In some classrooms, the role sheets became a hindrance, an obstacle, a drain—sometimes a virtual albatross around the neck of book club meetings. What had been designed as a temporary support device to help peer-led discussion groups get started could actually undermine the activity it was meant to support" (Daniels 2002, p. 13).

I have often seen literature circles where children take turns reading from their role sheets rather than sharing their thoughts in an interactive group discussion. We have to prepare students carefully for the purpose of literature circles, and model authentic interactive talk about books in the group discussions we lead after read-alouds or shared reading. Then, even though one child may come with formal questions to get the group started, hopefully the need for roles will fade as all the children participate fully in the dialogue.

Literature Circles in the Primary Grades

I have facilitated literature circles successfully in kindergarten and first-grade classes, where students met informally with their copies of the book in hand, read out their favorite parts, made connections to the story, and perhaps showed pictures they had drawn about the story. These groups were more like informal book clubs. They weren't concerned with a job or role they had to accomplish but simply brought their natural language and ideas to share. These young English language learners often rely heavily on speaking in the primary language, with another child translating if necessary. Sometimes I ask adult volunteers to read a book in English to English language learners if they want to participate in a book club with their friends but their English level isn't high enough to read the book themselves. A primary-grade literature circle could also evolve when participants in a guided reading lesson decide to meet again, reread the book or another book by the same author, and discuss it on their own.

Usually, though, literature circles in the primary grades need to be monitored and facilitated by the teacher. Sometimes I ask buddy readers or upper-grade children to help, but that doesn't always work because they want to lead and direct the group rather than facilitating talk by the younger children. I can ask adult volunteers to help, or I try to sit in on one literature group between my guiding reading groups just a couple of times per week. Starting with kindergarten, I also ask children to keep literature circle journals, where they record books they have read and their responses to the literature. Daniels (1994; 2002) and Peterson and Eeds (1990) have good suggestions on how to work with very young children in literature circles.

Literature Circles in the Upper Grades

I would like to share here some examples of literature circles in the upper grades in some very diverse schools in Southern California.

In one school I was consulting at in Huntington Beach, where every class included some English language learners, over half the teachers wanted to try out literature circles for the first time. They were especially interested in using literature circles to help in their management of independent reading

In the movie the Lord of the Rings', The Return of the King, Aragorn is king and has to do similar things like Jess and Leslie as rulers of Terabithia. The older students on the school bus sit on another side, away from the smaller kids, like at our lunch. Jesse is slower than Leslie, like I am to other people. I used to pretend like Jess and Leslie pretend about Terabithia. Jess and Leslie look forward to going to Terabithia like I look forward to some speical days. When May Belle said that her father gather Twinkies, it reminded me of of when one of my relitives go to a differer country, they get me something from there. When Leslie tells Jess stories, it reminds me of when people used to read to me. In the story, Leslie and her family don't have a T.V., but they have money, this is like my uncle who doesn't have alot of new things like a microwave and DVD player, but he has the money for them.

A student makes connections with *The Bridge to Terabithia* in literature response journal.

time so that they could meet with guided reading groups while other children were reading or meeting on their own.

One of the first things we did was take an inventory of all sets of books in teachers' classrooms. We found that there were more than enough titles to start literature circles right away because only five or six copies were needed per group, so teachers' sets of thirty could be split and distributed among the different classrooms. This provided a wealth of titles for children to choose from. One

fifth-grade class selected these titles to read: *The Bridge to Terabithia; Esperanza Rising; Hatchet; Sarah, Plain and Tall;* and *Number the Stars.*

To orient themselves, teachers checked out Daniels's books from the school's professional library, watched videotapes about conducting literature circles, watched me model how to get the groups started, and read the stories the children had chosen. Some taught all the roles to the children beforehand, others passed out new role sheets every day, and others just used a literature response log.

It was a learning process for the teachers as well as the children. As the literature circles progressed, as they sat in and listened to the conversations, as they saw when they needed to make suggestions and when they could sit back, the teachers became much more relaxed and comfortable. Control was definitely an issue for them because they were used to teacher-directed classrooms. But they saw that these student-led discussion groups could empower children who did not participate much in other settings. ELLs were able to share more confidently; shy children and special ed children took part more easily.

Some teachers told me that, as they had time during independent reading, they met with individual children, especially their English language learners, to make sure they were getting the gist of their reading assignment for the literature circle. I suggested other ways to help children who needed additional support to prepare for the group discussion because they might be having difficulty understanding tricky parts of the text. There were a lot of parent volunteers at the school who could be asked to read the books onto audiotape or to read individually to an upper-grade student (in another room or the school library, so as not to single him out). The mainstreamed special ed children took their books to the resource room, where the resource teacher helped them prepare for the next day's literature circle.

In the rich range of books available for literature circles, there will be some with unfamiliar geographic or cultural settings, historical periods, or nonstandard spelling indicating informal speech or dialect. This can be tricky, especially for ELLs, if children do not have the background knowledge to support their reading of the text. *The Bridge to Terabithia,* for example, contains a lot of informal speech or dialect and nonstandard spelling that native speakers, let alone ELLs, might have trouble with. The ELL in the group that chose this book was at very high language and reading levels, so he could handle it, and his response or connection to the text in his literature log was very high. But I have used this text in many classrooms and often have to scaffold it for the children. Scaffolding may just mean sitting in a couple of times with the group and highlighting a passage or two. But at other times—outside of

the literature circle, so as not to intrude on the student-led conversation—I focus on the tricky part more directly. The children and I read aloud some informal speech from the book, trying to say the words as they are spelled, to get a better understanding of what the characters are saying and their accent:

". . . but he, Jess, planned to give old Fulcher a
    le-etle surprise come noon."
"Whatcha drawing?"
"Ah, c'mon. Lemme see."
"I ain't gonna hurt nothing."

I point out to the students that this isn't correct speech but rather informal talk or dialect that people from different parts of the country sometimes use.

At another school I was consulting at in the inner-city of San Diego, in a Spanish bilingual fourth-grade class, most of the children except some recently arrived immigrants were reading in English. One literature circle was discussing the bilingual book *Friends from the Other Side/Amigos del otro lado.* I noticed that they were speaking all in Spanish, so I asked them in Spanish what they were reading, the English or the Spanish version? They all shouted, "The English!" "Okay," I said, and sat back to listen. They made lots of comments on what was happening in the story, what the author was trying to say, and what they had learned from the story, and they were answering each other's questions thoughtfully. At one point, one girl said, "*Dame más* details" (give me more details), and the others responded by giving more details in English, using examples from the English text.

English language learners naturally want to improve their English—they know it is the language of the classroom and of their new country. But they draw on both languages to express themselves when they are engrossed in thinking. I did wonder whether their speaking mostly in Spanish was due to just being more comfortable with it or not having enough English to tackle the in-depth questions they were considering. Either way, it was clear they had a good comprehension of the text. Would I have seen that, however, if their discussion took place only in English? They used their Spanish for a higher-level discussion. They switched to English to give the specifics, "the details," which they lifted from the book and in response to lower-level questions.

We need to continue to encourage the children to use their primary language when working independently to help them develop cognitively at a deeper comprehension level and thus help improve their knowledge of English at a higher proficiency level. How many of us, while learning a second language, still use our primary language to "think through" confusing texts or concepts in the second? I not only think it is fine to allow them to speak in their primary language, but I encourage it.

As I've mentioned, if the teacher does not understand the primary language of the children and is therefore unable to judge whether they are using higher-level thinking processes and comprehending the text, she would have to rely on other children, adult volunteers, or instructional assistants to translate the conversations. If we have no help in this regard, we need to ask the children to speak in English, whatever the level, and to listen to the quality of the response, not based on sentence structure, and to ask specific questions to elicit responses that reveal their comprehension or lack of it.

LITERATURE CIRCLES IN ACTION

These pictures of literature circles in action were taken in a fifth-grade classroom in a more suburban San Diego city school. The children started in a bilingual track and transitioned into the mainstream English program. Some of them are still considered ELLs at various stages of language proficiency, and others have been reclassified as fluent English speakers. The classroom teacher talked to the children about being in a book club and all having a responsibility to participate. Many adults attend book clubs and enjoy sharing with other people their interpretations of the chosen book, the connections they make to it, what they like or dislike about it, and questions they may have about it. This teacher had their literature circles meet every day for fifteen to twenty minutes, and then participants used independent reading time; first, to read the number of pages decided on by their group for the next day, and second, to go on with other books they are reading. They have two journals in which to record their responses—one for literature circle books and one for other independent reading books. The photos and captions on the next few pages describe the management of literature circles and independent reading time in this upper-grade classroom.

Watching children choose good books, read independently, and share their insights and connections with others are rewarding experiences for a teacher. It shows we have instilled in them the love of reading and valued their opinions as they construct meaning for themselves. By setting aside time and space for independent reading during the balanced literacy program, we emphasize for our students the importance of becoming lifelong readers.

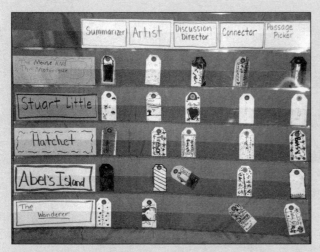

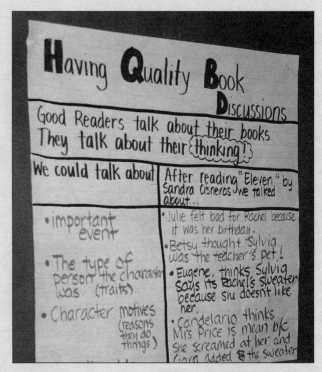

On an organizational wall chart, children can see which literature circle or book club they are in and which roles they are responsible for. They often change roles daily, moving their own tags. The chart allows the teacher to see what children are supposed to be doing in literature circles that day. She doesn't have to keep her own records. The children are responsible for doing this. A group stays together until it finishes reading its chosen text, sometimes up to a month if it is a long book. When the text is finished, individual children may choose to stay with the same group to read another book together, or change groups if they want to read a different title that another book club has chosen. In the latter case, they have to time the switch so that they can start up with the new group just as it is beginning.

A wall chart about "Having Quality Book Discussions" reminds children of the purpose and procedures of literature circles.

Taking part in one of five literature circles that are meeting simultaneously, these children are leading their own discussion. They are not sitting at their regular places but have moved to seats around a table to meet as a group.

The teacher is listening in on one of the book clubs. She is standing because she has just moved to that group from another group. By having all the literature circles take place at the same time, she can move freely from group to group to listen in on the discussions and assess whether any group needs help. Issues sometimes come up: someone has not done the reading assignment, or an argument has started. She asks the children how they think they should handle the problem and only steps in if they can't solve it. She might bring up the issue with the whole class later if she knows it has also been discussed in other groups.

Once literature circle time—approximately twenty minutes—is over, the teacher talks for a couple of minutes to the whole class to make sure that all the children have their reading and role assignments for the next day. She might comment briefly on something she has observed that is important for everyone. Then she asks the children to return to their regular seats or to find a place around the room for independent reading.

As the children take up their independent reading, the teacher meets with a guided reading group of three (two are shown). She works with one child while the others are reading silently on their own. Her guided reading assessment notebook is open, in which she has noted which guided reading groups she is working with, with which children and which books or articles. She also has put out some cards for words that these English language learners had difficulty with. During the lesson, she records in the notebook anecdotal notes about the children and what goes on in the lesson.

From her seat in the guided reading lesson, the teacher can see the rest of the students reading their literature circle assignments for the next day or their independent reading books. Two of the children are in the same book club, which just started reading *Shiloh*. They are checking the back cover before starting their reading.

Students choose new places to read as their teacher calls a new guided reading group. Because the children are all reading independently, she doesn't disturb them or worry about them missing an important discussion in their book club by calling guided reading groups at this time. Also, this gives her much more flexibility to call guided reading groups based on the needs of the children, which often changes daily. During her earlier tour of the literature circles, the teacher may have noticed that several children were having trouble with a strategy like summarizing. She now has the opportunity to interrupt these students' independent reading temporarily and call them over for an impromptu guided reading lesson focusing on that strategy, so that they will be better prepared to use it in their next book club meeting.

14

INDIVIDUAL INSTRUCTION

Like Water for Chocolate

When my in-laws were visiting from Argentina, they went to see the movie Like Water for Chocolate/Como agua para chocolate *with my parents. This Mexican art film, in Spanish with English subtitles, uses a cooking metaphor to talk about love and forbidden relationships. My in-laws often went to the movies in Buenos Aires, and they were used to seeing Hollywood films with Spanish subtitles. Now they would be able to ignore the subtitles and listen to the Spanish dialogue directly. My parents went to the movies less often, and rarely to foreign films, but they would be able to follow the action by reading the English subtitles. The movie was extremely funny but had some racy scenes in it. So, I wasn't sure all of them would like it, but at least each set of parents could enjoy it in their own language—or so I thought.*

As the movie went on, my mother and mother-in-law had no trouble following the story; they enjoyed the film and laughed at the funny parts. But my father and father-in-law had a more difficult time. My dad couldn't read the English subtitles fast enough, and when he did adjust to reading them, he couldn't look up at the same time and follow the scene being played on the screen. My Spanish-speaking father-in-law started by trying to read the English subtitles because he was so used to reading Spanish subtitles at home that he couldn't adjust to not reading them. Even after he realized that this wasn't necessary, he kept trying to match the English words in the subtitles with the Spanish dialogue on the screen, and thus lost the point of the story. For both fathers, finally, the combination of spoken and written media interfered with their understanding and enjoyment of the movie. By contrast, the two mothers, having thoroughly enjoyed themselves, walked out of the theater giving their husbands looks that said, What is your problem? All in all, it was quite an illuminating lesson on learning styles.

Perhaps many of you have had the same experience as my father and father-in-law while watching a foreign film. The cognitive demands of following the meaning of the film in another language while trying to read subtitles or with the distraction of subtitles can be too much for many people. It does take some getting used to. They got so into the details, they missed the big picture. How many of our students get so caught up in decoding words that they miss the overall picture? How many have trouble reading new genres and learning new strategies to read harder texts? They can improve with practice. But we have to take into consideration that all children (and adults) have different learning styles and different ways of making meaning for themselves. Some readers are very literal and try to translate literally from one language to another. Some are visual learners and depend heavily on pictures. Others are auditory learners and can move along best by reading along with audiotapes. Gardner (1983; 1993; 2000), in his theory of multiple intelligences, outlines seven different modes of learning, which we need to be aware of to optimize individual children's learning.

In this chapter I highlight ways that we can work with individual students who have diverse strengths and needs, and who deserve individual instruction even in our busy classrooms. I look closely at the assessments, including running records, and the observations sheets we use throughout our balanced program, and which I have highlighted throughout the book, which includes looking at a child's language level, a child's reading level, a child's strategy use, and also a child's learning style, in order to plan an instructional program that will meet each child's individual needs. I share with you extra reading practices that you can set up within your classroom in order to help your English language learners become better readers in English. I also share with you some highlights of individual conferences from a variety of children in a variety of classrooms I worked in—

both primary and upper grade—and how I then helped teachers plan for their instruction by recording information on conference sheets. I discuss how you have choices to then work with these children in small-group or whole-group lessons within your balanced program. And I discuss the importance of all children having individual time with you, the teacher, regardless of the needs of all of the other children in the classroom.

| GUIDING QUESTIONS |

How can I meet the needs of all of my children?
What do I do with the assessment information I have gathered?
Are there any extra reading activities that will help my English language learners?
How often do we conference with our children?
What do we learn about our children in our conferences that will help us shape instruction?
Are there different types of reading conferences or do they all look the same?

USING ASSESSMENT TO PLAN INSTRUCTION

Assessment provides us with opportunities to plan effectively and to set goals for instruction of individual children. We need to look at their developmental progression in reading and language since they arrived at the school and in light of their prior histories. If our ongoing assessment does not help us plan for instruction or reach the goals we have set for our students, there is no point in doing it.

Flexibility Is Key

Flexibility is key within a structured program. We can be very organized and do the same thing every day, but we need to allow for continual changes in the children's learning accomplishments and instructional needs. With ELLs, there are extra variables because they are all at different levels of English language proficiency and reading, and there may be multiple primary languages in the classroom. Therefore flexible groups are an important part of the literacy program.

I have found that the anecdotal notes I jot down during shared reading or guided reading lessons are very helpful in planning mini-lessons. It is also from these notes that I update checklists (Appendix A) once a month for each child to watch their long-term growth. Every week I look at the results different children have produced— their responses in reading and language folders, literature response journals, and literature circle logs; my notes on strategies they were using during guided reading; their miscues on running records—and compare them to the checklists to see if they are making progress in language and reading. Then I decide which children should be called for small-group work on particular skills, whether the whole class would benefit from a mini-lesson, or which children I need to work with one-on-one because the progress they have made is minimal. Day-to-day instruction will vary for each child and change based on ongoing assessment. If we always start with the child rather than the curriculum, the curriculum becomes much easier to teach because we know what each child needs and what each child already knows, and can plan our lessons accordingly.

The four children highlighted in a guided reading lesson in Chapter 12, for instance, all had different strengths and weaknesses. A teacher looking at her notes about Ivonne's need to work on sentence patterns could decide to gather Ivonne and several other children with the same instructional need into a shared reading group with a Big Book that had repetitive sentence patterns. Or, seeing that David needed practice with inferring, he could focus on this strategy with a small group. Observations of Gabriela's and Nayeli's reading showed that they needed to work on synthesizing information and summarizing. Perhaps the teacher's review of these two children's folders reminds her that in a fourth-grade class all children need to work on this, so during a shared reading lesson or read-aloud with the whole class she focuses on these strategies.

Throughout the book I have emphasized observing children, taking notes, and making ongoing assessments. Unless we use this information to plan individual instruction effectively, gathering it becomes just so much more busywork.

A Running Record

One of the most frustrating things for a child is to be constantly assessed by the teacher and yet not be told what he does well or what he needs to improve. In the context of assessing a child, of taking a running record, for example, we should share with him what we observe, highlight for him what he is doing well, and then tell him what he needs to work on.

Running records give us valuable information on what a child needs to work on to improve her reading, but with ELLs the English language proficiency level affects the score, and the record may not give us the whole picture unless we closely analyze the miscues.

For instance, during a one-on-one conference, I took a running record on Mayra's reading of *Car Trouble.* Mayra was in first grade when I met her in Huntington Beach. At that time, during a guided reading lesson with a level 2 book, I found she was a beginning speaker and an emergent reader who was using effective reading strategies while adding to her vocabulary (see Chapter 1). Now an early fluent reader in second grade, she scored 93 percent on the running record of *Car Trouble,* a DRA level 22 book at a strong second-grade level. She was thinking while reading, and anticipating words based on her knowledge of syntax. But she was not always correct and did not always self-correct. On page 2, she read "cars came *by*" instead of "cars came *and* [went]," which makes sense until the next word, *went,* is reached. Once she noticed the miscue, she should have gone back and self-corrected, but she did not. Again anticipating, she read "when they *got*" instead of "when they *had* [all gone]," but in this and most later instances she did reread and self-correct, which told me that she was reading for meaning. Other miscues—*repeated* for *replied,* for instance—were visually close and the same part of speech, and made sense, so I could tell she was using the graphophonic, syntactic, and semantic cueing systems. She read *Dad* for *Dad's* but had no trouble with *let's,* so she had the language proficiency to read contractions.

Mayra read "Dad probably had *a* car trouble" instead of "Dad's probably had car trouble." Perhaps in this instance she anticipated a sentence like "Dad probably had a problem"; in that case,

rereading would clarify the sense. But perhaps she thought "Dad probably had *a* car trouble" did make sense; in that case, she would need to work on sentence structure and improve her recognition of what correct sentences sound like. Mayra had trouble reading names—Claire, Greco, Jane (read as "Jan", page 4)—as English language learners often do because they are not familiar with common U.S. names. But these errors should be looked at differently when determining the appropriateness of the book for the child because they aren't that important. Without counting such errors one would conclude that the book really is well within her independent reading level rather than her instructional level.

After the reading, I told Mayra what she had done well and what she should work on. The running record and my comments to her went into her reading and language folder. The classroom teacher was also recording running records with Mayra about once a month and entering them into her reading assessment notebook which is kept inside the reading and language folder to plan for further instruction. She planned some shared reading and shared writing lessons focusing on sentence structure to help Mayra and other children who had the same instructional need.

TEST PREPARATION

Because of pressures for doing well on standardized tests, teachers often put English language learners, who score lower on those tests, through monotonous practice drills rather than teaching them strategies that will help them do better on the tests. One school I consulted with in San Ysidro school district was under the gun to raise its test scores. Through analyzing miscues and assessing retellings, by looking at reading strategy and language structures used in order to see what individual children in each classroom and grade level needed to improve, we were able to design lessons within the balanced literacy program to help them develop their language and reading proficiency and thus do better on the tests.

The ELLs in the upper grades were having trouble understanding complicated texts. They weren't asking the difficult questions they needed to think

Car Trouble — level 22

PM STORY BOOKS (Rigby)
Story by Kathryn Sutherland (Kathy Su) I don't know

Mayra

p.2

Cars come by/and went

Dad

When sc

or/roc Greg: said

here agreed

p.3 isn't sc

p.4

Jan's

Jan

driveway st/rang Stared

went

p.5

stop/ded (pronn.)

ro/lded sc

R

repeated

We stopped — Questions on inferencing & retelling — Comprehension was great. Good responses — details

Page 2
The bell rang loudly
at the end of the school day.
Children and parents were everywhere,
and cars came and went.

But when they had all gone,
Claire and her little brother, Lewis,
were still there, waiting for Dad.
He was late—again.

"Dad's probably had car trouble," said Lewis.
"Let's go back to the classroom
and wait with my teacher."

"No, let's wait here today," said Claire.
"Then we'll be able to see Dad coming."

Lewis wasn't sure that this was a good idea.
"But Miss Greco says we should wait with her
if our parents are late," he argued.

Page 3
"It doesn't matter. Dad won't be long,"
said Claire. "We'll stand here by the gate."

Page 4
Minutes later, a blue car
came around the corner.
"That's not Dad," said Lewis.

"No, but it looks like Aunt Jane's car,"
said Claire. "Maybe she's picking us up."

"That's not Aunt Jane in the car,"
said Lewis.

The car slowed down. The driver stared
at Claire and Lewis. Then she drove off.

Page 5
Soon the same car came past again,
and this time it stopped.

The driver rolled the window down
and called to Claire and Lewis.
"Who are you waiting for?" she asked.

"Our dad," Lewis told her.

"Your dad asked me to pick you up,"
replied the woman.
"Get in and I'll drive you home."

Mayra's running record on *Car Trouble*.

about in order to gain an understanding of what they read. They also had trouble understanding the questions being asked in the tests.

In one fourth-grade class, based on the same Big Book that they were already reading, *Earthquake Experts,* we gave a lesson with a focus on asking questions and answering them. I modeled a shared reading with this familiar text, and together the children and I wrote our own questions and possible answers. The children became the test writers in this shared reading/shared writing. They were very tricky, supplying answers based on the text that were only partly correct, just as they knew test writers do on standardized tests. Many articles and books highlight the importance of teaching children about how tests are constructed and the traps that test writers set for children (e.g., Calkins et al 1998; Santman 2002; Wolf and Wolf 2002; Walton and Taylor 1997).

Working together with the whole staff, we also planned mini-lessons based on the common but difficult vocabulary used in the test questions, which seemed to confuse all the English language learners. The vocabulary words in test questions seem to be written in a genre of their own, and by helping ELLs become familiar with them, they would be much more comfortable when they saw these words in a test question. Most of these words are also English-Spanish cognates, so at least the Spanish-speaking children had a handle on their meaning:

actual	actual
assume	asumir
compare	comparar
conclude	concluir
describe	describir
determine	determinar
indicate	indicar
mark	marcar
most appropriate	más apropiado
opinion	opinión
probable	probable
reasonable	razonable
sequence	secuencia
sum	suma
table	tabla

(See more examples of Spanish/English cognates in Appendix C3.) We made charts and wrote sample

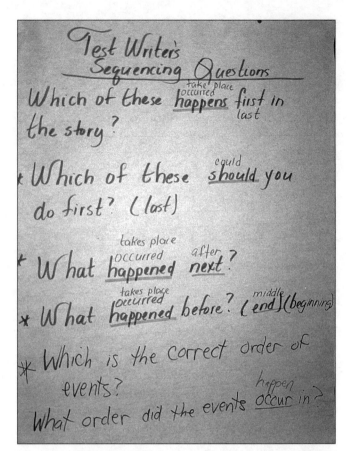

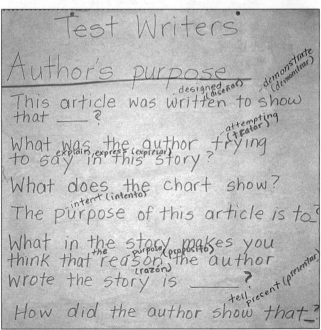

Children become the test writers to learn about standardized tests.

questions with these words and synonyms, so that children would have a better understanding of what they meant and how they were used.

We found that the best way to prepare children for the standardized tests was to continue teaching them effective strategies that they were already learning in the context of read-alouds, shared reading, and guided reading, and practicing in independent reading. The critical thinking that they developed, which included strategies like inferring, summarizing, analyzing, predicting, connecting, and using prior knowledge, helped not only their reading development and their language development, but also their test taking.

Their goal for their children was to increase their test scores, which they did rather effectively, but it was also to make them better readers and speakers of English and to have a life-long love of reading. They brainstormed together, both primary teachers and upper-grade teachers, on these common goals that they had for all of their children. They left their charts up for all to see in their teacher meeting room. Through small-group lessons in guided reading and whole-group mini-lessons in shared reading and read-aloud throughout the year, they were able to focus on the individual needs of their children, which were varied within each classroom. They made time for individual conferences with children to learn even more about each child's reading and language abilities. They also set up opportunities to have their English language learners have extra practice reading.

EXTRA READING PRACTICE

Children might need more opportunity to read one-on-one with an adult, a peer, or a small group of readers. This extra practice, which takes place during independent reading time, includes

---

★ Reading with the teacher or an adult volunteer
★ Buddy reading or cross-age tutors
★ Read-alongs
★ Choral readings
★ Reader's Theater

Reading with an Adult

Every child strives for attention from the teacher, and we have to make the time to respond. I have found that reading with children individually, even just two or three children for five minutes per day each, gives them confidence as readers and language users. Sometimes that bit of attention is all a

child needs to keep him moving and wanting to read independently. "Mrs. Cappellini, are you going to read with me today?" is what I often hear when I visit classrooms where I am helping teachers set up a more structured independent reading time. The children are excited at the possibility of reading one-on-one with me, even if it is only for a few minutes, and they are usually thrilled at the prospect of showing off how well they can read.

The teacher can't read with every child every day, but she might get help from retired people who would be willing to come in and read with the children. Sometimes we need to ask services clubs in the community to come to our assistance. College and high school students who need community service hours, or who are thinking about making a career out of teaching, are a great resource. And families, of course, should be our number one resource. If asked, and if they are literate, they would love to read not only to their own children but also to other children in the classroom.

Buddy Reading and Cross-Age Tutors

Another form of extra reading practice that is very helpful for ELLs is buddy reading. I have seen buddy reading implemented in several ways, and there isn't one right way to do it. Buddies can help each other with fluency and with strategies of figuring out unknown words or clarifying understanding of the text. They can just be two friends, two children who get together to spend time enjoying a book or talking about a book.

The children can select their own buddies, or pairs of readers can be selected by the teacher. Either way, feeling comfortable with each other is critical to the success of buddy reading, so we must be careful how these pairs of readers are selected. Personalities are always a factor. Once the children are paired up, they can take turns listening to each other read, helping and prodding each other when necessary, or they can read the book together as in choral reading, practicing fluency.

Sometimes teachers pair up a more advanced reader with a reader at a lower level in the same class. This can work if the children are comfortable with each other. But this becomes more like a tutor-student relationship than a friendship or buddy relationship. The better reader may try to show the

Buddy reading.

other child what to do, and the less-skilled reader may feel inferior, if they are in the same class. I am not saying this can't work, but if we are not careful with the personalities of the two, the buddy relationship cannot develop effectively. It is the same when two classes pair up as buddy readers. If there are fifth-graders with kindergartners, the older ones become teachers to the younger children. But if third-graders and first-graders or first-graders and kindergartners are paired, they will tend to consider themselves friends, look for each other on the playground, and send notes back and forth to each other. Thus, the relationship is different.

Many English language learners benefit from buddies who are closer in age and abilities, having a peer to share their enjoyment of what they are reading or learning. Others do better with cross-age tutors, older children working with younger children, usually three or four years apart. If a child needs a tutor, it is better to choose a child from another classroom rather than from the same classroom. *Buddy Reading: Cross-Age Tutoring in a Multicultural School* (Samway, Whang, and Pippitt 1995) is a helpful resource for setting up buddy reading. As the title indicates, the authors focus on cross-age tutoring.

It is also beneficial to pair buddies in the same classroom who might be reading at the same instructional level but have different levels of English proficiency. Reading with a peer who is a

native speaker or at a higher language level helps ELLs learn how to pronounce words and benefit from discussion with a good English model. Seeing a same-age buddy as a friend rather than as a tutor helps ELLs gain confidence as readers and speakers and builds friendships as well. It also shows the better English speaker that her buddy might be able to help with reading challenges in the text even though her English isn't at the same higher developmental level.

Read-Alongs

Read-alongs provide another opportunity for children to practice reading. They can be set up in the classroom with just a listening center and some good books on tape. Read-alongs are a crucial element in supporting ELLs in their development as readers. Because they do not have English models at home, they need to hear books read to them as often as possible. A listening center's purpose should be to have children read along with the tape, not just listen to it to improve fluency. Of course, ELLs also need to read new texts by themselves, but listening centers allow even fluent readers to improve their reading fluency and to enjoy reading.

I still remember hearing Meryl Streep read "The Velveteen Rabbit" on the children's channel on my airplane headphones when I took a trip across the country. It would have been even better if I had had the book in front of me, but it was wonderful to hear a story so well read. English language learners need the opportunity to hear well-read stories from as many sources as possible.

Many publishers produce in-class reading books with tapes. Big Books for shared reading come with little books and tapes. Books for read-alouds and guided reading come with tapes. In bilingual classrooms teachers can have the same book in English and Spanish (and some other languages) and the tape that goes along with each version (see Appendixes C4, E5, and F2 for lists of books on tape). If they are teaching in the primary language, they can place the same book in English in the listening center. In English-only classrooms teachers might have a primary language version of the tape in the listening center if children with that primary language are speaking at the beginning or

Reading along in the listening center.

early intermediate level in English, in order to reinforce the main ideas of the story.

The computer instead of the tape recorder can be a wonderful tool for children to read along with books. Although some teachers may not have an extra computer available for read-alongs, those that do have found that interactive books on CDs are a great resource and are wonderfully motivational. Bilingual books allow a child to read along in English and interact with the text by asking for the Spanish or Japanese translation of a word, for example, which helps connect to the primary language and build vocabulary. If a computer is not available in the classroom for this use, than the old-fashioned tape recorder with book works just fine.

Choral Readings and Reader's Theater

These are also wonderful techniques to have ELLs practice their English reading and speaking. Many teachers do not feel they have the time these days to have children perform choral readings or reader's theater. But I think we can have children do this during independent reading time occasionally without unduly taking away from instructional time. Children can benefit by meeting once in a while with a small group to practice and get ready to perform a choral reading or reader's theater for the class. This doesn't have to happen every week, but

perhaps once a month children can choose a text they want to read and prepare to perform it for the class. Choral reading and reader's theater help children with reading fluency and language development, and with being comfortable getting up in front of a group.

Choral reading is an extra reading practice activity, not an activity to be done during guided reading. The purpose of guided reading is to help children individually become better readers, even though they are in a small group. It is not the time for children to read aloud in unison. When children read in choral reading, they are part of a choir that relies on all of its members to read along. If one child falters a little, the others pick up the lapse, hopefully without the audience noticing that one faltered. If we did choral reading in guided reading, students would not be able to try out their own strategies to become better readers. Choral reading does help children gain confidence as readers and speakers, but it should be viewed as such—a time to build confidence while a group reads together.

Reader's theater, which is designed to have each child take a part, is a little more demanding on the ELLs who are at lower stages of language development. But there are usually main parts and small parts, so children can decide which parts they feel most comfortable taking. Even if a child takes only a small part, he will have a boost in confidence while taking part in the performance for the class. Reader's theater is an enjoyable way to explore literature and practice talk and reading.

READING CONFERENCES

When I am consulting with classroom teachers I am often asked to meet with individual children to get my opinion on the child's strengths and weaknesses in both language and reading development. This assessment provides us with valuable information to plan future mini-lessons or to help that child right on the spot. It also lets us just spend time reading with the child, and we can learn a lot about the child's choice of reading material and guide her in choosing appropriate and interesting books.

A one-on-one conference can be powerful for both the child and the teacher. As I mentioned, all children strive for individual attention. Setting up daily conferences, even if it is with only two or three children per day, tells students that they will have the opportunity to meet with the teacher individually every two weeks or so. They can wait for that if they know they will all have that chance. More information on conferences is given in Fountas and Pinnell (2001), Hindley (1996), Sibberson and Szymusiak (2003), and Taberski (2000).

Taking notes in conferences is important. The results can go into the child's reading and language folder, but when I am conferring with a few children per day, I like to keep a reading conference sheet (Appendix A2) listing the results for all the children with whom I conferred that day. I still would write comments in their individual reading and language folders, but I find that if I keep a master of what all the children are doing, it helps me in my planning to see if there are any patterns or if certain children can be grouped together. Otherwise, I'd have to go back to each individual child's folder, which I have them keep with them during reading, to compare notes and to decide which children to pull for which groups.

Jonathon, Mena, and Tania

The children that you see on the reading conference sheet come from that diverse classroom of English language learners and English-only children that my friend taught in Huntington Beach. Mayra was in that classroom as a second grader when Jonathon was a first grader. Now, new children with new and diverse backgrounds have arrived. One of them is Mena, from Afghanistan. She speaks Pashtu, Arabic, and is at an early intermediate stage of learning English. Tania was an immigrant from Mexico and Jonathon was Mexican American. He spoke primarily Spanish, but both he and Tania were now at an intermediate stage of English Language Proficiency. When I arrived in the room, the children were engaged in independent reading while the teacher was working in guided reading groups. Most of the children had their reading boxes with them and the conferences that day centered around what they had been reading in guided reading, since at least these three children had their book boxes filled with books they had read in guided reading and were now reading independently.

Jonathon, whom I met when he was a first-grader reading at level 4, had advanced to second grade and was reading at DRA level 16. In our conference he wanted to read me *The Careful Crocodile*. As noted on the reading conference sheet, he was self-correcting and trying to make sense of the text but had trouble with irregular verbs. In his retelling he was trying to use the future tense, although intermediate speakers are not expected to be able to use it yet, and his sentence structure was awkward. So I noted that in shared reading, shared writing, and cloze activities he could benefit from work on sentence structure and cause-and-effect statements that include the future tense ("If he walks there, he will slip on the mud").

Mena, a first-grader whose primary language was Pashtu, and Tania, a first-grader whose primary language was Spanish, needed help with sentence patterns using the present progressive and past tenses. Jonathon and other children in the class also needed practice with the past tense, so I would do a shared reading with a Big Book that had a repetitive pattern using the present progressive and past tenses. I would highlight the pattern while reading and then ask the children to practice it by writing their own sentences, writing on sentence strips, or acting out the story using the same patterns. In our conferences Mena and Tania shared

Reading Conference Sheet

To Monitor Reading and Language Development and to Plan for Instruction

Week of ____1/8____

Date/ Name of Child	Type of Conference Title of Book	Observed Reading Strategies and Language Used	Future Mini-Lessons Reading	Future Mini-Lessons Language
Jonathon 2nd grade (Span/Eng) intermediate speaker	Reading Progress: <u>The Careful Crocodile</u> Level 16	Reading: Self-corrected numerous times. Substitutions made sense. Had trouble with irregular verbs in text. Language: Sentence structure is awkward: "The mud will take him down the ground. It will slip him." He is trying to use future tense.	Cloze activities with meaning making being the focus: "What makes sense?"	Work on syntax: simple sentence patterns. Shared writing: Forming correct sentences.
Mena 1st grade (Arabic/Eng) (and Pashtu) early intermediate speaker	Reading Progress: Read a variety of books from her book box Level 8	Reading: Used many strategies: reread line for meaning, looked at the pictures, but had trouble retelling the story. Language: Knows articles, but uses them too much: "The dad, the mom, I like to read the books." Just developing present progressive, still makes errors.	Focus on retelling story. Model summarizing the main idea.	Work on syntax: Make lists of items using articles in simple sentences. Shared writing: Use sentences with present progressive.
Tania 1st grade (Span/Eng) intermediate speaker	Reading Progress: Read a variety of books from her book box Level 12	Reading: Cross-checked for meaning. Shared her favorite parts. Talked about characters. Language: Using short sentences. Needs help with the past tense. Used present progressive, but seemed to confuse patterns.	Highlight the main character and connection to the plot. Model self-correcting.	Shared reading: Use texts with repetitive patterns. Shared writing: Use sentences with past tense and with present progressive.

A reading conference sheet listing Jonathon, Mena, and Tania.

with me several books from their individual book boxes. They were reading at a lower level, so the books were quite short. They both used good reading strategies, including rereading, using the pictures, and cross-checking for meaning. Mena had difficulty retelling the story; she needed help with summarizing and figuring out the main idea. Tania focused on the characters, so I would use her interest to guide her to make connections between the characters and the plot.

All three children had filled their book boxes with books they had read in guided reading and were now reading independently. They could read these guided reading books pretty well but would benefit from writing in response journals to build deeper understanding. I would also encourage them to choose other books for independent reading, not just ones they had read in guided reading.

Jocelyn and Nayeli

This next conference sheet is from one fourth-grade classroom in the same school I consulted at in San Ysidro. During my visit the following school year, I conferred with individual children during independent reading time while the teacher also held conferences with other children. I was able to conference with two children that day and also do a guided reading lesson with a different group of children. I learned a lot about the four children in the guided reading group (see lesson comments and observation notes in next section), but I especially was able to learn a lot about Jocelyn and Nayeli through their conferences with me. They brought their books that they were reading which were covered in sticky notes with questions that they were asking of themselves as they read. (See Harvey and Goudvis 2000 for this technique.)

These fourth-grade girls were very different speakers and readers of English, although while reading independently they used similar strategies. Each brought to her conference a book covered with Post-it notes. Each asked questions while reading and recorded them on Post-it notes. Because I didn't know them as would their classroom teacher, I asked them to write down answers to their questions and bring them along to the conference, so that I could analyze their language and thinking. It is not necessary to have children do this if the

teacher works with them daily and can look at their response journals or literature circle logs.

Jocelyn's writing sample shows she asked higher-level questions, including some that couldn't be answered from the text but that she was curious about. On the Post-its she recorded the strategy she would use to answer her own questions: "think and search" or "in my head." She had to infer based on the information in the text. She answered her question on whether the BFG (Big Friendly Giant) and the other giants celebrate Christmas and give presents to each other in a very logical way: "I think they don't celebrate Christmas or give presents to each other because the BFG don't like the other giants because they eat children and people." Nayeli also shared with me the strategies she would use to answer her own questions: find them in the book or think about what might happen. She used a Spanish word when she couldn't think of the English one (*escondido* for *hiding*), and she told me she thinks about words a lot in her primary language.

Both girls seemed to need the most help developing their language proficiency, and I suggested to the classroom teacher future mini-lessons on helping them form correct questions in English. Jocelyn used the past tense correctly in statements ("I think Sophie liked the soda because I like soda"), but had difficulty asking questions in the past tense ("Does Sophie liked the soda?" "Does the BFG was scared?"). Nayeli had the same difficulty ("Why does he didn't like her if her is being good to he?"). These children as well as other ELLs in the class would benefit from small-group or whole-class instruction in shared reading or shared writing on asking questions.

Using Conference Sheets to Plan Guided Reading Lessons

As I looked over the sheets that the classroom teacher had kept on conferences with the students in this fourth-grade class in San Ysidro, I noted that certain children needed to work on similar things. Four children—Leslie and Viviana (early intermediate speakers), Jessica (intermediate), and Marcos (advanced)—needed help reading nonfiction. Although their language levels varied, they were all reading at second-grade level, guided reading levels

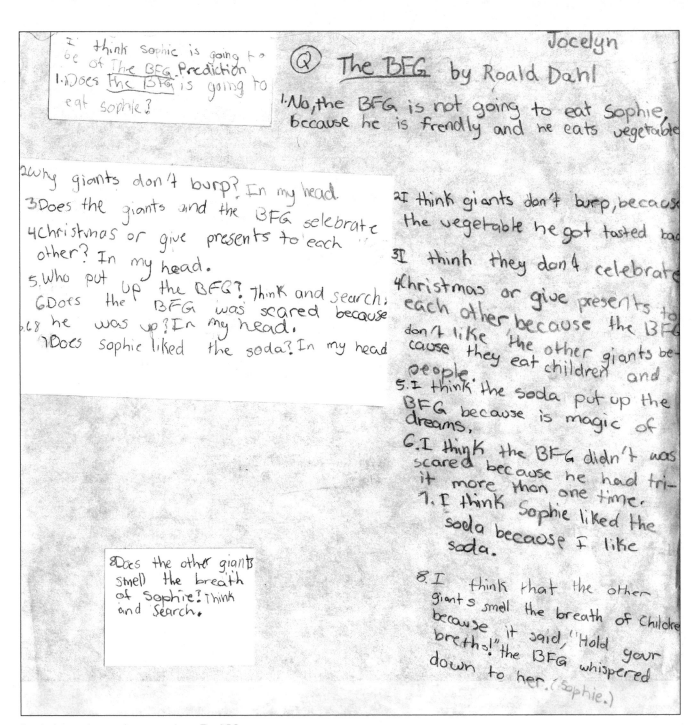

Jocelyn's questions and answers about *The BFG*.

K–M. They also had trouble with the reading strategy of asking questions. The teacher had focused on questioning during mini-lessons in shared reading but not in guided reading. Jocelyn and Nayeli had internalized questioning techniques and were using them while they read independently (see previous section), but these four children were not doing as well. A guided reading lesson with a nonfiction book and focusing on questioning would benefit them.

The nonfiction text *Fire! Fire!* is part of a series for older students reading below grade level. It was a good match because these children had background knowledge of the subject and would be interested in reading and discussing it: they were aware of devastating forest fires in the San Diego area that had closed their school for a week, and one child's aunt had lost her home in the fires. The book also highlights questions in speech bubbles that stand out on the page. We concentrated on the

Reading Conference Sheet

To Monitor Reading and Language Development and to Plan for Instruction

Week of ___1/16___

Date/ Name of Child	Type of Conference Title of Book	Observed Reading Strategies and Language Used	Future Mini-Lessons Reading	Future Mini-Lessons Language
Jocelyn 4th grade early advanced speaker (Span/Eng)	Reading Progress: The BFG Level Q	**Reading:** Shared self-questions on Post-it notes. Shared good strategies on how to answer the questions: Prediction In my head Think and search She then answered her own questions and recorded her answers – shows higher-level thinking **Language:** Sentence structure is very good in her responses, but she needs help with phrasing questions. Example (she wrote) Does the BFG was scared? Does Sophie liked the soda?	Continue to work on questions with deeper meaning. Work on inferring	Work on asking and writing questions. Develop the use of the past tense in questions.
Nayeli 4th grade intermediate speaker (Span/Eng)	Reading Progress: Prince Chuckie Level M	**Reading:** Shared her questions on Post-it notes. Answered the questions with logical answers, but had difficulty retelling me the main idea of the story. Seemed to get lost in the details. **Language:** Pretty good, but needs help with sentence structure, asking questions, pronouns, and the use of "it." She wrote: The girl it was the sister of Max.	Practice retelling, focusing on main idea, and summarizing.	Work on asking questions, use of "did" in questions and use of "it."

A reading conference sheet listing Jocelyn and Nayeli.

first story, "Forest Fires," and I modeled asking questions to get them to predict what it would be about. I asked questions about their own experiences and then as we read the text. We read questions from the book, such as "Why do you think helicopters with buckets are used?" The students came up with their own questions as we were reading and shared those in the discussion. I asked them to write down their questions after each page. At the end of the lesson I encouraged them to continue writing down questions as they read the other stories in the book. I also shared with them a copy of *Time for Kids* magazine with "Wildfire!" as the cover story. Many other resources, like newspaper articles, could be used to keep up their interest in reading about this nonfiction topic.

With a little guidance these students improved their ability to question while reading, although Leslie and Viviana, the early intermediate speakers, would need specific language instruction in order to succeed with more challenging texts. Their lower language level kept them from communicating in the past tense and understanding the complicated sentence structures in higher-level texts. These four students fit into the same guided reading group, however, because their reading levels and the strategies they needed to work on were similar. In a class of over thirty children we have no choice but to form groups as best we can.

Helping Children Choose Books During Conferences

Conferences can also be designed to help a child choose appropriate books or to check whether the choice a child has made is a good one. Children often choose to read books that other children are reading, or that they think are cool to read, regardless of whether they can actually read them. Other children are so motivated to read a book that they work very hard to get through it. We can check the appropriateness of a book for a child by asking him some questions about it and asking him to retell it or to discuss the main idea. If the child has difficulty with that or has trouble reading a section of the text, that is an indication that the book is too difficult. But we must be careful in our assessments of the appropriateness of books that children choose, especially because English language learn-

ers often don't have the background to be successful with numerous books. How can we carefully promote good choice without hampering the child's reading a book he really wants to read?

In one fifth-grade classroom I observed a reading conference with a child named Noel, who was determined to read one of the books from the *Amber Brown* series because her friends were reading it. She had already read four chapters but was having difficulty understanding parts of the text. The teacher asked, "Is this text too challenging? Should you abandon it?" The child agreed that it was too challenging. "You're almost ready for this book," the teacher continued. "I think you should abandon it now and come back to it at a later time. Maybe in a month you could read it." The child was a good sport about it. Yet I couldn't help but feel that she had invested valuable time in trying to read it and she hadn't seemed frustrated by the challenging parts. I wondered if there weren't another way that could have let her continue to read it. Could she have read it with a buddy or an adult volunteer? Could the teacher have worked it into her schedule to read with the child for ten or fifteen minutes once or twice a week?

I hate to have children get discouraged by thinking that they can't read something. They often work through a text even though it is difficult because they are motivated to do so. Jonathon is an example of that. He so wanted to read a text that he didn't want to realize it was too difficult for him. So I decided to read it with him. I also helped him with strategies that helped him manage parts of the text better while he read on his own. Our goal should be to have children recognize that texts may be difficult and to help them use strategies to construct meaning (Sibberson and Szymusiak 2003).

In Noel's case, I wondered whether the plot line was too difficult, whether Amber Brown was doing something that Noel could not relate to, whether there were just too many unknown vocabulary words, which hampered her understanding of the main idea. Without spending time with her in a conference myself to help her get through part of the story, I found it difficult to just discount that book for Noel.

One of my daughters in fourth grade got very excited about reading the first *Artemis Fowl* book, yet she had a lot of difficulty reading it. The main character was a wild child genius who was jet-setting across the globe, and my daughter couldn't follow what city or country he was in. I helped her look up some of the places in an atlas. There were also some difficult slang terms or idioms. She was motivated to read it, though, and refused to let some confusions stop her. She needed some clarification at times, and I was there to help her. She went on to read three more of the books and loved them.

Can we provide ELLs with the same kind of support that our own children receive at home? Can we make time in conferences to give a little extra help to children like Noel? I would hope so, especially if we make independent reading time an important part of our literacy block.

"PRIVATE READING LESSONS" WITH ELLS

Reading conferences with English language learners can look like private reading lessons. Instead of just assessing the children's reading skills, we can spend some time listening to them read and helping them grasp deeper meanings. Sibberson and Szymusiak (2001; 2003) talk about helping transitional readers who pick up chapter books and never quite finish them, and about encouraging older children to develop stamina and persistence as they read more difficult texts. It is common for ELLs who are starting to read fluently as independent readers to get into trouble with longer texts that have more complex plot lines. Literature circles are a good opportunity for ELLs to talk about books and help check their understanding of texts. But one-on-one conferences can offer ELLs the benefits of a private reading lesson. In a conference the child can shine all on her own and does not have to compete with more vocal children to get a chance to share what she knows.

When I conferred with Jonathon later in the school year (see previous section), he was reading at level 20 or 22, a strong second-grade level. But the classroom teacher was concerned with his progress, thinking he had hit a plateau and wasn't moving off it. I looked in his book box and saw he was using many guided reading books for independent reading. I also noticed a chapter book that stood out

among the guided reading titles: a *Magic Tree House* book called *The Knight at Dawn*. This book is classified at a second-grade level (Fountas and Pinnell 1999), and I was pleased to see that Jonathon had ventured out to a chapter book. I thought this would be a good starting point for a discussion.

"Are you reading this book?" I asked. "Yes," he said, "I'm on chapter three." "What's happening so far?" I asked, and he started a summary: "The kid was picking who would go with him. He picked his sister. He went to Magic Tree House. They read a book, then they went to the castle." I was surprised at how few details he included, and curious to know if he even understood the concept of the Magic Tree House taking Jack and Annie back in time. So I asked if he had read any other books in the series.

"[This is] my first *Magic Tree House*," he said. "How did you decide to read this book?" I asked. "Did your teacher pick it, or did you?" "I did!" he said. I also asked if he liked it so far and if he wanted to continue reading it. He confirmed that he liked it but when asked why, all he said was, "There's a Magic Tree House." "Is there any other reason you like it?" I asked. "That's all," he said.

So far I hadn't learned much about Jonathon's comprehension of the book. I did learn that his English sentence structure had improved greatly from the beginning of the year. But he wasn't elaborating on any of his responses. I asked if he would like to continue reading the book with me, and he said yes. So I decided to keep track of his reading by doing a running record. I told him what I was going to do, and he seemed fine with it. I didn't do a true running record but rather recorded what he read, and if he didn't self-correct his miscues, I asked him if they made sense and gave him a chance to rethink what he had read in order to help him sustain meaning. Doing this partial running record actually allowed me to help him while he was reading.

He started reading at the top of page 16, which was in the middle of a sentence. I suggested he might want to go back to the previous page and read a couple of lines or two to refresh his memory on what was happening. I shared with him that I often do that when I pick up a book I am reading that I haven't read for a few days. So he did go back a few lines. He made substitutions right away—

Anna for *Annie* and *give* for *gave*. Both of those made sense, yet they also showed me that he was having trouble with the past tense, so I figured that he was probably still at the intermediate language level even though he used the past tense earlier. He also self-corrected a word at the end of the next line.

In just a couple of lines he showed his use of meaning-making strategies. But when the text got more difficult, it seemed the only strategy he relied on was sounding it out, which was not very helpful with harder words. He often made four attempts on the same word, sliding through the letters to figure it out, relying heavily on the graphophonic cueing system. The words he came up with were close visually, but they were not making sense. He said *pick* for *peek* and *ground* for *groaned*. I often stopped him to check his comprehension because he just continued to read with the errors. When I asked him if it made sense ("I'm going to take a pick"), he said no. He seemed to understand that it didn't work, but he didn't have enough strategies to help himself. He couldn't give me another substitution for the word or think what would make sense. Since he seemed to be most comfortable with sounding out, I asked him what sound *ee* made and suggested he use that sound in the word. He then said, "Peek." "What does that mean?" I asked. "I'm going to take a peek," he said, and put his hand up to his eye, squeezed his fingers together, and looked through the hole he had made. "To look, like in a little hole," he said. It was as if he had just looked it up in the dictionary!

What I noticed with further discussion was that Jonathon had the language level to be successful with this text, although there was specialized vocabulary related to the Middle Ages that he didn't understand. But he did not have the reading strategies to be able to read the book independently. It was clear that he had excellent word analysis skills, but he also needed to use his knowledge of semantics and syntax to help him. The example with *peek* demonstrates that with help he did know if something made sense, but he needed to start to use that strategy on his own. Although he wanted to, he was definitely not able to read this book independently yet.

At this point I had a choice. I could continue to assess him and suggest that he read a different book

that he could read independently, or I could help him read this book. Then the conference would be a one-on-one reading lesson. I could let him read when he could and help him when he had trouble. Often a child just needs this encouragement to continue reading, but not to the point of frustration. And the child might not take on such a difficult task on his own without someone supporting him.

Jonathon wanted to continue reading the book. He was fascinated with the heavy armor and the thought of traveling on dangerous roads, and he loved the drawbridge that "go down and up." So I continued reading with him, but I put my nurturing hat on, trying to forget my role of teacher. Often we don't take the time to sit down and help a child read a book that he really wants to read. I found myself lost with Jonathon in the Middle Ages, with castles and moats and forty-pound armor helmets and feasts of pheasant pie. What was so nice is that the rest of the children in this classroom were all such well-trained independent readers that no one interrupted Jonathon and me. We were able to read together for about twenty minutes.

While we were reading, though, I still wanted to help Jonathon improve his reading strategies, which ultimately would improve his confidence. I suggested to him to forget about sounding out a word he didn't know. I told him that any time he didn't know a word to stop, cover it up, read on, and try to see what would make sense. I assured him he could do it if he had confidence in his own abilities. We read the next couple of pages together almost like a game. I stopped him at first because he kept forgetting to cover up the word after he had said the initial sound but couldn't get it. Then, miraculously, he started self-correcting most of the words he miscued, like *building, crossing, gate, studied, believe,* and *peering*—all because he used the context to help himself. What he couldn't solve by himself were new vocabulary words that related only to the content of the book, like *moat, armor,* and *windmill*. He seemed to have fun, though, acquiring this new vocabulary. We discussed why they had certain things in the castle and the purpose for them, like the moat, the drawbridge, or the knights' armor. His reasoning skills shone through. I asked, "Why do you think they wear armor?" "The bad guys have swords, so they can be killed," he said. "They have to wear the armor because they are so skinny." He seemed to have a reason for everything, even when he read a word wrong. He said *naughty book* for *notebook* (an interesting way to pronounce not/e/book) and described it as *naughty* because "it keeps falling down in his pocket." I laughed but complimented him on his explanation and reasoning skills.

If Jonathon didn't have the background knowledge to understand the new vocabulary, and if I couldn't describe the word well enough, I tried to draw a picture of it, like *windmill*. Unfortunately he thought my windmill was a flower! So we looked for a picture of it in the book. We didn't see a windmill, but we did see a knight going over a drawbridge, which was over the moat, which led into the castle. I think both of us realized at the same time that we could learn a lot from the pictures. This chapter book had supportive pictures throughout, though it was too bad they weren't always on the same page as the text. It was Jonathon who suggested, "Let's look at the pictures," reminding me that ELLs can benefit from a picture walk even through chapter books.

We flipped through the rest of the book looking at the pictures, and Jonathon made predictions along the way. On page 58, he saw a picture of Jack and Annie with the Knight, all on the Knight's beautiful horse. "Look," said Jonathon, "the knight is taking the two boys and the girl. They're taking them back to the Magic Tree House. They're going to go back home. Look, here's the last page. He's home." Then I was surprised what else Jonathon showed me in the pictures. He pointed to the M and connected it back to three other pages. He said it looked like a coin, and he was very excited. We talked about it a little, and then I asked him about the relationship between the Knight and Jack and Annie, and whether he thought the Knight was nice to them in the book. "Yes, he is their friend," he said.

I wanted Jonathon to be successful finishing this book after I left. I asked if he had an older brother or sister who reads English, and he said he only had a little sister. His parents don't speak English, but he did say he had a cousin who read English. I was hoping his cousin would read it to him. I asked him to remember what strategies helped him, and he said, "Skipping and reading again" and "Slide my finger." I reminded him to

Jonathon's vocabulary list from *The Knight at Dawn* and his self-constructed definitions.

ask himself, What would make sense here? and to rely more on context and background knowledge than graphophonic knowledge.

I also wanted him to remember the words he had learned. So before I left, I had him write them down. He found the words in the book and copied them all down. Then we closed the book and went back to the top of the list, starting with *Knight*. He wrote what he thought they meant in his own words and spelling. I was surprised how quickly he did this without much prodding from me. (He wrote all this in about five minutes.) I then asked him to write any other new words he learned while reading the later chapters. I hoped he would be able to do it. I also hoped that his cousin would take the time to read with him, or that he would find a buddy to read with him in class. He was so motivated to read this book that it would have been a shame if he weren't able to get the help he needed with his English and his reading strategies. He wanted to be successful, and he loved to read. Keeping that going is critical to help him become a lifelong reader.

I thought about Jonathon compared to my daughters (and compared to native English speakers.) They bring their chapter books home and they often just love to have me listen to them read. But I remember when they were struggling through their first *Magic Tree House* stories when they were a little younger than Jonathon. They stopped reading this same story *The Knight at Dawn* and chose a different title, because it was too challenging and because they weren't as interested in the topic as other adventures Jack and Annie took. But when they did decide to go back to it, and when they did decide to read other chapter books, I was there to help them. Jonathon doesn't have a mom who can do that. Not because she isn't an educator, but because she doesn't read in English.

If we want ELLs who come from homes with no English to succeed, it is our responsibility to spend extra time reading with them. We need to make every individual child a priority during reading time. And we cannot be afraid that a parent or a principal will come into the room and look askance because we are reading with just one child. We have to share what we believe in, that every child can learn and every child's strengths can be nurtured. We also have to let visitors know that we read every day with different children, either during conferences or independent reading time, so *all* have equal attention. Helping children become strong readers should be our top priority. Jonathon wanted to read another *Magic Tree House* book. He was motivated to read and he enjoyed it even with his intermediate level of English language fluency. We have to keep that same joy of reading alive for all of the Jonathons in our classrooms.

I like to learn words so my brain could get smarter. I like to get smarter so I could go to high-school. I also want to get smarter to get a job. I want a job so I could get money. When I get my job I'm going to turn it into a career.

APPENDIXES

Informal Language Assessment Record Sheet | A1

Name_____ Grade _____ Current ELD Level _____

Date_____ Type of Interaction _____

Language Structures Used Correctly	Language Structures Used Incorrectly	Types of Language Functions Used

Comments, Analysis

To Monitor Reading and Language Development and to Plan for Instruction

Week of _____

Date/ Name of Child	Type of Conference Title of Book	Observed Reading Strategies and Language Used	Future Mini-Lessons Reading	Future Mini-Lessons Language

Balancing Reading and Language Learning: A Resource for Teaching English Language Learners, K–5 by Mary Cappellini. Copyright © 2005. Stenhouse Publishers.

Developmental Checklist of Language Patterns for Beginning to Intermediate English Language Learners

Name _____ **D = Developing, S = Secure, NE = No Evidence**

English Language Proficiency Level	Skill	Date								
Beginning	Uses regular plurals									
	Uses prepositions									
	Knows how to use the verb *to be*									
	Can say a command									
Early Intermediate	Knows subject pronouns									
	Uses statements: *there is/are, here is/are*									
	Knows present tense									
	Uses present progressive									
	Can state a negative statement									
Intermediate	Uses habitual present: *she goes*									
	Knows subject/verb agreement									
	Uses adjectives correctly									
	Uses past tense									
	Uses simple contractions: *it's, isn't*									
	Uses comparatives									
	Asks questions in future tense									
	Uses possessive pronouns									

Developmental Checklist of Language Patterns for Early Advanced to Advanced English Language Learners   A4

Name _____ **D = Developing, S = Secure, NE = No Evidence**

English Language Proficiency Level	Skill	Date									
Early Advanced	Uses superlatives: *most, least*										
	Uses irregular past tense										
	Uses adverbs: *well* (vs. *good*)										
	Uses abstract nouns: *freedom, citizenship*										
	Uses gerunds: *going to school*										
	Uses conjunctions: *however, therefore*										
	Uses synonyms and antonyms										
	Asks questions in past tense										
Advanced	Uses perfect tenses: *has been, will have been*										
	Uses conditional perfect tense: *if he had worked harder, he would have finished*										
	Uses specialized adverbs: *already, still*										
	Uses auxiliary verbs: *could, would, should*										
	Uses auxiliary contractions: *couldn't, wouldn't, shouldn't*										
	Uses relative pronouns: *who, whom, whose*										
	Uses metaphors										
	Uses similes										

Name _____ D = Developing, S = Secure, NE = No Evidence

Reading Strategies and Language Functions	Date								
Pleasure Reading									
Participates in shared reading activities by memorizing rhymes, songs, repetitive phrases of Big Books									
Holds book and envisions self as reader									
Starts to read books independently									
Chooses own books out of classroom library									
Comprehension									
Develops a sense of story									
Uses pictures to gain meaning from stories									
Retells a repeated pattern in a book									
Tells an appropriate story to match a picture									
Retells a story maintaining the main idea									
Begins to understand cause and effect									
Begins to predict outcomes in new stories									
Print Awareness									
Recognizes print in books and the environment									
Holds book and turns pages properly									
Follows and tracks lines of print left to right									
Has one-to-one correspondence when pointing to words									
Word Analysis									
Begins to point to individual words in a familiar story									
Recognizes common words									
Develops an individualized sight word vocabulary									
Names some beginning or ending letters in words									
Begins to use sound-symbol relations to read words									
Matches words with predictions to self-correct									
Vocabulary Development									
Develops speaking vocabulary from wide variety of thematic units									
Starts to use words in short sentences									
Starts to use words heard in books and songs in own sentences									

Balancing Reading and Language Learning: A Resource for Teaching English Language Learners, K–5 by Mary Cappellini. Copyright © 2005. Stenhouse Publishers.

Checklist of Strategies Used by Early to Fluent Readers to Sustain Meaning

Name _____ **D = Developing, S = Secure, NE = No Evidence**

Context of Observation (lesson, conference) _____ **ELP Level** (B, EI, I, EA, A) _____

Reading Strategies	Date									
Predicts										
Uses context										
Uses background knowledge										
Uses pictures/visual cues										
Uses graphophonic cues										
Uses syntactic cues										
Recognizes miscues that disrupt meaning										
Self-corrects miscues that disrupt meaning										
Rereads/looks back										
Reads ahead										
Cross-checks using multiple strategies										
Asks for help										
Expects to get meaning from the text										
Uses punctuation to help gain meaning										
Makes connections to gain meaning										
Thinks what would make sense										

Name _____ D = Developing, S = Secure, NE = No Evidence

Context of Observation (lesson, conference) _____ **ELP Level** (B, EI, I, EA, A) _____

Reading Strategies and Language Functions	Date								
Predicting									
Inferring									
Summarizing									
Connecting									
Visualizing									
Analyzing									
Evaluating									
Synthesizing									
Paraphrasing									
Retelling									
Reflecting									
Self-questioning									
Integrating									
Sharing									
Enriching vocabulary									
Writing responses									

Balancing Reading and Language Learning: A Resource for Teaching English Language Learners, K–5 by Mary Cappellini. Copyright © 2005. Stenhouse Publishers.

Estimados Padres:

¡Bienvenidos a nuestra clase!

Me encantaría tenerlos como participantes y ayudantes en la educación de su hijo/a este año. Ustedes son una parte muy importante para asegurarse que su hijo/a sea exitoso/a en la escuela. No solamente yo, pero su hijo/a estará muy agradecido por su ayuda también.

Hay muchas maneras en que ustedes pueden participar y ayudar en la clase. Podrían ayudar durante el tiempo de lectura y escritura, o con matemáticas, ciencas, historia o ciencias sociales. Si tienen algún talento en particular ya sea en música, arte o educación física—o si tienen algún talento especial como hacer papel a mano, coser, o hacer aviones de modelos—su ayuda en esas áreas sería apreciada. Si les gustaría venir y ayudar haciendo fotocopias, preparando materiales para la clase, o corregir papeles, sería buenísmo.

En la siguiente página hay una breva encuesta para que llenen y asi poder saber como podrían participar en la educación de su hijo/a este año. Por favor, incluyan cualquier otra cosa que les gustaría hacer en las lineas que están en blanco. También, si no pueden venir durante el día, pero pueden preparar cosas para la clase en su casa, márquenlo en la encuesta.

Si no hablan inglés, no es problema. Me encantaría tenerlos como ayudantes, y si no puedo comunicarme bien con ustedes, buscaré una traductora para ayudarme—tal vez su hijo/a. La falta del dominio del idioma no debería ser una barrera para que ustedes no puedan participar en la educación de su hijo/a.

Gracias por su tiempo y su esfuerzo. Me encantaría verlos ayudando y participando este año!

Sinceramente,

Child's name _____

Name of parent willing to help _____

Phone number _____ **Home language** _____

I would like to help with the activities in my child's classroom. (Please place a check on the lines next to what you are interested in helping with.)

_____ **Reading**	_____ **Writing**	_____ **Math**	_____ **Science**
_____ Read to children	_____ Help publish	_____ Work with small group	_____ Help with experiments
_____ Conference with kids	_____ Edit	_____ Other	_____ Other
_____ Other	_____ Other		
_____ **History/Social Science**	_____ **Art**	_____ **Music**	_____ **PE**
_____ Work with projects	_____ Teach a lesson	_____ Teach a lesson	_____ Teach a lesson
_____ Other	_____ Other	_____ Other	_____ Other

I would rather help the teacher in the class with

_____ Making journals   _____ Making children's books   _____ Making copies
_____ Cutting and pasting   _____ Decorating the room   _____ Anything
_____ Other

I would like to help with preparing these materials at home _____

I would like to help with special events:

_____ Class parties and celebrations   _____ Field trips
_____ Author's tea   _____ Other

I would like to be the class Room Mom _____ (coordinate events with all the parents and the teacher)

I have a special talent that I would like to share with the class: _____
(Cook, build models, sew, paint, tell stories, . . .)

I am a _____ (nurse, author, gardener, veterinarian, . . .)
Please call on me when my expertise could be of help with any unit of study or if you need something that has to do with my profession. _____

I can help

Before school _____ After school _____ Anytime _____
During: Early morning: 8:00–10:00 a.m. _____ only at this time: _____
            Late morning: 10:00–12:00 p.m. _____ only at this time: _____
During the afternoon: 12:45–2:45 p.m. _____ only at this time: _____

I can help on these days:

_____ Monday   _____ Tuesday   _____ Wednesday   _____ Thursday   _____ Friday
_____ Any day

Please call me as a substitute or on an as-needed basis _____
Other: _____

Nombre del niño/a _____

Nombre del padre/madre que le gustaría ayudar _____

Número de teléfono _____ **Idioma en la casa** _____

Me gustaría ayudar con las actividades en la clase de mi hijo/a. (Por favor, marque con una X donde está interesado/a en ayudar.)

____ **Lectura**	____ **Escritura**	____ **Matemáticas**	____ **Ciencias**
____ Leer a los niños	____ Ayudar a publicar	____ Trabajar con grupos	____ Ayudar con experimentos
____ Conferir con niños	____ Revisar	pequeños	____ Otra
____ Otra	____ Otra	____ Otra	
____ **Historia/Ciencias Sociales**	____ **Arte**	____ **Música**	____ **Educación física**
____ Trabajar con projectos	____ Enseñar una lección	____ Enseñar una lección	____ Enseñar una lección
____ Otra	____ Otra	____ Otra	____ Otra

Prefiero ayudar al maestro en la clase con

____ Hacer diarios	____ Hacer libros de niños	____ Sacar copias
____ Cortar y pegar	____ Decorar el salón	____ Cualquier cosa
____ Otra		

Me gustaría preparar cosas para la clase en mi casa _____

Me gustaría ayudar con eventos especiales:

____ Fiestas y celebraciones de la clase	____ Excursiones
____ Te de autores	____ Otra

Me gustaría ser La Madre de la clase _____ (coordinar todos los eventos de la clase con todos los padres y la maestra)

Tengo un talento especial que me gustaría compartir con la clase: _____
(Cocinar, construir modelos, coser, pintar, contar cuentos, . . .)

Soy un/a _____ (enfermero/a, autor/a, jardinero/a, veterinario/a, . . .)
Por favor, llámeme cuando pueda utilizar mi experiencia con cualquier unidad de estudio o si necesita algo acerca de mi profesión. _____

Puedo ayudar

Antes de la escuela _____ Después de la escuela _____ Cualquier momento _____

Durante la mañana:	8:00–10:00 a.m. _____	solamente a esta hora: _____
	10:00–12:00 p.m. _____	solamente a esta hora: _____
Durante la tarde:	12:45–2:45 p.m. _____	solamente a esta hora: _____

Puedo ayudar en estos días:

____ lunes	____ martes	____ miércoles	____ jueves	____ viernes
____ Cualquier día				

Por favor, llámeme como substituto o cuando me necesite _____
Otra: _____

Balancing Reading and Language Learning: A Resource for Teaching English Language Learners, K–5 by Mary Cappellini. Copyright © 2005. Stenhouse Publishers.

LEALO SOLO

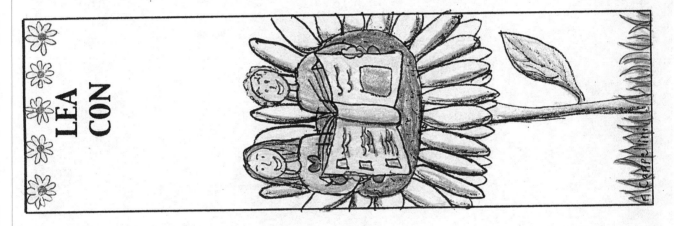

LEA CON

LEA A

Grade Level _____

Theme_____ **Time Frame** _____

Subtheme _____ **Time Frame** _____

Content Area _____ **Genre** _____

Content Area Concepts (Content Focus) _____
Science or History/Social Science Standards

Unit of Study (Literary Focus)_____
ELA and ELD Standards

Vocabulary Development (Language Focus)_____
ELA and ELD Standards

Reading To

Read-Aloud Books	Literary Focus and Reading Strategy	Language Focus and Language Pattern	Content Focus and Thinking Process	Teaching Group
Chapter Books: Picture Books:				

Mini-Lessons	How to Record Information

Continued on next page.

Balancing Reading and Language Learning: A Resource for Teaching English Language Learners, K–5 by Mary Cappellini. Copyright © 2005. Stenhouse Publishers.

Reading With

Shared Reading Books	Literary Focus and Reading Strategy	Language Focus and Language Pattern	Content Focus and Thinking Process	Teaching Group
Big Books: Other:				

Mini-Lessons	How to Record Information

Reading By

Guided Reading Books	Literary Focus and Reading Strategy	Language Focus and Language Pattern	Content Focus and Thinking Process	Teaching Group
Emergent: Early: Early Fluent: Fluent:				

ocean	océano
Pacific	Pacífico
Atlantic	Atlántico
Antarctic	Antártico
Artic	Ártico
Indian	Índico
gulf	golfo

habitat	habitat
island	isla
volcanic	volcánica
activity	actividad
coral	coral
reef	arrecife
tropical	tropical
surface	superficie
coast	costa
lagoon	laguna
continental	continental

climate	clima
atmosphere	atmosferica
air	aire
vapor	vapor
salinity	salinidad
temperature	temperatura
density	densidad
hurricane	huracán
storm	tormenta
current	corriente

zones	zonas
glacier	glaciar
polar	polar
north	norte
south	sur
east	este
west	oeste
exploration	exploración
expedition	expedición
explorers	exploradores

adjectives	adjetivos
exotic	exótico
enormous	enorme
incredible	increíble
similar	similar
immense	inmenso
colorful	colorido

(See other oceanography theme charts of English-Spanish cognates on page 87 in Chapter 5.)

Academic vocabulary/vocabulario académico used in content areas.

These are not exhaustive lists, but rather examples of the types of academic vocabulary that children might encounter in content areas in elementary grades.

Strategies/Estrategias
(Language Functions/Funciones de lenguage)

(Verbs listed are also cognitive thinking processes used for many content areas, including language arts, science, history/social science, mathematics, and ELD.)

predict	predecir
connect	conectar
describe	describir
analyze	analizar
synthesize	sintetizar
compare	comparar
contrast	contrastar
respond	responder
infer	inferir
assume	asumir
discern	discernir
conclude	concluir
evaluate	evaluar
paraphrase	parafrasear
demonstrate	demonstrar
differentiate	diferenciar
summarize	*resumir

*not exactly a cognate

admit	admitir
classify	clasificar
simplify	simplificar
simulate	simular
resolve	resolver
resist	resistir
respect	respetar
disappear	desaparecer
appeal	apelar
adjust	ajustar
conform	conformar
declare	declarar

Literature and Language/Literatura y lenguage

(humanities/humanidades)

author	autor
genre	género
poem	poema
text	texto
passage	pasaje
lyrical	lírico
metaphor	metáfora

simile	símil
analogy	analogía
hyperbole	hipérbole
paradigm	paradigma
paradox	paradoja
paraphrase	paráfrasis
annotation	anotación
semantic	semántico
syntactic	syntáctico
synthesis	sínteses
syntax	sintaxis
analysis	análisis
evaluation	evaluación
thesis	tesis
parenthesis	paréntesis
apostrophe	apóstrofo
verb	verbo
adjective	adjetivo
adverb	adverbo
conjugate	conjugar
past	pasado
present	presente
future	futuro
conditonal	condicional
perfect	perfecto

Science/Ciencia

(natural sciences/ciencías naturales, biology/biología, zoology/zoología, oceanography/oceanografía)

classification	clasificación
analysis	análisis
hypothesis	hipótesis
metamorphosis	metamorfosis
photosynthesis	fotosíntesis
photocopy	fotocopía
membrane	membrana
investigation	investigación
demonstration	demonstración
simultaneous	simultáneo
resistance	resistencia
reproduce	reproducir
cycle	ciclo

animal	animal
human	humano
mammiferous (mammal)	mamífero
carnivore	carnívoro

Continued on next page.

Balancing Reading and Language Learning: A Resource for Teaching English Language Learners, K–5 by Mary Cappellini. Copyright © 2005. Stenhouse Publishers.

herbivore	herbívoro
antenna	antena
insect	insecto
rodent	roedor
reptile	reptil
dinosaur	dinosaurio
extinct	extinto
zoo	zoo/zoológico

Mathematics/Matemáticas

number	número
multiplication	multiplicación
division	división
fractions	fracciones
problem	problema
numerator	numerador
denominator	denominador
difference	diferencia
sum	suma
equal	igual
reciprocal	recíproco
parallel	paralelo

History/Social Science/
Historía/Ciencias Sociales

civilization	civilización
democracy	democracia
responsibility	responsibilidad
republic	república
union	unión
constitution	constitución
federation	federación
federal	federal
confederation	confederación
United Nations	Naciones Unidos
United States	Estados Unidos
America	América
civility	civilidad
clemency	clemencia
vote	votar
democrat	demócrata
republican	repulicano
congress	congreso
legislature	legislatura
presidency	presidencia
circumstance	circumstancia
resignation	resignación
reform	reformar
difficulty	dificultad
annexation	anexión
public sector	sector público

Geography/Geografía

residence	residencia
city	ciudad
state	estado
nation	nación
region	región
continent	continente
hemisphere	hemisferio
globe	globo
dessert	desierto
mountains	montañas
peninsulas	peninsulas
islands	islas
lakes	lagos
rivers	ríos
gulfs	golfos
oceans	océanos
poles	polares
latitude	latitud
longitude	longitud
transportation	transportación
commerce	comercio
reserve	reserva
reservation	reservación

Art/Arte

painter	pintor
ceramics	cerámica
color	color
acrylic	acrílico
oil	óleo
perspective	perspectiva

Music/Música

musician	músico
instrument	instrumento
piano	piano
violin	violín
guitar	guitarra
flute	flauta
trumpet	trompeta
tempo	tempo
notes	notas

Dance/Danza

ballet	ballet
jazz	jazz
choreography	coreografia
rhythm	rítmo

Balancing Reading and Language Learning: A Resource for Teaching English Language Learners, K–5 by Mary Cappellini. Copyright © 2005. Stenhouse Publishers.

1. Reading To Children: Read-Alouds

The books listed in section 7 can also be used for read-alouds. Books marked with an asterisk are bilingual texts or also available in Spanish.

* *A House for Hermit Crab* by Eric Carle. Scholastic, 1987. Fiction.

A Swim Through the Sea: An Alphabet Alliteration by Kristin J. Pratt. Dawn Publications, 1994. Nonfiction.

Animal Safari: Sea Otters by National Geographic. Scholastic, 1999. Nonfiction.

* *Animals of the Seashore/Animales de la orilla del mar* by Mary Cappellini. Rigby, 1994. Nonfiction.

Big Al by Andrew C. Yoshi. Scholastic, 1988. Fiction.

Commerson's Dolphin Story, The, by D. Nuzzolo. Sea World, 2004. Nonfiction.

Dolphin: Prince of the Waves, The, by Renee Lebloas-Julienne. Charlesbridge, 2004.

Dolphin's First Day: The Story of a Bottlenose Dolphin by Kathleen W. Zoehfeld. Scholastic, 1994. Nonfiction.

Exploring Salt Water Habitats by Sue Smith. Mondo, 1994. Nonfiction.

Extraordinary Sea Creatures. Scholastic, 2001. Nonfiction.

* *Fish/Peces* by Jane P. Resnick. DDL Books, 1994.

Habitats of the World by Alison Ballance. Dominie Press, 1998. Nonfiction.

* *Inside a Coral Reef/Dentro del Arrecife de Coral Reef* by Katy Muzik. Charlesbridge, 1993. Nonfiction.

Isla by Arthur Dorros. Dutton Children's Books, 1995.

* *Island of the Blue Dolphins* by Scott O'Dell. Random House, 1961. Fiction.

O Is for Orca by Andrea Helman. Sasquatch Books, 1995. Nonfiction.

One Tiny Turtle by Nicola Davies. Candlewick Press, 2001. Fiction.

Orca Song by Michael C. Armour. Scholastic, 1994.

Penguins and Polar Bears: Animals of the Ice and Snow by Sandra Lee Crow. National Geographic Society, 1985. Nonfiction.

Plenty of Penguins by Sonia W. Black. Scholastic, 1999.

* *Rainbow Fish, The/El Pez Arco Iris* by Marcus Pfister. North-South Books, 1992. Fiction.

Rainbows of the Sea by Meredith Thomas. Mondo, 1998. Fiction.

Sea Animals by Amy Ericksen. Chronicle Books, 1995.

Sea Otters: A Natural History and Guide by Roy Nickerson. Chronicle Books, 1994. Nonfiction.

Sea Turtles by Gail Gibbons. Holiday House, 1998. Nonfiction.

Seal Pup Grows Up: The Story of a Harbor Seal by Kathleen W. Zoehfeld. Scholastic, 1994. Nonfiction.

Sharks by Gail Gibbons. Holiday House, 1993. Nonfiction.

* *Swimmy* by Leo Lionni. Scholastic, 1963. Fiction.

This Is the Sea That Feeds Us by Robert F. Baldwin. Dawn Publications, 1998. Nonfiction.

Underwater Counting: Even Numbers by Jerry Pallotta. Charlesbridge, 2000. Nonfiction.

Whale: Giant of the Ocean, The, by Valerie Tracqui. Charlesbridge, 2004. Nonfiction.

Whales by Gail Gibbons. Holiday House, 1993. Nonfiction.

Whales, The, by Cynthia Rylant. Scholastic, 1996. Fiction.

Who Lives in the Sea? by Sylvia M. James. Mondo, 1997. Nonfiction.

2. Reading With Children: Big Books

Books marked with an asterisk are bilingual texts or also available in Spanish.

* *Grandpa, Grandpa* by Joy Cowley. Wright Group, 1998. Fiction. Grades K–1.

Our Whale-Watching Trip by Sylvia Karavis. Rigby, 2000. Nonfiction. Grades K–1.

Exploring Salt Water Habitats by Sue Smith. Mondo, 1994. Nonfiction. Grades 2–3.

* *Greedy Gray Octopus, The,* by Christel Buckley. Rigby, 1988. Fiction. Grades 2–3.

* *Meet the Octopus* by Sylvia M. James. Mondo, 1996. Nonfiction. Grades 2–3.

Cousteau by Kevin Comber. Era Publications, 1991. Nonfiction. Grades 4–5.

Whale Rap by Joan Van Bramer and Janine Scott. Text and song. Rigby, 1992. Grades 4–5.

3. Reading With Children: Sing Along, with Music (CDs or Tapes)

Baby Beluga by Raffi. Knopf, 1990. Grades K–1.

Sing Along and Play in the Splash Zone by Linda Arnold. Monterey Bay Aquarium, 2000. Grades 2–3.

Whale Rap by Joan Van Bramer and Janine Scott. Rigby (Big Book), 1992. Grades 4–5.

4. Reading By Children: Guided Reading

Books marked with an asterisk are bilingual texts or also available in Spanish.

GR = Guided Reading Level; IL = Intervention Level; Note: DRA level is used above Level 28

GR/IL

F10 * *A Coat Full of Bubbles/Un abrigo lleno de burbujas* by Sherry Shahan. Richard C. Owen, 1998. Nonfiction.

N28 *Animals of the Arctic and Antarctic* by Paul Reeder. Wright Group, 2000. Nonfiction.

Continued on next page.

Balancing Reading and Language Learning: A Resource for Teaching English Language Learners, K–5 by Mary Cappellini. Copyright © 2005. Stenhouse Publishers.

B2   *At the Aquarium* by Keith Pigdon. Explorations, Okapi, 2003. Nonfiction.

M22 * *Big Catch, The,* by Mary Cappellini. Rigby, 1996. Fiction.

A1 * *Boat, The,* by Sue Fuller. Pacific Learning, 1999. Nonfiction.

N25   *Buried Treasure.* Wright Group, 2000. Fiction.

Q40   *Caught by the Sea* by Rosemary Keating. Pacific Learning, 1999. Nonfiction.

H14   *Coral Reef* by Christine Echomos. Newbridge. 1999. Nonfiction.

F10   *Corals* by Lola M. Schaefer. Capstone Press, 1999. Nonfiction.

E8   *Crabs* by Lola M. Schaefer. Capstone Press, 1999. Nonfiction.

R40   *Creatures of the Reef* by Angie Belcher. Pacific Learning, 2000. Nonfiction.

N26   *Deadly Sea Creatures* by Bill Francis. Wright Group, 2000. Nonfiction.

C4   *Divers, The.* Wright Group. Nonfiction.

L21   *Diving for Treasure* by John C. Fine. Richard C. Owen, 2000. Nonfiction.

E7   *Dolphins* by Martha E. H. Rustad. Capstone Press, 2001. Nonfiction.

F10   *Dolphins* by Sylvia M. James. Mondo, 2002. Nonfiction.

O29   *Dolphins* by Victoria St. John. Wright Group, 2001. Nonfiction.

L24   *Encyclopedia of Fantastic Fish* by Mignon Manhart. Rigby, 2000. Nonfiction.

N26   *Escape from the Deep.* Wright Group, 2000. Nonfiction.

D6   *Fish.* Wright Group. Nonfiction.

C3 * *Fish Print* by Mary Cappellini. Lee and Low, 2000. Nonfiction.

J18   *Fish That Hide* by Stanley Swartz. Dominie Press, 2000. Nonfiction.

M24   *Fishing Off the Wharf* by Don Long. Pacific Learning, 1993. Nonfiction.

T44   *Hawaiian Magic* by Rod Morris. Pacific Learning, 2000. Nonfiction.

H15 * *Hoketichee and the Manatee* by Kathleen Hardcastle. Richard C. Owen. Fiction.

N20   *Humpback Whale, The.* Wright Group. Nonfiction.

H14 * *Hungry Sea Star, The/La estrella de mar tiene hambre* by Sherry Shahan. Richard C. Owen, 1997. Nonfiction.

P38 * *Hurricane On Its Way* by Eduardo Aparicio. Rigby, 1997. Nonfiction.

P30   *I Am the Walrus* by Diana Motsinger. Wright Group, 2001. Nonfiction.

B2   *I Like to Find Things.* Wright Group. Nonfiction.

H14   *I Ride the Waves* by Rhonda Cox. Richard C. Owen, 1999. Nonfiction.

B4   *I Went to the Beach* by Lori Morgan. Richard C. Owen, 2001. Nonfiction.

D5   *Ice and Snow* by Lee Wang. Explorations, Okapi, 2003. Nonfiction.

B2   *In the Sea.* Wright Group. Nonfiction.

T44   *Island Beginnings* by Susan Paris. Learning Media. Nonfiction.

L20   *Islands* by Alison Balance. Dominie Press, 2001. Nonfiction.

H14   *Little Puffer Fish.* Richard C. Owen. Fiction.

M18   *Little Whale, The.* Wright Group. Nonfiction.

D6   *Look Out.* Wright Group. Nonfiction.

L24   *Mammals of the Sea.* Wright Group. Nonfiction.

T44   *Maui's Fish* by Susan Paris. Pacific Learning, 2004. Fiction.

N29   *Monsters of the Deep.* Wright Group. Nonfiction.

J18   *Mother Octopus* by R. Hugh Rice. Richard C. Owen. Nonfiction.

G12   *Night Diving.* Wright Group. Nonfiction.

M22   *Ocean by the Lake, The,* by Antonella Parisi. Celebrations Press, 1996. Nonfiction.

E8   *Ocean Facts* by Joan Chapman. Rosen Publishing, 2001. Nonfiction.

J18   *Ocean Tides* by Al Richter. Rosen Publishing, 2001. Nonfiction.

F10   *Octopuses* by Lola M. Schaefer. Capstone Press, 1999. Nonfiction.

M20   *Otters* by Graham Meadow and Claire Vial. Dominie Press, 2002. Nonfiction.

F9   *Parrotfish* by Lola M. Schaefer. Capstone Press, 1999. Nonfiction.

D6   *Penguin's Chicks* by Joy Cowley. Pacific Learning, 1994. Nonfiction.

N30   *Pirates.* Wright Group, 2000. Nonfiction.

D6   *Rays* by Martha E. H. Rustad. Capstone Press, 2001. Nonfiction.

M24 * *Sam and Kim* by Jocelyn Cranefield and Don Long. Pacific Learning, 2001. Nonfiction.

B3 * *Sandcastle, The,* by Jane Buxton. Pacific Learning, 2000. Nonfiction.

O34   *Saving the Yellow Eye* by John Darby. Pacific Learning, 1999. Nonfiction.

I16 * *Schools of Fish/Cardúmenes* by Stanley Swartz. Dominie Press, 2001. Nonfiction.

F10   *Sea Anemones* by Lola M. Schaefer. Capstone Press, 1999. Nonfiction.

J18   *Sea Dragons.* Wright Group. Nonfiction.

E8   *Sea Horses* by Lola M. Schaefer. Capstone Press, 1999. Nonfiction.

J18 * *Sea Horses and Pipefish/Caballitos de mar y agujas de mar* by Stanley Swartz. Dominie Press, 2001. Nonfiction.

K19   *Sea Lights* by R. Hugh Rice. Richard C. Owen. Nonfiction.

E7   *Sea Stars* by Lola M. Schaefer. Capstone Press, 1999. Nonfiction.

E7   *Sea Turtles* by Martha E. H. Rustad. Capstone Press, 2001. Nonfiction.

F9   *Sea Urchins* by Lola M. Schaefer. Capstone Press, 1999. Nonfiction.

Continued on next page.

D6   *Seals* by Martha E. H. Rustad. Capstone Press, 2001. Nonfiction.

J28   *Seals and Sea Lions*. Wright Group, 2000. Nonfiction.

P38   *Searching for Sea Lions* by Kim Westerskov. Pacific Learning, 1999. Nonfiction.

O34   *Shark! The Truth Behind the Terror* by Mike Strong. Capstone Press, 2003. Nonfiction.

Q25   *Shark Rescue*. Wright Group. Nonfiction.

L19   *Sharks*. Wright Group. Nonfiction.

L19   *Ships*. Wright Group. Nonfiction.

O27   *Shipwrecks*. Wright Group. Nonfiction.

D7   *"Smile!" said Dad* by Jane Buxton. Pacific Learning, 1995. Fiction.

G12   *Snap! Splash!* by Jane Buxton. Pacific Learning, 1994. Nonfiction.

S44   *Spoiled by Oil* by Mandy Hager. Pacific Learning, 2004. Fiction.

L20   *Starfish and Urchins* by Stanley Swartz. Dominie Press, 1997. Nonfiction.

I16   *Stingrays*. Wright Group. Nonfiction.

I16   *Tides*. Wright Group. Nonfiction.

S44   *Truth About Sharks, The,* by Mike Bhana. Pacific Learning, 2004. Nonfiction.

?   *Unusual Fish* by Christine Butterworth. Steck-Vaughn, 1990. Nonfiction.

J18   *Walrus Watch*. Wright Group. Nonfiction.

M24 *   *Watching Whales/Observamos las ballenas* by Brenda Parkes. Newbridge, 1999. Nonfiction.

D6   *Water* by Dona Herweck Rice. Time For Kids, 2002. Nonfiction.

C3   *Water Moves* by Jenny Feely. Explorations, Okapi, 2003. Nonfiction.

J17   *Waves*. Wright Group. Nonfiction.

T44   *Whale Tales* by Kim Westerskov. Pacific Learning, 1999. Nonfiction.

M28 *   *Whale Watching* by Mary Cappellini. Pacific Learning, 2000. Nonfiction.

E7   *Whales* by Martha E. H. Rustad. Capstone Press, 2001. Nonfiction.

O27   *Whales*. Wright Group. Nonfiction.

E8   *Whales in the Ocean* by Claudia C. Diamond. Rosen Publishing, 2001. Nonfiction.

H14   *What Lives in a Tide Pool?* by Lily Richardson. National Geographic, 2003.

N25   *What's Under the Sea?* by Claudia Diamond. Rosen Publishing, 2001. Nonfiction.

K20   *What's Underneath* by David Glover. Rigby, 1998. Nonfiction.

K20   *Why the Sea Is Salty* retold by Leanna Traill. Rigby, 1997.

Q40   *Wild Bird and Other Stories of Adventure* by Angie Belcher. Pacific Learning, 1999.

Z50   *Wreck Trek* by Angie Belcher. Pacific Learning, 2000. Nonfiction.

5. Reading By Children: Books Designed to Teach Phonics

Early level texts: one sentence per page.

By the Ocean (Learning the Long O Sound) by Abigail Richter. Rosen Publishing, 2002.

Sharks (Learning the SH Sound) by Ira Wood. Rosen Publishing, 2002.

Boats That Float (Learning the OA Sound) by Abigail Richter. Rosen Publishing, 2002.

Summer at the Beach (Learning the EA Sound) by Maryann Thomas. Rosen Publishing, 2002.

6. Reading By Children: Independent Reading

The books listed in section 1 can also be used for independent reading.

7. Reading By Children: Chapter Books for Literature Circles or Independent Reading

Andrew Lost Under Water by J. C. Greenburg. Random House, 2003.

Dive I: The Discovery by Gordon Korman. Scholastic, 2003.

Dive II: The Deep by Gordon Korman. Scholastic, 2003.

Dive III: The Danger by Gordon Korman. Scholastic, 2003.

Dolphin in the Deep by Ben M. Baglio. Scholastic, 2001.

Dolphins at Daybreak by Mary Pope Osborne. Magic Treehouse Series. Random House, 1997.

Finding Nemo: The Junior Novelization adapted by Gail Herman. Disney Pixar. Random House, 2003.

Grandpa at the Beach by Rob Lewis. Mondo, 1998.

Into the Blue by Ben M. Baglio. Dolphin Diaries Series. Scholastic, 2002.

Island I: Shipwreck by Gordon Korman. Scholastic, 2001.

Island II: Survival by Gordon Korman. Scholastic, 2001.

Island III: Escape by Gordon Korman. Scholastic, 2001.

Island of the Blue Dolphins by Scott O'Dell. Random House, 1961.

Kensuke's Kingdom by Michael Morpurgo. Scholastic, 1999.

Nim's Island by Wendy Orr. Random House, 1999.

Pirates Past Noon by Mary Pope Osborne. Magic Tree House Series. Random House, 1994.

Secret of Kiribu Tapu Lagoon, The, by Tandi Jackson. Rigby, 1995.

Wild Whale Watch, The, by Eva Moore. Magic School Bus Chapter Book. Scholastic, 2000.

Balancing Reading and Language Learning: A Resource for Teaching English Language Learners, K–5 by Mary Cappellini. Copyright © 2005. Stenhouse Publishers.

Name _____ **Title of Book** _____

How would you describe the main character's personality?

What happened to the character, or what one event changed the character somehow?

How did the character deal with it? What was the character's reaction?

What do you think of the character's response?

What would you have done?

How woud you compare yourself to the main character?

Balancing Reading and Language Learning: A Resource for Teaching English Language Learners, K–5 by Mary Cappellini. Copyright © 2005. Stenhouse Publishers.

These are my favorite books from my personal library that I have with classrooms full of multicultural children. The categories are ones that I feel are important for read-alouds. Books marked with an asterisk are bilingual texts or also available in Spanish.

1. Poetry Books

1.1 Multicultural

* *Belly Button of the Moon and Other Summer Poems/Del ombligo de la luna y otros poemas del verano* by Francisco X. Alarcón. Children's Book Press, 1998.

Border Voices: Poems by San Diego City Schools' Genre Studies Students edited by Jack Webb. San Diego, 2000.

* *I Am of Two Places: A Book of Children's Poetry/Soy de dos Lugares* edited by Mary Carden and Mary Cappellini. Rigby, 1997.

Love to Mamá: A Tribute to Mothers edited by Pat Mora. Lee and Low, 2001.

My America: A Poetry Atlas of the United States by Lee Bennet Hopkins, 2000.

* *My Mexico/México mío* by Tony Johnston. Putnam, 1996.

* *Songs to the Corn: A Hopi Poet Writes About Corn* by Ramson Lomatewama. Rigby, 1997.

* *Tamarindo Puppy and Other Poems, The: Poems in English Mixed with Spanish* by Charlotte Pomerantz. Greenwillow Books, 1980.

1.2 Classic, Humorous

A Light in the Attic by Shel Silverstein. HarperCollins, 1981.

Dinosaur Dinner: Favorite Poems by Dennis Lee selected by Jack Prelutsky. Scholastic, 1997.

Falling Up by Shel Silverstein. HarperCollins, 1996.

Good Books, Good Times! selected by Lee B. Hopkins. HarperCollins, 2000.

Mrs. Cole on an Onion Roll and Other School Poems by Kalli Dakos. Scholastic, 1995.

Sometimes I Wonder if Poodles Like Noodles by Laura Numeroff. Scholastic, 1999.

Unzip the Sky by Patricia I. Johnson and Jocelyn Kerslake. Steck-Vaughn, 1992.

Where the Sidewalk Ends by Shel Silverstein. HarperCollins, 1973.

2. ABC Books

2.1 Bilingual Alliteration

* *Albertina Goes Up: An Alphabet Book/Albertina anda arriba: El abecedario* by Nancy M. G. Tabor. Charlesbridge, 1992.

* *Alphabet Fiesta: An English/Spanish Alphabet Story* by Anne Miranda. Turtle Books, 2001.

2.2 Clever, Rhyming

ABC I Like Me by Nancy Carlson. Viking, 1997.

Chicka Chicka Boom Boom by Bill Martin Jr. and John Archambault. Scholastic, Simon and Schuster, 1989.

Dr. Seuss's ABC. Random House 1963.

Old Black Fly by Jim Aylesworth. Henry Holt, 1992.

2.3 Poetry

A Helpful Alphabet of Friendly Objects: Poems by John Updike. Knopf, 1995.

Gathering the Sun: An Alphabet in Spanish and English by Alma Flor Ada. Lothrop, Lee and Shepard, 1997.

2.4 Regional, Multicultural

A Is for Aloha by Stephanie Feeney. University of Hawaii Press, 1980.

A Is for Antarctica by Jonathan Chester. Tricycle Press, 1995.

Alaska ABC Book by Charlene Kreeger. Paws Four Publishing, 1988.

Capital! Washington D.C. from A to Z by Laura K. Melmed. HarperCollins, 2003.

O Is for Orca: A Pacific Northwest Alphabet Book by Andrea Helman. Sasquatch Books, 1995.

2.5 Multiple Lists

Oliver's Alphabets by Lisa Bruce. Bradbury Press, 1993.

2.6 Content Areas, Nonfiction

A Fly in the Sky by Kristin J. Pratt. Dawn Publications, 1996.

A Swim Through the Sea by Kristin J. Pratt. Dawn Publications, 1994.

A Walk in the Rainforest by Kristin J. Pratt. Dawn Publications, 1992.

Airplane Alphabet Book, The, by Jerry Pallotta and Fred Stillwell. Charlesbridge, 1997.

Eating the Alphabet: Fruits and Vegetables from A to Z by Lois Ehlert. Harcourt Brace Jovanovich, 1989.

G Is for Googol: A Math Alphabet Book by David M. Schwartz. Tricycle Press, 2000.

Icky Bug Alphabet Book, The, by Jerry Pallotta. Charlesbridge, 1990.

Ocean Alphabet Book, The, by Jerry Pallotta. Charlesbridge, 1991.

Q Is for Quark: A Science Alphabet Book by David M. Schwartz. Tricycle Press, 2001.

Spice Alphabet Book, The, by Jerry Pallotta. Charlesbridge, 1997.

Underwater Alphabet Book, The, by Jerry Pallotta. Charlesbridge, 1991.

Continued on next page.

3. Books with Rhyme, Rhythm, Rich Language, Humor, Idioms

3.1 Rhyme and Repetition

Boom Chicka Rock by John Archambault. Philomel, 2004.

Counting 1-2-3: An Early Learner Book by M. C. Leeka. Modern Publishing, 1991.

Counting Crocodiles by Judy Sierra. Scholastic, 1997.

Cows Can't Fly by David Milgrim. Scholastic, 1998.

* *Fifty on the Zebra: Counting with the Animals/Cincuenta en la cebra: contando con los animales* by Nancy M. G. Tabor. Charlesbridge, 1994.

* *Grandmother's Nursery Rhymes/Las nanas de Abuelita: Lullabies, Tongue Twisters, and Riddles from South America* compiled by Nelly P. Jaramillo. Henry Holt, 1994.

I Can't Said the Ant by Polly Cameron. Scholastic, 1961.

* *Is Your Mama a Llama?* by Deborah Guarino. Scholastic, 1989.

Jesse Bear, What Will You Wear? by Nancy W. Carlstrom. Scholastic, 1986.

Miss Bindergarten Gets Ready for Kindergarten by Joseph Slate. Scholastic, 1996.

Mrs. McNosh Hangs up Her Wash by Sarah Weeks. Scholastic, 1998.

Mud Is Cake by Pam Muñoz Ryan. Hyperion, 2002.

One Fish, Two Fish, Red Fish, Blue Fish by Dr. Seuss. Random House, 1960.

Tumble Bumble by Felicia Bond. Scholastic, 1996.

Wee Witches' Halloween by Jerry Smath. Scholastic, 2002.

What Do You Do with a Kangaroo? by Mercer Mayer. Scholastic, 1973.

3.2 Rhythm

Crocodile Beat by Gail Jorgensen. Rigby, 1988.

I See the Rhythm by Toyomi Igus. Children's Book Press, 1998.

I'm Still Here in the Bathtub: Brand New Silly Dilly Songs by Alan Katz. McElderry Books, 2003.

Snake Alley Band by Elizabeth Nygaard. Doubleday, 1998.

We All Sing with the Same Voice by J. Philip Miller and Sheppard M. Greene. HarperCollins, 2001.

3.3 Rich Language

Glorious Angels: A Celebration of Children by Walter Dean Myers. HarperCollins, 1995.

Goodnight Gecko, The: A Bedtime Story from Hawaii by Gill McBarnet. Ruwanga Trading, 1991.

* *Hairs/Pelitos* by Sandra Cisneros. Random House Children's Media, 1994.

I Love You the Purplest by Barbara M. Joose. Scholastic, 1996.

Mama, Do You Love Me? by Barbara M. Joose. Chronicle Books, 1991.

Moon Tiger by Phyllis Root. Henry Holt, 1985.

My Many-Colored Days by Dr. Seuss. Knopf, 1996.

On a Wintry Morning by Dori Chaconas. Viking, 2000.

On the Day You Were Born by Debra Frasier. Harcourt Brace, 1991.

One Hundred Is a Family by Pam Muñoz Ryan. Hyperion, 1994.

Owl Moon by Jane Yolen. Scholastic, 1987.

Rainbows of the Sea by Meredith Thomas. Mondo, 1998.

Snow Dance by Lezlie Evans. Scholastic, 1997.

Touch the Earth by Hane Baskwill. Mondo, 1999.

3.4 Humor

Chrysanthemum by Kevin Henkes. William Morrow, 1996.

Click, Clack, Moo, Cows That Type by Doreen Cronin. Simon and Schuster, 2000.

Falling for Rapunzel by Leah Wilcox. Putnam, 2003.

Giggle, Giggle, Quack! by Doreen Cronin. Simon and Schuster, 2002.

Hooray for Diffendoofer Day! by Dr. Seuss with Jack Prelutsky. Random House, 1998.

I Like Me! by Nancy Carlson. Puffin Books, 1988.

Late for School by Mike Reiss. Peachtree, 2003.

Miss Alaineus: A Vocabulary Disaster by Debra Frasier. Harcourt, 2000.

No Moon, No Milk! by Chris Babcock. Scholastic, 1993.

Sheila Rae, the Brave by Kevin Henkes. William Morrow, 1987.

Twinnies by Eve Bunting. Harcourt Brace, 1997.

3.5 Idioms

A Chocolate Moose for Dinner by Fred Gwynne. Simon and Schuster, 1976.

King Who Rained, The, by Fred Gwynne. Simon and Schuster, 1970.

4. Multicultural Picture Books

A Boy Called Slow by Joseph Bruchac. Putnam, 1994.

* *A Chair for My Mother* by Vera B. Williams. Scholastic, 1982.

* *A Day's Work* by Eve Bunting. Clarion Books, 1994.

A Handful of Seeds by Monica Hughes. Orchard Books, 1993.

* *Abuela's Weave* by Omar S. Castañeda. Lee and Low, 1993.

* *Amelia's Road* by Linda J. Altman. Lee and Low, 1993.

América Is Her Name by Luis J. Rodríguez. Curbstone Press, 1998.

Apple Pie 4th of July by Janet S. Wong. Harcourt, 2003.

Continued on next page.

Balancing Reading and Language Learning: A Resource for Teaching English Language Learners, K–5 by Mary Cappellini. Copyright © 2005. Stenhouse Publishers.

* *Baseball Saved Us* by Ken Mochizuki. Lee and Low, 1993.

Bracelet, The, by Yoshiko Uchida. Philomel, 1993.

Bus Ride, The, by William Miller. Lee and Low, 1998.

Caged Birds of Phnom Penh, The, by Frederick Lipp. Holiday House, 2001.

* *Camila and Clay-Old-Woman* by Mary Cappellini with Tito Naranjo. Rigby, 1997.

Carlos, Light the Farolito by Jean Ciavonne. Clarion Books, 1995.

Chato's Kitchen by Gary Soto. Putnam, 1995.

Coming Home: From the Life of Langston Hughes by Floyd Cooper. Putnam, 1997.

Dancing Dragon, The, by Marcia Vaughan. Mondo, 1996.

* *Day of the Dead* by Tony Johnston. Harcourt Brace, 1997.

* *Dear Abuelita* by Sofia M. Keane. Rigby, 1997.

December by Eve Bunting. Harcourt Brace, 1997.

Dragon Parade by Steven A. Chin. Steck-Vaughn, 1993.

El Chino by Allen Say. Houghton Mifflin, 1990.

* *Family Pictures/Cuadros de familia* by Carmen L. Garza. Children's Book Press, 1990.

Farolitos of Christmas, The, by Rudolfo Anaya. Hyperion, 1987.

* *First Day in Grapes* by L. King Pérez. Lee and Low, 2002.

Fishing Day by Andrea D. Pinkney. Hyperion Books, 2003.

For Every Child a Better World by Kermit the Frog as told to Louise Gikow and Ellen Weiss. United Nations Publication, 2001.

Gleam and Glow by Eve Bunting. Harcourt, 2001.

Goin' Someplace Special by Patricia McKissack. Simon and Schuster, 2002.

* *Going Home* by Eve Bunting. HarperCollins, 1993.

Goodbye, 382 Shin Dang Dong by Frances and Ginger Park. National Geographic, 2003.

Granddaddy's Gift by Margaree K. Mitchell. Bridgewater Books, 1997.

Gullywasher, The: A Modern Tall Tale by Joyce Rossi. Northland Publishing, 1996.

* *Harvesting Hope: The Story of Cesar Chavez* by Kathleen Krull. Harcourt, 2003.

Heroes by Ken Mochizuki. Lee and Low, 1995.

* *How Many Days to America: A Thanksgiving Story* by Eve Bunting. Clarion Books, 1988.

How My Parents Learned to Eat by Ina R. Friedman. Houghton Mifflin, 1984.

* *I Am America* by Charles Smith Jr. Scholastic, 2003.

I Love Saturdays y Domingos by Alma Flor Ada. Simon and Schuster, 2003.

* *I Speak English for My Mom* by Muriel Stanek. Albert Whitman, 1989.

Isla by Arthur Dorros. Dutton Children's Books, 1995.

Jalapeño Bagels by Natasha Wing. Simon and Schuster, 1996.

Maria Molina and the Days of the Dead by Kathleen Krull. Macmillan, 1994.

Messages to Ground Zero: Children Respond to September 11th edited by Shelley Harwayne. Heinemann, 2002.

* *Moon y Luna/Luna, Lunita Lunera* by Jorge Argueta. Children's Books Press, 2005.

My Brother Martin: A Sister Remembers—Growing Up with the Rev. Dr. Martin Luther King Jr. by Christine K. Farris. Simon and Schuster, 2002.

* *My Name Is Yoon* by Helen Recorvitz. Farrar, Straus, Giroux, 2003

Name Jar, The, by Yangsook Choi. Knopf, 2001.

* *Papa's Mark* by Gwendolyn Battle-Lavert. Holiday House, 2004.

Passage to Freedom: The Sugihara Story by Ken Mochizuki. Lee and Low, 1997.

Pot That Juan Built, The, by Nancy Andrews-Goebel. Lee and Low, 2003.

Read for Me, Mama by Vashanti Rahamn. Boyds Mills Press, 1997.

* *Remembering Grandma/Recordando a Abuela* by Teresa Armas. Arte Público Press, 2003.

Sachiko Means Happiness by Kimiko Sakai. Children's Book Press, 1990.

* *Sí, Se Puede!/Yes We Can! Janitor Strike in L.A.* by Diana Cohn, trans. by Sharon Franco. Cinco Puntos Press, 2002.

Smoky Night by Eve Bunting. Harcourt Brace, 1994.

* *Story of Doña Chila, The,* by Mary Cappellini. Rigby, 1997.

Story of Ruby Bridges, The, by Robert Coles. Scholastic, 1995.

Tea with Milk by Alan Say. Houghton Mifflin, 1999.

* *This Home We Have Made/Esta casa que hemos hecho* by Anna Hammond and Joe Matunis, Crown, 1993.

* *Tomás and the Library Lady* by Pat Mora. Random House Children's Media, 1997.

* *Too Many Tamales* by Gary Soto. Putnam, 1993.

* *Under the Lemon Moon* by Edith Hope Pine. Lee and Low, 2000.

Up the Learning Tree by Marcia Vaughan. Lee and Low, 2003.

* *Upside Down Boy, The/El niño de cabeza* by Juan Felipe Herrera. Children's Book Press, 2001.

* *Waiting for Papa/Esperando a Papa* by Rene Colato Lainez. Arte Público Press, 2004.

What's the Most Beautiful Thing You Know About Horses? by Richard Van Camp. Children's Book Press, 1998.

Whispering Cloth, The: A Refugee Story by Pegi D. Shea. Boyds Mills Press, 1996.

* *Who Belongs Here? An American Story* by Margy B. Knight. Tibury House, 1993.

Yoko's Paper Cranes by Rosemary Wells. Hyperion, 2001.

Continued on next page.

5. Multicultural Chapter Books

A Migrant Family by Larry D. Brimner. Lerner Publications, 1992.

Aleutian Sparrow by Karen Hesse. McElderry, 2003.

Amah, The, by Laurence Yep. Putnam, 1999.

Barrio: José's Neighborhood by George Ancona. Harcourt Brace, 1998.

Breadwinner by Deborah Ellis. Groundwood Books, 2001.

Colibrí by Ann Cameron. Farrar, Straus, Giroux, 2003.

Dear Mrs. Parks: A Dialogue with Today's Youth by Rosa Parks with Gregory J. Reed. Lee and Low, 1996.

* *Esperanza Rising* by Pam Muñoz Ryan. Scholastic, 2000.

House on Mango Street, The, by Sandra Cisneros. Vintage Books, 1984.

Journeys with Elijah: Eight Tales of the Prophet by Barbara D. Gold. Harcourt, 1999.

Key Collection, The, by Andrea Cheng. Holt, 2003.

Maldonado Miracle, The, by Theodore Taylor. Harcourt, 2003.

Pablo Remembers: The Fiesta of the Day of the Dead by George Ancona. Lothrop, Lee and Shepard, 1993.

Parvana's Journey by Deborah Ellis. Groundwood Books, 2003.

Tenement: Immigrant Life on the Lower East Side by Raymond Bial. Houghton Mifflin, 2003.

Under the Royal Palms: A Childhood in Cuba by Alma Flor Ada. Atheneum, 1998.

Voices from the Fields: Children of Migrant Farmworkers Tell Their Stories. Little, Brown, 1993.

6. Multicultural Legends

* *Arrow to the Sun* by Gerald McDermott. Viking, 1974.

* *Desert Mermaid, The/La sirena del desierto* by Barbara Paschke. Children's Book Press. 1992.

* *Magic of Spider Woman, The,* by Lois Duncan. Scholastic, 1996.

* *Mufaro's Beautiful Daughters: An African Tale* by John Steptoe. Scholastic, 1987.

People of Corn: A Mayan Story retold by Mary-Joan Gerson. Little, Brown, 1995.

* *Uncle Nacho's Hat/El sombrero de tío Nacho* adapted by Harriet Rohmer. Children's Book Press, 1989.

* *Story of Colors, The/La historia de los colores: A Bilingual Folktale from the Jungles of Chiapas* by Subcomandante Insurgente Marcos, trans. Anne Bar Din. Cinco Puntos Press, 1999.

* *Woman Who Outshone the Sun, The/La mujer que brillaba aún más que el sol* by Alejandro Cruz Martinez, Harriet Rohmer, Rosalma Zubizarreta, and David Schecter. Children's Book Press, 1991.

7. Variations on Traditional Tales

Cinderella Penguin, or, The Little Glass Flipper by Janet Perlman. Viking, 1993.

Cook-A-Doodle-Doo! by Janet Stevens and Susan S. Crummel. Harcourt Brace, 1999.

Fairy Tales told by Berlie Doherty. Candlewick Press, 2000.

Falling for Rapunzel by Leah Wilcox. Putnam, 2003.

Little Red Hen, The, by Byron Barton. HarperCollins, 1993.

Princess Knight, The, by Cornelia Funke. Scholastic, 2003.

Princess Smartypants by Babette Cole. Putnam, 1986.

Three Pigs, The, by David Wiesner. Scholastic, 2001.

* *True Story of the Three Little Pigs, The,* by M. Wolf as told to Jon Scieszka. Viking, 1989.

8. Author Study: Eve Bunting

* *A Day's Work* by Eve Bunting. Clarion Books, 1994.

A Perfect Father's Day by Eve Bunting. Clarion Books, 2000.

A Picnic in October by Eve Bunting. Harcourt Brace, 1999.

* *Cheyenne Again* by Eve Bunting. Clarion Books, 1995.

* *December* by Eve Bunting. Harcourt Brace, 1997.

Ducky by Eve Bunting. Clarion Books, 2004.

Flower Garden by Eve Bunting. Harcourt Brace, 1994.

* *Fly Away Home* by Eve Bunting. Clarion Books, 1991.

Ghost's Hour, Spook's Hour by Eve Bunting. Clarion Books, 1989.

Gleam and Glow by Eve Bunting. Harcourt, 2001.

* *Going Home* by Eve Bunting. HarperCollins, 1993.

* *How Many Days to America: A Thanksgiving Story* by Eve Bunting. Clarion Books, 1988.

In the Haunted House by Eve Bunting. Clarion Books, 1990.

Jin Woo by Eve Bunting. Clarion Books, 2001.

Memory String, The, by Eve Bunting. Clarion Books, 2000.

Night Tree by Eve Bunting. Harcourt, 1991.

Our Teacher's Having a Baby by Eve Bunting. Clarion Books, 1992.

Secret Place by Eve Bunting. Clarion Books, 1996.

Smoky Night by Eve Bunting. Harcourt Brace, 1994.

So Far from the Sea by Eve Bunting. Clarion Books, 1998.

Sunshine Home by Eve Bunting. Clarion Books, 1994.

Train to Somewhere by Eve Bunting. Clarion Books, 1996.

Twinnies by Eve Bunting. Harcourt Brace, 1997.

* *Wall, The,* by Eve Bunting. Clarion Books, 1990.

* *Wednesday Surprise, The,* by Eve Bunting. Clarion Books, 1989.

Balancing Reading and Language Learning: A Resource for Teaching English Language Learners, K–5 by Mary Cappellini. Copyright © 2005. Stenhouse Publishers.

Balancing Reading and Language Learning: A Resource for Teaching English Language Learners, K–5 by Mary Cappellini. Copyright © 2005. Stenhouse Publishers.

Shared Reading—Primary Grades
Focus Sheet of Outcomes for English Language Learners

E1

Beginning to Intermediate Speakers

Thematic unit _____

Mini-theme _____

Shared reading material _____

Features to Note in Text (examples):

Rhyming words:

Plurals/words ending in *s*:

Interesting vocabulary:

Punctuation:

High-frequency words:

Expected language outcomes (examples)

Beginning speakers

One-word response _____

Regular plurals _____

Early intermediate speakers

Repeat simple sentence _____

Use present tense _____

Intermediate speakers

Express understanding of text _____

Possessive pronouns/subject-verb agreement _____

Use past tense _____

Expected reading outcomes (examples)

Beginning speakers

Read aloud simple words in story _____

Early intermediate speakers

Identify and produce rhyming words _____

Intermediate speakers

Read simple vocabulary _____

Read phrases, sentences independently _____

All speakers

Tracking left to right _____

One-to-one correspondence _____

Outcomes based on performance standards from ELD Standards (California Department of Education)

Beginning to Early Advanced Speakers

Thematic unit _____

Mini-theme _____

Shared reading material _____

Features to Note in Text (examples):

Cognates:

Plurals/words ending in *s*:

Prepositions:

Verb tense:

High-frequency words:

Text format:

Expected language outcomes (examples)

Beginning speakers
One-word response _____
Regular plurals _____

Early intermediate speakers
Repeat simple sentence _____
Use present tense _____

Intermediate speakers
Express understanding of text _____
Possessive pronouns/subject-verb agreement _____
Use past tense _____

Early advanced speakers
Speak in complete sentences _____
Ask questions in past tense _____

Expected reading outcomes (examples)

Beginning speakers
Read aloud simple words in story _____

Early intermediate speakers
Identify subject, read short phrases _____

Intermediate speakers
Read simple vocabulary _____
Read phrases, sentences independently _____

Early advanced speakers
Read captions and glossary easily _____
State main idea, find supporting details _____

Outcomes based on performance standards from ELD Standards (California Department of Education)

Balancing Reading and Language Learning: A Resource for Teaching English Language Learners, K–5 by Mary Cappellini. Copyright © 2005. Stenhouse Publishers.

Shared Reading Planning Sheet

Date_____ Big Book _____ Which Reading _____

Purpose of Reading

Focus

Children's Needs

Introduction

During Reading

After Reading

Possible Follow-ups

Shared Reading
Observations and Notes from a Lesson

Date_____ Big Book _____ Which Reading _____

Language Level	Language Output/Participation	Reading Output
Beginning		
Early Intermediate		
Intermediate		
Early Advanced		
Advanced		

Books marked with an asterisk are bilingual texts or also available in Spanish.

1. Fiction Big Books

1.1 Creative Narratives
A Farm's Not a Farm by Brenda Parkes. Rigby.
Angus Thought He Was Big by Amanda Graham. ETA/Cuisenaire.
Beware! by Gail Jorgenson. Rigby.
* *Big Surprise, The,* by Melissa Leighton. Pacific Learning.
Creatures Features by David Drew. Rigby.
Crocodile Beat by Gail Jorgensen. Rigby.
Day of the Dead by Tony Johnston. Hampton Brown.
* *Days of Adventure* by Lyn Swanson-Natsues. Mondo.
Down They Rolled by Janeen Brian. ETA/Cuisenaire.
* *Excuses, Excuses* by Andrea Butler. Rigby.
Fiesta by Katacha Díaz. Macmillan.
From Here to There by Margaret Cuyler. Hampton Brown.
* *Grandpa, Grandpa* by Joy Cowley. Wright Group.
* *Greedy Cat* by Joy Cowley. Pacific Learning.
* *Greedy Gray Octopus, The,* by Christel Buckley. Rigby.
* *It Didn't Frighten Me* by Janet Goss and Jerome Harste. Mondo.
* *Judge for a Day* by Margarita González-Jensen. Rigby.
* *Look at the Moon* by May Garelick. Mondo.
Mrs. McNosh and the Great Big Squash by Sarah Weeks. Hampton Brown.
* *Mrs. Wishy-Washy* by Joy Cowley. Wright Group.
My Dog by Claude Belanger. Rigby.
Parrot, The, by Betty Zed. ETA/Cuisenaire.
Stuck in the Mud by Josephine Croser. ETA/Cuisenaire.
Tortillas and Lullabies by Lynn Reiser. Hampton Brown.
Tricky Truck Track, The, by Amanda Graham. ETA/Cuisenaire.
Two Feet by David Kennett and Gwen Pascoe. ETA/Cuisenaire.
Whale Watching by Josephine Croser. ETA/Cuisenaire.
* *What's Cooking?* by Shelly Harwayne. Mondo.
* *When Lana Was Absent* by Andrea Butler. Rigby.
* *Who's in the Shed?* by Brenda Parkes. Rigby.
* *Zoo Looking* by Mem Fox. Mondo.

1.2 Legends, Folk Tales Big Books
A Book of Fables. Era Publications.
* *Crying Mountain, The: A Mexican Legend* retold by Patricia Almada. Rigby.
Folk Tales: A Short Anthology retold by Jane O'Loughlin. Era Publications.

1.3 Poetry Big Books
Catch Me the Moon, Daddy by William Kaufman. Rigby.
* *I Am of Two Places: A Book of Children's Poetry* edited by Mary Carden and Mary Cappellini. Rigby.
Morning, Noon, and Night: Poems to Fill Your Day edited by Sharon Taberski. Mondo.
Songs of Myself: An Anthology of Poems and Art selected by Georgia Heard. Mondo.

2. Nonfiction Big Books—Science, History/Social Science

* *Alone in the Desert* by David Drew. Rigby.
Animal Lives. Rourke Classroom Resources.
* *Beavers* by Helen Moore. Mondo.
Big Bad Cats. Big Books by George.
* *Birds: Modern-Day Dinosaurs* by Kerri O'Donnell. Rosen Publishing.
Birds of Prey by Marilyn Woolley. Mondo.
Book of Animal Records, The, by David Drew. Rigby.
* *Bringing Water to People* by Katacha Díaz. Rigby.
Cat on the Chimney, The, by David Drew. Rigby.
Cousteau by Kevin Comber. Era Publications.
Deep in a Rainforest by Gwen Pascoe. ETA/Cuisenaire.
Different Faces from Different Places. Wright Group.
* *Earthquake Experts* by Patricia Almada. Rigby.
Elephants Never Forget. Wright Group.
* *From Father to Son* by Patricia Almada. Rigby.
Grizzly Bears by Marilyn Woolley. Mondo.
I Spy by David Drew. Rigby.
* *Inside the Sun.* Rosen Publishing.
* *Is This a Monster?* by Scarlett Lovell. Mondo.
* *It's Electric!* by Greg Roza. Rosen Publishing.
* *Journey to a New Land: An Oral History* by Kimberley Weinberger. Mondo.
* *Meet the Octopus* by Sylvia M. James. Mondo.
Night Diving. Wright Group.
Paper Skyscraper, The, by David Drew. Rigby.
Postcards from the Planets by David Drew. Rigby.
Primary Sources in Early American History by Janey Levy. Rosen Publishing.
Primary Sources of Immigration and Migration by Janey Levy. Rosen Publishing.
Red Eyed Tree Frog. Hampton Brown.
Save Our Earth by Ron Bacon. Rigby.
Should There Be Zoos? by Tony Stead. Mondo.
Skeleton by David Drew. Rigby.
* *Space Rocks.* Rosen Publishing.
Spiders by Esther Cullen. Mondo.

Continued on next page.

Balancing Reading and Language Learning: A Resource for Teaching English Language Learners, K–5 by Mary Cappellini. Copyright © 2005. Stenhouse Publishers.

* *Story of Sitting Bull, The.* Rosen Publishing.
What's Happening? A Book of Explanations by Patricia Relf. Mondo.
Which Is Which? by Josephine Croser. ETA/Cuisenaire.
You Are a Scientist. Rourke Classroom Resources.
Your Amazing Body. Wright Group.

3. Complete Series—Big Books, Posters, Tapes

A Chorus of Cultures. Hampton-Brown.
Avenues. Hampton Brown.
Bookshop. Mondo.
* Greetings! Rigby/Harcourt Achieve.
Into English! Hampton-Brown.
Let's Sing About It! Mondo.
Now I Get It! Mondo.
On Our Way to English. Harcourt Achieve.
* Orbit Shared Reading. Pacific Learning.
* Shared Reading Pack Sets. Wright Group.
Story Box, The. Wright Group.

4. Other Resources

e-Lective Language Learning by Jim Cummins and Sotirios Chascas. www.e-Lective.net. (This is an effective resource for independent reading in the content areas or with any text.)
My Picture Dictionary. Mondo.
Oxford Picture Dictionary for Kids, The. Oxford University Press.
Oxford Picture Dictionary for the Content Areas, The. Oxford University Press.
Picture Perfect Word Book. Hampton-Brown.
Picture Perfect Dictionary 1. Hampton-Brown.
Picture Perfect Dictionary 2. Hampton-Brown.

Balancing Reading and Language Learning: A Resource for Teaching English Language Learners, K–5 by Mary Cappellini. Copyright © 2005. Stenhouse Publishers.

Guided Reading—Text Features Form F1

Title ____________________

Author/Illustrator ____________________

Genre ____________________ **Series** ____________________

Stage ____________________ **Intervention Level** ____________________

Number of Running Words ____________________

Supports

Challenges

Interesting Features

Sentence Structure
(including verb tense)

Vocabulary and Theme

High-Frequency Words

Phonics Features

Punctuation

1. Multicultural Books

Books marked with an asterisk are available in Spanish.

* *A Surprise for Monica* by Katherine Maitland. Rigby, 1997.
* *Camila and Clay-Old-Woman* by Mary Cappellini. Rigby, 1997.
* *Chinese New Year, The,* by Andrea Hsu. Pacific Learning, 1997. Nonfiction.
* *Confetti Eggs* by Dani Sneed and Josie Fonseca. Lee and Low, 2002. Nonfiction.
* *Dear Abuelita* by Sofia M. Keane. Rigby, 1997.
* *Dressing with Pride* by Maria H. Acuña and Maly Ny. Rigby, 1997. Nonfiction.
* *Elena Makes Tortillas* by Clara Bowes. Pacific Learning, 1999. Nonfiction.
* *Everybody Wears Braids* by Adjoa Burrowes. Lee and Low, 2002.
* *Fish Print* by Mary Cappellini. Lee and Low, 2000.
  Friendship Garden, The, by Angela Medearis. Celebrations Press, 1996.
* *Going to America: Li Ming's Diary.* Pacific Learning, 2003.
* *I Play Soccer* by Mary Cappellini. Lee and Low, 2001.
* *Lac Hong Music Group, The,* by Mary Cappellini. Rigby, 1997. Nonfiction.
* *My Family* by Karen Hjembroe. Lee and Low, 2000.
* *One City, One School, Many Foods* by Argentina Palacios. Rigby, 1997. Nonfiction.
  Refugee, The, by Janice Marriott. Pacific Learning, 2000.
  Tomato Picking Day by Tom Pipher. Wright Group, 2000.
* *Trip to Freedom* by Andrea Nguyen and Patricia Abello. Rigby, 1997. Nonfiction.
* *We All Play Sports* by Diana Noonan. Pacific Learning. 1997.
* *We Dance* by Beth Becker. Pacific Learning, 1997. Nonfiction.
* *We Eat Rice* by Min Hong. Lee and Low, 2002.

2. Series

If a series has a counterpart in Spanish, it is listed in parentheses.

2.1 Emergent to Transitional Readers

These series as a whole are recommended because of the quality of the writing and illustrations, the range of topics and genres including nonfication, and the portrayal of multicultural children in the books.

Bebop Books Guided Reading in English (Bebops in Spanish). Lee and Low.
First Stories. Pacific Learning.
Guided Reading (Farolitos). Pacific Learning.
Literacy 2000, Stages 1–6 (Literatura 2000, Stages 1–6). Rigby/Harcourt Achieve.
Little Books Collections A and B, from Into English! Hampton-Brown.
Little Celebrations, Stages 1–3 (Pequeñitas Celebraciones). Celebrations Press.
Reading Safari. Mondo.
Storyteller (Sra. Sabiduría). Wright Group/McGraw-Hill.

The following series include only nonfiction books. Also recommended because of quality of writing, photographs, topics, and design of books.

Bridgestone Books. Capstone.
Discovery Links (Descubrimientos). Newbridge.
Explorations. Eleanor Curtain Publishing.
First Explorers (Primeros Exploradores). Wright Group/McGraw-Hill.
Leveled Readers Nonfiction. Dominie Press.
Nonfiction Guided Reading Kits. Mondo.
Nonfiction Readers. Time for Kids.
Pebble Books. Capstone.
Rosen Real Readers. Rosen Publishing.
Shutterbug Books. Steck-Vaughn/Harcourt Achieve.
Windows on Literacy. National Geographic.
Wonder World. Wright Group.

2.2 Early Fluent to Fluent Readers

These series as a whole are recommended because of the quality of the writing and illustrations, the range of topics and genres, the good content coverage, and the high interest level in short chapter books and short stories. The nonfiction series listed in section 2.1 are also appropriate. Grade levels listed are for approximate readability level.

Chapters (Capítulos). Pacific Learning. Grade 2.
Greetings! (¡Saludos!). Rigby/Harcourt Achieve. Includes Big Books.
Guiding Reading, Fluency Stage (Farolitos, Fluency Stage). Pacific Learning.
High Five. Capstone. Grades 2–5.
Literacy 2000, Stages 5–10 (Literatura 2000, Stages 5–10). Rigby/Harcourt Achieve. Grades 2–5.
Orbit Chapter Books (¡Capítulos!). Pacific Learning. Grades 3–6.
Orbit Double Takes. Pacific Learning. Grades 3–6.
Orbit Collections. Pacific Learning. Grades 3–6.
Safari Readers. Mondo.
Take Twos. Wright Group. Grades 2–5.
Wildcats. Wright Group. Grades 1–6.

2.3 Older Readers Well Below Grade Level

These series as a whole are recommended because of the quality of the writing, the illustrations, and the high-interest topics, especially nonfiction, that appeal to older readers. Guided reading levels and interest levels can be researched on the publishers' Web sites. Many series come with tapes for more practice and partner reading.

Boyz Rule! Mondo. (tapes)
Greetings! (¡Saludos!). Rigby/Harcourt Achieve. Includes Big Books. Grades 2–5. (tapes)
High Five. Capstone. Grades 2–5.
New Heights. Pacific Learning. Grades 1–3. (tapes)
Orbit Chapter Books (¡Capítulos!). Pacific Learning. Grades 3–4.
Take Twos. Wright Group/McGraw-Hill. Grades 2–5.
Toocool. Pacific Learning. Grades 2–6.
Wildcats. Wright Group/McGraw-Hill. Grades 1–6.

Balancing Reading and Language Learning: A Resource for Teaching English Language Learners, K–5 by Mary Cappellini. Copyright © 2005. Stenhouse Publishers.

Guided Reading Group _____ **Date** _____

Title of Book _____ **Level** _____

Name of Child	Overall Comments	Language Patterns and Vocabulary Used	Reading Strategies Used

Name _____

Title of Book _____ **Genre** _____

Author _____

New Words or Phrases	What I Know About the Words	What I Think They Mean	How They Are Used

Name _____

Title of Book _____ **Genre** _____

Author _____

Main Idea of Chapters/Paragraphs Supporting Details from Text	Heading/Page

Name _____

Title of Book _____ **Genre** _____

Author _____

What I Learned About the Topic and Vocabulary That Helped Me	Chapter/Page

Balancing Reading and Language Learning: A Resource for Teaching English Language Learners, K–5 by Mary Cappellini. Copyright © 2005. Stenhouse Publishers.

Fluent Guided Reading Focus Sheet—
K-W-L Chart

Name _____

Title of Book _____ **Genre** _____

Author _____

What I *Know*	What I *Want to Know*	What I *Learned*

Name _____

Title of Book _____ **Genre** _____

Author _____

Facts	Opinions

Balancing Reading and Language Learning: A Resource for Teaching English Language Learners, K–5 by Mary Cappellini. Copyright © 2005. Stenhouse Publishers.

Name _____

Title of Book _____ **Genre** _____

Author _____

What Does It Really Mean? Supporting Details from Text	Chapter/Page

Name _____

Title of Book _____ **Genre** _____

Author _____

What was the purpose of the story?

What was the author trying to say?

Problem:

Character What I know about the character	What I learned about the character
What is the character like at the beginning of the story?	How does the character change?
Character What I know about the character	What I learned about the character
What is the character like at the beginning of the story?	How does the character change?

Solution:

What did I learn from the story?

What was the author trying to say?

These books are high interest for all ages of readers regardless of grade level. Books are grouped by approximate reading level from beginning to more fluent series. Guided Reading Levels are also listed.

Beginning Chapter Books—Early Fluent Series	Guided Reading Levels
Henry and Mudge series by Cynthia Rylant.	J
Mr. Putter and Tabby series by Cynthia Rylant.	J
Nate the Great series by Marjorie W. Sharmat.	K
Commander Toad series by Jane Yolen.	K
Amelia Bedelia series by Peggy Parish.	L
Cam Jansen series by David Adler.	L
Jigsaw Jones Mystery series by James Preller	L
Horrible Harry series by Susy Kline.	L
Triplet Trouble series by Debbie Dadey and Marcia Jones.	L
Judy Moody series by Megan McDonald.	L

Intermediate Chapter Books—Fluent Series	Guided Reading Levels
Arthur series by Marc Brown.	M
The Magic Tree House series by Mary P. Osborne.	M
Flat Stanley series by Jeff Brown.	M
A to Z Mysteries series by Ron Roy.	N
Amber Brown series by Paula Danziger.	N
The Amazing Days of Abby Hayes series by Anne Mazer.	O
Ramona series by Beverly Cleary.	O

Advanced Chapter Books—Fluent Series	Guided Reading Levels
Baby-Sitters Club series by Ann M. Martin.	O
The Boxcar Children series by Gertrude C. Warner.	O
Fairy Realm series by Emily Rodda.	P
The Adventures of the Bailey School Kids series by Debbie Dadey and Marcia Jones.	P
Magic School Bus Chapter Books series by Joanna Cole.	P
Encyclopedia Brown: Boy Detective series by Donald J. Sobol.	P
Anastasia series by Lois Lowry.	Q
Dolphin Diaries series by Ben M. Baglio.	S
Artemis Fowl series by Eoin Colfer.	S
Harry Potter series by J. K. Rowling.	V
A Series of Unfortunate Events series by Lemony Snicket.	V

REFERENCES

CHILDREN'S BOOKS

The following books are those mentioned in the text or by students in journals or reading conferences. See also book lists in Appendixes C–G.

A Day's Work by Eve Bunting. Clarion Books, 1994.

A Farm's Not a Farm by Brenda Parkes. Rigby (Big Book), 1989.

A Friend for Me by Jane Buxton. Learning Media, 2000.

A Friend Is . . . (*Toy Story* character book). Disney/Pixar, 1996 (out of print).

A Migrant Family by Larry D. Brimner. Lerner, 1992.

Abuela's Weave by Omar S. Castañeda. Lee and Low, 1993.

Amber Brown series by Paula Danziger. Scholastic.

Amelia's Road by Linda J. Altman. Lee and Low, 1993.

Ancient Civilizations of Mexico. Time for Kids, 2002.

Artemis Fowl by Eoin Colfer. Hyperion, 2001.

Baby Animals by Sue Davis and Jeni Wilson. Rigby, 2000.

Baseball Saved Us by Ken Mochizuki. Lee and Low, 1993.

Baseball's Best by Phil Mettie. Learning Media, 2004.

BFG, The, by Roald Dahl. Scholastic, 1982.

Big Catch, The, by Mary Cappellini. Rigby, 1997.

Bracelet, The, by Yoshiko Uchida. Philomel, 1993.

The Bridge to Terabithia by Katherine Paterson. Crowell, 1978.

Bringing Water to People by Katacha Díaz. Rigby (Big Book), 1997.

Camila and Clay-Old-Woman by Mary Cappellini with Tito Naranjo. Rigby, 1997.

Canoe Diary by Nic Bishop. Learning Media, 1999.

Car Trouble by Kathryn Sutherland. Rigby, 1999.

Cat on the Chimney, The, by David Drew. Ginn, 1992.

Catch Me the Moon, Daddy by William Kaufman. Rigby, 2001.

Charlotte's Web by E. B. White. Harper, 1952

Chicka Chicka Boom Boom by Bill Martin Jr. and John Archambault. Simon and Schuster, 1989.

Click, Clack, Moo, Cows That Type by Doreen Cronin. Simon and Schuster, 2000.

Counting Crocodiles by Judy Sierra. Scholastic, 1997.

Cows Can't Fly by David Milgrim. Scholastic, 1998.

Cranes by Sally Cole. Wright Group, 2000.

Crocodile Beat by Gail Jorgensen. Bradbury, 1989; Rigby (Big Book).

Crying Mountain, The: A Mexican Legend retold by Patricia Almada. Rigby, 1997.

Dad Didn't Mind at All by Ngarangi Naden. Rigby, 1989.

Dance My Dance by Ned Osakawa. Wright Group, 2000.

Dear Abuelita by Sofia M. Keane. Rigby, 1997.

Dinosaur Dinner: Favorite Poems by Dennis Lee selected by Jack Prelutsky. Scholastic, 1997.

Dressing with Pride by Maria H. Acuña and Maly Ny. Rigby, 1997.

Esperanza Rising by Pam M. Ryan. Scholastic, 2000.

Exploring Saltwater Habitats by Sue Smith. Mondo, 1994.

Falling for Rapunzel by Leah Wilcox. Putnam, 2003.

Fish Print/Huella de pescado by Mary Cappellini. Lee and Low, 2000.

Fly Away Home by Eve Bunting. Clarion, 1991.

Folk Tales: A Short Anthology retold by Jane O'Loughlin. Era Publications, 1991.

"Forest Fires" from *Fire! Fire!* by Paul Reeder. Wright Group, 1999.

Friends from the Other Side/Amigos del otro lado by Gloria Anzaldua. Children's Book Press, 1995.

Grandma's Memories by Virginia King. Rigby, 1997.

Grandpa, Grandpa by Joy Cowley. Wright Group, 1998 (Big Book).

Green Footprints by Connie Kehoe. Rigby, 1997.

Hairs/Pelitos by Sandra Cisneros. Random House Children's Media, 1994.

Harry Potter and the Sorcerer's Stone and other books in the series by J. K. Rowling. Scholastic.

Harvesting Hope: The Story of Cesar Chavez by Kathleen Krull. Harcourt, 2003.

Hatchet by Gary Paulsen. Simon and Schuster, 1988.

Henry and Mudge and the Starry Night by Cynthia Rylant. Aladdin, 1998.

House on Mango Street, The, by Sandra Cisneros. Vintage Books, 1984.

Huggles' Breakfast by Joy Cowley. Wright Group, 1989.

I Am of Two Places: A Book of Children's Poetry edited by Mary Carden and Mary Cappellini. Rigby, 1997.

I Can Fly by Ruth Krauss. Golden Books, Random House, 1999.

I Can't Said the Ant by Polly Cameron. Scholastic, 1961.

I Spy by David Drew. Irwin, 1994; Rigby (Big Book).

I Wash by Mary Cappellini. Learning Media, 2000.

Is This a Monster? by Scarlett Lovell. Mondo, 1995 (Big Book).

Island of the Blue Dolphins by Scott O'Dell. Random House, 1961.

Jouanah, A Hmong Cinderella adapted by J. R. Coburn with T. C. Lee. Shen's Books, 1996.

Judge for a Day by Margarita González-Jensen. Rigby, 1997 (Big Book).

Key Collection, The, by Andrea Cheng. Holt, 2003.

Knight at Dawn, The, by Mary P. Osbourne. *Magic Tree House* Series. Random House, 1993.

Land of the Dragons by Rod Morris. Learning Media, 1999.

Living Rain Forest, The, by Nic Bishop. Learning Media, 2000.

Mrs. McNosh Hangs Up Her Wash by Sarah Weeks. Scholastic, 1998.

Mrs. Wishy-Washy by Joy Cowley. Philomel, 1999; Wright (Big Book).

My Cousin Far Away by Mary Cappellini. Learning Media, 2002.

My Dog by Claude Belanger. Shortland Publications, 1988; Rigby (Big Book).

My Special Job/Mi trabajo especial by Michael A. Solis. Learning Media, 1997.

Nim's Island by Wendy Orr. Random House Children's Media, 1999.

Number the Stars by Lois Lowry. Houghton Mifflin, 1989.

One Fish, Two Fish, Red Fish, Blue Fish by Dr. Seuss. Random House, 1960.

Owl Moon by Jane Yolen. Scholastic, 1987.

Paper Patchwork by Barbara Beveridge. Pacific Learning, no date.

Pets by Jennifer Beck. Rigby, 1988.

Poor Old Polly by June Melser and Joy Cowley. Wright Group, 1998.

Postcards from the Planets by David Drew. Rigby, 1988.

Prince Chuckie by Sarah Willson. Simon Spotlight, 2001.

Q Is for Quark: A Science Alphabet Book by David Schwartz. Tricycle Press, 2001.

Rainbow Fish, The/El pez arco iris by Marcus Pfister. North-South Books, 1992.

Ready, Steady, Jump! by Nic Bishop. Learning Media, 1995.

Red Socks and Yellow Socks by Joy Cowley. Wright Group, 1987.

Sarah, Plain and Tall by Patricia MacLachlan. HarperCollins, 1985.

Save My Rainforest/Salven mi selva by Monica Zak. Sitesa, 1989.

Scarecrow, The/Esos pájaros by Ron Bacon, adapted by Mary Cappellini. Rigby, 1997.

Sheila Rae, the Brave by Kevin Henkes. William Morrow, 1987.

Shells by Coral White. Rigby, 2000.

Shiloh by Phyllis R. Naylor. Atheneum, 1991; Aladdin, 2000.

Skeleton by David Drew. Rigby, 1994. Era Publications, 1994; Rigby (Big Book).

Sleepy Bear by Marcia Vaughan. Rigby, 1989.

Smoky Nights by Eve Bunting. Harcourt Brace, 1994.

Spots by I. N. Worsnop. Rigby, 1996.

Storm Trackers by Katacha Díaz. Rigby, 1997.

Story of Doña Chila, The, by Mary Cappellini. Rigby, 1997.

Superfudge by Judy Blume. Dutton, 1980.

Tomás and the Library Lady by Pat Mora. Random House Children's Media, 1997.

Tumble Bumble by Felicia Bond. Scholastic, 1996.

Water Boatman, The, by Joy Crowley. Pacific Learning, no date.

Whale Watching/Mirando ballenas by Mary Cappellini. Learning Media, 2000.

What Makes a Bird a Bird? by May Garelick. Mondo (Big Book), 1995.

When Jose Hits That Ball by Anne M. Bingley. Learning Media, 1997.

Which Is Which? by Josephine Croser.

"Wildfire!" *Time for Kids,* November 7, 2003.

Willie Wins by Almira Astudillo Gilles. Lee and Low, 2001.

PROFESSIONAL LITERATURE

Allington, Richard L. 2001. *What Really Matters for Struggling Readers: Designing Research-Based Programs.* New York: Longman.

Ayres, Linda. 1998. "Phonological Awareness Training of Kindergarten Children: Three Treatments and Their Effects." In *Reconsidering a Balanced Approach to Reading,* ed. Constance Weaver. Urbana, IL: National Council of Teachers of English.

Bear, Donald R., Shane Templeton, Lori A. Helman, and Tamara Baren. 2003. "Orthographic Development and Learning to Read in Different Languages." In *English Learners: Reaching the Highest Level of English Literacy,* ed. Gilbert Garcia. Newark, DE: International Reading Association.

Beaver, Joetta. 1997. *Developmental Reading Assessment Resource Guide.* Glenview, IL: Celebration Press.

Becoming a Nation of Readers. 1985. Ed. Richard C. Anderson, E. H. Hiebert, J. A. Scott, and I. A. G. Wilkinson. Report of the Commission on Reading. Washington, DC: National Academy of Education, National Institute of Education, and Center for the Study of Reading.

Calkins, Lucy, Kate Montgomery, and Donna Santman with Beverly Falk. 1998. *A Teacher's Guide to Standardized Reading Tests: Knowledge Is Power.* Portsmouth, NH: Heinemann.

Cambourne, Brian. 1988. *The Whole Story: Natural Learning and the Acquisition of Literacy in the Classroom.* Gosford, NSW, Australia: Ashton Scholastic.

Center for Research on Education, Diversity, and Excellence (CREDE). 2002. Research Evidence Five Standards for Effective Pedagogy and Student Outcomes. Technical Report No. G1. http://www.crede.org/research/pdd/5standevidence.html.

Chamot, A. U., and J. M. O'Malley. 1994. *The CALLA Handbook: Implementing the Cognitive Academic Language Learning Approach.* Reading, MA: Addison-Wesley.

Clay, Marie. 1979. *The Early Detection of Reading Difficulties.* Portsmouth, NH: Heinemann.

———. 1991. *Becoming Literate: The Construction of Inner Control.* Portsmouth, NH: Heinemann.

Collier, Virginia P. 1989. "How Long? A Synthesis of Research on Academic Achievement in Second Language." *TESOL Quarterly* 23, 3: 509–532.

———. 1992. "A Synthesis of Studies Examining Long-Term Language-Minority Student Data on Academic Achievement." *Bilingual Research Journal* 16, 1 & 2: 187–212.

Cummins, Jim. 1981. "The Role of Primary Language Development in Promoting Educational Success for Language Minority Students." In *Schooling and Language Minority Students: A Theoretical Framework.* Los Angeles: Evaluation, Dissemination, and Assessment Center.

———. 1989. *Empowering Minority Students.* Sacramento: California Association for Bilingual Education.

———. 1994. "Knowledge, Power, and Identity in Teaching English as a Second Language." In *Educating Second Language Children: The Whole Child, the Whole Curriculum, the Whole Community,* ed. Fred Genesee. Cambridge: Cambridge University Press.

———. 2001. *Negotiating Identities: Education for Empowerment in a Diverse Society,* 2d ed. Los Angeles: California Association for Bilingual Education.

———. 2002. "The Importance of Using Primary Language: To Help Make Literacy Stronger in Second Language." Presentation at International Reading Association Conference, San Francisco.

———. 2003. "Reading and the Bilingual Student: Fact and Friction." In *English Learners: Reaching the Highest Level of English Literacy,* ed. Gilbert Garcia, 2–33. Newark, DE: International Reading Association.

Daniels, Harvey. 1994. *Literature Circles: Voice and Choice in the Student-Centered Classroom.* Portland, ME: Stenhouse.

———. 2002. *Literature Circles: Voice and Choice in Book Clubs and Reading Groups.* 2d ed. Portland, ME: Stenhouse.

Daniels, Harvey, and Marilyn Bizar. 2004. *Teaching the Best Practice Way.* Portland, ME: Stenhouse.

Diller, Debbie. 2003. *Literacy Work Stations: Making Centers Work.* Portland, ME: Stenhouse.

———. 2005. *Practice with Purpose: Literacy Work Stations for Grades 3–6.* Portland, ME: Stenhouse.

Dorn, Linda J., Cathy French, and Tammy Jones. 1998. *Apprenticeship in Literacy: Transitions Across Reading and Writing.* Portland, ME: Stenhouse.

Dorn, Linda J., and Carla Soffos. 2001. *Shaping Literate Minds: Developing Self-Regulated Learners.* Portland, ME: Stenhouse.

Drucker, Mary J. 2003. "What Reading Teachers Should Know about ESL Learners." *The Reading Teacher* 57, 1: 22–29.

Echevarria, Jana, and Anne Graves. 1998. *Sheltered Content Instruction: Teaching English Language Learners with Diverse Abilities.* Boston: Allyn and Bacon.

Echevarria, Jana, MaryEllen Vogt, and Deborah J. Short. 2000. *Making Content Comprehensible for English Language Learners: The SIOP Model.* Boston: Allyn and Bacon.

Ellis, Rod. 1990. *Instructed Second Language Acquisition.* Oxford: Blackwell.

English Language Development Standards for California Public Schools. 1999. <http://www.cde.ca.gov/re/pn/fd/englangart-stnd-pdf.asp>.

Fay, Kathleen, and Suzanne Whaley. 2004. *Becoming One Community: Reading and Writing with English Language Learners.* Portland, ME: Stenhouse.

Fisher, Bobbi. 1991. *Joyful Learning: A Whole Language Kindergarten.* Portsmouth, NH: Heinemann.

———. 1995. *Thinking and Learning Together: Curriculum and Community in a Primary Classroom.* Portsmouth, NH: Heinemann.

Fitzgerald, J., and Jim Cummins. 1999. "Bridging Disciplines to Critique a National Research Agenda for Language-Minority Children's Schooling." *Reading Research Quarterly* 34, 3: 378–390.

Fountas, Irene, and Gay Su Pinnell. 1996. *Guided Reading: Good First Teaching for All Children.* Portsmouth, NH: Heinemann.

———. 1999. *Matching Books to Readers: Using Leveled Books in Guided Reading, K–3.* Portsmouth, NH: Heinemann.

———. 2001. *Guided Readers and Writers, 3–6.* Portsmouth, NH: Heinemann.

———. 2002. *Leveled Books for Readers, 3–6: A Companion Volume to Guided Readers and Writers.* Portsmouth, NH: Heinemann.

Freeman, David, and Yvonne Freeman. 2000. *Teaching Reading in Multilingual Classrooms.* Portsmouth, NH: Heinemann.

———. 2001. *Between Worlds: Access to Second Language Acquisition,* 2d ed. Portsmouth, NH: Heinemann.

Freeman, Yvonne, and David Freeman with Sandra Mercuri. 2002. *Closing the Achievement Gap: How to Reach Limited-Formal-Schooling and Long-Term English Learners.* Portsmouth, NH: Heinemann.

Freire, Paolo. 1978. *Pedagogy of the Oppressed.* New York: Continuum.

Gardner, Howard. 1983. *Frames of Mind: The Theory of Multiple Intelligences.* New York: Basic Books.

———. 1993. *Multiple Intelligences: The Theory in Practice.* New York: Basic Books.

———. 2000. *Intelligence Reframed: Multiple Intelligences for the 21st Century.* New York: Basic Books.

Genesee, Fred, ed. 1994. *Educating Second Language Children: The Whole Child, the Whole Curriculum, the Whole Community.* Cambridge: Cambridge University Press.

Gibbons, Pauline. 1991. *Learning to Learn in a Second Language.* Portsmouth, NH: Heinemann.

———. 2002. *Scaffolding Language, Scaffolding Learning.* Portsmouth, NH: Heinemann.

Goodman, Kenneth S. 1982. *Language and Literacy.* London: Routledge and Kegan Paul.

———. 1996. *Reading: A Common Sense Look at the Nature of Language and the Science of Reading.* Portsmouth, NH: Heinemann.

Goodman, Kenneth S., Lois Bird, and Yetta M. Goodman. 1991. *The Whole Language Catalog.* Santa Rosa, CA: American School Publishers.

Goodman, Yetta. 1985. "Kid Watching: Observing Children in the Classroom." In *Observing the Language Learner,* ed. A. Jaggar and M. T. Smith-Burke, 9–18. International Reading Association and the National Council of Teachers of English. New York: New York University Press.

Graves, Michael F., and Jill Fitzgerald. 2003. "Scaffolding Reading Experiences for Multilingual Classrooms." In *English Learners: Reaching the Highest Level of English Literacy,* ed. Gilbert Garcia. Newark, DE: International Reading Association.

Hahn, Mary Lee. 2002. *Reconsidering Read-Aloud.* Portland, ME: Stenhouse.

Halliday, M. A. 1989. *Spoken and Written Language.* New York: Oxford University Press.

Harvey, Stephanie, and Anne Goudvis. 2000. *Strategies That Work: Teaching Comprehension to Enhance Understanding.* Portland, ME: Stenhouse.

Harwayne, Shelley. 1992. *Lasting Impressions: Weaving Literature into the Writing Workshop.* Portsmouth, NH: Heinemann.

———. 1999. *Going Public.* Portsmouth, NH: Heinemann.

Hayes, Curtis W., Robert Bahruth, and Carolyn Kessler. 1998. *Literacy con cariño: A Story of Migrant Children's Success.* New ed. Portsmouth, NH: Heinemann.

Helman, Lori A. 2004. "Building on the Sound System of Spanish: Insights from the Alphabetic Spellings of English-Language Learners." *The Reading Teacher* 57, 5: 452–460.

Herrell, Adrienne. 1999. *Fifty Strategies for Teaching English Language Learners.* Upper Saddle River, NJ: Prentice Hall.

Hindley, Joanne. 1996. *In the Company of Children.* Portland, ME: Stenhouse.

Holdaway, Don. 1979. *The Foundations of Literacy*. Gosford, NSW, Australia: Ashton Scholastic.

Hornsby, David. 2000. *A Closer Look at Guided Reading*. Prahran, Australia: Eleanor Curtain Publishing.

Hornsby, David, and Deborah Sukarna with Jo-Ann Parry. 1986. *Read On: A Conference Approach to Reading*. Portsmouth, NH: Heinemann.

Hoyt, Linda. 1998. *Let the Learner Lead the Way. Primary Voices*. Urbana, IL: National Council of Teachers of English.

Keene, Ellin Oliver, and Susan Zimmermann. 1997. *Mosaic of Thought: Teaching Reading Comprehension in a Reader's Workshop*. Portsmouth, NH: Heinemann.

Krashen, Stephen D. 1981. "Bilingual Education and Second Language Acquisition." In *Schooling and Language-Minority Students: A Theoretical Framework*. Sacramento: California State Department of Education.

————. 1996. *Under Attack: The Case Against Bilingual Education*. Culver City, CA: Language Education Associates.

————. 2003. "Three Roles for Reading for Minority-Language Children." In *English Learners: Reaching the Highest Level of English Literacy*, ed. Gilbert Garcia. Newark, DE: International Reading Association.

————. 2004. "The Case for Narrow Reading." *Language Magazine* 3, 5: 17–19.

Krashen, Stephen D., and Douglas Biber. 1988. *On Course: Bilingual Education's Success in California*. Sacramento: California Association for Bilingual Education.

Krashen, Stephen D., and Tracy D. Terrell. 1983. *The Natural Approach: Language Acquisition in the Classroom*. Hayward, CA: Alemany Press.

Kress, Jacqueline E. 1993. *The ESL Teacher's Book of Lists. Center for Applied Research in Education*. New York: Wiley.

Kucer, Stephen D., Cecilia Silva, and Esther L. Delgado-Larocco. 1995. *Curricular Conversations: Themes in Multilingual and Monolingual Classrooms*. Portland, ME: Stenhouse.

Law, Barbara, and Mary Eckes. 2000. *The More-Than-Just-Surviving Handbook: ESL for Every Classroom Teacher*. 2d ed. Winnipeg, Man., Canada: Peguis Publishers.

Miller, Debbie. 2002. *Reading with Meaning: Teaching Comprehension in the Primary Grades*. Portland, ME: Stenhouse.

Mooney, Margaret E. 1990. *Reading To, With, and By Children*. Katonah, NY: Richard C. Owen.

Nagy, W. E., P. A. Herman, and R. C. Anderson. 1985. "Learning Words from Context." *Reading Research Quarterly* 20: 233–253.

National Center for Education Statistics. U.S. Department of Education. 2002. <http://www.nces.ed.gov/>.

National Council of Teachers of English and International Reading Association. *Standards for the English Language Arts*. <http://www.ncte.org/about/over/standards/110846.htm>.

Nieto, Sonia. 1992. *Affirming Diversity: The Sociopolitical Context of Multicultural Education*. Boston: Allyn and Bacon.

O'Malley, J. Michael, and Lorraine Valdez Pierce. 1996. *Authentic Assessment For English Language Learners: Practical Approaches for Teachers*. New York: Addison-Wesley.

Opitz, Michael F., and Timothy V. Rasinski. 1998. *Good-Bye Round Robin: 25 Effective Oral Reading Strategies*. Portsmouth, NH: Heinemann.

Parkes, Brenda. 2000. *Read It Again! Revisiting Shared Reading*. Portland, ME: Stenhouse.

Peterson, Barbara. 2001. *Literary Pathways: Selecting Books to Support New Readers*. Portsmouth, NH: Heinemann.

Peterson, Ralph, and Maryann Eeds. 1990. *Grand Conversations: Literature Groups in Action*. New York: Scholastic.

Reading for Life: The Learner as a Reader. 1996. Wellington, New Zealand: Learning Media.

Reading in Junior Classes. 1985. Wellington, New Zealand: Learning Media.

Reading Recovery Council of North America. <http://www.readingrecovery.org/>.

Routman, Regie. 1994. *Invitations: Changing as Teachers and Learners, K–12*. Portsmouth, NH: Heinemann.

——. 2000. *Conversations: Strategies for Teaching, Learning, and Evaluating.* Portsmouth, NH: Heinemann.

——. 2002. *Reading Essentials: The Specifics You Need to Teach Reading Well.* Portsmouth, NH: Heinemann.

Samway, Katharine Davies, Gail Whang, and Mary Pippitt. 1995. *Buddy Reading: Cross-Age Tutoring in a Multicultural School.* Portsmouth, NH: Heinemann.

Santman, Donna. 2002. "Teaching to the Test? Test Preparation in the Reading Workshop." *Language Arts* 79, 3: 203–211.

Saunders, William, and Claude Goldenberg. 1999. *The Effects of Instructional Conversations and Literature Logs on the Story Comprehension and Thematic Understanding of English Proficient and Limited English Proficient Students.* Santa Cruz, CA: Center for Research on Education, Diversity, and Excellence.

Shin, Fay. 2001. "Motivating Students with Goosebumps and Other Popular Books." *California School Library Association* 25, 1: 1549.

Short, Kathy, and Kathryn Pierce, eds. 1990. *Talking About Books.* Portsmouth, NH: Heinemann.

Sibberson, Franki, and Karen Szymusiak. 2001. *Beyond Leveled Books: Supporting Transitional Readers in Grades 2–5.* Portland, ME: Stenhouse.

——. 2003. *Still Learning to Read: Teaching Students in Grades 3–6.* Portland, ME: Stenhouse.

Smith, Frank. 1988. *Joining the Literacy Club: Further Essays into Education.* Portsmouth, NH: Heinemann.

——. 1994. *Understanding Reading,* 5th ed. Hillsdale, NJ: Erlbaum.

Snow, Catherine E., Wendy S. Barnes, Jean Chandler, Irene F. Goodman, and Lowry Hemphill. 1991. *Unfulfilled Expectations: Home and School Influences on Literacy.* Cambridge, MA: Harvard University Press.

Swain, Merril. 1985. "Communicative Competence: Some Roles of Comprehensible Output." In *Its Development Input in Second Language Acquisition,* ed. S. Gass and C. Madden. Rowley, MA: Newbury House.

Taberski, Sharon. 2000. *On Solid Ground: Strategies for Teaching Reading, K–3.* Portsmouth, NH: Heinemann.

Teachers of English to Speakers of Other Languages (TESOL). 1997. *ESL Standards for PreK–12 Students.* <http://www.tesol.org>.

Texas Education Agency (TEA). 1997. *English Language Proficiency Standards.* <http://www.tea.state.tx.us>.

Tharp, Estrada, Dalton, and Yamauchi. 2000. *Teaching Transformed: Achieving Excellence, Fairness, Inclusion, and Harmony.* Boulder, CO: Westview Press.

Thomas, William, and Virginia Collier. 1999. *School Effectiveness for Language Minority Students.* Washington, DC: National Clearinghouse for Bilingual Education.

Tovani, Cris. 2000. *I Read It, but I Don't Get It: Comprehension Strategies for Adolescent Readers.* Portland, ME: Stenhouse.

Traill, Leanna. 1994. *Highlight My Strengths: Assessment and Evaluation of Literacy Teaching and Learning.* Chicago: Rigby.

Trelease, Jim. 2001. *The New Read-Aloud Handbook.* New York: Penguin.

U.S. Department of Education. <http://www.ed.gov/>.

Van Lier, L. 1988. *The Classroom and the Language Learner.* New York: Longman.

Vygotsky, L. S. 1978. *Mind in Society,* ed. M. Cole, V. John-Steiner, S. Scribner, and E. Souberman. Cambridge, MA: Harvard University Press.

Walter, Teresa. 1996. *Amazing English.* New York: Addison-Wesley.

Walton, Sherry, and Kathe Taylor. 1997. "How Did You Know the Answer Was Boxcar?" *Educational Leadership* Dec/Jan: 38–40.

WIDA Consortium: Wisconsin, Delaware, Arkansas, District of Columbia Public Schools, Maine, New Hampshire, Rhode Island, Vermont, and Illinois. 2004. *English Language Proficiency Standards for English Language Learners in Kindergarten Through Grade 12 (K–12).* <http://www.isbe.state.il.us/bilingual/htmls/elp_standards.htm.>

Wilde, Sandra. 2000. *Miscue Analysis Made Easy: Building on Student Strengths.* Portsmouth, NH: Heinemann.

Williams, Joan A. 2001. "Classroom Conversations: Opportunities to Learn for ESL Students in Mainstream Classrooms." *Reading Teacher* 54, 8: 750–757.

Wolf, Shelby A., and Kenneth P. Wolf. 2002. "Teaching True and to the Test in Writing." *Language Arts* 79, 3: 229–242.

Yopp, Hallie. 1988. "The Validity and Reliability of Phonemic Awareness Tests." *Reading Research Quarterly* 23: 159–177.

INDEX